COMMERCIAL ACTIVITIES AND RURAL DEVELOPMENT IN SOUTH ASIA

(A GEOGRAPHICAL STUDY)

Proceedings of the International Conference of the I G U Study Group on Geography of Commercial Activities GORAKHPUR, 1985

Chief Editor
V K SHRIVASTAVA
Department of Geography
University of Gorakhpur
Gorakhpur-273009 India

ICSSR Consultant
Professor S L Kayastha

CONCEPT PUBLISHING COMPANY NEW DELHI-110015

The Indian Council of Social Science Research gave the financial support towards the publication of this work. However, the responsibility for the contents of the book -facts, opinions, conclusions etc.—are entirely that of the author not of the ICSSR

ISBN 81-7022-194-3

First Published 1988

V.K. **Shrivastava** (*b*. 1939 -)

Published by
Ashok Kumar Mittal
Concept Publishing Company
A, 15-16, Commercial Block, Mohan Garden
NEW DELHI-110059 (India)

Printed at
Taj Press
A 35/4 Maya Puri
NEW DELHI-110028

DEDICATION IN MEMORY OF OUR BELOVED PRIME MINISTER

Shrimati Indira Gandhi

Mrs. Indira Gandhi at the Canvocation of the University of Gorakhpur, 1984

DELEGATES OF THE INTERNATIONAL CONFERENCE

FOREWORD

Geographers, for a long time now, have been prodigiously and effectively cultivating the old-established specialisation of marketing geography. The corpus of literature is both expensive and expanding. For novitiates there is burgeoning wealth of bibliographies, books, themes, paradigms, questions, and techniques. Nor has the field been the sole monopoly of the geographers: some of the best research has been conducted by historians, economists, sociologists, and anthropologists. They have looked at the phenomenon of marketing from the perspectives that are unique to their disciplines. The plethora of perspectives has expanded the horizons of both research and understanding. What makes the contributions of the practitioners of the science of marketing geography merit consideration is their explicit concern with the role of market centres in organising the patterns of space, in consistently applying the spatial approach, and in placing the process of marketing in the context of space. From the role that the markets play in providing the principal nodes of nexus between the processes of production and of distribution and thus leading to consumption, it is axiomatic that they form the structure of the three principal components of economy, in the best of the traditional understanding of economics, production, distribution, and consumption and through their translation into the spatial dimension they contribute significantly to the regional structure, its formation, functioning, sustenance, and development.

Marketing, both permanent and periodic, religious and secular, is one of the three basic components of economy: production, distribution, and consumption. The three components are clearly linked together like the components of a functioning system. It is obvious that the components of an economy constitute sub-systems in themselves so that the processes and results of one are transferred to those of the second and third. On the other hand the different marketing systems constitute a cascading system - the genesis, survival, growth, and decay of an individual market or a system of markets, of any kind, really operates within the system of spatial organisation. Viewed in the perspective of a system, the salient characteristics of any market, reveal the input, process, output, feedback control and restriction. It will be highly interesting to examine whether the periodic markets and permanent markets of an area or of a large city function as a cascading system. Essentially this hinges upon the question whether one could exist and function without the other. Likewise, the smaller periodic markets form a functioning system with those of their larger counterparts. From this proposition it is only logical to move forward to suggest that Christaller's model really attains its true significance in providing us with a descriptive-analytical configuration of functional relationship and not so much any geometrical arrangement.

In the economic paradigm - production, distribution, and consumption, the third component is the immediately related to marketing, periodic and permanent but this component comes into play only as a result of the adequate and appropriate functioning of the preceding two components. Distribution in its turn is a process involving a large diversity of complexly inter-related variables of these, physical, economic, and social, of immediate consequence is the system of transportation. Transportation not only provides the basic infrastructure for distribution but also for the entire process of marketing : collecting and disposal. The relationship between all the three components of economy : production, distribution, and consumption on the one hand and transportation on the other hand is both symbiotic and inter-generating. Transportation leads both to collection of commodities and distribution and the latter is a sine qua non of consumption. Similarly the process of production will be stunted if the commodities produced in surplus cannot be transported to a distribution centre and, what would the transportation system survive on if there was to be no commodities to be transported to and from a distribution-collection centre.

From this inter-related system of production, distribution, and consumption, one can suggest that the multi-order integration of markets, periodic and permanent, in increasingly complex nexus will result in an expanding spectrum of commodities, both agricultural and non-agricultural and the associated services hinged upon the very process of production. The spectrum is the result of marketing process as also its generator. The market provides the goods needed by the population of the economic region but also prompts them to adopt commodities which were not a part of the traditional mix and thus creates a new need for expanding list. Along with these arrive a host of servicing functions which get located in the older markets and begin to dominate the newer ones. Together they generate implications for development.

In the backward areas, predominantly agricultural, villages, large or small, have no power to attract administrative functions and they have played role in rural development only by providing market centres. Even the smaller settlements have gained in size and economic significance by the gradual development of market functions. Where the markets have become permanent they have generated snow-ball effects and catalytic processes by prompting the transportation lines to converge on them. This, as a chain reaction, has brought into the village and the surrounding, smaller, subsidiary villages a diversity of functions and functionaries. It is through these processes that the market centre, originally rural and agricultural, develops into either rural and tertiary activity centre or into an urban and tertiary activity centre. Along with this spread of development processes the smaller villages are linked to the market centre and a functional-nodal region is developed. Thus, market centre has rightly been considered as a development centre in realistic feasible, and promising strategy of rural development of the under-developed agrarian areas. An implication of this formulation needs also to be emphasised. By locating new growth centres which do not correspond with the existing market centres or in the settlements which do not have the potentials of emerging as market centres the strategy for rural development has been already stunted at the point of initiation. It will be an abortive attempt. In effect we plead that the growth centres or focal points should be located in the already existing market centres, both permanent and periodic. In the latter through investment in infrastructure and implementing regulatory financial mechanisms the periodic market can be converted wholly or partly into a permanent market. On the other hand an arbitrarily chosen growth point or development focal point may or may not have a market, permanent or periodic, to begin with and since it has a lower-level concentration of only the institutional services it will have little potentialities to augment or initiate growth in production as an integral component of the economy's triumvirate - production, distribution, and consumption. Such a growth point will contribute to limited part in the growth spectrum. The distribution function and development function will then become spatially disjunct. This is mainly related to the fact the while a periodic or a permanent market emerges on the economic landscape as the result of an evolutionary process the focal point or growth point is entirely a created entity, a result of political manipulation rather than rational, optimising, decision-making process, overwhelmingly important in a system of chaotic democracy.

The Indian market is made unique by paradigms altogether different from those operating in the developed countries of the world. In our region the questions - where is the market located, what does it sell, when does it sell, and who sells what, are important to an understanding of the historical, traditional, and social economic contexts of the functioning of society in space and the lineaments of the modes of living. A market is not merely an economic mode, much more important is its function as a node of social network woven around it. This is the basis of its role in regional, social and economic development.

Earlier efforts in research in marketing geography addressed the question of morphology and function of a market or a system of markets as entities in themselves embedded in the traditional-historical matrix of specific regions. A market and its region were considered as one integrated systematic component of a region and even though the reflection of the region in a market was sought to be identified and portrayed in all its complex details the practitioners of the field did not concern themselves with the role of markets and systems and functioning in regional rural development. As proposed earlier this role is being performed through fulfilling the demands already in existence and creating demands for new commodities and services. In these processes new transportation lines emerge and the existing ones are reactivated, agriculture becomes gradually commercialised, and a wide spectrum of commodities emerge in a market. The market region is energized and gets nested into market regions of successively higher orders. Thus, the accessibility and complexity of the oxogenous and endogenous commodities and services are increased by a quantum jump. In the era of planning in general and regional planning in particular the periodic and permanent marketing systems and indeed the entire gamut of commercial activities, mainly the tertiary activities, have played the generating and sustaining roles. They have provided, what is easily, the most efficient nodal-functional region for the spatial organisation of society and economy.

Dr. V.K. Shrivastava's highly commendable effort in collecting, together in one volume, not less than forty five full length papers is really an illustration of the brief remarks made earlier in this writing. The meaningful title of the edited book 'Commercial Activities and Rural Development in South Asia : A Geographical Appraisal' would raise a lot of promise. The book contains as many as 45 research papers grouped under four theme sections: current status and trends of research in Commercial Geography containing 3 papers, Analysis of Commercial Activities contaning 23 papers, Rural-Urban Linkages and Development containing 7 papers, and Rural Development: Issues, Strategies, and Planning Policy containing 12 papers.

It was pleasant surprise to find the good, old, and widely-used, and universally understood term 'Commercial Geography' around which the first three papers are woven. Since the days of its final disappearance from higher academia 'Commercial Geography's main concerns have expanded to staggering horizons to include diverse activities with manifold facets. In one paper geography has been related to business pursuits and the case has been made very convincingly even though it is not quite clear whether it could not have been subsumed under Economic Geography by simply expanding its scope. Nonetheless, the point is made and strongly that there could be geographical dimensions of business activities. From business to markets is a smooth movement. Periodic markets, however, are genetically, morphologically, and functionally radically different from large business activities and the former does not get nested in the latter. This paper proposes generalisations which have very great coverage and potentialities for wider application. Strengthened by several innovative models and diagrams this paper can be easily considered as the leader in this genre of thinking.

The 23 papers in the second section cover an expansive ambit of papers dealing with rural markets, periodic markets, vegetable markets, fruit markets, identification of central places, and mandis. When such a large number of papers are compressed into one omnibus theme one does get an impression of material getting diffused. The papers are morphological and functional in the widest sense of the term. There are extremely interesting research reported in this section: one paper analyses human resources utilization in commercial activities in rural areas, another-focuses on cultivation population dynamics, and yet another investigates seller's travel behaviour. Most of the papers balance their material between nomothetic and idiographic search and thus provide information and propose conceptual formulations. Almost all of them are based on premises and hypotheses and they have generated a fund of knowledge about the local areas and distinctive regions. The role of commercial activities on changing patterns of agriculture and on agricultural development has also attracted the close consideration of some authors. From a close perusal of these 23 papers one could derive certain conclusions: (i) scholars continue to be interested in morphological analysis for whatever it is worth, (ii) marketing geography is, in practice, much more comprehensive than has been sought by the practitioners to be the limits, it does include infrastructure, marketing organisation, central places, and even commercial farming, and (iii) it is necessary for marketing geography to gradually merge itself into geography or commercial activities-not merely tertiary activities of the traditional economic classification but also those which were definitionally put out of its circumsference. Marketing geography, thus should include as many themes as are related to the central activity of sale and purchase.

There was a period in the development of marketing geography when most studies concentrated on the individual market, their morphologies and functions. Both rural and urban markets were investigated and information and generalisation were generated but mainly the two systems were considered as separate entities and analysed as such. In the later phases the scholars of the fields became aware of the intrinsic linkage between the two and the imperatives of analysing them together. It became clear that even though one was not the putative of the other and generalisations on one could not be transferred without critical modification to the other, the two systems could, and should, be merged together through proper integration. This concern, thus, has led to the realisation of linkages not only between the marketing systems but also between the rural and urban economics.

It is also significant that development planners consider it axiomatic to have a firm system of functioning rural-urban linkages as an integral component of regional development. This realisation is reflected in as many as six papers which explore, inter alia, the role of periodic markets in spatial development, urbanisation and regional development., and non-convergence of central functions and rural underdevelopment. The authors of these papers must be meanwhile engaged in elaborating upon these themes by additional investigations for rural-urban linkages as translated through commercial activities do constitute an important set of requirements for a comprehensive regional development. As a matter of fact, the linkages operating through commercial activities become closely integrated with special infrastructure of development leading to more effective re-location of developmental activities. All the papers exploring these perspectives not only examine the development processes but also suggest new policies and strategies for spatial development.

Theme three papers lead one logically to the Theme Four papers numbering twelve. These papers are explicitly devoted to the questions of rural development and are fascinating investigations of a wide spectrum of themes going beyond the concensus boundaries of marketing geography. One paper deals with the dynamics of rural transformation in India and another, very intriguingly, analyses the relationships of electoral participation, political consciousness, and regional development. Nor has the traditional paradigm of ecological basis of geography been ignored: there is one model paper on the ecological studies for commercial activities and rural development.

Easily Dr. Shrivastava's book is the most comprehensive treatment of the theme of commercial activities and its integration with rural development. One would read the papers with gratification of having found a substantial evidence of the two-way relationship of commercial activities and rural development. They do indeed develop and prosper together.

On behalf of the prospective readers I would like to most heartily congratulate Dr. Shrivastava for his efforts in assembling this interesting intellectual fare.

Chandigarh
December 10, 1987

A B Mukerji

List of Contributors

Ahmad, Asmah
Department of Geography, University Kebangsaan, Bangi, Malaysia.

Bansal, S.C.
Department of Geography, J.V. Jain College, Saharampur, U.P.

Bera, A.K.
Department of Geography, Surendra Nath College for Women, Calcutta.

Bhagwan Deo
Department of Geography, Digvijay Nath Degree College, Gorakhpur, U.P.

Bhole, Hans, G.
Geographisches Institut der Universitat Gottingen D-3400 Gottingen West Germany.

Chauhan, P.R.
Department of Geography, University of Gorakhpur, Gorakhpur, U.P.

De, N.K.
Department of Geography, University of Burdwan, Burdwan, West Bengal.

Dixit, R.S.
Department of Geography, I.T. College, Lucknow, U.P.

Dikshit, S.K.
Department of Geography, University of Gorakhpur, Gorakhpur, U.P.

Gurung, B.S.
Department of Geography, Tribhuan University, P.N. Campus, Pokhra, Nepal.

Gurung, K.B.
Department of Geography, Tribhuan University, P.N. Campus, Pokhra, Nepal.

Gurung, T.B.
Department of Geography, Tribhuan University, P.N. Campus, Pokhra, Nepal.

Islam, Nazrul
Department of Geography, University of Dhaka, Dhaka, Bangladesh.

Jamkar, A.G.
Department of Geography, S.S.V.P. Science College, Dhule, Maharashtra.

Lal, H.
Department of Geography, University of Gorakhpur, Gorakhpur, U.P.

Lal, Nirankar
Department of Geography, University of Gorakhpur, Gorakhpur, U.P.

Lal, V.N.
G.B. Pant Institute of Social Science, Allahabad, U.P.

Misra, R.P.
Department of Geography, (Ex. Vice-chancellor, Allahabad

University) Delhi School of Economics, Delhi University, Delhi.

Mukerjee, A.B
Department of Geography, Punjab University, Chandigarh, Punjab

Nath, Triyugi
Department of Geography, University of Gorakhpur, Gorakhpur, U.P.

Pandey, J.N.
Department of Geography, University of Gorakhpur, Gorakhpur, U.P.

Pondel, P.C.
Department of Geography, Tribhuan University, P.N. Campus, Pokhra, Nepal.

Prasad, Mahatam
Department of Geography, Bapu Degree College, Peppeganj, Gorakhpur, U.P.

Rai, J.P.
Department of Geography, D.C.S.K. Degree College, Mau, Azamgarh, U.P.

Ranasinghe, Mrs. P.C.H.
Department of Geography, University of Colombo, Colombo, Sri Lanka.

Rao, P. Parthasarthy
Research Associate, Economics Unit, International Crop Research Institute for Semi-Arid Tropics, Patencheru, Andhra Pradesh.

Rehman, A.
Indian Council of Social Science Research, 35. Ferozshah Road, New Delhi.

Routray, J.K.
Department of Geography, Utkal University, Bhubaneshwar, Orissa.

Saxena, H.M.
Department of Geography, Government College, Sriganganagar, Rajasthan.

Sharma, K.D.
Department of Geography, Punjab University, Chandigarh, Punjab.

Sharma, M.L.
Department of Geography, Lal Bahadur Shastri Degree College, Gonda, U.P.

Sharma, N.
Department of Geography, L.N. Mithila University, Darbhanga, Bihar.

Sharma, S.C.
Department of Geography, M.L.K. (P.G.) College, Balrampur, Gonda.

Shrivastava, Mrs. K.R.
19, Ka, Hirapuri Colony, University Campus, Gorakhpur, U.P.

Shrivastava, V.K.
Department of Geography, University of Gorakhpur, Gorakhpur, U.P

Shukla, B.M.
Department of Chemistry (Ex. Vice-chancellor, Gorakhpur University), Banaras Hindu University, Varanasi

Shukla, S.K.
Department of Geography, Dr. H.S. Gaur University, Sagar, M.P.

Sinha, B.R.K.
Department of Geography, M.S. University, Baroda, Gujarat.

Sinha, R.N.P.
Department of Geography, M.S. University, Baroda, Gujarat.

Singh, J.
Department of Geography, University of Gorakhpur, Gorakhpur, U.P.

Singh, D.K.
Department of Geography, Utkal University, Bhubaneshwar, Orissa.

Singh, R.S.
Department of Geography, University of Gorakhpur, Gorakhpur, U.P.

Singh, R.N.
Department of Geography, University of Gorakhpur, Gorakhpur, U.P.

Srivastava, H.O.
Department of Geography, M.M.T.D. College, Ballia , U.P.

Srivastava, R.C.
Department of Geography, P.P.N. College, Kanpur, U.P.

Swaminathan. E.
Department of Geography, Sri Krishnadevaraya University, Anantpur, Andhra Pradesh.

Tiwari, K.N.
Department of Geography, Degree College Malikpura, Ghazipur.

Tripathi, M.P.
Department of Geography, Thribhuan University, P.N. Campus, Pokhra, Nepal.

Trivedi, Miss Venu
Department of Geography, Government Girls' College, Indore, M.P.

Verhagen, Hetty
Research Scholar, Economics Unit, International Crop Research Institute of Semi-Arid, Tropics, Patencheru, Andhra Pradesh.

Verma, J.S.
Department of Geography, Lal Bahadur Shastri Degree College, Anandnagar, Gorakhpur, U.P.

Verma, S.S.
Department of Geography, University of Gorakhpur, Gorakhpur, U.P.

Yadava, H.R.
Department of Geography, Madan Mohan Malviya Degree College, Bhatpar Rani, Deoria, U.P.

CONTENTS

Theme III - Rural - Urban Linkages and Development

Theme IV - Rural Development : Issues, Strategies and Planning Policy

CEREMONIES

PREFACE

Geography, which is rightly called the 'mother science', is uniquely relevant to current concerns both with the environment and ecology and with regional contrasts and imbalances in human welfare. So is the spatial manifestation of commercial activities.

In an all embracing manner commercial activities include primary, secondary and tertiary sectors of human activities. It is through commercial activities that the wealth is generated and distributed. Human welfare is imbedded in the distributional aspects of generation and distribution of wealth on the surface of the earth and of the distribution of income generated by them. Environment and ecology are deeply interwoven with commercial activities. Each and every commercial activity involves utilization of some elements of environment, both natural and social. The elements of environment are so interlinked that their minutest utilisation generates a chain reaction manifested through ecological changes. This unique synthetic quality of geography enabled to undertake academic debate on commercial activities, environment, ecology and human welfare.

I

Majority of the world's population is rural. A vast majority of this rural population lives below the standard a human being is supposed to live. This may be said to be true of all those nations which become independent in the latter half of the twentieth century. South Asia represents one such unit which comprises of nearly 1/3 of the world's population, an overwhelming majority of which is engaged in primary activities. The gradual independence of various nations has initiated structural and functional changes in the socio-economic setting of these nations concerned. The intensification and diversification of agriculture, a greater utilization of natural resources, expansion of manufacturing activities at small, medium and large scales, improvement in literacy and in the educational standard at formal and technical levels, realization of human resource potential and a consciousness towards the limitations of nature are some of the many factors which have influenced the process of development in South Asia. The political consciousness to initiate or to percolate the benefits of developmental efforts at grassroots levels has had an awakening effect on the rural masses. The first sign of development in rural areas, besides the improvement in agriculture, is manifested through the initiation of tertiary activities. Human organization is nodal. An increased mobility of the masses coupled with the generation of wealth has naturally lead to the establishment of central place activities at nodal points. It is because the rural population is no longer self-sufficient. The benefits of science and technology have revolutionised the economy upto farm level. The farmers have to catch up with a minimum level of modern technology in the form of new varieties of seeds, fertilizers, pesticides, facilities of disposal of their produce, market intelligence, market news etc. For this they have to move to central places - big and small. This fundamental trend strengthens the development of tertiary activities.

Tertiary activities alone cannot lead to an overall development. They must be supported by secondary activities. Commercial activities, therefore, lay an equal stress on manufacturing industries from cottage industry level to the level of industrial complexes. Given the will and power, manufacturing activities can be installed even in space at present. But in the context of South Asia in particular, such activities are still either bound by resources or by market. Industrial planning, therefore, still requires the considerations of environment and resources.

With a high density of population and even higher population growth rate on one hand, and the need of expansion of commercial activities on the other, environment has been a casuality in South

Asia. It was first exploited for export of resources to the erstwhile colonial powers and later for the provision of the basic needs of food, clothes and shelter to the growing masses. The paradigms of development, till recent past, were either a continuation of the superimposed ideology of development (Malthusion approach) of the so called advanced world or were borrowed, under superficial connotations like 'green revolution', 'trikling down effect', 'commercial development', 'extension programmes' etc. etc. These paradigms deflected attention from the need for conservation of resources rather exploitation, from the need for better distribution of benefits among the masses rather than for concentration of increasing production in limited pockets. The failures gradually turned out to be boons in the sense that they gave rise to a consciousness towards human welfare and degradation of the ecological complex. It has now become more than obvious that commercialization with care and for the welfare of the rural masses should be the motto of development in the world in general and in South Asia in particular.

II

In order to focus attention on the importance of commercial activities in the upliftment of the masses, the 25th International Geographical Congress held at Paris in 1984, rightly approved the formation of a Study Group on Geography of Commercial Activities. Commercial activities are a common phenomenon of the developed, developing and under-developed world alike. There are backward areas in advanced countries as well and the upliftment of those areas is as much of conern to geographers as of the backward areas of the developing and under-developed world. In the fitness of the things, therefore, the Study Group approved the idea of focussing attention on the role of commercial activities in development through holding conferences, symposia, workshop etc. in Afro-Asian countries as well, along with European and other advanced nations. India was chosen as the venue for a conference on South Asia. Without any financial support from the I.G.U. sources, six south Asian nations (Bangladesh, India, Malaysia, Nepal, Sri Lanka and Thailand) could be represented in addition to Kenya. A small window on east Africa has been provided among the contributions on South Asia as it deals with a very vital issue of rural development.

III

The deleberations of the conference were invited with due consideration to the objectives of the Study Group. The articles selected for publication in this book exhibit great variety on diverse topics. The organization of the book first of all traces the status and trends of research in commercial geography and related fields. It is followed by an analysis of commercial activities at regional and local levels. Later, rural-urban linkages, a vital missing link in the context of development of predominantly rural areas, have been examined. The book concludes with the issues, strategies and planning policy of rural development in South Asia. The text book type approach was bypassed in favour of providing a wider window on the themes selected and for leaving an open-ended debate rather than a closed one. It is presumed that the book will initiate more discussion on problems related to commercial activities and development rather than provide a conclusive debate. The shortcomings have crept in due to the limitations of time and money on the part of the editor rather than those of the authors.

The book has been organised into two parts. The first part consists of the academic programme in which the articles discussed in the conference have been presented. The second part gives a glimpse into the liturgiological aspects of the organization of the conference.

The first part comprises of four themes under which the papers presented have been arranged. Three articles, out of the 45 articles presented, have been placed in the first theme. V.K. Shrivastava has presented a trend report on the status of geography of commercial activities in brief which is mainly based on the papers presented at the 25th International Geographical Congress at Paris in 1984. It is followed by a searching paper explaining the relevance of geography to business pursuits by Professor R.N.P. Sinha, Professor A.B. Mukerji has made significant generalisations on periodic markets of India as these are the only outlets available to rural population for commercial and social exchange. He has further highlighted their developmental implications.

Theme II contains articles dealing with the analysis of commercial activities. This has been sub-divided into two parts, i.e. regional aspects of commercial activities and case studies of individual town or village markets.

Mrs. Ranasinghe critically analyses the structure and process of rural marketing in Sri Lanka and points out to the inefficiency of public marketing agencies. Tawde and Gophane have discussed marketing organization and commercial fruit farming in the Konkan region of Maharastra- whereas P.R. Chauhan highlights the salient features of spatio-temporal pattern of agricultural development in Madhya Pradesh. Following him Sharma draws attention to changes in the cultivation of commercial crops in the *Tarai* region where as Singh establishes the role played by cultivation-population dynamics in intra-regional economic situations. The umland of Pokhra town of Nepal provides promising potentials for the development of commercial activities as observed by Gurung et al. B.R.K. Sinha draws attention to the human resource potential model and argues that a proper orientation of human resources can lead to better commercial out put. Mrs. K.R. Shrivastava has taken a view of the not so far off future when the commercial potential of distant and fore lorne areas like the Antarctica will be put to use for the survival of mankind. Tamskar has pointed out the multifarious economic functions performed by weekly markets whereas Jamkar emphasises the role of historical factors in the origin and evolution of periodic market places in Dhule district of Maharastra. The two articles by H.M.Saxena and R.C. Srivastava reveal rural marketing systems in area like Rajasthan and Bundelkhand respectively. Dixit follows with the identification of hierarchy of market centres in Hamirpur district, a part of Bundelkhand. Gedam, Vishwanath and H.O. Srivastava and Tiwari deal with consumer behaviour and market area regions in context of areas like the Wardha Valley, the *Avadh* plain and the Saryupar plain respectively. Ram Surat has putforward the characteristics of wholesale agricultural *mandis* in eastern U.P. whereas Mahatam Prasad has demonstrated the method of identification of central places through field investigations. Swaminathan and Km. Venu Trivedi deal with the methodological aspects of the identification of the hierarchy of central places in Coimbatore (Karnatka) and Indore (M.P.) districts respectively. There are three papers dealing with case studies of individual market places. H. Lal has manifested the evolution of commercial activities in Gorakhpur city. V.N.Lal and Bansal have studies two rural markets of Rai

Bareilly and Saharanpur districts of U.P. and have emphasised the role that rural markets can play in commercialisation of rural areas.

Themes III deals with articles presented on rural-urban linkages and development. Agnes Musyaki and Professor Obudho have examined the role of periodic market systems in spatial development from a case study of Kenya. Their brief presentation suggests how the returns can be maximised and losses minimised through reorganising the market systems. Professor D.K. Singh argues how rural market-potential can be used as a measure of regional development whereas K.D. Sharma examplifies how non-convergence of central functions can lead to underdevelopment. J.P. Rai has drawn attention towards unifying role of growth centre and central place concepts for micro-level planning.

Mrs. Asmah Ahmad has made an elaborate study of rural-urban migration in Malaysia and has posed a question as to whether such migration is a challenge to development. Parthsarthy Rao and Hetty Verhagen have taken-up the semi-arid tropical (SAT) India for the study of marketing of commercial farm-inputs and have discussed the formal and informal channels of distribution at rural and urban levels. Verma links regional development of Rohilkhand Plan with urbanization.

Theme IV considers issues, strategies and planning policy in so far as rural development is concerned. In an interesting study Nazrul Islam has examined the role of *Upzila* (sub-district) centres in rural development of Bangladesh. Such studies give an opportunity to examine the out-puts of public policy schemes. Coming to the role of industrialization in rural development, Afzalur Rehman and Sharma have established that agro-industries can help in a large way to accelerate development of rural areas. Two development *block* level studies further emphasise the arguments of Rehman and Sharma. S.K. Shukla has studied the role of commercial activities in the development of Sagar block in M.P. whereas Professor N.K. De and Bera have high-lighted the approaches to Integrated Rural Development (I.R.D) through *block* level attempts in West Bengal. Tripathi has further demonstrated the impact of developmental activities (planned through public policy) in the rural hilly area of Nepal. Hans-G.Bohle examines polarised distribution systems from an empirical study in south India and demonstrates the way in which the spatial polarisation of the rural distribution system can lead to underdevelopment of marginal farmers and petty traders. Following Bohle, Nandeshwar Sharma rightly calls for reorganisation of commercial complexes which is a core mechanism of rural growth processes. Professor Jagdish Singh, though very briefly, has putforward the dynamics of rural transformation in India. J.N. Pandey has outlined a strategy for rural development which incorporates the suggestions made for rural development in other articles. Professor De cautions towards ecological consequences of commercial activities and the resultant development. Lastly, but not least, Dikshit shows that political consciousness plays a silent but decisive role in regional development.

V K Shrivastava

ACKNOWLEDGEMENTS

We are grateful to the University Grants Commission, the Indian Council of Social Science Research, New Delhi and to the Association of Marketing Geographers of India, Gorakhpur, for sponsoring the International Conference on Geography of Commercial Activities and Rural Development, held in the Department of Geography, University of Gorakhpur, Gorakhpur (India), from Dec. 21-23, 1985. Our thanks are due to the Govt. of India, Ministry of Human Resource Development, New Delhi, for permitting us to hold the conference. The financial support extended by Shri Vir Bahadur Singh, Chief Minister, Uttar Pradesh, is also acknowledged with thanks. We are also obliged to the International Geographical Union Study Group on Geography of Commercial Activities for agreeing to hold this conference in India. The I.C.S.S.R. have further come up with a publication grant which has made it possible to bring out the proceedings of the conference in a book form, for which we are grateful. Lastly, but not the least, we are grateful to all contributors of articles and to our research students for providing cartographic assistance.

Mr. Naurang Rai, Concept Publishing Co., New Delhi, have taken up the challenging task of printing this book in a short time. We are thankful to them for coming up to our expectations.

V K Shrivastava

Theme I

Current Status and Trends of Research in Commercial Geography

ONE

V.K. Shrivastava

Geography of Commercial Activities: A Trend Report

Commercial activities have been changing their form and functions according to man's perception of physico-cultural environment. Man's knowledge of the earth surface, his status of education, science and technology, his traditional background etc. have been the factors that have controlled the initiation, development and spatial expansion of commercial activities in general.

Till mid-nineteenth century man was discovering new lands, exploring and inhabiting newly discovered areas. His activities were confined to mainly primary production. Commercial activity was confined to the exchange of primary products. The industrial revolution in 1850 marks a major breakthrough in orienting commercial activities towards manufacturing and distributional aspects. For about a century onwards the growth and development of large scale industry and commerce was confined mainly to the European countries and to the U.S.A., with the exception of Japan in the eastern hemisphere. Since 1950 onwards, with the gradual end of colonial rule in the south and the south-east Asian countries, a new phase of commercial activities started in the so called 'Third World' Same was the case with many African and Latin American nations. New sources of raw materials were discovered, exchange of raw materials underwent a change and the exchange of technology and know-how became more important. The traditional political outlook of the major power blocs thawed. The communists, capitalists and socialist countries initiated and executed exchange of goods, services, ideas and people among themselves. The phase again broadened the scope and nature of commercial activities.

The application of space technology for human welfare added a new dimension for the scope of commercial activities. Remote sensing technique enabled the discovery of mineral and power resources in hitherto unexplored areas. Experiments in the field of manufacturing activity in space by the United States and the U.S.S.R. during their lengthy space missions store a new future for many industrial activities. The exploration of Antarctica and the territorial claims made by seven nations give an indication that the seventh continent of the world may become a focus of commercial activities in future. It controls not only the heat budget of the earth but it may also control the financial budget as well.

In context of the foreseable future of commercial activities a survey of research papers related to commercial activities has been made. This is based on the papers presented to the 25th. International Geographical Congress at Paris in 1984. Out of a total of 742 papers pertaining to 40 themes nearly 18% of the papers were devoted to some aspects of commercial activities and about 14% of the total number of papers were devoted to ideas related to developmental activities. The following themes particularly emphasized the study of commercial activities :-

a Utilization of ocean resources (Theme 4).
b Utilization and conservation of woodlands (Theme 5).
c Manufacturing Industries (Theme 6).
d Recent changes in farming and rural societies in the developing countries (Theme 7).
e Agricultural trends and rural communities in industrialised countries (Theme 9).
f Secondary and tertiary economic activities and urbanization in the third world countries (Theme 7).
g Natural resources, their management and development (Theme 12).
h Types of economic organizations in mountains (Theme 22).
i Ecological conditions as the basis and limits of development in the mountains (Theme 24).

Out of the papers related to various aspects of commercial activities five key papers can be identified.

The first paper entitled 'mankinds' economic and cultural differentiation: Its interaction with environment' (7.1) is by Andrianor Boris and Doskach Anna (U.S.S.R.). The authors have emphasized the combination of economic activities with cultural types. They have also laid emphasis on the role played by natural zones in various parts of the earth in the evolution of types and combinations of economic-cultural activities. The peculiarities of such types and combinations represent the principle pertinent to their spatial evolution.

Czyz Bronislaw of the Polish Academy of Sciences has discussed about 'Socio-economic dislocation' resulting from agro-technical transformations in the lake Chad basin of Africa (7.6). The dislocation of local pastoral economy and the introduction of entirely new social and economic pattern is highlighted in the paper.

M.J. Troughton (Canada) talks of Agricultural industrialization, its impact on farming operations and the rural environment (9.23). The paper makes a synoptic view of the impacts of agricultural industrialisation both at an operational level and at the rural systems level. It describes industrialisation as the latest 'revolutionary' stage in the agriculture of developed countries. The paper concludes that the exclusive landscape created by and required for industrial agriculture goes against the amenity goals of rural development and planning.

The role of trans-national corporation (TNC) and the land-scape of agricultural commodity production in the third world countries catches the attention in the series of key papers being discussed in context of geography of commercial activities. M.E. Fliot Hurst (7.14) mentions that 'since the early 1960's the pattern of ownership and control in food production, marketing and processing has become increasingly concentrated on a global scale in the hands of a few Transnational Corporations (TNCs). 85% of coffee, cocoa and tea marketing, 90% of tobacco and wheat, 70% of bananas and rice and 60% of global sugar trade is in the hands of less than 15% transnationals. The export oriented evolution of production has generated low purchasing power and landscapes of deprivation'. This analysis can be repeated for all food products, agricultural raw materials and minerals.

Last, but not the least Jack David talks of ecological constraints of development (24.7). The paper draws attention to the fact that the development (of commercial activities) and technical aid projects will have little chance of success until the underlying political and socio-economic causes are recognized. Many third world nations will face ecological, socio-economic and political chaos unless present day trend can by reversed.

To sum-up in brief, the following trends in the geography of commercial activities may be summarised :-

i. The avenues of development of commercial activities in space are far numerous than they were at any one time in the recent past. It is because of the efforts of new independent nations to explore their resources and the advances made in science and technology.
ii. Commercialization of traditional agriculture has increased the potential of this traditionally subsistence sector of economy towards commerce and trade.
iii. Land use planning is gaining momentum in developing countries.
iv. Socio-economic dislocations are being forced on the society due to land reforms and the role of Transnational corporations (T.N.C.).
v. The trans-border commuting and politico-economic conditions in developed and underdeveloped nations are both influencing the regional economy in terms of re-grouping of nations like the European Common Market etc.
vi. An increasingly greater attention is being paid to retailing and consumer behaviour.
vii. Outlook towards energy sources is being transformed in context of environmental quality and development.
viii. Spatial hierarchical principle is being applied in local government reforms.
ix. Commercial activities are being viewed in terms of ecological constraints.

TWO

R.N.P. Sinha

Relevance of Geography to Business Pursuits

Uninformed or poorly informed people may say that geographers have no business to talk about business, they should mind their own business, otherwise we would send them about their own business. But I must say something about the relevance of geography to business pursuits. With a view to clearing the misconception or misinformation which is at the back of such assertions.

By now it might have become clear that there are varied senses in which this term 'business' might be used. It is not an easy task to define this term to the satisfaction of every one. The Oxford English Dictionary defines it very broadly as the state of being engaged in anything; occupation, profession, or trade; a piece of work, a job; commercial transaction or engagements; a commercial enterprises. This seems to cover too wide a field. In a more concise way the term has been defined as referring to 'all such activities' establishments, institutions and organisations which operate to produce goods and services to satisfy the needs of consumers and which seek some point of location over the geographic space'.

Any business concern aims at gaining profits which depend on the following six factors:

1. Selecting favourable location for capital investments.
2. Determining the growth potential of its service and market areas.
3. Understanding international markets and investment oppor-

tunities.

4. Meeting environmental impact standards.
5. Developing effective strategies for corporate planning.
6. Getting quick analysis and presentation of masses of statistical data for business decisions.

Now let us see, what is geography and what a geographer does. Geography is a science of space relationship. The geographer studies the spatial relationship of earth's phenomena. In this process he studies both natural and social sciences. The natural science include topography, natural resources, soils, climate and weather, vegetation, and water supply. This gives the geographer an understanding of the world's natural conditions and forms the basis of interpreting the impacts between the elements of social sciences viz. the social, economic, cultural and political activities on the one hand and the diverse environments of the world on the other. Geography as taught and practised today focusses on four closely knit kinds of problems: (1) Locational analysis, (2) Environment and area analysis, (3) Interdisciplinary approach, and (4) Data management.

Having viewed the aims of business concerns and the type of studies geographers make, let us see how far these types of geographic studies and expertise go towards the furtherence of business objectives.

1. Locational Analysis

By this type of study geographers attempt to understand and predict the location of human activities. Every firm is concerned with the problem of where to invest its money. The spatial locational skills of geographers (concerned with business studies) are uniquely beneficial in the solution of this kind of problem. A geographer by this type of skill is capable to find profitable location for spatial investment. Each business has special problems of locational choice. The geographer by virtue of his advanced mathematical, statistical, and map techniques is able to identify sites/promise lowest costs or highest returns for/that/almost any kind ofbusiness or service activity.

Locations also change character through time. An initially good location may lose its attractiveness with changing conditions. Both urban geographers and economic geographers make such change studies. Urban geographers study patterns of urban growth and decline and identify trends that upgrade or downgrade parts of a city and its suburbs. They can help business managers reach decisions on where to invest in land for future industrial, recreational, residential, wholesale, or retail use. Economic geographers deal with changes in resources availability and use, labour supply, regional cost pattern, and other conditions that affect profitability of manufacturing, wholeselling, or retailing sites.

Transportation geographers are specially trained to deal with problems related to the movement of goods and people to business sites. For all business location decisions transportation studies are a must. Such studies help to predict the efficiency of materials flowing from producer to consumer, and of people travelling from homes to places of employment or to places where they purchase goods and services. Transportation companies in planning routes and schedules, use geographic network analysis to determine distance, direction, extent, and density of routes to improve the accessibility of all points in their system. Geographers come handy for such jobs.

2. **Environment and Area Analysis**

This type of exercise is sound to make in-depth studies of specific regions. Area analysis reveals the complex inter-relationships and interactions between human activities, including those of business, and the differing natural and human environments in which those activities take place. This knowledge and the techniques used to acquire it help solve many business problems such as

i. They can estimate present and future domestic markets. The growth potential of its market area is a major concern of most businesses. Geographers using the techniques of area analysis, can predict the growth of decline of these areas.
ii. They can also assist market areas to reach their growth potentials by helping prepare programmes for industrial, commercial recreations and residential development.
iii. Area studies can also help in designing urban and regional planning programmes and forcasting of resource opportunities.

iv. Such studies can also help in identifying international markets and manufacturing opportunities. Any business with international operations or one that is considering foreign investments needs information on geopolitical, economic, social, and natural conditions overseas that will affect its planning. Many geographers are specialists in some areas outside their own country. They are familier with the natural and human characteristics of their chosen region, including its language. They can report quickly and correctly on market opportunities, resource availability, prospective plant locations, and other aspects of areas under consideration.

   In an increasingly closely knit yet uncertain world, geopolitical assessments have assumed particular importance. Business decision must be made quickly, and a geographic foreign area specialist can furnish the necessary information.

v. Environmental Impact statements can also be prepared on the basis of area studies. It has become now almost essential to prepare environmental impact statements before a proposed plant or factory, or mining etc. is approved by the government. Such impact statements avoid the costly delays and other difficulties that result from environmental agencies. This also avoids unforeseen 'traps' during the construction of new facilities. The geographer trained both in natural and social sciences is the ideal professional for directing and coordinating the work of interdisciplinary teams involved in such impact studies.

3. Interdisciplinary Approach

Most corporations and big business concerns have many decentralised departments and divisions. Each provides its own piece of the puzzle. The problem is how to fit together the pieces of the corporate planning puzzle. The geographer being able to 'talk the language of a wide varriety of specialists, can help solve the problem. They in staff positions can use their broad knowledge and their presentation studies to correlate and condense information from these diverse sources to prepare comprehensive and understandable maps and position papers for decision makers.

4. Data Management

Most geographers have a common inventory of skills that they can apply to business needs. These skills are in data gathering, analysis and presentation, specially in map form. Most geographers have experience in person to person interviewing, questionnaire design and analysis, and direct field observation of economic, social, and natural characteristics of areas. They are well trained to find and use the masses of economic and social information available in libraries government publications and other secondary sources of data. Many geographers have expertise in air photo and remote sensor interpretation. Modern geographers use advanced analytical, mathematical and statistical techniques to solve problems. These, together with special computer techniques, have resulted in the development of unique geographic methods of location, and environment analysis.

Data presentation in map form is the speciality of a geographer. Every geographer is experienced in map compilation and interpretation. Computer has added a new dimension to the map making process. It analyses and converts into maps great mass of economic and social information in a fraction of the time and with much lower cost than in the past. Such maps communicate their findings quickly to business executives and manager.

In addition to their unique skills in map compassion and use, geographers are trained to write concise, yet comprehensive, reports on the conclusions stemming from their data gathering, analysing, and presentation techniques.

Building on this broad background, an increasing number of geography students in the western countries are being trained to assume business careers. Many geography department now have interdisciplinary programme with economics and business departments. Most of these include internship arrangements with private firms to give students practical experience in business problem solving. As a consequence, geographers in business are being employed as transportation analyst, consumer behaviourist, appraiser, interviewer, map interpreter, manager, media analyst, trading area analyst, sales projector and advisor.

In India this realization has not come yet. This attempts to bring to the notice of business concerns the utility of geographer's expertise in the furtherance of their objective, and goad the geographers to rise to their expertise by acquiring all the requisites skills and expertise thus harbingering a new, mutually beneficial relationship between geography and business.

THREE

A.B. Mukerji

Periodic Markets of India: Characteristics and Developmental Implications

Periodic markets have been and continue to be widespread through different historical periods and areas. While in Europe they are characteristically mediaeval in occurrence, in India their antiquity goes back to the pre-Christian centuries as is very firmly documented in the Jatakas, Vedas, Puranas, Brahmans and other religious texts and folk lores. Their diverse origins can be reduced to a rather simple set of axioms of economic exchange systems but the place and site of where they are held are essentially cultural and historical contingencies to an extent that these elements could be considered fortuitous. All quantitative, analytical, positivistic models are actually ex-post-facto explanations. If there is a rationality, it is rational in the context of the given specificities of local or regional cultures. Although the site and place of periodic markets are not derived from deterministic explanations they are, in their own turn, determinants of their essential characteristics and developmental implications.

On Place and Site

To the local people the primary identity of a periodic market is derived from its place and site. This place is always referred to in terms of an existing village and town although in behavioural terms, in their movements to and from the market, the sellers and buyers name the market after the village or town . Immediately two different questions pertaining to the two attributes are raised: why is the market located in a particular place and why is the market set on a particular site? These two questions, inpart, are related to teach other because the site sits within place but the answers to the questions are neither the same, nor supportive, nor complementary. Place and site, both conceptually and empirically, are differentiated not only in terms of scale which is not so important to their genesis and evolution. The former,whether created or evolved, involves selection, rational or fortuitous. The latter is the result of its changing responses to the local, regional, and supra-regional economic processes. Creation of transportation lines, appearance of other modes of travel other than pedestrian, and gradual intrusion of industrial products will represent the widening regional and supra-regional contact and economic changes. It is obvious that the level of economic and social development of the locality will,to a considerable extent, influence the responses of the markets to the external stimulii.

There are three kinds of relationships between the place and site of the periodic market: (i) the place is older than the site which means that the market appeared later to the emergence of the place in which its site is embedded,(ii) the site of the market and the market functioning constitute, in fact, the raison de etre of the place, which means that the market is antecedent to the place and in many cases in India these sites form the nucleus of the place as well, and (iii) the place and the site are totally unrelated which means that they originated and developed independently of each other even though they are located in the same general locality and both depend on their survival on the local population and economy. To some extent, in all the three conditions, there is an element of symbiosis.

A site is a place on minute scale but it has also regional relationships of varying orders.A site has a locational grid intersection and a situation which can be generalized. Both are important to its functioning. Regional topography, history and culture are filtered through the situation over to the site. Here, the general subsumes the specific, in the site general is concretised into the specific.

As the diagram (Fig. 1) clearly and effectively demonstrates any site is anchored in the locality, hitched to the region and linked to the supra-regional territories. The place of a site is located within the area produced by the intersection of the locality within the area produced by the intersection of the locality regions. This site place is, therefore, a sub-set common to the two intersecting locality regions. Within this region created by the intersection of regions within which the two localities are embedded The new sub-set is common to the two locality areas and the two regions simultaneously and is smaller than the first sub-set. As a matter of fact, the second subset is of higher order than the first because it is a setting in a much larger territory, and has linkages with a larger functional area. Finally, one observes the site area or plac e is sitting in the national territory itself, a superior region. Thus, a site, at once, has local, regional, and supra-regional dimensions which are hierarchically ordered in terms of significance and linkages, This systemic relationship is related to the commodity structure, transportation linkages in linkages, and the evolution of markets.

FIG. 3.1

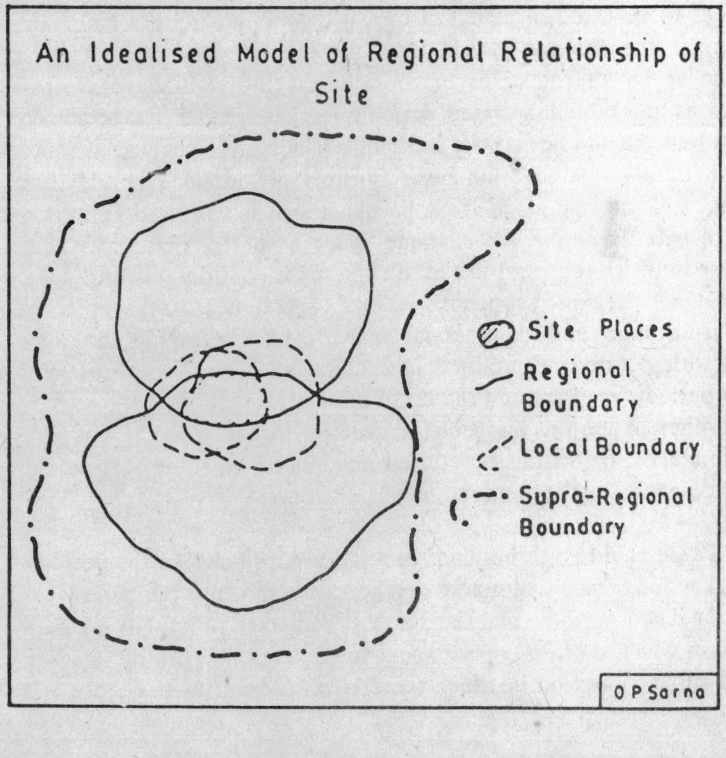

I Periodicity

Easily the most obvious characteristic of the periodic market of India, as indeed of another country, is its periodicity. In the country periodicity varies from one region to another through one-day a week, two -days a week, and three-days a week. However, the first and second systems of periodicity are the most common. The attribute of periodicity cannot be fully understood without awareness of the existing system of markets in which each member has a periodicity that complements but does not overlap the periodicity of the other.Periodicity is axiomatic in a system of periodic markets spread over a fixed territory. One could be tempted to conjecture that the rise of the levels of development would be reflected in the gradual decline in the number of days constituting the periodicity. This would simply mean that the frequency will diminish and the periodicity will be lenghtened.The corollary of this hypothesis could be that at a high level of development the periodic, fluctuating, market and market system would altogether disappear. This hypothesis needs to be ested in actual historical context but cannot be easily done in the absence of adequate and reliable data. What can be done as an alternative is to consider the differentially developed regions and their associated periodic market systems synchronically and find out the periodicity in them.Excluding the regions in which periodic markets have not been a historical trade-in, one does find that, in some regions at least,the hypothesis is validated.The backward tribal regions, for example, have a shorter periodicity than those in which the rural-urban dichotomy is considerably abridged. What is, perhaps happening in this context is that the enlarged transportation and commercial networks are pumping in larger quantities of diverse products in addition to those of local origin at the periodic markets and the establishment of new market towns on the other. When this happens the need for higher frequency of periodic market is drastically reduced and,indeed, in some regions the periodic markets become redundant.

There could be three kinds of relationships between the periodic market and permanent market: (i) condition in which the permanent market: and periodic markets co-exist with each other, (ii) a condition in which there is a permanent market but no periodic market, and (iii) a condition in which there is no permanent but there is a periodic market.

There are development implication of these relationships.In the first condition th the development level is only medium, both are fulfilling the needs of the local populace with a range of commodities and services which stand at different orders. The permanent market is providing all the higher order goods plus some lower order goods and services while the periodic market provides for all the lower order goods and services.a clear case of nesting of the orders of goods and services. It must be emphasised, however, that the goods and services being provided by both kinds of markets are derived from a necessity that is clearly created by a particular way of living, in brief, a particular culture. For the buyers and sellers, therefore, the goods and services constitute an expected category.

In the second condition there is permanent market and either no or a very few periodic markets. This condition is associated with high level of development.There is a clear indication of low or no necessity of goods and services which are generally available in the periodic markets alone.On the other hand the permanent market is sufficiently evolved so as to provide for a fairly wide spectrum of goods and services of large range of orders. Apart from the application of the Central Place Theory principles the phenomenon may be entirely historical and cultural.In the State of Haryana,in most parts,the absence of the periodic markets has been attributed to, inter alia,the diet of the local populace that does not include fresh vegetables or is based entirely on pulses. Now,the absence of the need for vegetables which throughout the country constitute the main commodity of the periodic market knocks out the need for the periodic market.Historically, this has been a region of strong agrarian communities comprised of the entire spectrum of production organisation system classes which were capable of fulling the needs of the community, at the prevailing level of demand diversification. Something that was essentially and mainly historical and cultural has become more or less frozen in time.

In the third condition the periodicity of the periodic market becomes very high and the intervals are shortened. This condition, brought about by the absence permanent market, is accompanied by a low level of development. The nature of the commodity,the dietic habits, rites and rituals, cycles of festivals, an old-established system of itinerant traders travelling over short distances, and an essentially agricultural and agrarian economy and society with restricted horizontal extension are associated with this context. Obviously, the production rate is low and there is marked specialisation in the products form one village to another so that the demands of daily living can be fulfilled only by a short-range high frequency periodic marketing system. Rural Bengal, Orissa, Assam, Bihar, and parts of eastern Uttar Pradesh and tribal areas would answer the description of this condition.In such areas we find interestingly the co-functioning of itinerant trade, service functionaries, and jajmani elements. Unless there is radical change in the economic configuration of the region the periodic market continues to prove for all the commodities and services, in a sense, hindering the emergence of a permanent market or market town or a diversified economy which promotes the coagulation of basic factors in one place.

II Periodic Markets, Itinerant Traders, and Jajmani System

In many parts of India the rural areas are serviced by itinerant traders and the traditional jajmani system. That both periodic markets and the jajmani system are simultaneously present in a rural area is an interesting fact. By the very nature of the restricted range of commodities and services provided by the itinerant traders and the sources of these commodities outside of the region the itinerant trader performed a function that was not performed by any other segment of tertiary activities. Such a trader would supply commodities of industrial origin, sugar, kerosene, matchbox, and salt. In many areas the transaction involved barter since the economy is not completely monetized. While the system of itinerant trader has its root in economic development the jajmani system is an integral element of the feudal rural social structure comprised of four classes: landowners, artisan, service, and labourers. Indeed the the latter is the essential complex of the rural production organisation system. Since neither of these two sectors provided for the commodities of the purely local nature the functioning of the periodic market become quite obvious. Equally well many of the services related to modern industrialisation, umbrella repair, lock repair, and the repair of kerosene became characteristic of the periodic markets. The beat or the movement territory of the itinerant trader is larger than that of the jajmani system and the hinterland or catchment of the periodic market is the largest. Although, there is, to some extent, overlapping of the functions provided by the three components of the tertiary sector, they, nevertheless, are coterminous. Since functional specialisation is the more marked of the characteristics they are not in competition with each other. As the area undergoes social and economic transformation all the three components lose gradually their dynamism and at different periods of change they, individually, disappear altogether. It is in the less developed areas that all the three survive for the longest duration. It needs to be emphasised that the three form a functioning system in which a change in none influences the other. However, the extent to which the feedbacks, positive and negative, are generated does not seem to be clear. What is clear is that their survival and their disappearence are related to larger, regional conditions of development.

III Site and Situation

Easily the most characteristic feature and one that strikes us immediately and is obvious in all periodic markets is the permanence of their site and the impermanence of their structures. There is cycle of life and death in the functioning of the periodic market. There remains a dead, empty site where there was bursting life generated by the interaction of sellers and buyers. In all the periodic markets one can easily observe the traditional manners of displayers and storing the commodities, the wherewithals using the locally produced arrangements and articles. An earthen pitcher, a basket, a mat, ajute bag or spread of cloth or leaves form the repetitive display support. These are brought along with the commodities and servicing equipments. In most periodic markets there is hardly any or no notion of fixed seat or place for the individual seller, thus, further reducing any need for a permanent structure.

Once occupied by a periodic market its site survives for long the historical changes. The site is everywhere rooted in the location and situational nexus. Unless there are dramatic changes in these relationships the site stays put where the market site retains its permanence. Although there are no permanent structures related to retail trade activity on the site there may be other secular or religious structures which will defy the ordeal of spatial change processes. These structures are always and everywhere as old as the site, indeed they are antecedent to the latter.

IV Site and Religion

Most sites have religious, topographic, and economic dimensions. They are not always simply fortuitous, nor are they everywhere secular. If one is impressed by consideration other than chance in the selection and occupance of a site by a market it is entirely because of the determinants being lost in history and not easily retrievable. The character of a king, the mandate of a local leader, the blessings of a local leader, the blessings of a local goddess, all can be related to the emergence of market site.

In India what are merely topographical features, physical and cultural, have deep symbolic significance. Many acre associated with rites and many are ritualistic. A well, a mango or a neem or a banyain tree, a tank, ,a ridge, a river, a temple or a shrine, a spring- all can be the raison de etre of a periodic market site's much as those of settlements. In many setting a site might even be a part a sacred space of a sacred structure. The deity ensures protection and preservation. In less developed areas, both agrarian and tribal, the temple or shrine, a well, a tree, is almost a sine qua non of the site. There is a strong theoretical possibility and empirical support for the gathering of devotees with their small offerings at the ritualistic symbol characterised by a cycle of time that corresponded with the cycle of worship. A well might have drawn people for water, a tree for shade and respite, both equally well religious symbols. The site became sanctified.

Interestingly, the site stands at the crossing of ancient routes traversed through hundreds of years by tribal or simple peasant groups. Formerly the routes were mere foot-paths. A they travelled on these paths, dangerous alignments through forests or hills, the pedestrians felt the need of a protective eye, a deity, and shrines were built. Many paths criss-crossed the country and formed the crossings, the site of a shrine and the site or the subsequent periodic market. Many paths lead to and diverged from a point, a crossing, linking the intra- territory and inter-territory localities, and later promoting the gathering of sellers and buyers. A ford on a river, a pass in the hills, the hill-plain contact, needed deity to protect the travellers during their dangerous journey. This deity shrine became a market site.

Periodic markets, at many places, share their sites with religious fairs. The periodicity of the two are totally synchronous and they mutually invigorate themselves. As a matter of fact, at such sites, the survival of the periodic market is fully assured by the continuance of the religious fair which once having come into existence can hardly ever disappear. Where this conjunction has been established the religious fair day or its periodicity corresponds to the Hindu system of year, seasons, months, days, and time (praharas) and these also become the time setting of the periodic market. In the realm of India this fusion of religious and secular is widespread through the entire spectrum of life activities. At such a complex even the structure of commodities is comprised of two sets: those which are used in worshipping and those which are used for domestic purposes.

V Periodic Markets and Service Areas

Periodic markets function in diverse kinds of areas, having different levels of socio-economic development, different degrees of accessibility, different kinds of economy, different culture groups, and different history. They are observed in both rural and urban places and reflect the persistence of old habits and traditional ways of living carried by the people from the rural to urban places. What is at once paradoxical is their survival with the same strength and dynamism as of the earlier periods even in the more developed areas undergoing transformation by modern economic technologies: mining, industries, and canal irrigation. Western Uttar Pradesh, Maharashtra, and South Bihar are good illustrations. Indeed in cities such as Dlhi and Meerut and Calcutta we have the periodical markets of ancient and recent origins. They are in competing relationship with permanent markets of these sites in that they are providing commodities and services at cheaper rates to certain classes, mostly lower middle and lower. Without these two classes it is certain that the flourishing and large periodic markets in the towns and even large cities would not have survived let alone prospered. The vast proletariat emerging out from the process of urban-industry-administration nexus fully assures the continuance of these markets which provides the buyers with a mind boggling variety of commodities, both for daily consumption and long-term use. In many cases these periodic markets have had their origins in a rural settlement serving several villages which, subsequently, were incorporated within the city territory on its extension and the redrawing of the municipal boundary.

Some of these urban periodic markets are undoubtedly of recent origin, many of the post-Independence periods; in areas of sudden city development and the influx of vast populations. These urban periodic markets are characteristically strong for a mile or so along the main road or cover the whole of a building lot or a large piece of declared vacant land.

In the hinterland of large cities too the periodic markets survive as of yore. In eastern Himalaya, in Sunderban Delta, in the Brahmaputra Valley, in the metropolitan region or Delhi, in Konkan and Marathawada, and in Gujarat we have chains and systems of periodic markets. Why are there no periodic markets in Haryana, Punjab, Himachal Pradesh, and Jammu and Kashmir has not been answered? Is their marchland location the answer? Throughout the country the periodic markets are linked with each other in terms of a hierarchical arrangement, thus, promoting a sustained system of service areas which at a certain level function exclusive of each other while the service areas of the lowest order periodic markets are obviously enmeshed in those of the next higher- order members, the former have no interplay, no intersection, and therefore are exclusive of each other. (Figs. 1 and 2) Generally, the local periodic markets are placed in the fabric or they emerge historically in it is such a way that the buyers and sellers can complete their journey from their residence (origin) to the periodic market (destination) and back and the hours spent in the market itself within one day, from sunrise to sunset. This is absolutely necessary because the market place is a functional entity, not a resting point.

For a long time now he service areas or the functional areas of the periodic markets have been supported by ancient paths having the sanction of tradition and the sanctity of pilgrimage and aligned with nature- topographical features, a spring, a river, a hillock, and pass,a patch of forest would attract or repel the alignment. The market place would everywhere be a node of convergence of paths coming from several directions.The service areas are themselves traditional, folk areas,small culture areas, or areas that report on the dominance of caste, tribe, or clan. Each such area is anchored in a small physiographic- ecologic niche, of specific mode of living, and an area of specific economic characteristics. But as the new periodic markets emerged on the landscape and some of the old ones gradually disappeared the functional areas revealed a pattern of flux.

FIG. 3.2

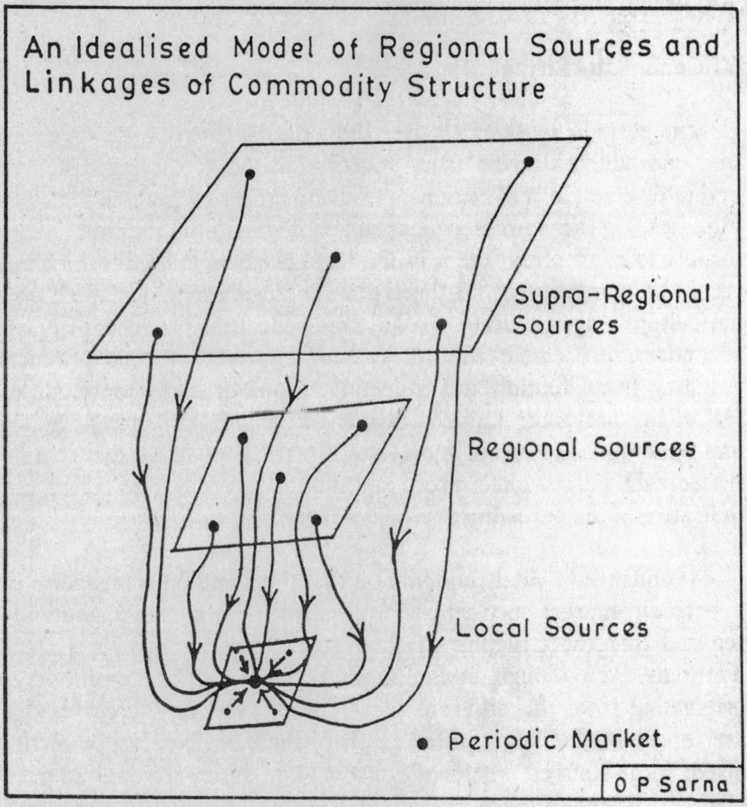

With the introduction of new routes, technological creations related in different ways than the traditional paths to the same topographic-physiographic features, new sites emerged, old markets shifted to new sites, and thus the functional areas displayed various kinds of change, expansion, shrinkage, attention, and regularisation. From a functional area based on pedestrian movement it was changed into one that involved, trucks, automobiles, auto -rickshaw, cycle- rickshaw, cycle, and varieties of carts. Technologically superior transportation systems and vehicles and mode of transportation reduced the time-distance and increased the volume of commodities resulting in an increase in the volume of trade and expansion of he functional areas. Human back, animals, and boats, however, continued singly in some areas and in complementary relationship with advanced transportation in some other areas.

VI Commodity Structure

The periodic markets all over India display a very wide spectrum of commodities derived from sources located at varying distances and in diverse kinds of regions. A sieving process separates the commodities of the lowest order and originating in the immediate locality to concentrate them in the local periodic markets which are the most numerous of all the types. These markets deal with pre-agricultural, agricultural, artisan, and industrial products-primary, secondary, processed, semi-processed, unprocessed, and products resulting from hunting and collecting. Many of these commodities reflect the prevailing mode of living: forest products such as honey and bark, fish and meat, and related to tribal mode of living while the cereals, pulses, ghee, processed milk, edible oils, and cotton are indicative of the agricultural mode of living.

Although it is widely understood that the commodity structure of a periodic market has a very wide spectrum, it is not generally realised that the structure of their source regions reveals a clear hierarchy even though in the same periodic market commodities originating from the different hierarchical levels of source regions are represented. Clearly, three levels of these regions can be recognised: local sources, regional sources, and supra-regional sources (Fig. 2). Through these commodities and hierarchically structured source regions as well, a periodic market, a tiny dot on the vast space of India, becomes integrated with the national economy and culture. This is apparent in the concurrent functioning of the permanent and periodic markets at the same place, thus further expanding the spectrum of the commodities and the services as well as, of course, the buyers and the sellers. We do find periodic markets being held in urban centres of all orders, from the Metropolitan cities of Delhi and Calcutta to the humblest *qasba* town located in a remote, backward area. Expectedly, therefore, the commodity structure assumes an incredibly wide spectrum. What makes the concurrent functioning phenomenon interesting is the unidirectional gravity influence condition, an unique kind of flow of manufactured goods from the permanent to the periodic marketing system, sarees, shoes, plastic software articles of daily household use, aluminum and steel products, and inexpensive furniture items. There is no exchange and therefore no flow of goods in the reverse direction. Nevertheless, the relationship is symbiotic in that the periodic markets support their permanent counterparts by providing to them an effective and efficient alternative channel of outflow and sale of their commodities while the permanent markets help in expanding the spectrum of commodity structure of the periodic markets. The permanent member of the marketing system does not have an exploitative relationship with the periodic member. In a periodic market located in an urban centre having permanent market the former displays an expected and striking mix of two sets of commodities (Fig. 3). Set I is comprised of the low-cost,unsophisticated, manufactured goods which are of use to a wide spectrum of class-neutral buyers and Set II is comprised of processed and semi-processed agricultural products and artisan products. The sets intersect to produce a subset that represents the agglomeration of the commodities of the two sets and is located at a periodic market, both located in an urban centre, the sub-set nature of the periodic market commodity structure is quite striking. In these conditions there is a clear spatial separation of the two sets linked by a network of transportation and exchange-system lines. In the periodic market illustrating the sub-set condition (Fig.3) the commodities, in terms of the uses, are mutually exclusive and non-substitutable in that the manufactured goods cannot be replaced by the artisan products and vice-versa and of course there is no substitute at all of the agricultural products, fresh, processed, and semi-processed. This explains the ever-expanding spectrum of the commodity structure of periodic markets in the sub-set condition. Apart from this is a type of periodic market that sells primarily the Set II commodities (Fig. 3), original and processed, and a large variety of region-characteristic artisan products which are entirely traditional in raw material, design and technology and are produced within the agrarian, production organisation system. This obviously reflects a class structure that is constructed of landowning, artisan, service, and labourer classes. Although the Set II commodity structure in a condition in which it is not intersecting the Set I and creating a sub-set is independent, the range of the commodities is small.

FIG. 3.3

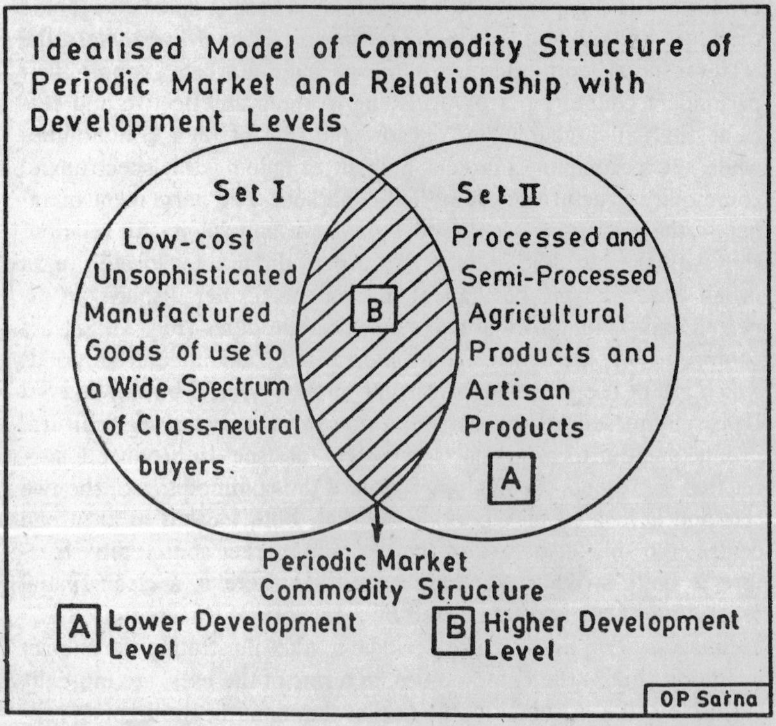

On the basis of the commodity structure it can also be proposed that there can be five different kinds of period markets : three single-criteria based and two compound-criteria based. There are periodic markets which derive their commodities from local, regional, and supra-regional sources severally answering to the description of the first kind of classification and there are periodic market which derive their commodities from local and regional; and from local, regional, and supra-regional sources (Fig. 2). It is clear, therefore, that the five types represent hierarchical levels, the local representing the first order and the local plus regional plus supraregional the fifth order of periodic markets.There is really no periodic market that does not derive its majority commodities from the local sources, In different levels the dominance of commodities originating from local, regional, and supra-regional sources display relative variations. In the periodic market based on the local-origin commodities, the local origin commodities fill the entire spectrum of commodities with none deriving from the regional and supra-regional sources. The regional type has a commodity structure that has a dominance of the local-source over the regional-source commodities. The supra-regional type is characterised by a commodity structure in which the local-origin dominates over the region-origin and the latter dominates over the suprea-region-origin commodities. In the fourth type the local-origin commodities are balanced with region-origin ones in the spectrum. Lastly, the fifth type is characterised by an approximate equalization of the commodities of different source regions.

The commodity structure in every periodic market reflects the needs of the people articulated in response to the demands of culture, environmental resources, history, and traditional linkages. The commodities are both indigenous and exotic and everywhere they tend to fulfill an incredibly large spectrum of needs, secular and religious., Nor is the commodity structure constant through time, it displays marked temporal variations that would correspond to the charts of socioeconomic markets placed in the hierarchical order display an increasingly widening spectrum of commodities and increasing complexity of the same with the elevation of their orders. The local-origin commodity structure of the simplest type of periodic markets has a surprising rigidity in its response to the changing web of socio-economic impulses. The periodic markets drawing their commodities from the regional and supra-regional sources show a far greater flexibility and resilience in their response to the oxygenic impulses of socio-economic development. They very promptly forge their linkages to an expanding network of channels of distribution and prompt and promote the intrusion of traders from a larger region, thus widening the spectrum of commodity structure. Obviously, the regional and supra-regional reflections in the periodic markets, in their own turn, also generate a larger exchange and monetary dealings. What is most surprising is that the agricultural and local bases of the commodity structure are never eroded let alone destroyed. This integrity is phenomenal.

Vll **Periodic Market Sellers**

There is a tremendous variety of sellers operating in the periodic markets. They represent a diverse spectrum of social, cultural, and economic groups. Various castes and religions are represented among them, Everywhere the types of sellers reflect the social and economic characters of the regions and the social-economic structure of the agrarian production organisation system. A periodic market is nowhere dominated by a mercantile community or a caste group of vaishyas nor is it true that the Brahmins and Kshattriyas are totally excluded from the structure of sellers. Essentially, the sellers of the periodic markets are retailers. Small volumes of products, the surplus of the agrarian production nexus, arrives and is disposed in the periodic markets to the buyers who are regular visitors to such a place of exchange and purchase. No where in India is there a specific caste group whose main occupation is to sell agricultural or other products at the periodic markets. Except for the large land-owners and zamindars or those who own the means of production in large measure, any member of the agrarian community , cultivator, collector and hunter, artisan, servicing group, and labourers are represented among the sellers.

Apart from the social types the sellers can also be classified on two additional taxonomic bases : area of origin and mode of dispersal. On the former basis one could distinguish between the local and regional sellers and the latter basis results in the barter sellers and the sellers whose dealings have become monetized. The local and regional sellers originate at different levels of areas and hence represented different spans of the range of commodities, the local selling fewer and unspecialised and small quantities of commodities. On the other hand the regional sellers spread their net wide over the spectrum of commodities of different levels of sophistication, needs, and price. Even now in many periodic markets in India one finds sellers who accept commodities in exchange for the commodities sold. These barter sellers are more characteristic of the rather backward and less accessible regions where the range of production is limited in comparison to that of the needs and the volume of a product available for sale is limited.The barter practise is a very old tradition and is continuing in many areas in many kinds of dealings. The barter sellers in particular, deal with agricultural produce, either raw or semi-processed. The monetised sellers are now ubiquitous. Obviously they sell only the agricultural and artisan produce of daily use and daily consumption, thus promoting frequent visits of the buyers to periodic markets. It needs to be remembered that these producers - sellers can bring to the periodic markets only small quantities of commodities as they move from one to other market as halting points in a circuit.The A system is most characteristic of underdeveloped areas having subsistence agriculture. They are more or less closed economic areas best illustrated by tribal territories.

The B system is somewhat larger and involves the entrepreneurs of lower levels with their own beasts of burden or a cart or a bicycle. There is intrinsic movement. The purchase by the itinerant trader from the producer directly involves a sustained trust which is promoted by an old tradition. The nexus of the producer, the itinerant trader, and the periodic market seller or the intermediate seller almost never changes. It is more or less a symbiotic system. This nexus shifts large quantities of commodities through the three links of the chain, the itinerant shifting much less than the intermediate trader. The beats and the territories are practically fixed and so they remain over pretty long time.Quite often the first two links are sustained by the crops pledged to the intermediate trader by the producer against either loan or advance money, both traditional practices. The B system is representative of the more productive areas and also of the regions which have more productive areas extending adjacent to the less productive areas. There is a larger surplus in the former areas that flows into the latter kinds of areas. These intermediate traders and the periodic market sellers deal with much larger quantities than their counterparts in A System and the periodic markets in this system need to be larger but more specialised.

FIG. 3.4

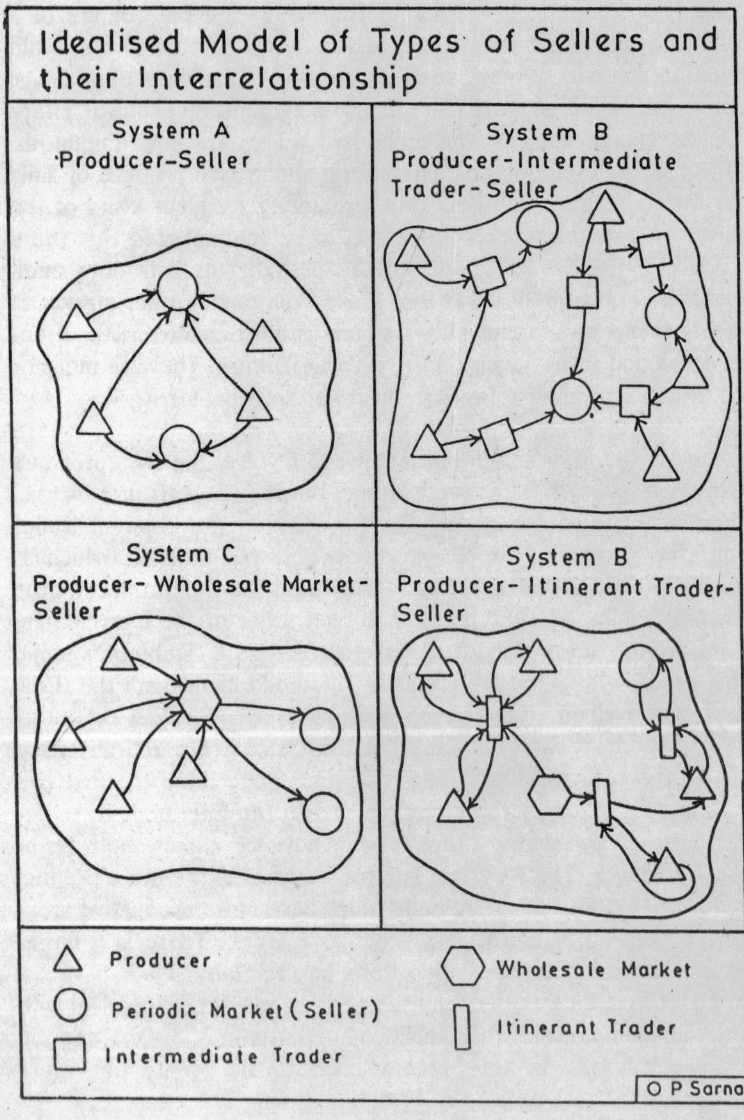
Idealised Model of Types of Sellers and their Interrelationship
System A
Producer–Seller
System B
Producer-Intermediate Trader-Seller
System C
Producer- Wholesale Market-Seller
System B
Producer- Itinerant Trader-Seller
Producer
Periodic Market (Seller)
Intermediate Trader
Wholesale Market
Itinerant Trader
O P Sarna

In the C System and the producer sells his surplus directly to the wholesale market (mandi) which it self might be periodic in nature (It could even be a periodic regulated market) and from here it is transferred to the periodic market seller. In this system, therefore, the intermediate trader or the itinerant trader is missing. Obviously, this system can function in area of open system and of much higher level of accessibility, production, and general socio-economic development. In this system the movements are far more complex, the volume involved is large, and the network of transportation has a higher level of accessibility. There is also a small system of hierarchically structured layers of points of outlets (the periodic markets and the large but specialised wholesale markets). All the three Systems, A, B, and C can function in co-existence in urban areas.

VIII Developmental Implications

One of the most widespread exchange systems, the periodic markets of India, have also played, and are playing, their humble role in regional socio-economic development.

The periodic markets, to begin with, have played a magnificent supportive role in the development and diffusion of consumerism. Through all kinds of periodic markets, rural and urban, and local, regional, and supraregional, the several channels of information create an awareness of and demands for a continuously expanding diversity of consumer products rolled out by large industrial establishments. Consumerism, as is well understood is essentially based on the hunger, most often unsuitable, for products which are exotic, not available in the local region and not produced in the local region. These goods are not absolutely necessary for the survival of the populace but are parts of a paraphernalia of fads, fashions, and fancies. Nonetheless their diffusion and increase in volume of trade and increase in money exchanges have been accelerated by the network of periodic markets. This has been possible because of the hierarchical ordering of periodic markets and their linkages which transport and filter the commodities from a higher order to lower order markets. Consumerism has also been promoted by periodic markets by becoming the channels of absorption and flow of the several alternate varieties of the same product having similar prices over a large network of periodic markets as in the permanent markets of large villages, *qasbahs* and towns of various size. Consumerism, as a phenomenon, is not a value-neutral concept but nonetheless in enlarging the range of market goods it directly contributes to the growth of trade and indirectly to the development of a whole series of industries.

The network of periodic markets of the local, regional, and supraregional orders promote inter-regional movement of goods either differing in kinds or in volume. Although such movements are also channelised through permanent markets and itinerant traders the periodic markets play no less an important role in the same process. In particular the goods specific to particular regions are moved from the regions of specialisation of one kind to those of another. Without the periodic markets there will be no transfer of specialised goods of one region of production to the other. Since all the regions are simultaneously of production and consumption the periodic market exchange system becomes inevitable. Also, through the hierarchical network the specialised goods move out from one region to another. A network of periodic markets thus converges on an influential node of spatial organisation outside of this particular region.

Apart from the fact of inter-regional movements prompted by differences in production and demand the periodic markets also display monopoly products, they do seem to have monopoly in the collection and sale of certain products specific to the local areas - - biotic products and agricultural produce alike. This condition enables the periodic markets to survive the stiff competition offered by other more organised and stronger exchange systems. The monopolistic tendencies originate not only from the environmental resources of the region but also from certain old traditions in crops, cottage industries, and forest products and livestock articles.

Since the phase of Independence and that of planned development the periodic markets have also emerged as spatial nodes of clusters of services. Even though these services are of elementary level and their number is small they do perform some important developmental functions of a lower-level. A post-office, a primary school, a primary health centre are found clustered along the site of the periodic market enabling the place to emerge as a low-order central place. These clusters are not found in all the periodic markets but many have them and more are attracting these clusters. Many development planners use these periodic markets in formulating their regional development strategies as nodes or hearths of diffusion of development impulses. These nodes are created functional landscape features which have been imposed upon the evolved periodic markets. Their acquired or inherited nodality, physical and traditional, encourages the location of clusters of services along and adjacent to them. While some of these services function more frequently than the periodicity of the periodic markets some functions some functions coincide in time with those of periodic markets. Family planning clinics and publicity camps, exhibitions relating to agricultural diversities of agricultural equipments and small agro-industrial tools are also located in these periodic markets. The agencies can reach a large, potential clientele without moving to their villages. More than their current advantages the periodic markets have large potentialities to function as diffusion centres of development. A recent phenomenon has been the establishment of periodic markets selling fresh vegetables, fish, and fruit products by the farmers' and producers' co-operatives in urban areas and also in certain rural areas. While the clusters of the institutional, state financed and administered, services become permanent in functioning, the periodic market continues to function as periodic system.

Many of the periodic markets have fairly large potentialities of evolving into *mandis, bazars,* and permanent markets.In the eventuality of such a change the number of shops, the commodity range, the structure of services, and the sale and purchase will undergo impressive increase. Particularly, where the periodic markets are held at places which have break-of-bulk locations or at junctions of two or more economic areas the change could be accelerated by the already existing network of roads, railway, steamer routes or paths. In those regions, which are even now not fully integrated with regional spatial economic organisation system there is government intervention through industrial activities, hydroelectricity establishments, or a large range of constructional activities, and the inhabitants are rapidly drawn into the realm of monetised life system resulting in an increasing demand for commodities which need to be imported. Here there is a sudden expansion of shops and commodities and the out-turn of the periodic markets. This has been a remarkable development in the tribal areas of Bihar, Orissa, and southeastern Madhya Pradesh.

For a long time now the periodic markets have been the centre of diffusion of information that concerned the populace of the local area comprising of, may be, 8 to 20 villages. With these information diffused through the local area the village communities could partake of joys and sorrows and evolve strategies for the solution of common problems. Local political gatherings and *panchayat* meetings found a suitable local in the periodic markets helped the villages in their hinterland to evolve into a local community transcending, for the purposes of cooperation and mutual support, the individual villages.

For the government and institutional services it becomes easier to operate in a much more effective manner from a periodic market. The multiple movements to reach a large number of villages are obviated by placing the services at the periodic market. Event private medicinal services are promoted by the periodic markets.

Lastly, it must be made clear that the periodic market assures at least some income to the farmers and the rural producers. In their absence the small surplus would never be exchanged either to bring money or other needed commodities. The intermediate trader (middleman) is simply not interested in picking up small surpluses which have their only outlet in the periodic markets. The idea of small surplus or small quantities of commodities sold in the periodic market is important in the context of environmental preservation as well. Whether, it is forest produce (a little honey, bark, herbs, particular kinds of grasses, leaves, roots, fish, hunted animals and birds, and fuelwood) or artisan products, the objective everywhere is to exploit the environmental resources in moderate amounts. This leaves enough time to the environmental resources to regenerate themselves. This is far more important in the tribal and subsistence production areas where the environment is fragile and where exploitation has to be moderate, selective, and cautions.

IX Conclusions

The periodic markets of India are a part of its old historical tradition. They are located in both rural and urban areas but they are far more common in areas of low socioeconomic development inhabited by tribal groups and subsistence agrarian communities of small landholdings and small surplus. The sites of the periodic markets are not everywhere explainable by the logic of transportation lines; religion, symbols, ancient paths of pilgrimage, and chance factors have been important determinants. The institutions of itinerant traders and the *jajmani* system have been supportive of the periodic markets. Periodic markets have usually a commodity structure that is characteristic of the regions in which they are located.In response to external stimulii created by industrialization, urbanisation, and evolving transportation network the commodity structure undergoes an expansion. The structure now draws commodities from the local, regional, and supra-regional sources. As a corollary, the service areas have expanded considerably. Periodic markets involve several kinds of sellers belonging to different social, economic, and functional groups. Contrary to the prevailing idea of periodic markets as inert, humble, economic system, their role, both actual and potential, in generating development processes, by acting as the nodes or centres of diffusion of development impulses, is significant. The lack of convergence between economic development and social development is reflected in the character of periodic markets. The structural element of the society related to the periodic markets is best revealed in its hierarchical structure. Hence, in an urban periodic market as well as in a permanent market there is confluence of functioning. The families of lower and lower middle classes who are not bothered about their association with the humble periodic markets visit them regularly. These classes are not concerned a bit about status. On the other hand the upper classes, highly conscious of their status, prefer the permanent markets. Thus, there can be a concept of status of market in relation to status and class of people.

Acknowledgement

The author is grateful to Mr. O.P. Sarna for drafting the sketches and to Dr. V.K. Shrivastava (Gorakhpur University) for inviting me to contribute this paper to the volume he has edited.

Theme II

Analysis of Commercial Activities

FOUR

P.C.H. Ranasinghe

A Critical Analysis of the Structure and Process of Rural Marketing in Sri Lanka with Special Reference to the Marketing of Vegetables

Sri Lanka is basically an agricultural country. 35% of the Gross Domestic Product is provided by agriculture. 50% of the total employment and 80% of the export earnings are supplied by the agricultural sector. Out of the total population, about 78% - 80% are rural and their main source or livelihood is agriculture and related activities.

Agriculture falls into two major categories, viz. plantation and domestic. In the domestic sector paddy, subsidiary food crops and vegetables are the main cultivations.

IMPORTANCE OF VEGETABLES

Vegetables constitute an essential item in the daily diet of the Sri Lankan population and forms the second important component after rice. Estimated average expenditure of an average family unit on vegetables is about 9% - 10% of the total food bill. Hence, the price fluctuations in the vegetables are reflected in the cost of living as far as the average consumer is concerned. Thus, vegetables occupy a significant position in the domestic production and consumption. Therefore, the proper and efficient marketing of vegetables is of vital importance at least in two ways: to enhance the well-being of the rural farmer and to bring down the cost of living of the consumer, especially the urban consumer.

FIG. 4.1

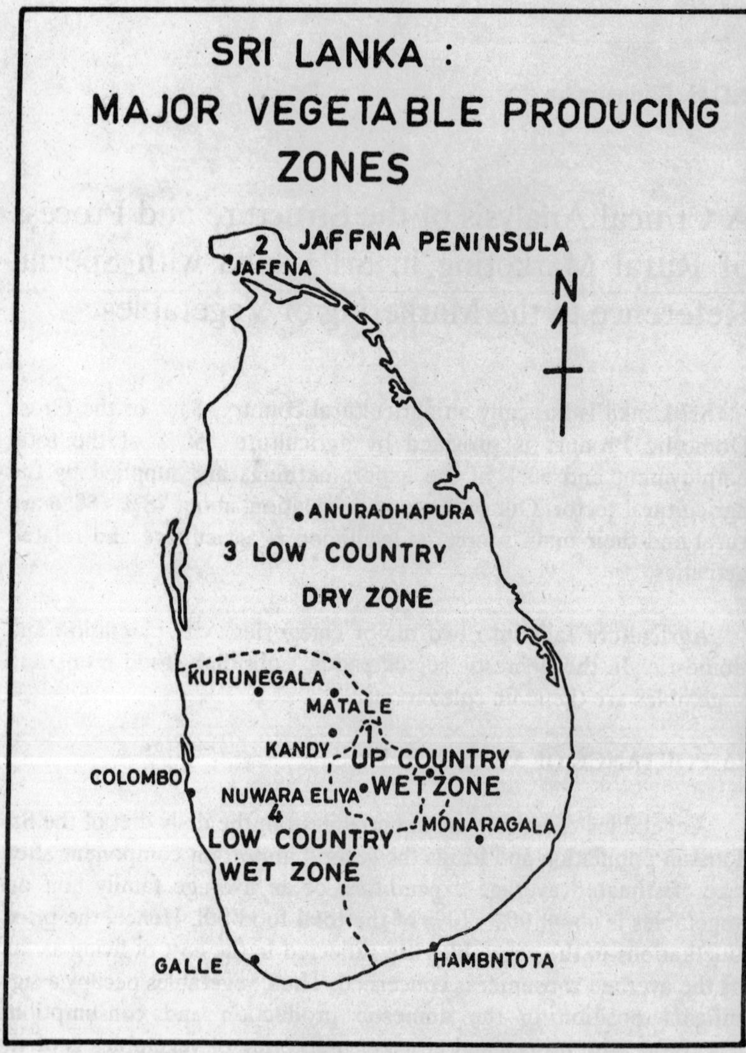

It is estimated that roughly about 61,000 metric tons of vegetables are produced annually in Sri Lanka in an area of about 122,000 hectares.

SPATIAL AND TEMPORAL DISTRIBUTION OF PRODUCTION

Generally, vegetables are grown almost every part of Sri Lanka. Yet, certain vegetables demonstrate regional specialization. Hence, four broad vegetable producing zones can be identified based on regional variations in agro-climatic conditions. These four zones are: the up-country wet zone, the low-country wet zone, the low-country dry zone and the Jaffna Peninsula (Fig. 1).

Vegetables which are grown in Sri Lanka can be divided into two major categories: viz. exotic vegetables and indigeneous vegetables. Exotic vegetables are mainly grown in the hill country where there is a temperate climate, although, and some of these, also can be grown in the Jaffna Peninsula. This type of vegetables are cultivated through out the year; but the supply varies seasonally, the two major seasons being March, April and May; and September and October. On the otherhand, indigeneous vegetables are grown in the low country wet zone and also in the Jaffna Peninsula. In the low country dry zone these vegetables are grown under 'chena' or 'slash - and - burn' system. The main supply is during July - August till February - March while January and February are the peak months. In the wet zone during the rainy season they are cultivated as highland crops; and after the paddy harvest the vegetables are also grown in the paddy fields. In the wet zone the largest supply of vegetables comes during April and August. Thus, it is clear that there is a seasonal fluctuation in the supply of vegetables in Sri Lanka. This seasonal variation has a definite impact on the price structure of the retail sales of vegetables.

MARKETING SYSTEM

The marketing system of vegetables involves the collection of produce from various parts of the island and redistribution of vegetables to the consumers mainly in the urban areas. Before the vegetables are sold to the consumer there are many functions involved in the process such as packing, transport, bulk-breaking, pricing and retailing etc.

MARKETING PROCESS

Producer Rural Areas → + Collecting + Packing + Transport + Bulk-breaking + Pricing + Financing + Retailing → Consumer Urban

However, the marketing system for vegetables can be identified in three categories:

Marketing Systems

Private | Government | Co-operative

All these three categories operate at all levels, although there are spatial and temporal variations in the intensity of their operation.

Level of out-lets

There are three levels of operation in the process of vegetable marketing in Sri Lanka.

Marketing outlets

Primary | Wholesale | Retail

However, the studies so far done in Sri Lanka reveal that, at all three levels 80% of the vegetables are marked by the private sector (Indraratne, 1975).

Primary Level Outlets

This is generally the marketing of produce at farm level. There are several forms of outlets in the primary level.

People who collect the produce from the farmers for another collector or seller. They usually keep a margin of profit varying from 5% - 8%. They are also called 'assembling agents' because they collect vegetables for some other trader.

Traders who come in lorries or vans collecting vegetables either direct from the farmers or from the assembling agents. They usually keep a margin of profit varying from 5% - 8% They are also known as 'trucker buyers'.

Wholesalers who undertake the selling for the farmers on commission basis which is usually 10% of the selling prices.

Farmers themselves sell their produce in the village fairs. This category of farmers are generally small producers.

Government sponsored outlets such as Marketing Department and Co-operative also collect vegetables, but the producers are not willing to sell their produce to these organizations due to numerous reasons such as bureaucratic procedure, excessively strict enforcement of quality tests, corruption, inability to accept deliveries due to lack of storage facilities. These factors invariably reduce the efficiency of the Marketing Department and Co-operatives as buying agents.

Out of the farmers interviewed 95% sell their produce to private traders and only about 5% dispose their vegetables through the government organizations.

Wholesale Level outlets

Pettah (Colombo) market is the chief centre for wholesale in the vegetable trade. This is the main collecting centre for almost all urban areas in and around Colombo District. The field survey revealed that about 95% of the produce which comes to this centre is through private traders such as private wholesalers and commission agents. It was also noticed that the Marketing Department (MD) and the Co-operative Marketing Federation (MARKFED) also handle a small quantity of vegetables.

Private wholesalers in the main market collect their produce through two main sources :

i. Transport agents
ii. Producers and traders who supply them directly.

MARKFED and MD collect their produce through their collecting centres and transport them in their own lorries.

In the hill country, Kandy is the main wholesale market for vegetables. Private traders and commission agents dominate the wholesale market in this city as well. MD stall in this city acts as a regional collecting point. Normal system of collection by the private trader operates in two ways:

i. the producers themselves send their vegetables to the wholesaler through commission agents on a commission basis,
ii. or wholesalers visit the farms in their own lorries and collect vegetables direct.

Apart from the two main wholesale markets in the island, bulk-breaking and wholesale marketing is carried on in almost all principal cities in the country such as Matara, Kalutara and Kurunegala.

Retail level outlets

At retail level as well, all three categories of marketing process operate. The private retailers include, stall keepers at main market centres which a are found almost in every urban centre, stall holders at traditional fairs, pavement vendors and hawkers and travelling retailers. In addition to these some of the food selling firms also are engaged in retail vegetable selling through their super markets mainly in cities. It is interesting to note that some of these private retailers themselves are producers or collectors at primary or wholesale level.

Marketing Department and the MARKFED sell the vegetables they collect through retail stalls in the urban centres. In addition, Marketing Department supplies vegetables to Government institutions such as hospitals, prisons, armed forces, and universities etc;

while MARKFEDl provides vegetables to ships and various government institutions.

The vegetable marketing system in Sri Lanka is, however, very complex and characterised by too many channels. The impact of this complexed system is felt on the price structure and in the distribution pattern.

Various functions involved in the Marketing Process

Before the vegetables reach the consumer there are various functions involved in the process of marketing. Some of these functions are formal while majority are informal. Among many functions the following could be indentified during the field survey.

1. **Cleaning of vegetables**

In Sri Lanka at firm level no cleaning or minimum cleaning takes place before the produce is sent to the market. It was observed that such cleaning was, if at all, confined to removal of spoiled or damaged produce in vegetables such as snake gourd, bitter gourd or brinjals, removal of leaves which are of bad quality with regard to leafy vegetables and removal of excess soil from root vegetables. However, some vegetables necessarily need no cleaning as in the case of beans, ladies fingers, pumpkins etc. Since cleaning of vegetables at the farm level is not accepted as a part of the marketing process the vegetables reach the wholesale market often in an uncleaned condition.

It was observed that at the wholesale outlets as well no cleaning of vegetables are undertaken. Hence the vegetables are brought by the retailers in the same original condition as they arrive at the wholesale market. However, the consumers pay much attention to the appearence and to the cleanliness of the vegetable, hence it is the retailer who cleans the vegetables before being sold. Yet, even at the retail level it is the private trader who pays much attention to the cleanliness of the vegetable when compared to the retail outlets of the Government marketing institutions.

2. **Grading and sorting**

Grading or vegetable can be defined as separating vegetables which have the same qualities into different lots.

There is a difference between the private buyer and the Marketing Department as far as the grading is concerned, Private trader usually pay a flat rate for produce without any sorting while the Marketing Department buys the vegetables from the producer based on grades. Therefore, the producer prefer the private trader to the Government buyer.

It was observed that the private buyers are not concerned about the grades of the vegetables but they insist on removal of damaged vegetables. The main problem faced by the producer is that the grading systems applied by the Marketing Department are obscure, therefore, the producers prefer to get a flat rate from the private trader without some of the produce getting condemned.

At the wholesale level it was observed that even the private trader sort and grade the vegetables and fix the price accordingly. Most interesting feature in the retail marketing of vegetables in urban areas is the relationship between the grades and quality of vegetables and the retail prices and also the level of selling points.

Good quality, better grade vegetables are sold in the Supermarkets which are sponsored by the Government but where the stalls are run by the private traders. Second grade vegetables are sold in various shops and market stalls and inferior quality vegetables are sold on the road-side stalls and by mobile vendors. However, at the retail level, grading is according to cleanliness, size, appearence and the freshness of the vegetables.

Packing

Transport of vegetables from the producing areas to wholesale markets usually takes one to one and a half days. Therefore, to avoid the vegetables being damaged or spoiled proper packing should be done.

Producers use gunny bags to pack vegetables such as beans, cabbage, beet-root, carrots etc. Wooden boxes are used to pack tomatoes and capsicums. Some vegetables are just bundled by tying with coir ropes. Producers try to minimize the cost of packing by getting the maximum quantity of produce into one container. Usually about 50-100 Kg. are packed in one container.

It was observed that the packing methods and systems applied by the producers are most unscientific and technically inefficient, yet, there is no incentive for the producer to use more modern methods of packing. Applying modern methods would only increase the cost and would further reduce the profit margin of the producer. Lack of proper transport and wearhousing facilities further discourage the producers to apply new techniques of packing.

Cold storage is virtually absent for private trader and only in the Marketing Department a limited facility of cold storage is available to keep the vegetables over-night.

Transport

In the localities where the observations were made most of the vegetable farms are not accessible by motor vehicles. Farmers transport their produce from the farms to the nearest collecting centre through head portage employing either family or hired labour. Collectors or transport agents welcome this system since it saves time and the transport cost to them. Normally collectors visit the farms if the quantity of produce is fairly large and the farms are accessible by lorries. Sometimes the farmers transport their produce by ox-driven carts or hand carts or even by tractortrailers from the farms to an assembling point. Farmers who bring the produce themselves to the major terminal markets or periodic rural markets use hired lorries, carts bicycles and even public transport.

In areas not served by proper farm to market roads, transport becomes an arduous and time consuming operation. Due to the difficulties of transport the farmers often come under the control of the middlemen who undertake to transport their goods. These middlemen purchase the produce at a price considerably lower than what prevails in the market. This is done because the purchases are made by such traders at the farm level.

However, marketing conditions in the village do not help the producer to obtain the the best price for his produce.

Weighing

This also an important function. Almost all the farmers interviewed said that they weigh their produce before selling to the collectors or wholesalers. Some farmers had their own system of measurements. However, 80% of the farmers reported that they are not quite happy with the systems of weighing applied by various buyers. Private traders usually keep a broad margin of weight of containers, excessive moisture, drying, spoiled vegetables etc. Most of the farmers are of the view that the collectors or traders use incorrect weight mostly through faulty scale.

Even at the retail level incorrect weight is observed. This is mainly done to recover the loss due to low prices on damaged good.

Mechanism of Marketing and vegetable Prices

Marketing Coast Profit Margins and Price of vegetables

Several main components can be indentified into the formation of the retail price of vegetables.

a. Cost of production
b. Producers' profit margins
c. Cost of marketing
d. Middlemen's profit margin
e. Loss, and waste of produce in handling and transit.

Marketing Costs Marketing costs comprise of the following:

Transport Coasts

Transport cost which the producers have to bear varies according to the outlet through which they sell their produce. If they sell their produce to the commission agents they have to bear the total transport cost. Farmers who sell to the village assembling agents or trucker buyers have to bear only the transport cost which would incur from the farm to the assembling point.

Transport cost varies according to many variables such as conditions of road, the supply of vehicular facilities. However, over the years transport cost have increased due to increasing cost of fuel, vehicles, and the spare parts, and wages. For instance in 1964 the transport cost per 50 Kg. from the hill country to Colombo was about Rs. 1.50 and in 1974 it increased by about 350% and in 1984 it has increased almost by another 460%.

Cost of containers: Some commission agents supply containers to the producers but most of the producers have to use their own containers. Gunny bags can be used only there times and wooden boxes for about one month duration and cadjan can be used only once.

Labour charges: Farmers have to pay both loading and unloading charges when they sell their produce through the commission agents. Charges are mainly on piece-basis. When the producers sell their vegetables to trucker-buyers, they have to pay only for loading.

Commission and Broker Fees: Commission agents normally 10% of the proceeds of sales payable to the vegetables producers as their commission.

However, it is difficult to compute the actual charge of commissions as it varies from area to area and from produce to produce.

Retailers have to pay a commission of about 10% to the brokers in the wholesale markets.

Market levies and Taxes and Rent etc.: Producers who are selling their produce at fairs have to pay a tax to the Local Body.

There are four grades of whole stalls in the Pettah market. The annual rent payable to the Municipality varies according to grades.

Wastage: Shrinkage and spoilage cause loss of weight from the farm upto the sale point. If was observed that 14% - 16% weight is lost in this way. The producers reported that they have to bear this loss. At the retail level, cleaning, washing, spoilage and shrinking also takes about 17% of weight. This is usually transfered to the consumer through the retailer.

Conclusion

The basis of this paper was the data and information through field observations and various published sources.

The study reveals that the prices of vegetables have gone up especially during the recent years. However, it is difficult to calculate the increase in prices throughout years since the vegetables have such a variety and also the supply of different varieties are subjected to physical factors. Nonetheless, the study has helped to find a few factors which are responsible for the present structure and pattern of price fluctuations in vegetables, especially related to marketing.

Transport Coasts

Transport cost have increased considerably with increases in prices of fuel, spare parts, vehicles and wages. It was also revealed that the concentration of transport services among a few people prevents any reduction of transport charges which should really have had a different effect with the liberalization of import of vehicles. Coast of packing material and containers, labour charges, market levies, taxes rents and the cost of communication have also gone up considerably which have contributed for the increase in prices of vegetables.

Inefficiency of Government Marketing Institutions such as Marketing Department and MARKFED

These organizations could not provide a reasonable competition to the private trader.

Consumer demand

It is not possible to calculate the demand for each vegetables over-time. However, available sources such as food balance sheets, socio-economic Surveys and consumer finance Surveys show that there has been a progressive reduction in per capita consumption of vegetables. Decreasing per capita consumption suggests relatively lower quantity of production and simultaneous increases in total population.

Profit margings of the producer

It was observed that the total marketing costs incurred by the producer varies according to the outlet. For example when they sell their produce to the commission agent they have to incur more cost than the producers who sell their produce to the "trucker buyers". Several individual vegetable prices were analysed and found that in general the net price received by the producer is as much as 50% less than the consumers' buying price.

Proper Packing

The wastage is more due to bad and unscientific packing. Yet the producers are not prepared to improve the system of packing since it is not going to increase their profit margin.

Middlemen

Various elements of imperfections operate at various levels of marketing with the results of limiting the competition among the traders which in turn leads to a low producer prices and exceptionally high profits to the middlemen.

In conclusion it can be said that the producers do not get a reasonable price for their produce and at the same time the consumers pay very high prices for vegetables due to many factors, such as the behaviour of the middlemen, the monopolistic operation of the transport, poor storage facilities provided at the government collecting centres etc. The government should enforce legislation to prevent the specialization of routes by private transporters and collectors and try to assure a more equitable distribution of transport facilities. The collecting centres should have better storage facilities. It is important to eliminate the operation of the middlemen or brokers at the primary level and also the touts at the wholesale level. These two groups increase the marketing cost for the producer and reduce the profit margin considerably. Physical conditions of the markets should be improved along with the infrastructure in the producing areas. Markets informations such as the prices and demand should be diffused in an effective manner.

Finally, producers should organize themselves into various unions where they can have their own system of collection and transportation to the wholesale markets.

FIVE

M.D. Tawade and
B.N. Gophane

Marketing Organisation and Commercial Fruit Farming: A Case Study of Konkan Region of Maharastra State

The Konkan region, the coastal part of Maharashtra, is famous for fruit farming. Often it is referred to as the "California" of Maharashtra. Maharashtra State is comprised of four major regional divisions - Vidarbha, Marathwada, Western Maharashtra and Konkan. Amongst all the regional divisions, Konkan carries the highest proportion of land under fruit cultivation. It is not just the outcome of " Green Revolution" or "agricultural innovation" in the recent past, but this region has been traditionally known for its fruit farming bias in agriculture, as a natural growth in response to the conducive geographical environment. Though there were no human efforts in the orientation of Green Revolution, the land has provided natural impetus for this specific enterprise. The type of soil, the climate and the physiography are very good bases for cultivation of fruits. Besides, the traditional endeavour has been helping the regional economy.

However, this commendable fruit farming has been lacking marketing organisation. Due to this significant lacuna, the pattern of fruit farming has been getting a set back. The impact of this unorganised marketing system has ultimately proved to throttle up the commercial farming. It is the backbone of the regional economy. The Kondan region is, therefore, inevitably declared by the scholars as a "problem region" of India.

Theoretical base

A good marketing system is a pre-requisite for maintainance of a pattern of production suited to the geographical environment and for ensuring economic stability of a region. It is vertical linkage which is very essential to provide assurance of distribution in a proper manner to nourish the agricultural activities. A region devoted to commercial agriculture, naturally indulges in surplus production of certain monopolistic varieties. Obviously, in this process the region remains dependent upon other regions for meeting its needs of other commodities. Further, if the basic commercial crops fail to bring home the desirable returns, the entire agricultural economy crumples and the related repurcussion of economic instability become evident.

The "on farm" activities and the "off farm" activities are to be complementary to each other. If the "off farm" activities in the shape of a healthy market channel upto the consumer are not systematised properly, the "on farm" activities suffer and ultimately the farmer gets affected. In the commercial farming, thus, the marketing organisation plays a vital role.

A good marketing organisation warrants market intelligence at farmer's level, existence of minimum number of middlemen, a smooth traffic flow, efficient collection and storage system and reliable monetary feed back. The occupation of agriculture has not yet been given the status of an industry. The entire price fixation and the distribution of goods is in the hands of the middlemen who prove themselves as exploiters, rather then beneficiaries. The cultivators are helpless and are at the mercy of the middlemen. The product is taken by the farmer to the market, where the fate of the farmer and his farming enterprise is at stake. Whatever price is fixed by the middlemen, has to be accepted by him. When in such circumstances the producer is exploited, the regional economy deteriorates. To improve the regional agricultural economy, it is, therefore, necessary to examine the entire market system.

The Konkan's fruit farming

The Konkan region is comprised of five districts, including the

Bombay region. It is the coastal region of Maharashtra, a strip running north-south. It is marked to the west by the Arabian sea and to the east by the sahyadrian ranges. Due to its narrowness, (40 Km. width on an overage) and the hilly terrain only 30% of the land is available for agriculture. The entire region is very weak in industrial development. The physiographic inconveniences are coupled with unreliable rainfall. These are certain significant adversities for the routine agricultural field cropping. The farmers have to seek some alternative in this situation. They have to look for some substitute for the field crops. The field crops in the poor agro-economy are not commercially viable.

The agronomic base of the region is favourable for fruit farming. Mango, coconut, betelnut, jackfruit, banana, chiku and cashewnut are the main fruit crops of this region.[1] Considering the agronomic bases in this region every expert committee (in all seven committees so far), appointed for suggesting means for regional development, has recommended fruit farming as the main base for the development of this region.

The natural growth of fruit farming, in spite of absence of organisational incentives, has been commendable in the recent two decades. The acreage under the fruit crops has been doubled. In the paucity of irrigation (only 4% irrigation) and moderate net sown area (30% of the total area), the farmers have pinned their hopes on fruit farming. To make fruit farming a good economic proposition, some planning measures are necessary. Planning of land use under fruit farming on the basis of suitable environment, improvement in the fruit farming varieties and provision of good infrastructure with a better marketing system and agro industrial units are the requisite measures for exploiting the favourable geographical bases of fruit farming.

Marketing of fruits

The marketing system for the fruit farming activity in the Konkan is important for development. The entire process of agricultural operation and innovation is ultimately dependant upon the cash in the hands of the farmer. The land holdings in the Konkan region are already small, i.e. less than 1.2 hectares per agricultural worker.

These land holdings do not permit the farmers for going in different experiments. The lack of agricultural education and paucity of funds for progressive agricultural investment are two major handicaps that the farmers face. A good marketing system would be able to increase the economic strength of the farmers. The present market system is highly unfavourable for the farmers. It is not able to pay proper dividend to the cultivator.

The marketing channel:

The marketing of fruits is extremely mal-organised. The channel starts from the preharvest period itself, especially with regard to mango. Though the fruits are ready for sale in April, the transactions start in December-January, i.e. 5 months in advance. There are "preharvest village level contractors" who decide the price of the fruit tree for the season by observing the intensity of its flowering. The grower (its farmer) is not the decision maker. Naturally the contractor plays very safely and gives minimum price for the prospective fruits. The poor farmer accepts the bargain as inevitable one. the same process is followed with some modifications in the case of all fruits produced in the Konkan.

There are five middlemen in the entire process, till the fruits reach the urban consumer. It will be seen that when a consumer pays Rs. 100/-, then the producer at the lowest stratum gets only Rs. 18-30 (Table I). This meager income can never be expected to boost either the morale of the farmer or the status of the regional economy. Due to this paltry return, the fruit farming has not been proved as a good economic proposition.

There are two adverse repercussions. Firstly, the fruit farming activity is not able to reach the status of commercial proposition. Secondly, the farmer is not in a position to spare some money, after meeting his expenses, to invest for innovative measures in his farming activity. This is a vicious circle making the economy more and more unstable. The returns are progressively diminishing. The fruits like mango, cashewnut and coconut have acquired reputation in the consumer market. However, this good reputation has been bringing dividends to the middlemen who do not know the basics of fruit farming. The farmer is away from any benefit.

The analysis brings home one significant point. The benefits of fruit farming are nullified by the faulty marketing organisation as far as the farmers is concerned. He is devoid of any dividend. Thus, even though the natural resources have have potential for commercial fruit farming, the economy remains at subsistence level. The farmer is unable to invest for improvement of his fruit garden. There are 18 big fruit cooperative estates in the region. Out of these 12 are stagnant and 6 gardens have already declined.

TABLE - I : MANGO PRICING AT BOMBAY MARKET

Shareholder	Per cent
Grower	18.30
--	
Watching 1-80 | Packing 5- 70 | Harvesting 2-80 |	10.30
--	
Loss & Damage	5.00
Preharvest Contractor	18.10
--	
Coolic charges 0-50 | Transport & Octroi 12-30 | Commission Agent 5-60 |	18.40
--	
Whole Seller	13.30
Retailer	8.30
Hawker	8.30
Consumer	100.00

Cartels of Middlemen

The cartels of middlemen have been sucking the major share of the price paid by the consumer. The trade in cashewnut and arecanut can serve as a good examples. Cashewnuts are collected by the local itinaries or agents at the weekly markets or by going from door to door. The farmers do not know the market channel. They do not know where their products will ultimately go. The price of arecanuts is fixed first at the terminus (Bombay) market and then at the local (Konkan) markets, The "trade formula" in this ıse is as follows :

$$Li * \frac{Bi \times 2}{3}$$

Li = Local market price
Bi = Bombay market price

According to this formula, the price differences should be 33.3%. But the cartels of middlemen fix the prices keeping the differences upto 50%. The farmer at the receiving end has to accept the price given. The weighing of the product and fixing of the price are done by the middlemen. They (middlemen) are organised but the farmers are not. This helplessness is caused by two factors - the absence of market intelligence at the farmers level and a lack of collection as well as storage facilities.

Market intelligence

The market intelligence is a function at farmers' level. It comes out of the agricultural education mode available to them. It can be given directly to them or through regulated markets established at strategic locations. Both the channels are not available in the Konkan. The farmer is perilously devoid of the knowledge. The lack of market intelligence at the farmers' level is convenient to the middlemen. In this situation they can exploit the producers. Good organisations to disseminate market intelligence to farmers are formed in Western Maharashtra. They have improved the lot of the farmers and exposed the cartels of middlemen. But such innovations are yet to be introduced in the Konkan.

Collection and storage facilities

These facilities are especially essential in fruit trade where most of the fruits are perishable. They are to be taken to the consumer market as quickly as possible. The producer cannot afford to keep them with him for a longer time. In such a rush, there can be a "glut" in the market. Such a glut bring the prices down. Such unwanted or unwarranted floods in the markets are to be avoided. This can be achieved by creating collection centres, storage and agro-industrial units at proper places on the basis of assessment the flow of fruit supply from different parts of the region.

Conclusion

The components of marketing organisation as discussed above play very vital role in all agricultural products in general and the fruit farming in particular. It is ecause, fruit farming is necessarily a commercial proposition. In an economy like that of the Konkan, where the nature or the geographical setting has destined the region to rely solely or exclusively on the fruit farming, it is rather imperative to design a market system strategy. For doing away with cartles of middlemen smooth marketing channel, provision of market intelligence and organisation of collection, storage and processing centres are the requisite measures. These will be proper means to remedy chronic ills in the case of a "problem region" like the Konkan of Maharashtra.

NOTES

1. Government of Maharashtra, Deptt. of Agriculture "**Agricultural development schemes in Konkan and facilities of them**" Bulletin No. 374, April, 1970, P. 11, 15, 18.

SIX

P.R. Chauhan

Spatio-Temporal Pattern of Agricultural Development in Madhya Pradesh

Introduction

Agriculture occupies most important place in the economic structure of Madhya Pradesh. It is mainly because of the diversified nature of the cultivation. Agriculture thus provides one of the fundamental bases for economic growth of the study region. The spatio-temporal pattern of agriculture, therefore, controls the socio-economic development of the State.

The dominant role of agriculture in the state economy may be seen in the fact that more the 87% of the state's total main workers are engaged in agriculture and provide livelihood to more than 79% of the total population (1981). So far as the land use is concerned, out of the total geographical area of the state 42.6% is net sown area, followed by 31.7% forested area, 10.3% not available for cultivation and the rest as follow and cultivable fallow lands. Agriculture, including animal husbandry in the state at current prices accounts for 48.4% of the net state domestic product.[1] Due to lesser population it provides surplus foodgrains and other agricultural products. In this way, the state plays an important role in the economy of the country.

Taking into consideration the importance of agriculture in the economic development of the state and of the country, it would be useful to analyse the regional and temporal pattern of agricultural development so that an over all view of economic development may be assessed.

Data Base

In order to highlight the regional pattern of agricultural development, the selection of indicators has been made in such way that each indicator may be reflective of agricultural development on one hand and capable to point out the regional imbalance on the other. This situation calls for a large number of indicators and their spatio-temporal analysis. In case of the present study, the following 13 indicators have been selected for the year 1971-72 and 1981-82 respectively.[2]

Indicator

1. Net area sown in '000 hectares
2. Net irrigated area in '00 hectares
3. Gross cropped area in '000 hectares
4. Area under foodcrops in '00 hectares
5. High yielding varieties coverage in '00 hectares
6. Consumption of fertilizers in '00 tones
7. Per hectare consumption of fertilizers in kg.
8. Irrigational pumpsets and tube wells energised.
9. No of tractors
10. Production of total puleses in '00 tones
11. Production of total cereals in '000 tones
12. Production of total oilseeds in '00 tones
13. Production of total commercial crops (Fibers) in '00 bales.

Methodology

On the basis of the above indicators, a district level analysis of spatio-temporal pattern of agricultural development has been attempted. 'Proportional Standardised mean' method (Srivastava, 1983) has been used to find out the composite indices of the agricultural development. Since all the indicators are not equal in nature and do not contribute equally to the levels of agricultural development, weights have been alotted to each indicators to bring them on an equal level. The $\frac{\bar{x}}{\sigma}$ is weight of any indicator where:

?

x = mean of the indicator 'X'

σ = standard deviation of the indicator 'X'

The composite indices have been derived according to the following formula :

$$\text{Composite indices (C.I.)} = \frac{x1 \frac{\bar{x}1}{\sigma 1} + x2 \frac{\bar{x}^2}{\sigma 2} \text{-------------} x^n \frac{\bar{x}^n}{\sigma n}}{\frac{\bar{x}^1}{\sigma 1} + \frac{\bar{x}^2}{\sigma 2} \text{-------------} \frac{\bar{x}_n}{\sigma n}}$$

Here, tne weights alotted to each indicator are 13.40, 6.70, 16.49, 4.93, 8.84, 7.26, 8.09, 3.98, 6.44, 10.93, 2.90, 7.07 and 2.90 (1981) respectively. Gross cropped are finds the maximum weight of 16.49 followed by 13.40 weightage of net area sown. The lowest weightage (2.90) is noted in the case of pulses and commercial crops. Taking Madhya Pradesh as 100, districtwise composite indices have been calculated. According to the indices the districts have been grouped into four categories of the levels of agricultural development (1971-72 & 1981-82).

Indices	Level of Agricultural Development
> 150	Very high
115 - .115	High
85 - 115	Medium
< 80	Low

The results are mapped in fig. Nos. 1a & b.

The Findings

The maps show the regional pattern of agricultural development. The range of composite indices varies from 249.06 (Raipur District) to 32.75 (Datia District) for 1981-82; and 225.05 (Mandsaur district) to 45.76 (Damoh district) in 1971-72.

FIG. 6.1 (A & B)

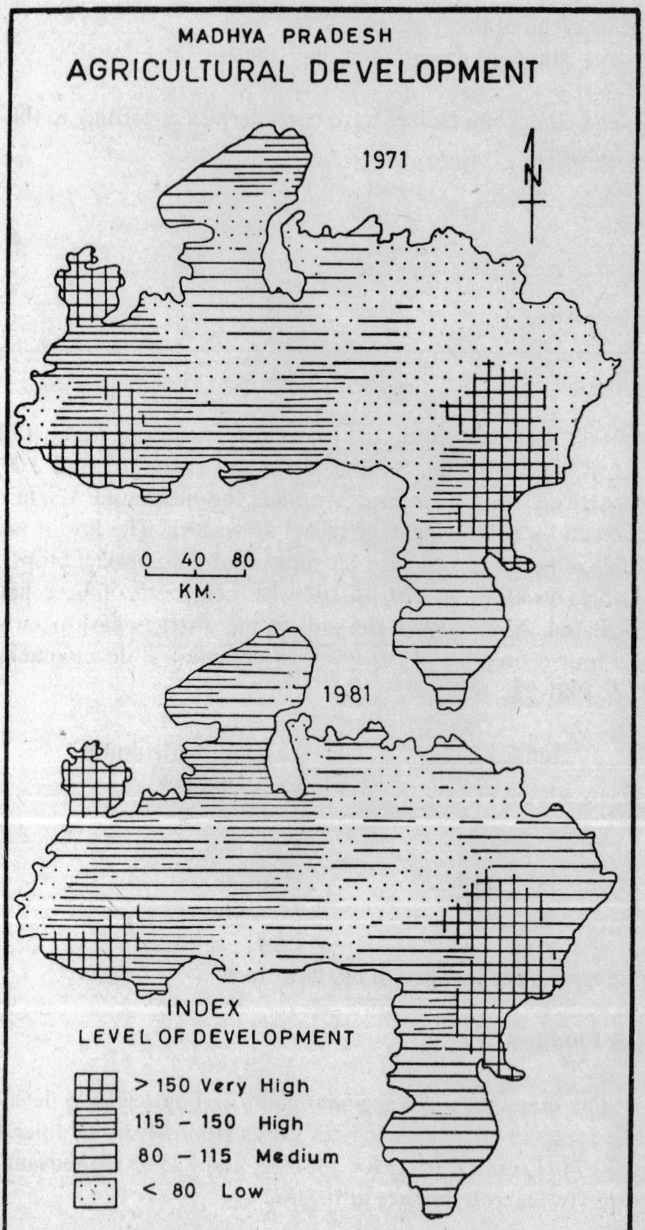
MADHYA PRADESH
AGRICULTURAL DEVELOPMENT
1971
N
0 40 80
KM.
1981
INDEX
LEVEL OF DEVELOPMENT
> 150 Very High
115 – 150 High
80 – 115 Medium
< 80 Low

It is observed that the areas of very high agricultural development lie in the Chhattisgarh plain (Raipur, Bilaspur districts) and in the western parts (Mandsaur, Kharagone districts) of the state. It is well known that these districts are facilitated with high intensity of irrigation, high percentage of HYV crops, expansion of new technology, and existence locations of a large number of regulated markets (Kumar, 1983) etc. It is also noteworthy that the western part possesses black soils suitable for commercial crops, specially cotton, while the districts of Chhatisgarh Plain are situated in the 'Rice Bowl' of the state. The second category of high agricultural development areas are scattered in the districts of North Western black soil tract (Dhar, Ujjain, Vidisha, Shivpuri, Sagar, Khandwa and Dewas), and Durg district of Chhattisgarh plain. These areas are adjacent to the areas of very high agricultural development. Therefore all these districts in this category possess almost the same facilities.

In this way medium level of agricultural development comprises the districts of Madhya Bharat (Bhopal, Shajapur and Indore districts) Central Mahakashal, North Eastern plateaun and the Dandkaranya regions. These districts have less irrigational facilities and fertile lands. The districts of Madhya Bharat, specially of the Chambal region are facilitated with irrigational infrastructures and fertile land, and therefore are countered in this category. Other districts are undeveloped in agricultural infrastructures due to hetrogenous topography. The agriculturally low development areas occupy the districts of North Central, and South Western parts of the state. These regions have scarce water supply undeveloped irrigation and less fertile lands and above all these are far from innovations, i.e., HYV crops, use of chemicals and fertilisers etc.

Spatio-temporal Pattern

More or less the regionalisation of agricultural development is almost the same in both the time periods of 1971-72 and 1981-82 with a few exceptions. there are 18 districts above the state average of agricultural development. A slight fluctuation is found in case of Indore district which has shifted its position from the first category (1971-72) to the third category in 1981-82. Narsinghpur, Dhar, Ratlam, Gwalior and Chhindwara districts have similarly shown a down word shifts in 1981-82 from 1971-72. The districts of Eastern Plateau and Madhya Bharat regions have shown an upward shift (Fig. 1). In this way the change in the agricultural development between 1971-81 may be observed in parts of Chhattisgarh, North-Western Madhya Bharat and Central Mahakoshal regions of the state where the expansion of irrigation, diffusion of innovations and infrastructural development have helped to a positive transformations of agricultural development. It is notable that some of these findings are similar to Sharma's findings (1980).

Conclusion

It may thus be mentioned that there are considerable disparities in agricultural development because of differences in soil fertility, variation in irrigation facilities and variation in the capacity of cultivators to utilise the fertilizers, chemicals and HYV crops. The regions having assured water facilities and expanded irrigational facilities like electrified pumps, canals and well developed pattern of infrastructures like rural electrification, network of marketing system etc. have shown steady progress. These facts indicate that there is a need for the expansion of irrigational facilities, innovations and agricultural infrastructure specially in the areas of Eastern Plateau, North central Mahakoshal and Bundelkhand regions.

NOTES

1. Agricultural Statistics 1982, Directorate of Agriculture M.P., Bhopal.
2. Agricultural statistics, M. P. 1972 & 1982 C.M.I.E., Bombay, 1982.

SEVEN

S.C. Sharma

Spatio-Temporal Changes in the Cultivation of Commercial Crops in the Tarai Region of Eastern Uttar Pradesh

Commercial crops play a very important role in the rural development of a region where agriculture is the mainstay of the people. They not only provide nutritive dish, but are highly remunerative also. Commercial crops may fetch high prices in the market and thus add to the prosperity of the rural community. As such, in any planning which aims at the coherent and balanced development of the rural masses, proper attention has to be paid to their cultivation.

The paper attempts to analyse the land use of the *Tarai* tract of eastern Uttar Pradesh under some important commercial crops, viz., sugarcane, oil-seeds and vegetables, with a view to explain the changes that have occurred during the period 1955-57 to 1980-82.

The region under study stratches in a narrow strip of land along the Indo-Nepal border between the river Ghaghra on the west and the river Gandak on the east with gently rolling low-lying land criss-crossed by streams and possessing fertile soils characterized by high moisture in the sub-soil and high clay factor. It has high temperature and high humidity and moderately heavy rainfall. Of the total cultivated area 26.3 per cent and 40.2 per cent is under irrigation and double cropping respectively. The net cropped area accounts for 77.9 per cent of the *Tarai* area of the region. The region has poor means of transport and communication and has long suffered stagnation and under-development (Shrivastava, V.K. 1983).

The commercial crops which comprise of sugarcane, oilseeds and fruits and vegetables cover 48,250 hectares, i.e. 7.9 per cent of the *kharif*, 6.8 per cent of the net cropped area and 4.2 per cent of the total cropped are in the *kharif* season; and 35,478, i.e., 9.2 per cent of the *rabi*, 4.9 per cent of the net and 3.6 per cent of the total cropped area in the *rabi* season. Together, they claim 7.8 per cent of the total cropped area of the region as against about 21 per cent in the case of the country as a whole. Generally, their concentration, is higher towards the west and the east.

The area of the commercial crops in question has increased from 50,967 to 83, 728 during the last 25 years. The volume of change in the area as a whole is to the tune of plus 2.6 per cent (+ 1.1 in the first 10 years and +1.5 in the later 15 years). There are micro-level variations which may be discussed in the case of some important crops.

SUGARCANE

Among the commercial crops, sugarcane ranks first, it covers an area of 43,496 hectares or 7.1 per cent of the *kharif*, 6.1 per cent of the net and 4.4 per cent of the total cropped area of the region, although these figures are lower than that of the state of Uttar Pradesh where 9.5 per cent of the net sown area and 7.1 per cent of the total cropped area is devoted to the cultivation of sugarcane (1975-76).

Sugarcane flourishes well on heavy loam with good drainage and slightly acidic to alkaline soils. Its moisture requirement is considerable (1250-1500mm). It requires care culture, heavy manuring and adequate irrigational facilities and demands more labour. All these agro-climatic and socio-economic conditions and competition from other crops affect the spatial distribution of this crop within the region (Fig. 1-A).

Three eastern most blocks, viz., Khadda, Nebua Naurangia and Bishunpura have very high concentration (above 20 per cent). In 2 blocks (Siswa and Nichlaul), it is high (10-20 per cent) and in 2

(Gainsari and Ghughali), it is moderately high (5-10 per cent). In 12 blocks (Bansi, Balrampur, Khuniaon, Phanwapur, Tulsipur, Pachperwa, Barhni, Maharajganj, Mithaura, Laxmipur, Pharenda and Brijmanganj) it is moderate (2-5 per cent) and in the remaining 12 blocks, it is low (2 and below) with almost negligible in all the blocks of Bahraich and Basti districts.

FIG. 7.1 A AND B
THE TARAI REGION OF EASTERN UTTAT PRADESH

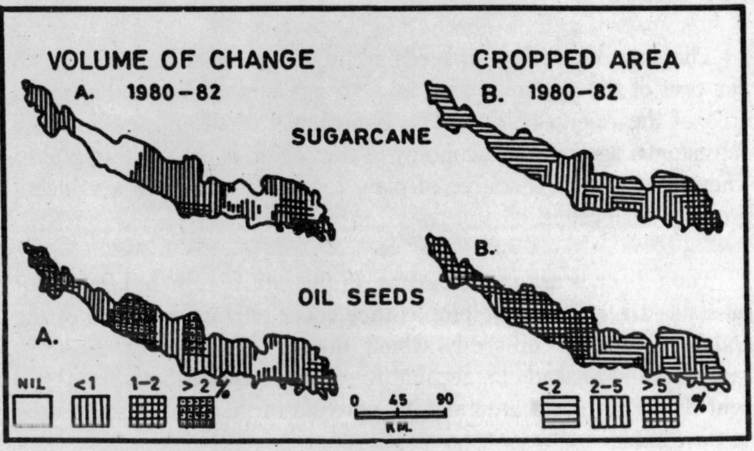

From the above discussion, it emerges that higher concentration areas lie generally towards east, where the conditions suitable for its cultivation are comparatively better. There has been an increase of 74.9 per cent in the area under sugarcane during the period of 25 years from 24,859 to 43,496 hectares), with some blocks experiencing an increases higher than 400 per cent.

The number of blocks in the low concentration category has decreased from 19(1955-57) to 12 (1980-82) and in the moderate category, it has increased from 6 to 12. The number of blocks in the moderately high concentration group has decreased from 5 to 2, as some of these blocks have shifted to the higher categories.

The volume of change in the area under sugarcane amounts to

the tune of plus 1.5 per cent (Fig. 1). There are micro-regional variations. Of the 13 blocks experiencing increases, 5 are in the high (above 2 per cent) category with Nabua Naurangia (14.9 per cent) and Bishunpura (25.0 per cent) having very high figures. Two blocks (Laxmipur and Brijamanganj) experienced moderate changes (1-2 per cent) and 6 (belonging the central part) low (1 and below). It is in the 4 blocks that the conditions have remained static. The decennial variations are also not very remarkable.

OLD-SEEDS ·

The area devoted to oil-seeds accounts for 34,510 hectares or 4.8 per cent of the net sown area and 3.5 per cent of the total cropped area of the region (Fig.1). The importance of the oil-seeds in the subsistance agricultural economy of the region is next to foodgrains. They also serve as a source of plant food and constitute a valuable group of cash crops.

The oil-seeds are mainly grown in the *rabi* season and the *kharif* oil-seeds are quite negligible, as they cover only 0.6 per cent of the *kharif*. The *rabi* oil-seeds which mainly comprise of mustard, rapeseed and linseed etc. account for 6.0 per cent of the *rabi*, 4.3 per cent of the net sown area and 3.1 per cent of the total cropped area of the region.

The spatial distribution of the area under oil-seeds (Fig. 1-B) shows that the zones of the high concentration (6-8 per cent) and that of moderately high concentration (4-6 per cent) are in the western districts of Bahraich and Gonda. In the moderate category, there are 11 blocks (2-3 per cent), only 2 of which (Balrampur and Jamunaha) belong to the western part. Of the 13 blocks in the low category (2 and below), only Nawabganj hails from the western part. It may be noted here that excessive moisture is harmful to *rabi* oil-seeds and the loamy sand soils preferably alluvium are suitable to their growth. This may explain, to some extent, the higher concentration of these crops towards west.

The hectareage under oil-seeds has increased from 24,090 (1955-57) to 34,510(1980-82) hectares, showing a percentage increase of 42.0. Fig. 1-B shows that there is not much variation in the distributional pattern of different categories of blocks, except that the number in the moderately high and high and high categories has increased from 3 to 4 and 1 to 43 respectively. The block Mihipurwa, the westernmost block of the region, has stepped down to one category lower.

As regards the volume of change, there is a slight addition of 0.7 per cent of the total cropped area in the area of oil-seeds. As many as as 17 blocks have experienced increases, most of which belong to the middle and the western parts where the concentration of the area under oil-seeds is high. Of the 14 blocks which have experienced decrease, a larger number belongs to the eastern part where wheat, sugarcane and some other crops are dominant and the importance of oil-seeds has decreased.

FRUITS AND VEGETABLES

The fruits and vegetables cover a very meager area which accounts for only 0.6 per cent of the total cropped area of the region (*kharif* 0.1 and *rabi* 0.5 per cent). The various types of vegetables grown for household consumption are beans, tubers, root crops like carrots and potato, pumpkins, ladyfingers, tomato, leafy vegetables like cauliflowers etc. Potato is the most important crop. Mango, banana, jack fruits and papayas etc. are the main fruits. The heactar-age under these crops has increased but quite insignificantly.

Conclusion

The foregoing discussion reveals that any attempt to ameliorate the nutritive and economic standard of living of the people and rural transformation warrants not only an increase in the heactar-age under these crops, but also a substantial increase in their yield and better marketing facilities. There is enough scope for the augmentation of the area and the per hectare yield of these commercial crops together with some others like jute etc. for which proper steps can be taken by introducing modern technological innovations in farming operations and by providing necessary post-harvest infra-structures etc. This will undoubtedly help this forbidden and under-developed tract in becoming one of the developed and prosperous areas of the country.

EIGHT

R.N. Singh

Cultivation-Population Dynamics in Barabanki and Deoria Districts: A Comparative Study

Introduction

This paper attempts to study the state of agriculture and the degree of population pressure in context of two districts, i.e. Barabanki and Deoria. Barabanki lies in the central part of U.P. near Lucknow and Deoria is situated in the north eastern part of U.P. A combination of the two elements, i.e.agriculture and population, helps in identifying potential, stagnant and problemetic areas.

The Study

Two fundamental elements, viz. the state of agriculture and the degree of population pressure determine the salient characteristics of space economy. In order to determine variable dynamics of these two elements so as to differentiate the level of development and appreciate the nature of problem, a composite ranking index has been prepared. All the 16 development *blocks* of Barabanki and 29 development *blocks* of Deoria have been ranked separately according to their average score of deviation index of food and commercial crops as also of the score of population pressure. These three ranks have been averaged out and thus a composite index has been obtained placing the order of *blocks* on the basis of their relative overall situation with respect of these three vital elements. The rank thus determined has been categorised into three, i.e. high - 4, intermediate - 4.1 - 8 and low 8.1 + for Barabanki; and high -7, intermediate - 7.1 - 14 and 14 - of Deoria (Table-I & Table-II).

The first group is invariably characterized by relatively low population pressure. In some extreme cases it is even under populated to the extent of 50/km.[2] These areas have been designated as potential in the sense that population pressure is not a major hindrance considering the stage of cultivation. As such, there is enough scope for producing surplus with a little enhancement in the agricultural efficiency.

The second group covers the blocks having moderately developed cultivation as indicated by deviation indices, but the pressure of population in these *blocks* is also moderately high (Fig. 1). Thus even if some advance is made on the agricultural front it may not yield better results as these *blocks* have exhausted the soil resources with the existing level of technology. Unless a break-through occurs on the technological front, these areas will not be able to produce a surplus. Therefore, these are called stagnant areas.

FIG. 8.1

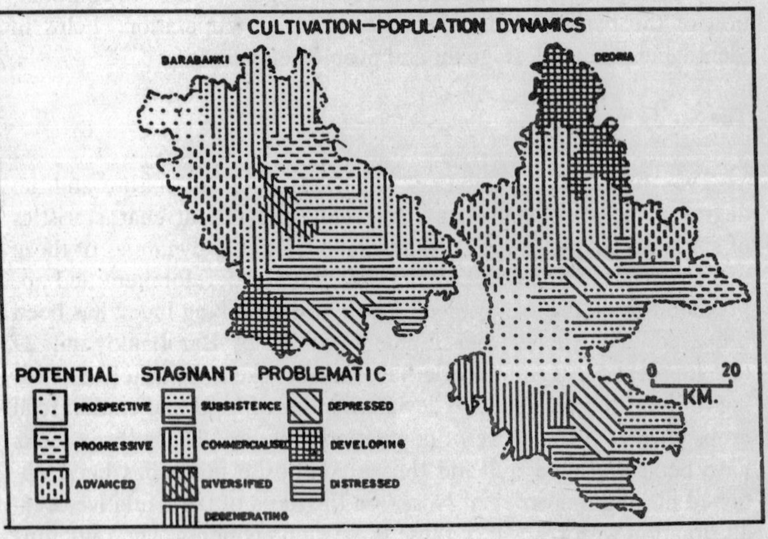

TABLE I : DEVELOPMENT BLOCKS - DISTRICT: BARABANKI

Developement blocks	Net sown area ha	Area under food crops ha	Area under food as % of net sown area	Area under food crops deviation index	Area under cash crops ha	Area under cash crops as % of net sown area	Area under cash crops Deviation index	Population pressure per Km^2	Ranking food crops deviation index	Ranking cash crops deviation index	Ranking population pressure	E Rank	Rank col 13	carrying capacity persons $/Km^2$
1	2	3	4	5	6	7	8	9	10	11	12	13	14	15
1. Banki	13668	19670	144	+1.01	1000	7.3	+1.20	94	8	8	14	30	8	457
2. Masauli	12932	19241	149	+1.04	998	7.7	+1.24	-45	5	7	4	16	2	454
3. Dewa	15619	24896	159	+1.11	1322	8.5	+1.37	86	1	6	13	20	3	319
4. Harakh	16462	21187	129	-0.90	1513	9.2	+1.48	22	15	4	9	30	8	437
5. Fatehpur	20668	27337	132	-0.92	2086	10.1	+1.63	31	14	2	10	26	70	444
6. Suratganj	23611	29424	125	-0.87	2954	12.5	+2.02	-11	16	1	7	24	6	407
7. Ramnagar	20905	29225	140	-0.98	2087	10.0	+1.61	-200	9	3	1	13	1	640
8. Nindura	19008	29469	155	+1.08	287	1.5	-0.24	-47	3	16	2	21	4	450
9. Daryabad	21625	31168	144	+1.01	909	4.2	-0.68	-40	7	10	6	23	5	432
10. Puredalai	23546	31349	133	-0.93	2129	9.0	+1.45	-41	13	5	5	23	5	428
11. Mawai	16944	23158	137	-0.96	526	3.1	-0.50	56	12	13	11	36	10	400
12. Rudauli	20035	31553	157	+1.10	755	3.8	-0.01	-46	2	11	3	26	7	400
13. Banikodar	17139	26020	152	+1.06	485	2.8	-0.45	-7	4	14	8	26	7	426
14. Haidergarh	16663	24275	146	+1.02	211	1.3	-0.21	56	6	15	11	32	9	401
15. Trivediganj	13941	19443	139	-0.97	469	3.4	-0.55	134	10	12	15	47	11	405
16. Sidhapur	17735	24576	138	-0.965	944	5.0	-0.81	76	11	9	12	32	9	421

TABLE II : DEVELOPMENT BLOCKS - DISTRICT: DEORIA

Developement blocks	Net sown area ha	Area under food crops ha	Area under food as % of net sown area	Area under food crops deviation index	Area under cash crops ha	Area under cash crops as % of net sown area	Area under cash crops Deviation index	Population pressure per Km^2	Ranking food crops deviation index	Ranking cash crops deviation index	Ranking population pressure	E Rank	Rank col 13	carrying capacity persons /Km^2
1	2	3	4	5	6	7	8	9	10	11	12	13	14	15
1. Kaptalinganj	14599	21895	150	+1.17	3184	22	+1.52	56	3	7	2	12	1	218
2. Khadda	24259	18571	77	-0.60	4744	20	+1.38	445	22	8	29	59	12	410
3. Nebua - Naurangia	18304	16960	93	-0.73	6429	35	+2.42	213	21	1	21	43	12	514
4. Motia-hak	13551	17716	131	+1.02	3497	26	+1.80	126	12	4	5	21	2	475
5. Ramkola	18210	16863	93	-0.73	6051	33	+2.28	196	21	2	17	40	11	475
6. Sukrauli	12988	18260	141	+1.10	2926	23	+1.59	133	8	6	7	21	2	467
7. Hata	13494	17156	127	-0.99	2555	19	+1.31	172	14	9	12	35	8	451
8. Kasia	15832	20672	132	+1.03	2130	13	-0.90	232	11	11	24	46	15	354
9. Tamkuhi	20437	22823	112	-0.88	2372	12	-0.83	190	19	12	15	46	15	415
10. Dudhi	15328	21818	142	+1.11	4234	28	+1.94	208	7	3	20	30	7	358
11. Pardrauna	24134	28121	117	-0.92	5829	24	+1.66	225	17	5	23	45	14	415
12. Fazilnagar	13425	15422	189	+1.48	918	7	-0.48	301	1	15	25	43	12	386
13. Bishunpura	19356	18871	97	-0.76	3753	19	+1.31	27	20	9	25	54	18	393
14. Seorahi	17888	22704	127	-0.99	6225	35	+2.42	181	14	1	14	29	6	369
15. Gauri Bazar	17479	24920	143	+1.12	2159	12	-0.83	106	6	12	4	22	3	424
16. Deoria	14776	21489	145	+1.13	1242	8	-0.55	151	5	14	9	28	5	401
17. Desai Deoria	10720	15698	146	+1.14	695	6	-0.41	207	4	16	19	39	10	449

18.	Patherdewa	14033	18301	130	+1.02	1036	7	-0.48	173	12	15	13	40	11	491
19.	Baitalpur	12645	19429	154	+1.20	1832	14	-0.97	205	12	10	18	30	7	331
20.	Rampur Bar-khana	12456	16842	135	+1.06	1181	9	-0.62	84	10	13	3	26	4	377
21.	Rudrapur	20508	25570	125	-0.98	342	2	-0.14	44	15	21	1	37	9	383
22.	Bankata	12262	16176	132	+1.03	1589	13	-0.90	166	10	11	11	32	8	366
23.	Barhaj	11858	13650	115	-0.90	478	4	-0.28	130	18	20	6	44	13	428
24.	Bhagalpur	11920	13497	113	-0.88	573	5	0.35	351	19	19	28	66	21	46
25.	Bhatani	12320	16886	137	+1.07	592	5.3	-0.37	214	9	17	22	48	17	318
26.	Bhatpar	11958	15721	131	+1.02	578	5.1	-0.35	158	12	18	10	40	11	439
27.	Bhaluani	16331	19469	119	-0.93	1075	7	-0.48	145	16	15	8	39	10	30
28.	Lar	12936	16394	127	-0.99	165	1	-0.07	194	14	17	16	47	10	419
29.	Salempur	13785	17700	128	+1.00	691	5	-0.35	289	13	18	25	57	10	417
				3708			x419.91		x191.1				x385		408.17
				x127.86											

The third group comprises of the areas located within high population pressure group so that despite the great advance made on the front of commercialization of agriculture (as is the case with the sugar belt in Deoria) some areas have recorded lowest overall ranking. Despite all possible efforts in the foreseeable future designed to augment the agricultural productivity the population pressure is not likely to be eased unless a major shift in the occupational structure takes place. Therefore, this group of *blocks* is designated as problematic.

Conclusion

It may thus be seen that taking cultivation population dynamics into account an altogether different intra-regional picture emerges. The stagnant and problematic areas can be further studie and measures can be adopted to develop them.

NINE

B.S.Gurung, P.C.Pondel and
K.B.Gurung

Commercial Activities within the Umland of Pokhara: A Case Study of Hill and Mountain Region of Nepal

Introduction

The mountain region of Nepal is poorly developed in terms of commercial activities. There occurs a small number of markets and that too of the subsistence level in the hilly and mountainous regions like the one under study. It is due to the rugged topography of these areas which has made accessibility difficult. The interaction among settlements is restricted. The distribution of population is sparse and agricultural surpluses are marginal. In remote areas trade is even restricted to barter. Periodic markets do not exist in such areas.

Pokhara is the commercial headquarters in the middle of Nepal. It is located 200 km. south west of Kathmandu, the capital of Nepal.

This paper makes an attempts to identify the nature and characteristics of commercial functions being carried out in the area of study.

Historical growth of marketing and trading affairs in the region

Marketing, in this part of the country, was negligible till the mid-18th. century. Till then Kathmandu, Lalitpur and Bhakatapur were the only towns of any significance in the midland (*Pahar*) region of the kingdom. At that time the country was divided into small principalities, whose chiefs were collectively called the '*baise*' (22) and '*choubise*' (24) *rajas*. Kashi Kot, three hour walking distance from from Pokhara, located on the Kaski ridge (1591 m.) was one of the principalities belonging to '*choubise*' *rajas* groups. Till this time most of the settlements were concentrated fortified hills (*Kot*) and the lower places were not favoured for the settlement on account of their weaker strategic location. Gorkha, Tanhunsur, Lamjung, Kaski and Syangja Nuwakot were the main settlements. But these settlements were created as garrison centres to serve the military and administrative needs of the expanding empire, carrying out minimum commercial activities.

Trading towns came into existance in this region only after the conquest of western Nepal by the Gorkha empire in the mid 18th century and, the foundations of one strong kingdom led to the decline of the strategic importance of fortified settlements (Regmi,D.R., 1956). With the restoring of peace and political stability, places with advantageous nodality grew to become large settlements and consequently commercial activities gained momentum. Another important event responsible for the acceleration of the trading activities in this region was the spread of *Newars*, the trading People of Kathmandu valley. Where ever these people settled trading flourished. As for example Bandipur, Baglung and Pokhara and Baglung developed along the traditional trans-Himalayan trade route whereas Bandipur grew on the Pokhara on the Pokhara-Narayanghat route.

Trading along the trans-Himalayan region gave birth to several market centres. In region north of Pokhara, beyond the Himalayas, in the absence of good cultivation, the inhabitants have no option but to depend upon some kind of trade for their subsistance. The tribal people of the region, the *Thakalis* of Thak Khola and *Bhotes* of Lo and Dolpo have always involved themselves in some kind of trade. In the past these people used to trade all along the traditional Kali Gandaki Trans-Himalayan trade route right from Tibet to the towns of the Indian *Tarai*(Shrivastava, V.K., 1983). This region was known for salt and wool trade both south from their source region, Tibet. The *Thakalis* had monopolised this trade with trading centre at Tukuche, their home station located just beyond the main Himalayas on the bank of the Kali Gandaki river between the Annapurna and the Dhaulagiri Himalayas. Thus Tukuche was serving as entrepot.

This sort of trade remained till 1928 when salt monopoly business was abolished, wool trade however, survived till the accession of Tibet to China in 1959 (Hamindorf, C., 1975). Apart from this no other type of trade affair was pronounced in this region. Other business and trade were of small scale serving mainly the needs of the local people.

Pokhara the trading centre and its umland

Today Pokhara is the major urban centre of the central hill region of Nepal. It is the 6th[1] largest town of the country which has grown from a small settlement with only 3500 population in 1961 to a town containing about 50,000 people in 1981. This fast growth rate is because of the combination of several socio-political factors like the eradication of the once dreaded malaria from the valley resulting in the influx of the hill tribal people from the surrounding hills to seek better future prospects, opening of two highways in the early 70's making this town easily accessible by land transport, its designation as headquarters of the Western Developmental Zone which has subsequently caused development works in the valley.

Pokhara's umland[2] covers extensive areas of Kaski, Lamjung, Probate, Gorkha, Mustang and Kusma districts of Gandaki and Dhaulagiri zone (Fig. 1). The umland extends from mountainous to hilly region bisected by numerous rivers and streams and a large part of the area lacks modern means of transportation. The two highways with a few kilometer of feeder roads are the only means of available surface transport. One of the centres, Jomson, is linked by air transport from the regional centre Pokhara. Economically, the region is based on subsistence agriculture. Hard crops like corn, millet, and buckwheat are the major crops of the mountainous area and the rice cultivation is mostly limited to valleys and terraced hills (Gurung, H.B., 1965).

Nature and characteristics of the commercial functions

As mentioned earlier the nature and characteristics of commercial functions of hill and mountains differ from the plain. The economy of the region is poor with low purchasing power. The commercial functions in most markets are of low level. For the purpose of this study various functions have been identified, identical functions have been grouped and ordered according to their local importance. Functions like banks, veterinary services, electric appliances are considered as lower order functions in developed countries. These become higher order functions in developing countries like Nepal. Bearing in mind the prevailing conditions of the study area the following commercial functions have considered as higher and lower order ones.

FIG. 9.1

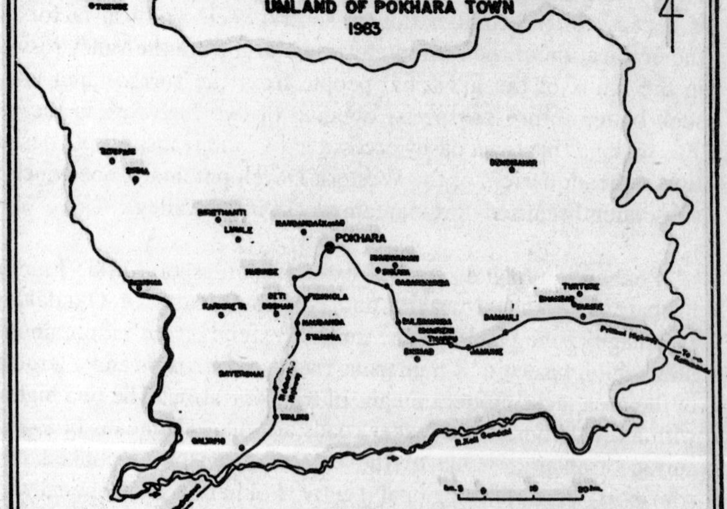

Retailing is one of the most common and basic commercial functions of Nepal. Most markets possess a handful of retail shops dealing with mainly a few number of convenient retail goods. Grocery, cigarettes, and country liquor, are the dominant commercial goods. Drug store, provision and bookstall, stationary shops donot occur in small markets. Similarly other convinience goods like meat and vegetables are also not sold in open market. However small markets located along the trekking routes consume a considerable amount of provision and cold drinks.

TABLE 1: Major functional group and their order in the Pokhara region (1981)

S.No.	Functional Group	Functional Units.
1.	Retail convenience goods	a.Grocery, b. Vegetables, c. Cigarette, d.Country liquor (LO); e.Drug Stores f. Provision and Cold drinks (HO).
2.	Retail non-convenience goods	a.Clothing store, b. Shoe store, c.Electric goods, d.Metal shop, e.Furniture, f.Hardware, g.Stationary (imported goods), h. Book & newspaper, i.Readymade garments, j.Optical store, k.Glass shops (HO).
3.	Whole saling	
4.	Retail industry	a.Tailoring, b.Watch reparing, d.Auto repairing, e.Rice/oil press mill, f.Ornamental works (HO).
5.	Personal service	a.Hair dresser,b.Washerman, c.Dry cleaner (HO).
6.	Professional service	a.Doctor's clinic, b.Lawyers firm, c.Photographer (HO).
7.	Catering	a.Hotels and lodge, b.Resturants, c.Tea-stall, d.*Bhatti*(HO).
8.	Finance	a.Commercial bank, b.Agricultural development bank,c.Co operative bank (HO).

N.B. LO = Lower order; HO = Higher Order functions.

Among the retail non-convenient goods, clothing store frequently occurs but in small markets there is hardly a shop dealing solely with clothings. It has been noted that shops generally deal with mixed retail goods, i.e. a portion of the shop used for grocery and other goods, and the other portion given to clothing.

Non-convenience goods like electric appliances, furniture, hardware, opticals, cosmetics, glass are sold only in Pokhara or in large markets like Damauli, Syangaja, Walling, Dumre which have location in highways.

At all large markets which have a highway location wholesaling business has come into existence.

Tailoring, rice,/oil press mill and ornamental work are the dominant industries occuring in majority of the market centres. Professional commercial functions occur only in large towns.

Functions belonging to catering include resturants, hotels, and bhattis (traditional bhattis are those mostly run by Thakalies women, where food and liquor are served and charged but lodging is either free or nominally charged). However, bhattis are gradually being replaced by hotels particularly along the busy trekking routes.

As regards the last commercial function finance, all the major markets have the facilities of either all the three available banks or of at least one.

Commercial Functions in Pokhara town:

Pokhara is the main trading centre of the region. As mentioned earlier its umland covers an extensive area. Though opening of the highways have certainly improved the trade volume in the region, it has also affected the area of trade influence of Pokhara town. Along these highways several markets have sprung up curtailing the trading domain of Pokhara. These markets now serve areas previously dominated by Pokhara town. However, towards north, Pokhara's trade influence is still unchallenged.

Pokhara town actually encompasses a radius of about 3.5 Km with the original old market in the centre and other five distinct areas of new developments in different directions. Generally market area of the town has developed along the road in north-south and east-west direction in a linear pattern. The linearity is more distinct in the old section of the town. Thus, two distinct zones of market old and new with different spatial pattern and developmental phase are remarked within Pokhara town.

Before 1960 Pokhara was a market centre belonging to a village panchayat. Ramkrishana *tole*[3] Nalamukha, Bhairab *tole* and Mohariya *tole* were the residential cum commercial zone. Till the opening of the Sidhartha highway (1968) and the Prithawi highway (1971) market was confined within the same old area. However onward 1968, different market areas like Ram Bazar in south eastern part of the town near Indian army's pension paying office, Pardi Birauta at the starting point of the Sidhartha highway in the southwest of the town, Mahendra Pool market at the southern end of the old market, and Bagar market at the northern end of the town. All these new markets have developed in different directions away from the old market centre.

Different factors are responsible for the development of these markets. Ram Bazar developed to serve the army pensioners coming from the surrounding districts to collect their pension. Pardi Birauta market developed after the construction of the Sidhartha highway. The development of Mahendra Pool is associated with the combination of factors like the construction of the bridge over the Seti Gorge, extension of the metalled road down to airport and to lake Fewa and the presence of a large piece of flat land for the parking of the vehicles and for the further outward extension towards airport in the south and towards Chipledhunga in the west. Apart from these its central location has also made it the central business district of Pokhara town. The development of Bagar bazar is mainly due to the establishment of different levels educational institutions. This market also enjoys better locational advantage since it is located in the northern end of the town and close to the non market surrounding areas.

A detailed urban land use survey of Pokhara town made along the road in 1982 reveals that there is no marked segregation of specialised commercial function like a separate wholesale market. Market is mostly dominated by retail function. Grocery, clothing, imported goods and garments, are stationery and the major retail functions. The nature and concentration of retail function varies in different markets of the town. The following table attempts to prevent the nature and distribution commercial functions in different markets of the town (Table II).

The table reveals that out of total commercial activities 32.35% are concentrated in old section, whereas 20.20% in Bagar 27.24% in Mahendra Pool, 15.60% in Ram Bazar, and 4.60% in Pardi Birauta market centre respectively.

TABLE II : Nature and Distribution of Commercial Functions in Different Marmet Sections Ppljara Town (1982)

Sl. No.	Commercial-Functions	Old Section	New Section			
			Bagar	Mahendra Pool	Ram· Bazar	Pardi-Birauta
	%	%	%	%	%	%
1.	Grocery	28.85	31.65	16.90	26.23	13.89
2.	Clothing	11.07	8.23	5.63	8.20	11.11
3.	Catering	2.37	9.49	9.86	0.82	2.87
4.	Imported Goods	3.16	4.43	7.04	2.46	--
5.	Stationary	1.18	1.90	4.23	--	--
6.	Tea Stall	7.51	6.33	5.63	19.67	41.67
7.	Goldsmith	5.14	2.53	0.47	14.75	--
8.	Godown	3.95	2.53	0.94	3.28	13.89
9.	Provision Shop	1.89	0.63	4.23	--	--
10.	Metal Works	5.14	1.27	3.29	2.46	2.78
11.	Drug Store	3.16	1.90	4.23	2.46	2.78
12.	Others*	26.48	29.11	37.56	19.67	11.11
Tota		100%	100%	100%	100%	100%
Percentage of total functions in the town		32.35	20.20	27.24	15.60	4.60

Source : Research project submitted to the Institute of Humanities and Social Sciences, Tribhuvan University, Kathmandu, by P.C. Pondel (1982)

* Other include more than 19 types of commercial functions (bicycle repair, ring, glass work, watch and radio repairing, transport companies, barber, poultry, butchery, printing press, photo studio, arts, cobbler, dry cleaner, vegetables, electric appliances etc.)

An analytical insight on the above table presents that in all market centres grocery tops the list. Clothing occupies second position in old section of the town, whereas catering is in the second position in Bagar and in Mahendra Pool. The third important category of shops in the old market is tea stall followed by goldsmith, godown, and metal works. The table also shows that the old market is mainly associated with goods of daily needs like grocery and other essential goods like clothing. But the situation is different in new markets particularly in Mahendra Pool. Here catering, imported goods and garments, and provision shops associated with modern urban life dominate the commercial function.

The unplanned layout of the street, traditional design of the buildings, and geographical inertia are the main reasons for more concentration of traditional type of commercial activities in the old market of the town. The situation of street layout, design of the buildings are more or less planned in the new market zones of Pokhara town, as a result this market has attracted the business mainly associated with the modern amenities.

While dealing with the commercial functions it has been generally observed that shops dealing with identical commercial goods tend to display clustering tendency or affinity for each other. An attempt has been made in this regard to identify the number of shops belonging to identical functions located nearest to each other in ground level, i.e. at least one side of the examined shop must be neighboured by the shop belonging to the same functional group. The study reveals that in Mahendra Pool 54% hotels and restaurants and 24% grocery shops are clustered together. In different shopping centres such clustering is of different retail functions. As for example, at Bagar it is the meat shop (58%) and at Dhobigaunda-Mohariya it is goldsmith shops (28%). Further, grocery, the top retail function, shows affinity to its own group in every market centre. The lowest percentage of affinity among grocery shops occur in the main business centre at Mahendra Pool. (24%) and highest in Dhobigaunda. (41%). Not only the grocery shows affinity to its own group, it also neighbours with every major retail function in every market centre with a fairly good percentage. Thus it is the most widely distributed retail function of the town.

The clustering has resulted mainly because of two reasons: (i) Certain types of shops can pay more than others for a preferred location in the town, so shops dealing with imported goods and garments and tourist class hotels which can afford the preferred location are mostly located in the main business centre at Mahendra Pool. (ii) Clustering has resulted also because of some social factors such as most of the castes or certain occupational classes tend to live in a group. Clustering of goldsmith and meat shop is the result of this factor.

Location of markets within the umland;

Within the umland of Pokhara thirty one market centres have developed. All of these centres are either located in the newly opened highways or along the busy foot trails. Eight centres have location in the Prithawi highway, seven in the Sidhartha highway, three in the Dumare-Beshisahar seasonal road (a feeder road to Prithawi highway), three in Syangja-Baglung trail, seven in the Pokhara - Jomsom trekking route (trans-Himalayan trade route) and the rest in other important trails. However most of these have location in east or south of Pokhara within 8 to 9 hours of journey. Immediately north of Pokhara, not a single higher market of any significance exists. This is because of Pokhara's own location in close proximity to the main Himalayas. The main Himalaya range of Annapurna runs east west only 29 km north of Pokhara. However, in north-west along the Kali Gandaki a few markets have developed beyond the Himalayan range.

So far their topographical location is concerned, most of them have location on the upper flat terraces of rivers. A few of them are either located on ridges or in low river basins. All except three have location in the hill region. The three markets Jomsom, Marpha, and Tukuche belong to mountain region.

The distributional characteristics of commercial function in thirty one market centres located in the region shows following characteristics:-

i. Of the total commercial functions retailing is the most dominant (48%), followed by catering (32%), retail industry (10%), wholesale (5%), professional (2%), and finance and personal (1%) each respectively.

ii. Only six centres Damauls, Syangja, Waling, Kushma, Dumre and Bhimad serve with all the available commercial functions. As regards the distribution of individual commercial function, these markets differ slightly from each other. As for example two centres Dumre and Bhimad have more wholesale business than others, where this particular function accounts for 12 and 9 per cent of their total commercial functions. Similarly, the two centres Syangja and

These six centres together contain 50% of the total commercial functional units available in thirtyone markets. As regards the individual commercial function these six centres control 46% wholesale functions of the region. Professional and personal services are virtually monopolised by these centres.

iii. There are four market centres performing six commercial functions. One of the noticeable features of these market is the non-occurance of personal services. Among these Beshisahar contains the largest number of commercial functional units, which is mostly dominated by catering. Its location on the busy Dumre-Manang trekk and its role as the district headquarters may be accounted for the presence of a large number of hotels and lodges.

iv. Six centres of the region perform five of the total available commercial functions. Among these Jomsom is located in trans-Himalayan zone. It is a district headquarters and an important tourist resort. Seti Dobhan and Gallyang are the wholesaling markets. Khaireni and Dulegaunda are small markets developed only 3 km apart each other on the Prithwi highway. The other market Turture is located along Dumre-Behisahar trail.

v. While considering the total number of commercial functions occuring in these markets, it becomes clear that there exists a distinct heirarchial order among the market centres. In this study these markets have been hierarchically ordered according to the number of functions performed by these market centers. Hence centres performing all seven functions are placed in Ist order, centres performing six functions are placed in 2nd order, and so on so forth C Table III).

vi. These market centres which have been classified in hierarchial order also differ in population size. The number of commercial functions and the commercial functional units range from two of seven and nine to two hundred and eighty respectively, with a

TABLE 3: Manor Commerccial Functions in Different Market Centres Located Within the Umland of Pokhara, 1983

Sl. No.	Market centre	Popu-lation	Retail	Whole-sale	Retail-ind.	Profess-ional	Personal	Cate-ring	Finance	Total funtions
1.	Damauli	1761	x	*	*	*	*	*	*	7
2.	Syangja	1561	x	*	*	*	*	*	*	7
3.	Waling	1580	*	*	*	*	*	*	*	7
4.	Kushma	1535	*	*	*	*	*	*	*	7
5.	Dumre	543	*	*	*	*	*	*	*	7
6.	Bhimad	376	*	*	*	*	*	*	*	7
7.	Boshisahar	714	*	*	*	*	x	*	*	7
8.	Naudanda (Kaski)	329	*	*	*	*	x	*	*	6
9.	Tharpu	281	*	*	*	*	x	*	*	6
10.	Gagan Gaunda	327	*	*	*	*	x	*	*	6
11.	Jomsom	889	*	*	*	x	x	*	*	6
12.	Seti Dobhan	587	*	*	*	x	*	*	x	5
13.	Khaireni	223	*	x	*	*	x	*	*	5
14.	Dule Gaunda	493	*	*	*	*	x	*	x	5
15.	Gallyang	428	*	*	*	x	x	*	*	5
16.	Turture	493	*	*	*	x	*	*	x	5
17.	Naudyang (Syangja)	528	*	*	*	x	x	*	x	4
18.	Siswa	414	*	x	*	x	x	*	*	4
19.	Shikha	778	*	x	*	*	x	*	x	4
20.	Khudi Muhan	235	*	*	*	x	x	*	x	4
21.	Bhansar	182	*	*	*	x	x	*	x	4
22.	Birethanti	195	*	x	*	x	x	*	x	3
23.	Tukuche	530	*	x	*	x	x	*	x	3
24.	Karki Neta	286	*	x	*	x	x	*	x	3
25.	Phedi Khola	347	*	x	*	x	x	*	x	3
26.	Jamune	157	*	x	*	x	x	*	x	3

27.	Tatopani	239	*	x	*	x	x	*	x	3
28.	Marpha	483	*	x	*	x	x	*	x	3
29.	Lumle	103	*	x	*	x	x	*	x	3
30.	Kubinde	101	*	x	*	x	x	*	x	3
31.	Bayer Ghari	129	*	x	x	x	x	*	x	2

Source : Field Survey 1982.

* = Present
x = Absent

population range from 101 to 1761. It is generally agreed that the number of functions offered at a market centre increase with the market's size. In order to ascertain the relationship between these two variables in the study area, the correlation has been computed, r = +0.849 which is high and significant.[4] Hence the degree of relation is high.

Conclusion

This study made in the hill and mountain region of Nepal reveals that the commercial activities are mostly of subsistance level. Markets are few and that too are unevenly distributed. Poor accessibility is the main reason which has left many areas still isolated. Interaction among the settlement is low resulting in the existence of an unorganised marketing system.

However the opening of roads have played significant role in the development of markets in this region. Roads have made many areas accessible and, in such areas, because of the frequent movement of the people markets have developed. These markets performing central place functions serve the surrounding rural areas. Thus it can be said that roads have brought markets, markets have given birth to commercial activities and the latter subsequently have caused development. In other words opening of roads seems to be the first stage in the development of marketing activities.

Before the construction of the two highways, the Sidhartha and the Prithwi (early 1970s), markets in this region were concentrated in different trails radiating from the regional centre Pokhara. Pokhara till that time had an extensive catchment area. But soon after the construction of two highways several markets have sprung up reducing the commercial catchment area considerably. At present around Pokhara the regional commercial centre, several markets of different hierarchical orders have emerged creating an organised marketing system particularly in the eastern and southern part of the study area.

NOTES

1. Kathmandu, Patna, Bhaκatpur, Biratnager, Birganj.

2. Umland of Pokhara has been demarcted considering the following indices:- milk supply zone, food supplyzone, wholesale trade zone and clientele of P.N. Campus.

3. Tole is equivalent to the words or 'mohallas' of a town.

4. r value has been 't' tested and found significant at 0.05 level of significance.

TEN

Braj Raj Kumar Sinha

Human Resources Utilization in Commercial Activities in Rural Area: A Case Study of Dhanarua Block (Patna District)

Dhanarua Block is located 20 km. south of Patna. It is bounded by 25'16' - 25'27' N Lat. and 85'2' -85'4' E Long (Fig. 1). It is a rural Block consisting of 122 villages (Fig. 3). It is almost a flat Plain, a segment of South Bihar Plain. Its total geographical area is 18555 ha.

Agriculture is the main stay of the people of this block which absorbs nearly 67% of the total utilized human resources.

Total population of the block was 114971 according to the 1981 census. The total number of main workers in 1981 was 33986. Both sexes constituted only 30 % work force of the total population. Only 29% of the total population was literate and educated. Since human resources (as an invaluable asset) change every aspect of life in the society and play a very significant role in the production and consumption of all resources and constitute the ultimate basis for regional development, the main thrust of the present paper is to pin-point the utilization of the human resources of Dhanarua Block in commercial activities.

Commercial activities (of tertiary sector) involve only services required in transferring, selling or exchanging the useful or desirable goods and the product. Indeed "tertiary production is commercial output of services rather than goods" (Thoman, Richard, and Corbin, 1974, p.4).

FIG. 10.1

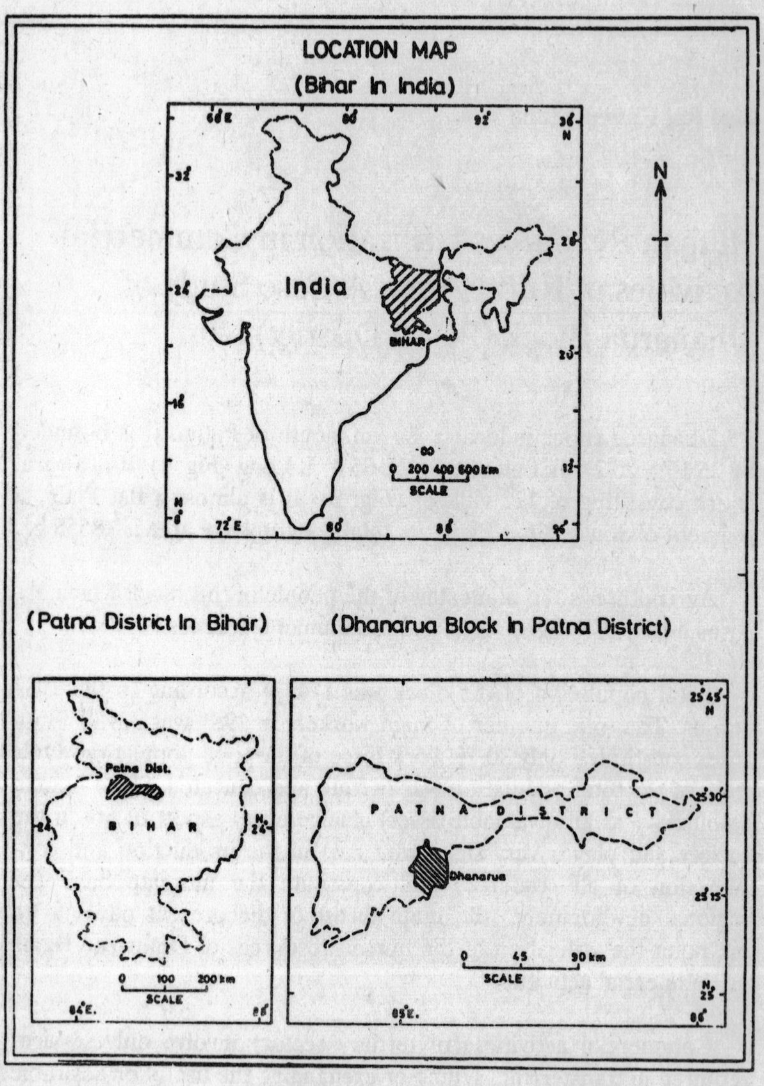

In this way, goods from their raw stage to the finished stage and to consumable form have to pass through three stages of actions of primary, secondary and tertiary human resources.

The quality of products of services depends upon the quality of human resources. The acceleration of economic and social growth depends upon intensifying measures for the appropriate utilization of human resources. In fact "the all round promotion and perfection of the economy and culture, social relations and political organisation" (Progress, 1976, pp. 23-24) depend upon the builders of a society, i.e, its manpower, thus human resources utilization in commercial activities for the development of the region is natural.

OBJECTIVE

In view of the above facts the main objectives of the present study are:

i. to find out the types of commercial activities and the levels of utilization of human resources in them,
ii. to assess the quality of commercial activities and the quality of human resources engaged in them, and
iii. to extend possible suggestions for the efficient and rational utilization of unutilized human resources for the furtherance of commercial activities in the overall development of the block.

METHODOLOGY

Fulfilment of above objectives is based on the primary data collected from the fourteen sample villages selected on the basis of stratified random sampling method. In order to measure the perfect differences in human resources utilization in commercial activities two types of villages - cultivator dominated and agricultural labourer dominated - were selected which appear to be approximately evenly distributed in the block. Data on variables such as, age of the individuals, types of work, hours worked, educational attainment, caste, etc. were collected.

Age has been divided into four groups, viz. 5 - 14 (children of under working age group); 15 - 34 (more active human resources of younger working age group); 35 - 59 (less active resources of older working age group); and 60 & + (superannuated or over the working age group).

TABLE I : Human Resources Utilization in Commercial Activities (1984)

	Age Group	5 - 14		15 - 34		35 - 59		60 & +		Total	
	Sex	M	F	M	F	M	F	M	F	M	F
	Total %	1 (2.04)		22 (44.90)		19 (38.78)	1 (100)	7 (14.28)		49 (100)	1 (100)
UNDER UTILIZED	i+					1 5.26	1 100	2 28.57		4 (6.12)	1 (100)
	ii	1 100		2 9.09						3 (6.12)	
	iii										
	iv										
						GRAND TOTAL				(12.24)	(100)
ASEQUATELEY UTILIZED	i			2 9.09		2 10.53		2 28.57		6 (12.24)	
	ii			6 27.27		3 15.79		1 14.29		10 (20.41)	
	iii										
	iv										
						GRAND TOTAL			(32.65)		
OVER UTILIZED	i			3 13.63		5 26.32		1 14.29		9 (18.37)	
	ii			6 27.27		6 31.58		1 14.29		13 (26.53)	
	iii			3 13.63		1 5.26				4 (8.16)	
	iv					1 5.26				1 (2.04)	
						GRAND TOTAL	(55.10)				

* Levels of Education:

i. Illiterate ii. Below Matriculate iii. Matriculate & above iv. Professional/Technical

Bracketed Lower Figures Indicate % to Total Male or Female workers Unbracketed lower Figures indicate % within particular age groups

Total human resources engaged in commercial pursuits have been divided into three categories, viz., underutilized (whose yearly average work hours is less than 6 hours); adequately utilized (whose average work hours runs for 6 to 8 hours throughout the year), and over utilized (who work more than 8 hours throughout the year).

Educational attainments have been divided into four categories, viz.

i. Illiterate,
ii. Below Matriculate,
iii. Metriculate and above,
iv. Professional/Technical.

RESULTS AND DISCUSSION

In commercial activities, there were 5.22% males and 0.53% females to total male or female utilized human resources in the block.

Table - I and diagram (Fig. 2) show the utilization pattern of human resource engaged in commercial activities in the block.

In the age group of 5 - 14, there was only one male child labour (2.04%). It is observed that the child labour below matriculate level of education was under utilized in their own shops. Their shops are a source of side income to maintain big families. The parents, being engaged in other activities, often use their children for shop keeping. It is mainly because the children of such families are usually unwilling to go to schools. Such examples are more common in backward castes. There was no child labour in other two categories of utilization.

Of the total males engaged in commercial activities, the younger working age group of 15 - 34 comprises of 22 males (44.90%). This age group consists of the largest percentage of manpower engaged in commercial activities.

Of the total males of this age group, 9.09% were under-utilized and all of them were below matriculate. They were self-employed vegetable and fruit vendors. It is observed that such activities are

FIG. 10.2

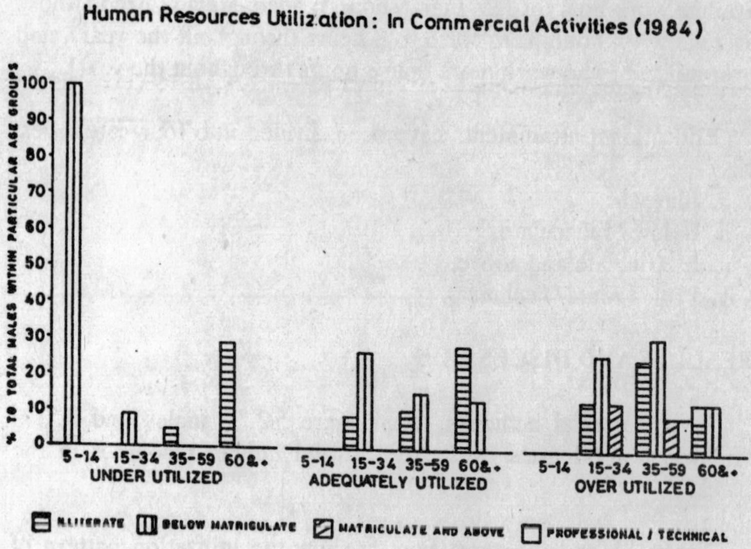

carried on by the poor and landless people with other source of livelihood.

In adequately utilized category, there were 36.36% males in which 9.09% (2) were illiterate and 27.27% (6) were below matriculate. All these illiterates were engaged in their own grocery shops, and sell some most wanted edible commodities such as salt, oil, cereal, species, bidi, tobacco, etc., daily requirements of the households. They take either cash or kind or both from the purchaser.

Of the total percentage of males of below matriculate category, 13.64% were engaged in their own grocery shops, 4.54% were engaged in cloth shops (particularly in the village where bi-weekly markets are held), 4.54% were engaged in selling vegetables and 4.54% were grain dealers purchasing surplus grains from the farmers and selling in the big *mandies* or nearby towns.

FIG. 10.3

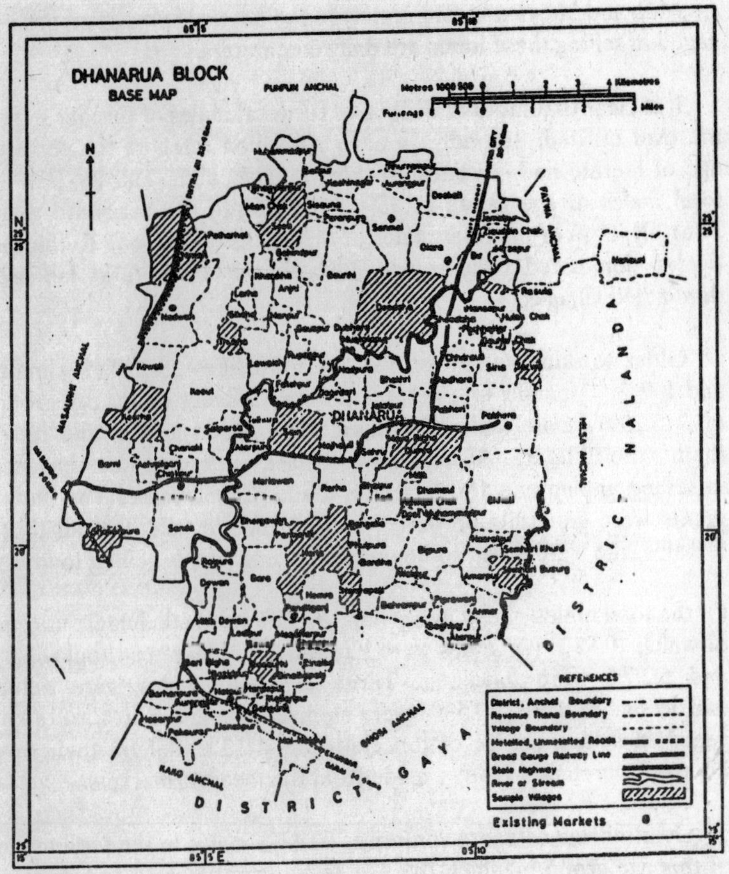

In over utilized category of this age group, there were 54.53% males in which 13.63% (3) were illiterate. Of them, 4.54% were engaged in selling home prepared milk product (khoya), 9.08% were engaged in grocery shops. 27% (6) were below matriculate and of them 13.63% were engaged in selling milk and another 13.63% were engaged in selling *khoya* or *mava* (Milk Product). Three (13.63%), were from matriculate and above category and of them 9.09% were engaged in selling grocery goods to the villagers and 4.54% were engaged in selling milk.

Milk and khoya are sold mainly in the nearest towns. Persons engaged in selling these items are daily commuters.

It is clear that more than 50% of the total males of this age group are over utilized. Secondly, in each utilization category the percentage of literate and educated workers is fairly high. Thirdly, 95% of total males of age group of 15 - 34 belong to the backward casts. Fourthly, 64% of the total males of this age group belong to the cultivator dominated villages and 36% to the agricultural labourer dominated villages.

Older working age group (35-59) constitutes 38.78%(19) males and 100% (1)female. Of the total males or females of this age group, one (5.26%) male and all females were under-utilized and all of them were illiterate. All males were blacksmiths and were engaged in selling implements for agricultural and domestic use. The implements were generally prepared at their own hearth. But all those females who were doing some thing were engaged in selling toddy.

Of the total males of this age group, 26.32% were adequately utilized of which 10.53% (2) males were illiterates, 5.26% were shopkeepers and 5.26% were hawkers. Three (15.29%) males were below matriculate in which 10.53% were shopkeepers and 5.26% were engaged in selling coarse cotton cloth prepared either on their own looms or purchased ready - made from the nearest markets.

Over utilized category comprises 68.42% males to the total males of this age group in which five (26.32%) were illiterate and most of them were engaged in milk and khoya selling and some of them were engaged in their tiny grocery shops. Six (31.58%) were below matriculate and all of them were engaged in selling *khoya*, skimmed and unskimmed milk in the nearest towns. One (5.26%) was from matriculate and above category and engaged in fair - price shops. All of them belong to forward caste. One (5.26%) male was professional medical practitioner.

It is obvious from the above that the percentage of over-utilized workers in this age group is highest as against the workers of other age groups of this category. This is mainly because of the greater sense of responsibility, and the family burden. Secondly, in each category (except under utilized), the percentage of literate and educated workers is fairly high. Thirdly, 89% of the total workers of this age group were of backward castes and most of them were in cultivator dominated villages.

Over-working age group (60 & +) comprises only seven (14.28%) superannuated or less utilizable males engaged in commercial activities in the block.

Out of total males of this age group, two (28.57%) were under utilized and they were illiterate. One was engaged in selling wood materials used in agricultural activities or for modestic purposes, and another one was engaged in selling toddy in his home.

In the adequately utilized category there were 42.86% of males in which two (28.57%) were illiterate and one of them was engaged in selling toddy and another one belonging to the muslim community did the business in animal flesh (they are locally called "Chicks"). One (14.29%) male was below matriculate and was engaged in his small grocery shops.

In the over utilized category, there were 28.58% males of which, 14.29%(1) was engaged in *khoya* selling and was reported illiterate. Another 14.29%(1) was engaged in selling mils and was below matriculate.

It is apparent from the above that the percentages of under utilized and adequately utilized males of over-working age group is higher than males of other age groups, except for the under-working age group. The highest percentage in under utilized and lowest percentage in over utilized categories is because of their old age. But, in persons of adequately utilized indicate the pressure of their socio-economic burden and in such circumstances they have to work in commercial activities. Secondly, in each utilization category, the percentage of literate is higher. Thirdly, more than 50% of the total males of this age group were in agricultural labourer dominated villages and most of them were of backward castes.

At all age groups, in all utilization categories, it is found that the child labour of under working age group were highest in under utilized category. Secondly, in the adequately utilized category, the over working age group manpower constituted highest percentage. In over utilized category, the manpower of working age groups constituted the highest percentage, in which the participation of older working age group (35-59) is highest, this may be because of their sense of responsibility towards their families.

In respect to educational attainment, it is observed and found that almost in each age group and in each utilization category (except in the utilization category of over working age group and, in under utilized category of older working age group) the percentage of below matriculate males is higher than other levels of education. It is also observed that the percentage of below matriculates is higher in rural commercial pursuit.

Second observation is that the percentage of literate and educated manpower decreases with increase in age. It indicates the growing awareness (for the need of education) among the workers of under-working-age group and younger working age group. This fact is supported by Table II.

TABLE II

Age Groups	5-14	15-34	35-59	60 & +
% of literates and educated workers	100	77	58	29

Third observation is that the workers who possess higher levels of education are over-utilized and those with lower levels of education are under-utilized in commercial activities. On this basis we can say that as the levels of education increases the percentage of over utilization of human resources in commercial activities increases. It means the development of commercial activity like other activities depend largely on the development of the human resources because educational level of the labour force affects the volume of production and each level of capital intensity requires a labour force with a determined level of education (Correa, 1963, p.183).

Fourth observation is that in each category, and in each age group, the percentage of backward castes workers is higher and with the increasing age group their percentage of participation decreases whereas the participation of the same age group of the scheduled caste and muslim workers has been found increasing in commercial activities.

Fifth observation is that out of the total male human resources engaged in commercial activities. 86% were of backward castes and out of them 37% were engaged only in selling milk and milk products (*khoya*, cream, etc.) All of them are over utilized as they have to commute everyday. It takes more than 8 hours of their time (daily) throughout the year. 33% were engaged only in a smaller *kirana* or grocery shops. Most of them are over utilized. 16% were engaged in other commercial activities such as in selling vegetables, fruits, etc., either sitting at one place of moving from village to village.

Out of the total utilized human resources engaged in commercial activities 2% were forward caste workers and all of them were engaged in fair price shops and are over-utilized. 4% were Muslims and 50% of them were engaged in coarse textiles trade. Another 50% were engaged in sale and purchase of live goats. All of them were adequately utilized. 8% were scheduled caste workers and most of them were engaged in selling *toddy* (toddy is country liquor) and other goods, either prepared in their house-holds or collected from the surrounding area.

All females of scheduled caste were found engaged in selling toddy and other things and are under utilized.

CONCLUSION AND SUGGESTIONS

Over all it is found that out of the total human resources engaged in the commercial activities, 12.24% males and 100% females were under-utilized in which 6.12% males and all females were illiterate. Another 6.12% males were below matriculate. 32.65% only males were adequately utilized and 55.10% only males were over-utilized and in both category the percentage of literate and educated manpower is fairly high.

From the census information it has been found that there are seven big villages namely Oiara, Sonamai, Pabhera, Cistipur,

Nataual, Panditganj, and Nadwan (Fig. 3) where markets are held twice a week and some essential goods are marketed. Yet these markets donot fulfill the needs of local villagers of the area and often they have to go the near by towns to purchase their goods not available in their local bi-weekly markets. Larger demands and less supply requires the expansion of the existing local markets. Therefore, the development of the existing markets is essential for the efficient and rational utilization of unutilized human resources available in the block. Some new market centres may also be developed to meet the needs of the villagers.

Almost all categories of human resources engaged in commerce are self-employed which is a good sign of developing rural economy. Therefore, they should be provided credit and other impetus from the cooperative societies, bank and government agencies. For this purpose particularly cooperative societies and other financing institutions should be incorporated in the area which may also provide employment opportunities for the un-utilized manpower particularly educated human resources. This would be a step forward in the rural development.

Particular emphasis should be laid to promote the house hold industries in the block. There are about 23% males and 49% females (1984) from the working age groups lying un-utilized. If these activities are promoted, a fraction of them may avail a fair chance of employment. It would further promote commercial activities in the area in which another fraction of the total unutilized human resources may avail a change of employment. This would contribute to the development of rural economy of Dhanarua block.

It is to be noted that there is a slow shift in workers participation rate from the primary activities to secondary and tertiary activities. The percentage of male workers in commerce has shown a growing trend of their utilization during the period of last 14 years. In 1971 the percentage of male workers to the total male workers engaged in commercial activities was only 2.21% whereas the percentage of females in the same occupation and during the same period has declined from 0.79% to 0.53%. This clearly shows that participation of males in the commercial activities is increasing whereas it is decreasing in case of females. However, a proper incentive for more benefits may promote the interest of females for these activities. The rising percentage of males is a healthy sign of the inclination of the people for better and more profitable self-contained activities assuring more dependable measures of prosperity. If incentives, financial support and proper guidance are extended to these people, it may be consequential to a rapid development of the rural economy of the block.

ACKNOWLEDGEMENT

The author expresses his gratefulness to Prof. R.N.P. Sinha, Head, Department of Geography, The Maharaja Sayajirao University of Baroda, for his guidance for the present work and to Shri S.M.H. Rizvi for going through the draft and making valuable comments.

ELEVEN

K.R. Shrivastava

Commercial Potential of Antarctica

Introduction

Antarctica is the world's seventh continent. It has remained largely unexplored because of its isolation and extreme weather. World economic relations have been changing with resource potential and political situations over the centuries. Till early twentieth century Great Britain was supposed to be the centre of world economic activity due to its large over-seas empire and due to the naval power she possessed. No body knows that in near future Antarctica may become the focus of world economic activity. The paper highlights the resources that may be available in Antarctica and may give rise to commercial activities in future.

The region

Antarctica is a stable platform. The geological history reveals that during the mesozoic era Gondwana Land had a common land mass consisting of Africa, Antarctica, Australia, India and Latin America. Later, these continents drifted away. Rock samples of gneiss and granite of Antarctica are similar to that of the Peninsular India.

Antarctica is 990 km. away from Cape Horn, the nearest land area to it. (It is 8000 km. away from India). Its average height is 1830 m. (Fig. 1). The mountain ranges of trans-Antarctica divide it into two parts, i.e. eastern and western. Vinson Massif is the highest point in the continent (5140m).

The eastern part is geologically older as compared to the western part which comprises of folded mountains. In between the two is a plateau, about 4000 m high. Most of the continent lies below the sea level due to the weight of the perpetually falling ice. The thickness of the ice varies between sea level and 4.5 km. Due to the presence of the Trans-Antarctic mountain the ice flows towards the Ross Sea and to the Weddell Sea.

FIG. 11.1

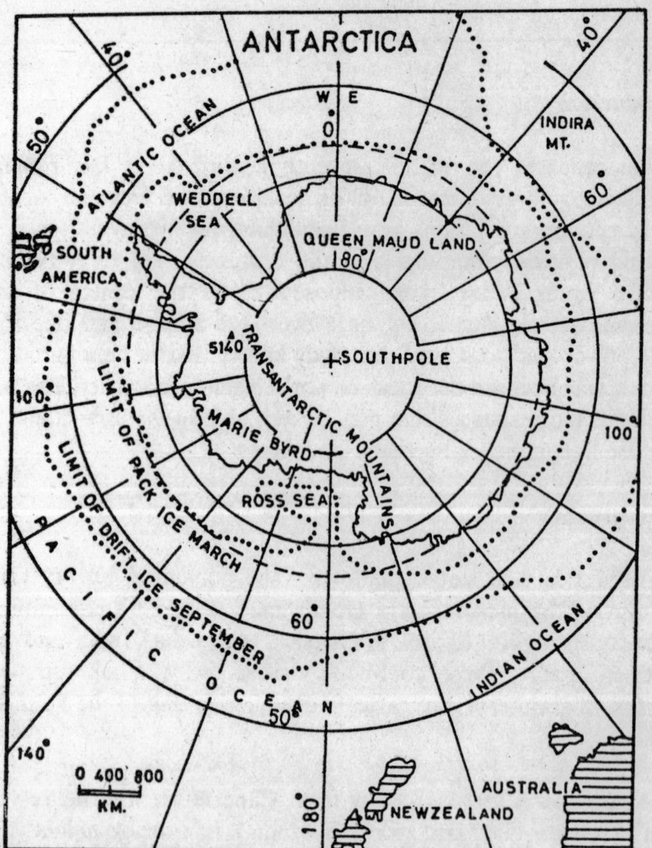

The ocean bottom toprography has revealed a mountain at a depth of about 4500 m. It is 185 km wide at the base and 135 km wide at the top. Its highest peak reaches within 88m of the ocean surface. It has been named as *'Indira Mount'* (53 '40' S and 47 '56' E).

The area receives a large intensity of solar radiation, 80% of which is reflected back (Qasim and Joshi, 1984). The heat balance is positive only during the two summer months of December and January. Minimum temperature may reach -29°C and the highest + 80° C. Wind speed may exceed 80 km/hr at times. Winds generally blow from the south and the south-east sectors. The ice melting rate was 35.8mm/day which is equivalent to about 20mm. of water. The flora generally consists of lichens and mossess, common to such areas. It grows on rockey substratum. The summers being very short no other form of flora has been reported so far.

Resource Potential

Inspite of its drawback of isolation, extremely cold and stormy conditions, attempts have been made to discover the resource potential of Antarctica. The Antarctic Treaty consists of 16 countries including India. India has organised three expeditions (1980-81, 82-83 and 83-84) under the Department of Ocean Development. The country has contributed much to discover the resources.

Ice

The major and commercially exploitable resource of the Antarctica is fresh water in the form of ice. Ice covers 90% of the total land mass of the study area with a thickness ranging from 1.6 km to 4.5 km. The huge ice sheet contains 90% of the world's ice. The shape of the ice sheet is like a dome and it has a height of 4000 m. A.S.L. The total volume is 30 million km^3. It is estimated that if whole of this ice sheet melts the sea level would rise by 60 m. The ice-cap contains nearly 70% of the world's store of fresh water. The area of the ice-pack varies between 2.6 million km^2 in March to 18.8 million km^2 in September. The northerly winds blowing in this area are very powerful. The ice gets disbursed towards the three oceans. It has been reported by the first Indian expedition team that the icebergs start appearing from 55'S lat. and keep on increasing in number as one moves south.

It is interesting to note that these ice- bergs can be towed to some of the dry areas and one can use them as a source of fresh water. The annual ice break-off rate is estimated to be about 1.4 trillion tonnes. It goes into the southern oceans. The towing of ice bergs will be economically viable. An iceberg weighing 85 million tones can be towed through the Indian Ocean for a distance of about 8000 km. Whatever remains of the ice-berg after the long journey will produce fresh water at a rate of about Rs.6.50/m^3. Desalined water in Saudi Arabia costs about RS.12/m^3. Besides there exist four fresh water lakes in the region of Dakshin Gangotri, established by the Indian Ocean expedition. This can be used by the explorers who may reside there in future.

The bio-mass

Another potential of the Antarctica may be its bio-mass. Lichen and moss have already been reported to be growing there. The bacterial flora is dominated by *baccillus, Micrococcus* and *Corynebacterim.* The essential nutrient salts of nitrogen and phosphorus are found in the fresh water lakes. Due to low temperatures through out, phytoplankton production is restricted to two summer months. The biological productivity of the Antarctic waters is high and with a regular input of nutrients primary production will be high. The Zooplankton biomass value is also very high. Higher type of flora, however, will be naturally restricted due to continuously low temperatures.

Minerals

Antarctica is said to be a part of the erstwhile Gondwana land. Rocks and minerals associated with the Deccan plateau and the African plateau are naturally expected to be present in Antarctica. Among them coal, iron ore, uranium, copper, oil, lead and gas are important. Rocks from the Dakshin Gangotri have confirmed the presence of these minerals.

Other resources

Among other resources which may indirectly help commercial activities are the clean and unpolluted environment which is similar to the one noted in the Himalayas. Manufacturing process of pure metals, which require such environment, and scientific investigations can make use of this unique gift of nature. The scientific experiments will also help in enhancing the knowledge about the *monsoons* on which the economic activities of the Indian sub- continent depend. An eye may be kept on world climate as well. Weather forecasting may be improved and this can save the economy from drought, floods etc.

It is observed that Antarctica may become a centre for world economic activity in supplying raw materials for food, water and industries in future.

TWELVE

B.G. Tamaskar

Economic Functions of Weekly Market Places

Introduction

Weekly market-places generate cash income to various sections of the people involved directly or indirectly with their operations. A comparative measure of relative significance of each market-place can be the amount of cash income generated by it in its service area, (Scott, 1972). It can be an objective index of ranking market places in a hierarchical class-system. However, data on their income-generating capacity are not readily available. This income yielding capacity of an individual weekly market-place depends upon its favourable site, amidst some productive region with relatively high density of population in its service area, efficient transport linkages and infra-structural facilities for agglomeration of men, materials, and services, congenial tax-structure, low overhead costs and defensive pricing to attract buyers to the place.

Weekly market-places are the first tier of marketing system in general. These are mostly, but no exclusively, rural market-places. They have been estimated to be more than 22,000 in number in 1983, all over India. In Maharashtra State, more than 3200 weekly market-places have been recorded in 1961.

HYPOTHESIS

We may hypothesise that weekly market-places in most cases on a small scale reveal two categories of economic functions i.e., (1) direct, within the market-place premises/campus to seller participants as well as to others, and (2) indirect, to other than actual participants on account of their occurrence on the economic landscape, for examination and verification.

METHODOLOGY

The data-base constitutes the author's former studies on weekly market-places on the Sagar-Damoh Plateau, the Chhattisgarh Plain, Mediaeval Maharashtra, the Arvi Upland and Gedam's study on the Wardha Valley and other published literature on the theme in India and abroad.

SITES

Having alluded to broadly the main economic functions of weekly market places and variables concerned with their successful operation at the outset, the categories of sites may be examined in brief. Whatever may be the physical site of a weekly market-place, associated characteristics are essential for its successful accomplishment of economic functions and continued growth and development. Sites, conducive to the fulfilment of its role in economic functioning, are normally contact zone of two differing economies, such as Theni Allinagaram in Madurai District (Jamuna & Swaminathan 1983), border zone of natural regions or an administrative/political boundary, particularly on a neutral ground (Bromley, 1975), transit and contact zone, exemplified by Pollachi in Coimbatore Nilgiris region (Parvathi, 1978), well-established trade route, e.g. as in cause of one type of West African house trade (Hill, 1971), or close to the Eastern Road in the Chhatisgarh Plain (Tamaskar, 1978:A), resource zones of Baghelkhand (M.P) (Shrivastava, K.R. 1983) etc. In the recent past, sites of weekly market places exhibited focussing point of very different order than of settlements, and are even independent of the existence of the latter, when located in them. They have tended to prefer their placement close to places of public assembly, viz., a shrine or *dharamshala* (inn) and at cross routes. The points of exchanges set in the rural milieu in the past witnessed their marked preference for nodes of former communication lines. (Fogg, 1932) and close to sources of water-supply on dry surfaces of ground, without being dusty in dry season. Such sites may be on banks of rivers/streams, springs, tanks, even canals serve to solve the problem of water-supply of the large gatherings of men and animals, though not altogether absent on interstream areas, (Tamsakar, 1978 B). In the arid region of Morocco the placement of these places lies close to some source of water-supply, such as wells, large springs or rivers. These sites even suffer migration within a range of a few kilometres to obtain water by digging a few feet below the ground surface.

GENERAL CHARACTERISTICS

With these introductory remarks, it is pertinent to examine in some details, the generic features of weekly market-places. This type of trading plays a great role in the economic organisation of space in developing countries. It has been estimated in general that contribution of commerce to GDP under discussion ranges between 8 and 18 per cent. In some selected parts of the world, it may rise as high as 28 per cent. (Beaujeu-Garnier and Debolez, 1979). The income from agricultural trade in the Chhattingarh Plain of India has been estimated to be around 5 per cent (Tamaskar, 1978 A). Approximately, more than 10 per cent of active population finds employment in this category of marketing activities. It may be remembered that this sort of self employment is merely a source of supplementary earning to a large number of part-time vendors. It is conjectured that commerce in developing countries occupies only fourth place as source of employment after agriculture, domestic services, handicraft and industry. This self employment in trading at weekly market places does not require any formal education or training. Though this is the last resort of the unemployed, there is relatively less scope for employment opportunity in this class of trading.

MOTIVE FORCES

It has been revealed that the motive forces of venture in weekly market-place hardly extend beyond making a living rather than making increasing profits. In other words, it is more or less a subsistence commercial activity. Likewise, most of the buyers are interested in procuring 'convenience' goods or commodities for their immediate consumption. Under such circumstances these market-places tend to attract relatively small number of visitors, as compared to these at urban centres. The total business transactions at such market-places are visibly on small scale, though there may be a few interesting exceptions to the general rule, such as pollachi (in the coimbatore-Nilgiri Region), Theni Allinagaram (Madurai District in Tamil Nadu) etc.

COMMERCIAL MECHANISM

We may, now, turn to the operational 'processes' or mechanism of marketing activities at weekly market-places. The most outstanding marketing process, in general,is retailing of goods directly to buyers. The central core of market process constitutes the distribution of agricultural products and essential goods of every-day life, needed by consumers. A few exotic 'foreign-made' goods trickle down or can be injected into weekly market-places.

The process of bulking cereals/food-grains seems to have come to a halt with the imposition of compulsory levy system for their procurement direct from producers to be stocked in government storage system, particularly, in Maharashtra State. The local supply of stable food-grains in villages and weekly market-places has dwindled sharply in quantity and consequent incapacity of villagers to encounter scarcity conditions on account of partial or total failure of rains in 1985 with increased prices. However, the process of bulking butter or curd by rural vendors at a few weekly market-places on the Arvi Upland by agents/representatives of a few rich urban dealers of Wardha and Nagpur has been vogue (Tamaskar (1978 B). Likewise, some commodities other than food-grains, such as lac, honey, etc., may be involved in the bulking process in favourable localities/regions. It is evident that vertical trade exists at a small scale at these market-places for re-sale of agglomerated goods in urban markets.

Cloth, clothes, grocery items, footwear, cheep consumer goods, sundry items, obtained from urban centres by vendors at periodic market-places, find their outlets to these market-places, and are vended by mobile traders normally, or by local shop-keepers. This brief discussion points to the economic integration between rural and urban areas, and implies their mutual dependence and the absence of total isolation and seclusion from each other. This has helped to usher in open-system of society, breaking down in the time-honoured closed system of self-sufficiency though not completely. Agricultural products and village crafts move up to urban centres and exotic factory made consumer and other goods move down from urban centres to rural market-places. The system of Alute-Balute in existence since at least the 13th Century in villages of Maharashtra made then almost self-sufficient in nearly all respects. The system provided services and crafts to villagers in lieu whereof craftsmen received grains (Balkrishna, 1940). It can be very well realised that only with the division of labour and regional specialisation in production, did the market-place exchange system came into existence. The periodic marketing system has undergone changes in the post-Independence period in India. The agricultural production in the service area of the periodic market place was geared to feed factories in England and food-grains were exported in the pre-independence period. The items included for export to England were bulked at periodic market-place and directed towards sea-ports from where they found out-lets to England, Such port-oriented trade for export to colonial powers was prevalent in other colonial countries and has been designed as dendretic market system (Johnson, 1975).

COMMODITY STRUCTURE

The goods sold at weekly markets places can be readily classified into three categories, viz. perishable, semiperishable and durable (Table I). However, it may be borne in mind that commodity structure reflects the regional food habits, their availability, production of specific crafts in the region, efficiency of transport linkages for goods brought for sale from different places, the nature of marketing system, etc.

This does neither exhaust all articles available for sale, nor indicate that the commodity structure has remained unaltered from that in the past. Slaves and bondsmen and girls, and women were offered for sale at weekly market places in the mediaeval times in India (Tamaskar,1966; 1978 A) and also in African countries (Meillassoux, 1971).

Most of the business transactions are made on card payments.

However, credit may be available in some cases where intimate bond has been established between buyers and sellers. Nearly 80% village sellers bring their produce for sale for securing cash to buy their necessities of life and return home to resume their agricultural or craft production on the remaining days of the week. In other words, these village producers are part-time sellers. Even mobile vendors cannot earn any conspicuous margins of profit but their transactions are more or less subsistence in effect and purpose.

TABLE I: General Commodity Stryctyre of Weekly Market-Place

Regional Goods (a)	Exotic goods/Factory-made article (b)
A. Agricultural Products:	1. Mill-made Cloth
1. Vegetables	2. Ready-made Garments
2. Fruits	
3. Cereals and Pulses	
4. Spices	
B. Animals and Animal Products	
1. Goats and Sheep for meat.	3. Hoisery items
2. Fishes and other aquatic animals	4. Luxury articles
3. Hides and Skins	
4. Butter and clarified butter (Ghee)	
C. Other Food Articles	5. Salt
1. Vegetable oils	6. Kerosene oil
2. Gur/Local Sugar	
3. Sweets	
D. Artisan Products	7. Small Iron and Steel products
1. Earthenwares	8. Tobacco
2. Wicker work e.g. baskets, fans, etc.	9. Soaps
	10. Biddi: indigenous cigarettes
3. Local made footwears	11. Plastic goods
4. Hand-loom cloth	12. Match Boxes
5. Indigenous agricultural implements, appliances etc.	13. Socks, Keys, etc.
	14. Others.
6. Wooden articles	
E. Forest Products	
1. Fuel wood	
2. Local Fruits (Wild)	
3. Honey, wax, etc.	

Source : Field work

GENERATION OF INCOME

Weekly market-places in general generate income to a certain group of participants who may be classified under direct economic and indirect economic functions.

DIRECT ECONOMIC FUNCTIONS

The direct economic functions of weekly market-places concern themselves with the sale of commodities and services, repairs, entertainments, and other sundry activities. All these categories of activities may be full-time, part time or even occasional. These market-places serve as outlets for rural products such as grains, vegetables, and items of handicrafts from their service areas. Normally, village peasants visit market-places to gain cash for purchase of convenience goods, such as food-stuffs, oil, kerosene, salt, grocery, cloth (Ganguly, 1984) and other items regularly and occasionally procure agricultural implements, seeds, fertilizers etc.

SERVICES

The normal categories of services available encompass sharpening of domestic applicances, repairing of agricultural implements, hair-dressing, massaging, earwax removing, shoeing of hoofs of animals, stiching dresses, mid-wifery, astrological consultations, (provided in India by *Jyotishis*) etc. By way of illustration, a few more services may be added, which differ from region to region according to local/regional cultural traits. In south Manbhum (India), it has been noted that the distribution of postal articles is arranged at weekly market-places (Sinha, 1961). Another allied service, namely, letter-writing is recorded to be in vogue in rural China. (Skinner, 1964), Morocco (Fogg, 1932), Search for canoe-men, masons, soldiers, brick-layers, interpreters linking with trade in Ghana from the locations of carpenters, blacksmiths. tile-layers, etc. is made at market places (Karve and Acharya, 1970). The availability of services of goldsmiths, foundary-men, grinder in corn-mills, tailors, carpenters, shoe markets in Ghana etc. and its coastal region the services of midwives, tailoring, butchering also may be added to the list. As most of visitors to market-places stay throughout the day at market places, their need of food and beverages, eatables and meals are met with in temporary stalls, and permanent hotels selling these items (meillossoux 1971: Geetha, 1979). The sale of rice-balls in the Mediaeval times of the Deccan history in India (Tamaskar, 1978 C) may also be observed. Tea-stalls in rural China play a significant role in socio-econo-interactions. They are convenient places for socialisation and also constitute form for taking decisions concerning certain social amenities (Skinner, 1964). Loans may be available from local bankers, where they are sought for in these weekly market-places. The payments of debt is done in these market places by debtors. However, modern banking system at large-sized market-place in India is making its slow appearance to replace the traditional banking, specifically for the purchase of improved seeds, fertilisers and other agricultural operations. The procedural impediments and malpractices of some persons in the modern banking system and disinclination to pay off outstanding debts render the smooth operation of banking a knotty problem. There is no scope for book-keeping, accountancy, administrators and bankers in this marketing system, at least in India. Surveying and measurement of plots of land may be undertaken by certain qualified individuals by setting up their temporary offices at such markets-places (Jamkar, 1985; personal communication).

REPAIRS

Repairs may be varied. Bicycle repairs in Uganda (Good 1975), repairing of rural houses before the onset of the *monsoons* specially roofs and actual repairs undertaken at market places in some parts of India, repairing of footwears, umbrellas, locks, and others may be enumerated among a wide range of repairs. In some weekly market-places in Tamil Nadu repairs of bullockcarts are also in evidence.

COUNTRY CLUB

The market-places are also considered as country clubs (Sinha et al, 1964). They provide apart from services and repairs, a certain category of common and cheap entertainments and amusements to visitors, on small payment or gratification, such as vocal and instrumental music, jugglery, acrobatics, snake charming, animal shows, even gambling on some occasions. Story telling has been found to be an interesting source of entertainment, amusement and diversion from normal chorces of human life in rural China, and Morocco (Fogg, 1932).

INDIRECT ECONOMIC FUNCTIONS

Apart from these active participants, income may be derived from the very existence of weekly market-places such as the organisational set-up, vested with power and authority of control, supervision, and superintendence over marketing activities, transportation system, utilized for marketing purposes, incentive to production of agricultural commodities, and certain professionals, viz., lawyers, physicians, surgeons, dentists, etc. approached by visitors to the these market-places for consultation and advice where these services may be available or their proximity, within their service.

ORGANISATIONAL SET-UP

The organisational body charged with the control, superintendence, supervision of market-places, derive small revenue from taxes, ground-rents, ferry tolls, fines levied for a certain categories of crimes or lapses. This revenuc may vary from a few hundred to a few thousand rupees per annum. A striking example of Choutra Umbare (Umbariyal) of Sarkar (sub-division) can be readily and convincingly cited to illustrate this point. This market-place developed to such an extent as to yield Rs. nine *lakhs)* and hence, it had earned the name of *Navlakh* Umbare (i.e. yielding Rs. Nine *lakhs* early in the 18th Century (Tamaskar, 1978 C). The biggest and oldest periodic market-place at Pollachi in South India contributed Rs. Six *lakhs* in 1978 to the revenues of the local municipality (Parvathi, 1978). A host of employees in the service of the organisational set-up obtain regular salary. Market-places serve to generate employment to a few unemployed individuals. In the medieval period of Indian history, an escort was provided en route to protect their merchandise. These escort procured some remuneration for the service rendered by them.

TRANSPORT FACILITIES

The transport system serving periodic market-places are vital for the circulation of men and materials. They may be broadly classified into two categories; Pre-modern and modern. The pre-modern means of transport exclusively comprised of pack-animals such as bullocks, horses, asses camels, etc. and bullock-carts, human backs, heads and shoulders; and modern means of transport cover bicycle, trucks, buses, metadors, three wheelers, auto-rickshawas, trailors of tractors and jeeps, and railways. However, both types are pressed into service for movements of men used by these who can bear its cost. Owners of animals obtain hire for services rendered by these animals (Parvathi, 1978).

INCENTIVE TO AGRICULTURAL PRODUCTION

The weekly market-places give rise to processing of farm produce for marketing them such as clearing, grading, unloading, repacking, measuring, etc. It may give employment to some persons, if farmers are unable to undertake any of these petty jobs. Some of the rural crafts like baskets, winnowing pans, cradles made of bamboo, pottery and ropes, (Geetha, 1979), receive patronage in these market-places. In the southern portion of Manbhum district of Bihar 14 types of rural crafts have been noticed, prior to 1961, such as bark rope, basketry, black-smithy, broom-stick making, bell-metal work, carpentry, cotton-weaving, comb-making, leather-work, mask-making, oil pressing, pottery, and wool-weaving (Sinha, 1961)

INCOME TO LOCAL PRIESTS

In the end, it may be observed that visitors to these market-places may make it a point to visit local shrines and temples. This may be a source of some additional income to priests of these place of worships on market-day. It has been emphasised that the trip to the market-place is multi-purpose elsewhere. Visitors to market-place avail of the market-meeting and other professionals visit to legal practitioners etc. From these visitors to relative categories of professionals some income may be derived on this day of market-meeting. This leads to the obvious conclusion that weekly market-places generate economic integration within their individual service areas. It has been revealed elsewhere that they also monitor social integration. However, it remains to be concluded that economic functions of weekly market-places are not only varied in their range but also their mechanism is equally complicated and complex. The following model promises the economic functioning of periodic market-places (Table - II). The business transactions at periodic market-places are not motivated by any large margin of profit. If peasants produce enough to feed, and procure clothing for family with some decency and meet social obligations, then their economic activities are considered successfull. The traditional production and exchange system serve to support a relatively large number of participants, many of them, with a low level of living (Beals, 1975). The exchange system covers transactions from the village to the market-place, the market-place to the village, and market-place to market-places , after purchase. Traditional market-places are noted for lesser variety of industrial products, smaller number of buyers and sellers, few stores or shops of permanent character and small ones that in modern stream of marketing activities. There are hardly any consideration of capital except in small degree by fruits-sellers and buyers. In several categories of vendors, there is hardly any staying power, particularly bulky goods, and perishable commodities like fruits vegetable, etc. This tends to make the exchange system exploitative for for unscrupulous buyers. All this point to unimpeachable conclusion that the sellers involve making a living rather than making increasing profits. The primary goods and services imply their demand and supply, cost of production, overhead costs, the concept of fair or market price, attitude of buyers, holding out capacity of sellers, urgency for cash etc. In brief, the market makes the price. This exchange system functions with a less sophisticated information system and has limited accounting practices. It has to be borne in mind that the village farmer enters the market-place to satisfy his own needs. This fact generally remains unrecognised. This exchange system serves both consumption and distribution systems and is noted for a seasonal fluctuations of market activities, with requirement of several reasons. In some big villages/small towns, there is an increased demand of local produce, due to the immigrations of teachers, officials, etc. In the absence of competition the cost of good is higher than that in large urban centres. These immigrants also take to farming on their purchased lands.

It has been observed that the periodic marketing system is not simply residual, it is actually tending to expand and remains very healthy (Tamaskar, 1983, Beaugeu-Garnier and Deboles, 1972). It has been revealed that 'new' forms of periodic marketing systems

TABLE II: ECONOMIC FUNCTIONS OF WEEKLY MARKETS.

A. DIRECT

1. Full time Part time & occasional sale and purchase of commodities.

2. Full time Part time & occasional sale and purchase of services.

3.
- a)Foot wears
- b)Umbrellas
- c)Locks & Keys.
- d)Building & roof repairs
- e)other.

4. Entertainment, Amusements etc.
- a)Vocal & Istru-meental music
- b)Magic shows
- c)Snake-charming
- d)Animal shows
- e)Mobile cinema
- f)Acrobatics
- g)Wrestling
- h)others.

5. Others
- a)Brokrage
- b)Commission Agency
- c)Assistanc
- d)Portage
- e)Miscellaneous

B. INDIRECT

1. Organising body:
- a)Employment to officials.
- b)Revenue from taxes, Iround rents cesse etc.
  - 1 Within
  - 2.Enroute

2. Transport (employees, hire etc.)
- 1.Pre-modern.
- 2.Modern

3. Incentive to production in villages of service areas
- a)Grains
- b)Vegetables
- c)Crafts
- d)other food-stuffs.
- e)agro-based industries.

4. Professional
- a)Lawyers
- b)Physicians
- c)Surgeons
- d)Dentists
- e)Veterinary Surgeons
- f)Temple/ Shrine Priests
- g)Others

have made recent appearance in developed countries of the world (Tamaskar, 1983; Gormsen, 1984). The system can adopt itself to changes in consumption or radical changes when competition with well-established shops appears. This has a great social significance in enabling the poor to survive. It must be admitted that the participation in market-place trade yields only extremely low earning. This may be additional income to the regular earning to secure at least subsistence. The weekly market system, obviously can be recognised as a part of a complex survival system serving substantial proportions of the rural poor (Bohle, 1979). It has been established that socio-economic attributes and working regimes of the periodic marketing system are an index of the wider socio-economic environment than that generally is in our mental focus. Barring a few honourable cases, low degree of specialization, scarcity of capital, as well as risk and uncertainty of agricultural production, are evident features of a majority of weekly market-places. The motivation does not involve maximization of the potential income of participants by specialisation in a particular occupation but they are inclined to operate in diverging economic spheres to minimise their risks (Good, 1975). In a nutshell, one of most characteristics features of weekly market-place participants, as revealed by several and personal studies, is adoption of a strategy which may be designated as maximum participation consistent with minimum risk.

The small-scale operation of weekly market place poses a question whether their abolition can be justified. The answer is a strong 'No'. The past attempt, during the communist revolution in China, totally paralysed the distribution system, causing hardships to a large number of rural consumers (Skinner, 1964). Moreover, it has been manifested that the modern marketing system and periodic marketing system are mutually complementary.

Attempt to equate these market-places with central places does not seem to be convincing and conclusive (Shrivastava, 1980). It has been averaged that central place theory may offer a promising way of analysing this marketing system but it too has its own limitations (Beals, 1979).

THIRTEEN

A.G. Jamkar

Origin and Evolution of Periodic Market Places in Dhule District (Maharashtra)

Introduction

There can be hardly any denying the common and impressive number of market-places as the wide-spread human phenomenon, and its significant position in the internal exchange system and economic and social structure in developing countries including India (Bromley, 1974 pp. 530-37). Periodic market-places have their intimate association with the informal (traditional) sector. There are direct as well as indirect circumstancial evidences to butress up the exogenous theory of origin-conditions of market places, shedding light on their close relationship with external trade. Trade routes stimulated, fostered and promoted the birth of periodic market-places along them or in their immediate proximity (Tamaskar, 1981). It has also been shown that in case of periodic market-places of mediaeval Maharashtra that the power and authority for their organisation were vested in local authorities by the State Government. Now, as far as the origin and evolution of periodic market-places in Dhule district are concerned, it is rather inconclusive to state authoritively about their origin due to fragmentary and meager data on this theme.

Like any other periodic marketing system in Maharashtra the existing periodic marketing system in Dhule district seems to be deeply rooted in the past, and it has undergone notable transformations with changing socio economic and demographic variables, resulting in the present day pattern, induced by the former long-distance inter-regional exchange system.

Methodology

A set of maps has been prepared on the basis of the available data on contemporary historical documents and factual information recorded in gazetteers. These maps depict two important aspects - (1) the spatial pattern of periodic market-places, their relation with the existing routes, the past and present transport network in the district and adjoining regions, and (2) the settlements with socio-economic significance.

Theories of Origin

The main objective of this paper is to investigate the possible and relavent origin-conditions of the periodic market-places in Dhule district (Fig. 1A). It is pertinent to examine the prevalent theories on the origin of periodic market-places and match them with the present and former market-places.

FIG. 13.1

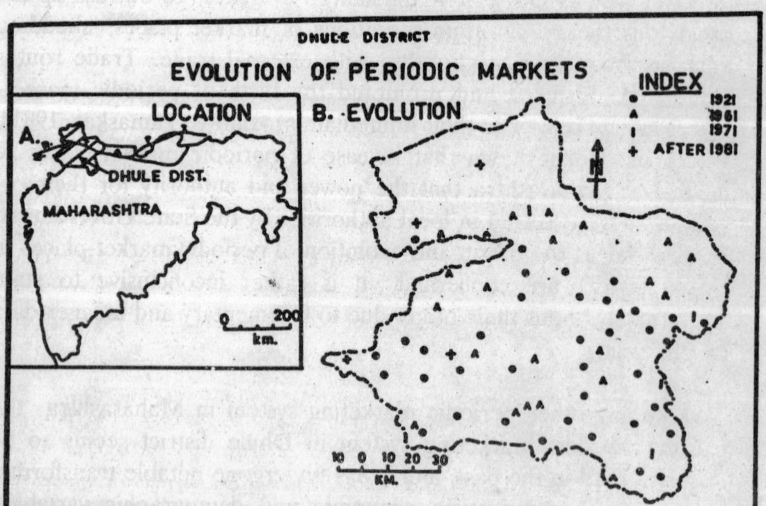

At present, there are two main theories in the field which throw light on the origin conditions of periodic market places. The are:

1. The endogenous theory, i.e. and individual's propensity to barter commodities.

2. The exogenous theory, i.e. springing up of periodic market-places as a result of the well-established and regular inter-regional or inter-national exchange systems along frequented routes or paths operating since long.

It will be helpful to consider at some length the central idea of the above theories. The endogenous theory is considered to be orthodox which sets out the individual propensity to barter, even involving silent barter, stemming from the necessity for local exchange, the division of labour and local markets, and finally the necessity for long-distance or at least external exchange or trade links (Bohannan and Dalton 1962). To put it in other words, the starting point reveals local exchange and local market-place, only a few of which can attain a status of important market-places, associated with long-distance trading, because of some fortunate circumstances. Quoting Hodder (1965) "barter exists among the most isolated and inaccessible societies, and the wordless exchange of goods, made without witnesses, in the further most recesses of jungle in Asia, America and Africa, is the evidence of an economic need. As confidence grows between individuals exchanging their respective goods, local markets spring up; and in more advanced countries wide use may be made of money in the more important markets or regional fairs". The following model can illustrate the implications of the theory;

The exogenous theory on the origin conditions of periodic market-places reverses the above sequence of events, indicating that trade with its associated phenomena can hardly arise within a community, for trade, it is claimed, is "an internal affair involving different communities" (Hodder, 1965). Market-places cannot spring up into existance put of the demands of purely individuals or local exchange. "Markets are primarily induced by external exchange of complementary products with an alien population". (Bohannan and Dalton C., 1962). In accordance with this view point, market-places are not the starting point but rather the out-growth of long-distance trading, which in its own right, is the result of division of labour and variable location of goods of nearby or distant region. The true sequence of events in the light of the arguments will embody i) trade route, ii) market-place as a network of tracks or roads develop.

BARTER ECONOMY

Subsistence level existence	Nothing to trade	No marketing system	
Subsistence level existence	Small surpluses	Silent trade mutual exchange of gifts.	
Self contained and self sufficient village communities	Little complementary production with dominance of farming.	Vertical trade transit inter-regional exchange system	Seasonal or annual exchange system en route.

(Refer Mckey and Smith : New-Zealand Geographical Society, 1974).

The Case Study of Dhule District

The origin of the periodic marketing systems have not been examined extensively in India so far but for a few attempts (Shrivastava, V.K., 1980).

From the maps prepared for this study the following routes become obvious. They are (a) Burhanpur - Surat road, which kept close association with the Tapi basin and passed through the then "Khandesh" region (Fig. 2). There is yet another reference from the same documents of the Agra - Surat road passing through Sironj - Burhanpur - Nandurbar - Navapur (b) Surat Golconda road Bardoli - Pimpalner - Deogaon-Daulatabad - Nanded - Golconda. It is quite possible that the same route was used for commercial activities between Paithan and Baroach (Motichandra, 1953). Approximate alignment to inferred routes, connecting the forts from this region, such as, a) Parōlā - Galna Bharmel - Mulher, b) Thalner - Songir -Lamkani - Bhamer - Pimpalner - Mulher, c) Thalner - Songir - Laling - Galna, d) Thalner - Torkhed - Sultanpur - Toranmal, and e) Thalner - Saindhawa is noted.

FIG. 13.2

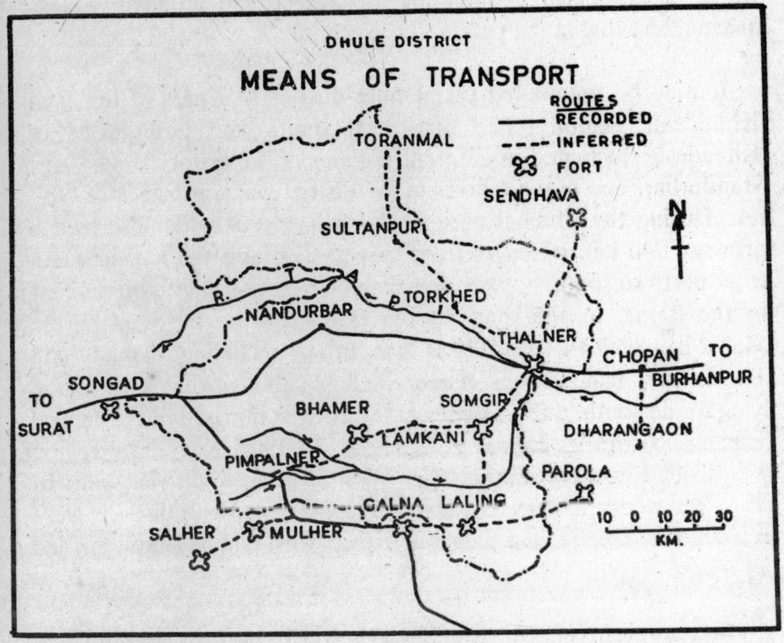

Fig.3 indicates the following categories of settlements in and around Dhule district : in (a) ancient (b) mediaeval (c) recent. The same map also depicts (i) forts & check posts (ii) fair centres, (iii) commercial centres, (iv) military - cum - administrative centres, and (v) industrial centres.[1] (Gazetteer of Dhule district - Maharashtra State revised, 1974).

Fig. 1-B sets out the growth of periodic market-places in Dhule district at observed time intervals, (a) S.O.I. topographical maps published in 1921, (b) Weekly periodic markets in Maharashtra-1961 census, (c) Dhule district census handbook - 1971, (d) Gazetteer of Dhulia District, Maharashtra State, revised edition 1974, (e) personal data collection, 1984.

From the maps it may be safely concluded that some of the existing periodic market-places have a fairly long history though such market-places seem to be few and far between. Afterwards, with the growth of population, increased out-put of agricultural, vegetable and fruit produce and fast transport facilities on all-weather roads, market-places began to multiply in number and attained a close spacing than that in the past.

It may be mentioned that Dhule district is a part of the then 'Khandesh' region. The territorial limits and boundaries of 'Khandesh' fluctuated in different regimes of the historical past, *e.g.*, Mandurbar, one of the talukas in the district was a province of Gujrat. During the Mughal period, the 'Khandesh' region "formed a province 240 km. in length from east to west and 160 km. in width from north to south, bounded on the north by the Malva, on the east by the Berar, on the south by the Galna and on the west by the Malva to which the districts of Nandurbar, including Shahada and Taloda were handed over. It contained 32 sub divisions. This region lying to the south of the Satpura hills mostly comprised of the central Tapi basin with its capital at Ashirgad. In 1906 'Khandesh' region was divided into two districts (a) 'West Khandesh' district, and (b) 'East Khandesh' district. On 21st of 1960, both of these districts were renamed as 'Dhulia' and 'Jalgaon' respectively. Dhulia is now spelled as Dhule.

Secondly, the people 'Khandesh' is conspicuous by its reference in historical writings, *e.g.* "Fruits grew much at Khandesh in Gujrath" (Srivastava, 1975). The same work mentions places like Burhanpur, Nandurbar, Nawapur, Thalner, Galna etc. as the centres of commercial activities.

Prakashi (Pra-Kashi meaning equivalent to Kashi) is regarded as having a contemporary temple of 'Lord Shiv' with that at Kashi. It is one of the important fair centres in Dhule district, with a big annual fair in *'Magh'* (December - January). The fair is still bigger at the time of 'Siemvasta' (rituals to be performed on the banks of holy river); besides there occurs comparatively small fair on every Monday of *'Shravan'* (July-August). It is a fact that such fairs attract large number of people from their neighbouring areas; and perform important commercial and marketing activities. Prakash probably is the first market place in the district. The other fair-centres with unknown past are Boris, Chadvel, Dhadne, Khapar, Mhasdi, Mudawad, Sarangkheda, Shirpur, Shirud and Toranmal (Fig. 3).

FIG. 13.3

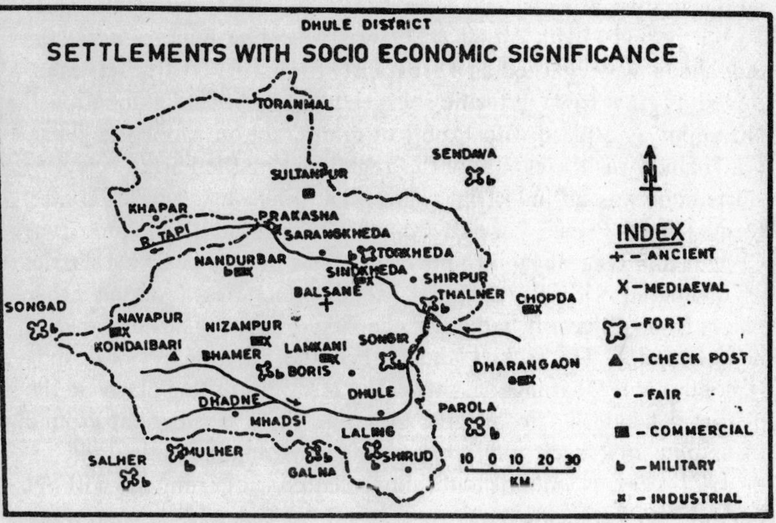

Fair centres at Khapar and Toranmal are noted for their tribal population of Bhil tribe. During fairs there is a large gathering of the Bhil community from the Satpura region.

Like fair centres, there are important forts and administrative centres at Torkhed, Thalner, Songir and Bhamer in the district recorded in Mughal, Maratha and British periods. Ashirgad, Parola, Galna, Mulher, Salher, Songad, Rajpipla and Sendhava are the other forts and administrative centres around Dhule district. Laling, Salbari, Kondaibari etc. were the check posts in those periods. Besides, there are 'Gadhis' (castles) at number of places in the district. There is sufficient ground to assume that these forts, particularly Thalner, Galna had a sizeable population of their own. Such large military and administrative stations could not be without market facilities, though their antiquity cannot be ascertained with certainty.

The settlements at Sindkheda, Nandurabar, Nawapura, Dhayta, Nimgul, Lamkani, Nizampur etc. in the district and a number of others outside the present domain of the district like Chopada,

Dharangaon, Burhanpur etc. appear to be ancient or mediaevel settlements. These settlements were either military, commercial, administrative or industrial centres. (i)Nandurbar, during the early Faruqi period (1370 - 1660 A.D.) was a leading military post, (ii) Sindkheda was regarded as a great dirty town, (iii) Dhayta was mentioned as great town in fertile soils, (iv) Salblank in 1609 mentioned Nizampur as a place with export of grains, cotton, wool and sugar, (v) Thalner was the capital of this region during the Faruqi rule, (vi) Burhanpur was an industrial centre. The English received '*farman*' (order) from Prince Perviz to open a factory at Burhanpur, (vii) Chopda and Dharangaon (quite close to the border of Dhule district as compared with Burhanpur) also had factories. Among other places Sivaji (Shavaji) had burnt the English factory at Dharangaon near Erandol. He sacked and burned the great marts of Copda (Chopda) and Dharangaon, two of the most flourishing places in the district 'Khandesh'. From these examples there is sufficient ground to assume that such military, commercial, administrative and industrial centres mentioned above could not remain without periodic-marketing system.

The middle of the 17th century was the time of highest prosperity for the province of 'Khandesh'. During the British period the town of Dhulia grew in its importance. The headquarters of the regular troops were fixed at Malegaon and Captain Brings as political agent took his residence at central station of Dhulia.

The British rulers took interest in the construction of roads and railways. In 1853-54 some progress was made in improving the cross routes in the district. Gradually, the road transport was supplemented by railway links. At present there are two rail routes, (a) The Bhusawal-Surat broad gauge, which was known as 'Tapti-Valley Railway'. (b) The Chalisgaon-Dhule broad gauge linked with the main Bombay-Howrah and with Delhi via Bhusawal. The expansion of road network is distinctively and impressively clear than rail network. The national highway No. 3 from Bombay to Agra and national highway No. 6 from Nagpur to Surat pass through the district. They intersect each other at Dhule. Burhanpur-Ankaleshwar national highway no.27 runs through Shirpur, Shahada, Taloda, Akkaleshwa.Nandurbar - Aurangabad a state highway also passes through Dhule; besides, there are a number of district road-ways sprawling the district. This road and rail network helped much in setting and promoting the periodic market-places, particularly at the junction of two highways, *e.g.,* Dhule or where there is rail road crossing, e.g. Dondaicha, Nardhana etc.

The demographic variables also control the distribution of periodic market-places. This region was peopled with the beginning of historic times. The first known historic reference of the people of 'Khandesh' Occurs in the Ptolemy's writtings (A.D. 150), mentioning the occupance of this land by Bhils. Later on the immigrants from Gujrat came inside the Tapi valley. During the regime of Yadav to Faruqi there were many immigrants from all sides. The estimated population in 1821 of the then 'Khandesh' region was 418021 persons, which further increased as shown in Table No.I

TABLE NO.I

Year	Population
1821	4,18,021
1837	4,78,457 (estimated)
1852	6,86,003 (estimated)
1872	10,28,042

The total population of the then 'Khandesh' region in 1905 must have exceeded the last 10 lakhs. In 1906, the 'Khandesh' region was partitioned into two districts (a) 'West Khandesh' district (Dhule), and (b) 'East Khandesh' district (Jalgaon). The major share of population passed on to the 'East Khandesh' because the 1901 censusreport records as many as 4,48,432 persons in 'West Khandesh' district which further shot up to 20 lakh (Table II).

TABLE II

Year	Population	Year	Population
1901	4,48,432	1941	8,45,776
1911	5,59,519	1951	10,60,278
1921	5,94,191	1961	13,51,236
1931	7,14,998	1971	16,62,181
		1981	20,50,294

It could be inferred safely that the total number of present periodic market places outnumbered than those in the past. There were as many as 38 periodic market-places till 1921 (The Survey of India Topographic maps), which increased relatively rapidly afterwards. Table no. III indicates the progressive increase of periodic market-places in the observed decades.

TABLE III

Year	Total No. of market-places	Population	No. of persons Surved
1921	38	5,94,191	15,636
1961	61	13,51,236	22,151
1971	65	16,62,181	26,802

It is obvious from table III that the total number of periodic market-places increased with the increase in population of Dhule district at the observed years. Another interesting point to note is that there is successive steady increase in the number of persons served by each periodic market.

Conclusion

In conclusion, it may be pointed out that complete information is not readily available about the origin and evoluation of market centres in the study region. But it is learnt from unofficial but reliable sources that the barter system is still in existence in some of the tribal areas of the district. There are sufficient direct as well as indirect circumstantial evidences to stress upon the exogenous theory of origin and evolution of periodic market-places. Doubtlessly, trade routes stimulated, fostered and promoted the birth of market-places along them or their immediate proximity. The following points clearly emerge from the discussion - (a) the existing periodic marketing system in the area under study is deeply rooted in the past, (b) the demographic variable is keeping close and positive association with the growth of periodic market places in Dhule district. The conclusions thus drawn may be considered tentative and desire further research.

Other Concepts

i. **Buyer Vs Trader Optima**

These two groups have a great concern in the locational spacing of periodic market-places in their origin (Smith, 1971). But it has been disclosed that in case of periodic market-places of mediaeval Maharashtra, the power and authority for their organisation were vested in local authorities by State Government (Tamaskar, 1977 b). As far as the study area is concerned, it could be the case that the local authorities in the past took care of time schedule of the adjacent market-places to avoid unhealthy competition and damaging the same day market meetings. This generated market meetings on different days particularly in proximate places.

ii. **Continuous Period of Peace and Security**

It is quite obvious from the historical records that the study area never enjoyed a stable rule in the pre-British times. The known historical documents indicate that the 'Satvahanas' ruled over this region till A.D. 250, followed by the 'Abiras', the 'Vakatakas', the 'Rashtrakutas' etc. In the last quarter of 12th. century A.D. the 'Yadavas' of 'Deogiri' extended their sway over this region. This was succeeded by the power of 'Delhi' Sultanat. The 'Faruqis' ruled over this region between 1370 and 1660 A.D. Then the Mughals established their power in the 'Khandesh' region. Towards the end of the Mughal period and in Maratha period, this region as a whole or in parts experienced toss in its power. All these happenings must have direct as well as indirect repercussion on the growth of periodic market-places. After the year, 1820 this region came under the British control, though the relations between the local *'Adivasi'* (tribal) rulers and the British rulers were hostile. The British rule brought about period of relative peace security and stability, which persisted in the post independent period.

iii. **Protection against insecurity and provision of positive incentives**

Favourable and benevolent policy decisions and positive incentive can only infuse vigour and stability in any periodic market-system. The same was noticed in Maratha period. Shivaji had encouraged marketing activities in all their ramifications possible in later half of 17th century (Navare 1927).

It may thus be concluded that there should be undisturbed, uninterrupted and continuous peaceful community life for the orign and evolution of periodic market-places the decision taking authorities should create positive incentives to cater the needs of both buyers and traders, and lastly, they should protect the interest of both of them.

NOTES

1. Gazetteer of Dhule District, Maharastra State, revised, 1974.

FOURTEEN

H.M. Saxena

Rural Marketing Pattern in Rajasthan

Rural market forms the basic blocks of the present day complex market place exchange system. On the one hand they are the farmer's first contact point for the disposal of their products while on the other hand they are complementary to urban market centres. The study of rural marketing pattern is more important in countries like India, where more than 80 per cent population lives in villages far removed from towns.

The objective of the this paper is to present the rural marketing pattern of Rajasthan as it exists today. The scope of the paper is limited to the identification of the types of rural marketing systems in various parts of the state. The paper is based on the information collected during field work as well as on secondary sources.

Rural Base of the Region

Rajasthan State (23 '3' to 30 '12' N lat. and 60 '30' to 78' 17 'E. Long) is a unique geo-economic and historical region covering an area of 3,42,274 km.*S*[2] According to 1981 Census the total population of the state was 34,261,862 out of which 84.85 per cent was rural. This indicates that the state, like the whole of India, is predominantly a rural region. The rural population is distributed throughout the state in 34,968 villages of various sizes. The following table indicates the number of villages according to their size in the state.

TABLE 1: Villages classified by population size in Rajasthan (1981)

Village Size According to their population	Total number of Villages
Less than 200	7,861
200-499	10,425
500-999	8,537
1000-1999	5,468
2000-4999	2,335
5000-9999	321
10000-Above	21
Total	34,968

Rural Marketing Pattern

Marketing activity involves interaction in space in order to facilitate exchange of goods and services. Since communities are not self-sufficient, their demands are to be fulfilled through trade or marketing. Thus, a simple hypothesis regarding the development of rural marketing is 'greater the demand more will be the marketing activity'. Similarly, surplus production involves flow of products, resulting in marketing at certain points known as market places.

Because of the diversified physical, economic and cultural conditions, the marketing pattern of the state is also diversified. The rural marketing pattern of the state differs from one region to another and still remains rudimentary and unsystematic. It is combination of periodic and permanent marketing. After an intensive survey, the author has identified the following forms of rural marketing pattern in the state (Fig. 1).

A Periodic Markets/Marketing
  i Weekly or bi-weekly markets, and
  ii Fairs.
B Marketing through mobile traders,
C Permanent village markets.

A-1 - Areas of weekly markets
B-2 - Fairs (Figures denote number of fairs in each district)
C-3 - Frequent
4 - Restricted
5 - Minimum

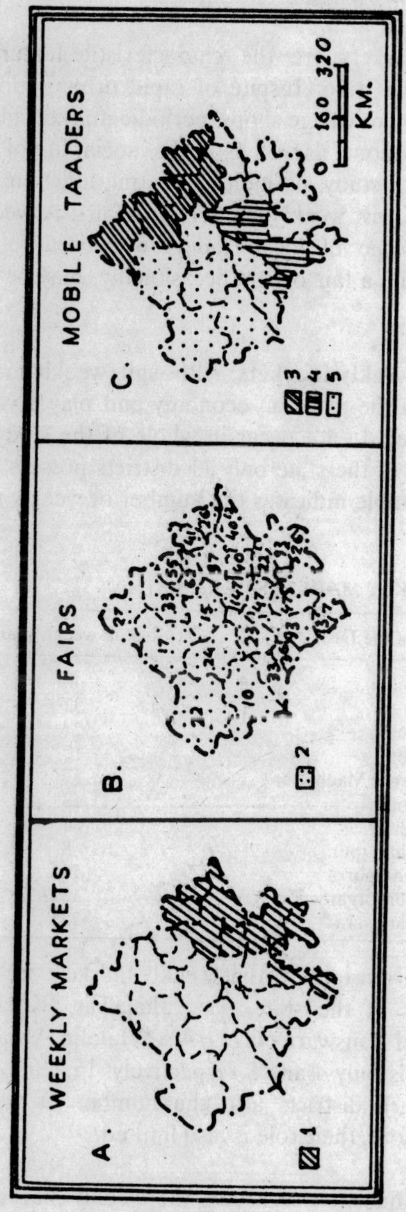

FIG. 14.1

(A) Periodic/Marketing

Periodic markets are the characteristic feature of the rural marketing in the state. Inspite of rapid urbanisation and development of permanent village shops, periodic markets play an important role in rural economy as well as in the social life of the villagers. In the region under study, periodic marketing function is performed by two institutions, viz. weekly markets and fairs. A weekly market is a weekly assemblage of local traders organised to facilitate retail operations; while a fair occurs occasionally, may be once or twice a year.

Weekly or bi-weekly markets: Although, weekly market are closely associated with the agrarian economy and play a vital role in rural society, but they do not occur in whole of the study region. Out of the 27 districts of the state only 11 districts possess weekly markets. The following table indicates the number of weekly markets in these districts.

TABLE II : WEEKLY MARKETS IN RAJASTHAN

Name of the District	No. of weekly markets
1. Jhalawar	42
2. Kota	52
3. Bundi	27
4. Tonk	10
5. Sawai Madhopur	59
6. Jaipur	18
7. Alwar	4
8. Bharatpur	8
9. Dholpur	14
10. Chittorgarh	12
11. Banswara	25

It is clear from table II that weekly markets are more in number in 15 districts of the state, viz. Jhalawar, Kota, Bundi, Swai-Madhopur and Banswara (Fig. 1-A). While in Alwar and Bharatpur their number is only 4 and 8 respectively. In Tonk, Jaipur, Dholpur and Chittorgarh districts also the number of weekly markets is limited, therefore, their role is also limited.

The basic question regarding the weekly markets is why weekly markets exist only in certain parts of state? Several geographers have explained the cause of the origin of weekly markets in developing countries. Stine (1962) has pointed out that two or more merchants meeting the same location at the same time are apt to sell more if the time of their visits were not co-ordinated. Hodder's (1968) theory, starts from the individual's propensity to barter, deduces from this the necessity of local exchange, the division of labour and local markets. While Bromley, Symanski and Good (1975) have developed a model and believe that periodic markets result from and persist because of the needs of producers, the organization of time, entertainment and comparative advantage.

The paper examines and reaches to the conclusion that in Rajasthan the existance of weekly markets in certain parts and their absence in adjoining areas cannot be explained by any theory or hypothesis as described by foreign geographers. It can be explained both in terms of geo-economic and historical-regional perspectives. The following points are notable:

(i) Weekly markets in the state (Where ever exist) have developed during the mediaeval period, specially during Rajput period of the Rajasthan history, as well as during the British period.

(ii) After independence their further growth remained static, therefore, there is no addition in their number except a change in site. This is because of government policy towards these markets.

(iii) Although these markets are closely associated with rural agricultural economy, but this is not true for all the districts where weekly markets are held. Alwar and Bharatpur districts have an agricultural base but possess a few weekly markets. On the other hand Banswara district is a hilly and forested region having quite a good number of weekly markets. There are several other districts which are agriculturally rich but without periodic markets.

(iv) Physical conditions are also responsible for the non-existance of such markets as in Western Rajasthan, which is arid. As many as ten districts of the state are having arid and semi-arid climate, where both production and demand are at their lowest level, therefore, weekly markets have not developed.

(v) The primary cause of the development of weekly markets in certain areas is historical. The whole of Rajasthan was governed by Royal chiefs and their Zamindars. Where ever the king happened to be interested in such weekly gathering, markets were established. Gradually their growth started, because of their role in the retail trade and also in promoting social contacts. This is the reason, that in adjoining districts there are weekly markets while in another there is complete absence of such markets.

The weekly markets in Rajasthan are locally known as *'hat'* or *'hatwara'* and exchange in these markets is based on mutual relationship between producer, trader and consumer.

Fairs-Fair is an important rural trading institution, although very little attention has been paid towards the study of fairs. A general concept regarding fairs is that they are simply an occasion for the recreation of rural folk. But, in fact, fairs are most important for rural people, because they provide an opportunity for yearly or half-yearly purchases, sale and purchase of cattle, local handicrafts and also a source of social intercourse.

Unlike weekly markets, fairs are held throughout the state, irrespective of their geographical conditions (Fig. 1-B). The total number of fairs held in Rajasthan are about 1500. But out of the total, about 1200 are one day fairs associated with festival days. Such fairs are held only for a few hours in the after-noon time and have very little economic importance. On the other hand there are fairs which continue from 2 to 15 days and are of considerable importance for sale and purchase of items of daily use farm equipments and trade in cattle. There are as many as 65 fairs in state where trade of cattle is performed. Among the cattle fairs 9 are organised and controlled by state Animal Husbandry Dept..

(B) **Mobile Traders**

When the maximum range is smaller than the threshold requirement of the firm (market), the firm either ceases to functions or else it becomes mobile (Stine, 1962). The mobile traders are those salesmen who visit rural areas in an individual capacity, and on the days they like best with their small amount of goods. Actually, in this case a shop reached to the consumers doorstep. This practice has been developed because these areas are having very low density of demand and/or high friction of distance (Bromley, 1975). Such mobile traders are although common throughout the state but they are more regular and frequent in districts of Ganganagar, Ghuru, Jhunjhunu, Sikar, Alwar, and Bharatpur (Fig. 1-C). In Ajmer, Bhilwara, Udaipur, Chittorgarh, Dungarpur and Sirohi their mobility is restricted by hills and forests. On the other hand their frequency and number of visits are minimum in arid western part of the state. These mobile traders used to supply articles of daily use, toys, utensils, cloth etc. to rural consumers. Although their role in rural marketing is minimum but they fulfil the limited demands of the rural folk.

(C) **Permanent Village Market**

There is a misconception regarding rural marketing that it is only periodic on the contrary a number of villages also have permanent shops or even markets in some cases. A sample survey of more than 150 villages indicate that shops have developed in villages having more than 2000 population. Although, these shops are very rudimantary and their number is less than 10 in case of villages having population between 2000 to 3000. But their number becomes more as the size of village increase. Table No. I indicates that in Rajasthan as many as 321 villages are having population between 5000 to 10000 and 21 villages are having more than 10,000 population. These villages also have markets along the main village road and/or near bus-stand. These markets and/or shops not only fulfill the demands of the residents of that particular village but also of the limited surrounding region.

CONCLUSIONS

The above analysis indicates that weekly markets perform rural marketing function in south-eastern, central and eastern parts of the state, with varying intensity, while fairs provide occasional marketing opportunity in the whole of the state. Mobile traders also play a limited role in providing certain items of daily use to rural folk. On the other hand big villages are also having permanent shops.

In fact, rural marketing is an important aspect for integrated rural development. But so far very little attention has been given to the study and development of rural marketing system. The present analysis is a preliminary survey of rural marketing pattern of the state, but it provides a base for further study and planning.

FIFTEEN

R.C. Srivastava

Marketing System and Problems in the Patha Area of Bundelkhand (U.P.)

Introduction

The backward and economically depressed regions develop a weak spatial organization on account of uneven economic topography, particularly in the absence of a sound network of market centres. Due to a wide gap between rural areas and market centres on one hand and poor accessibility to transport routes on the other, backward regions suffer a lot in the free flow of essential inputs and regular disposal of produc.Among manifold problem of marketing in a backward area the problem of agricultural marketing is prominent.

The Patha areas lies on the south of the first Vindhyan range in the district of Banda (Fig.1). It is the most backward area of Bundelkhand (U.P.), Covering a total area of 1149.55 km.^{2}, it includes 107 inhabited villages of Karwi and Mau *tahsils*. It is a drought-prone area because of its lithology, physiography and and climatic conditions. Agriculture is the backbone of the economy as it provides employment to about 88% of the total workforce.The Patha area produces only foodgrains, particularly wheat, barley, maize, millet and pulses. The area produces foodgrains in surplus. Livestock rearing is mostly practised as supplementary to the agriculture on mixed farming basis in the whole area (Srivastava & Ali 1979-80 p.1). Among livestock produce milk is a marketable surplus item. Industrial sector plays a minor role as only 2% of the working population is engaged in household industries and manufacturing.

FIG. 15.1

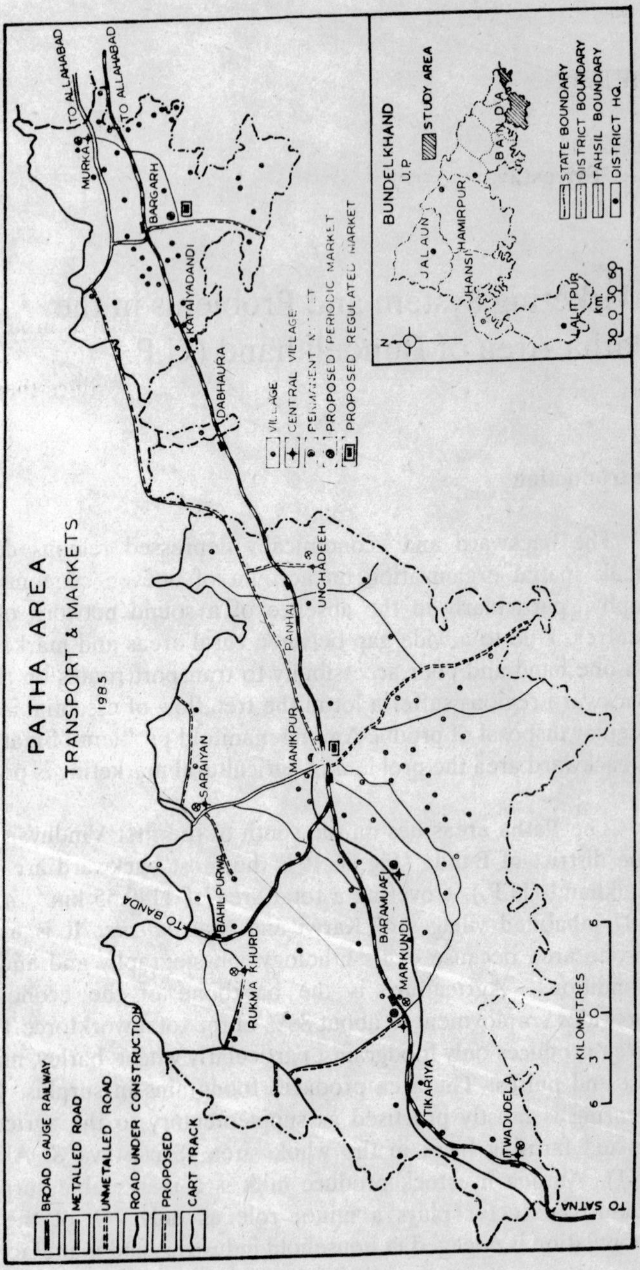
PATHA AREA
TRANSPORT & MARKETS
1985
BROAD GAUGE RAILWAY
METALLED ROAD
UNMETALLED ROAD
ROAD UNDER CONSTRUCTION
PROPOSED
CART TRACK
VILLAGE
CENTRAL VILLAGE
PERMANENT MARKET
PROPOSED PERIODIC MARKET
PROPOSED REGULATED MARKET
KILOMETRES
6 3 0 6
TO ALLAHABAD
TO ALLAHABAD
MURKA
BARGARH
KATAIYADANDI
DABHAURA
UNCHADEEH
PANHAI
MANIKPUR
SARAIYAN
BAHILPURWA
TO BANDA
RUKMA KHURD
BARAMUAFI
MARKUNDI
TIKARIYA
ITWADUDELA
TO SATNA
BUNDELKHAND
U.P.
STUDY AREA
JALAUN
HAMIRPUR
JHANSI
BANDA
LALITPUR
Km.
30 0 30 60
STATE BOUNDARY
DISTRICT BOUNDARY
TAHSIL BOUNDARY
DISTRICT HQ.

In the Patha area (68197 persons in 1971) 89% of the total population lives in villages. The density of population is very low, i.e. 66 persons/km^2. The area also enjoys the services of two railway lines which connect it to the southern and western parts of Bundelkhand, eastern U.P. and Madhya Pradesh. Road network of the area is not well developed as the length of both the metalled and metalled roads is 33 and 47 km. respectively (Fig. 1). The density of metalled and metalled roads is very low as their length per 100 km^2. and per 10,000 persons comes to 9 km. and 15.4 km. respectively. The poor rural-urban relations, absence of periodic markets, low density of roads and poor communication linkages have made Patha an area of a backward economy (Srivastava, 1980). Manikpur is the only urban centre which provides the major part of social and economic facilities of the area.

OBJECTIVES AND METHODOLOGY

In the light of overall orientation of development polices of a backward area the study of distribution of markets, farmer-seller travel patterns, marketing systems and their problems becomes essential for developing a framework for economic development. A cohesion of spatial, functional and institutional characteristics *pari passu* the techno-economic considerations are necessary for developing efficient marketing system (Srivastava, 1981). The paper aims (i) to explain the spatio-temporal distribution of market centres, (ii) to identify the farmer-seller travel patterns, (iii) to analyse the existing system of agricultural marketing, (iv) to highlight the problems of agricultural marketing, and (v) to recommend strategies for improving the present defective agricultural marketing system for the integrated rural development of this backward area.

The present study is mainly based on primary data which have been collected with the help of village and household schedules covering all inhabited villages. In order to find out space preferences for marketing 10% of the households of each village were randomly selected. Questions were asked about the mode of sale of agricultural and animal produce, type of marketing agencies and channels used, and problems faced in the disposal of surplus produce.

SPATIO-TEMPORAL DISTRIBUTION OF MARKET CENTRES

Market centres emerge only after goods began to move to consumers in exchange system transcending the limits of the house holding unit or the immediate social group (Berry, 1967 p.106). So long as the resulting exchange of goods was sporadic, market centres did not develop. The major part of the study area was covered with dense forests during the 19th century. Among the inhabitants, *kols* outnumbered as well as dominated for a long period. The exchange of goods was prevalent under barter system in the traditional society till the Independence. Manikpur could develop itself as a market centre only after the construction of Allahabad-Jabalpur rail line in 1889. Bargarh, the second important market centre, attained the status of a permanent market in the second decade of this century.

The two market centres, i.e. Manikpur and Bargarh, act as growth centre in two different parts of the Patha area. Manikpur (6512 persons), which is a *block* headquarters and an important rail junction of Bundelkhand region, is a developed permanent market centre. This centre caters to the daily and periodic needs of its own population and of the surrounding areas. Besides the retail shops of grain, cloth, hosiery, grocery, footwear, electrical goods, hardware, utensils, medicines and stationery, this centre also deals with the wholesale trade of food grains and cloth. For areas visit this centre. Bargarh (2378 persons) is the second important permanent market centre which caters to the need of the whole Burger Patha area. It also enjoys the facilities of retail cloth, hosiery, *kirana* and grocery. Markundi is emerging as a third important market centre in Manikpur Patha area. Some retail shops of cloth, hosiery and kirana have come up at this centre. Besides these three permanent market centres, some of the villages have a few retail shops which deal with grocery items, sweets and cosmetics. 42% of the villages have grocery shops while only two have retail shops of cloth.

SYSTEMS OF MARKETING

The system of marketing in backward agrarian area differs from a developed area where marketable surplus is high, transport network is thick and other infrastructure facilities are good. Marketable surplus in agriculture is the very foundation on which the whole structure of our development stands. Among marketable surplus items, wheat, maize, millet, gram as the agricultural produce, and milk and *'khoya'* as the livestock produce, are significant in the study area. Products of household industries are insignificant and do not find place among marketable surplus items. So far as the food-grains are concerned, the marketable surplus of the area is very low. This is because of (i) low productivity per hectare, (ii) the increasing propensity to hoard, (iii) poor road network, (iv) consumption of better cereals in place of inferior cereals, and (v) physical barriers, such as mountain ranges and forests.

Since there are no periodic markets the question of gathering of farmer-seller doesn't arise in rural areas. The usual channel for the marketing of agricultural produce in the study area, particularly wheat, maize, millet, and gram has been marked in three forms: (i) producer- village shopkeeper-wholesaler-retailer-consumer channel, (ii) producer-intinerant trader-wholesaler-retailer-consumer channel, and (iii) producer-primary wholesaler-secondary-wholesaler retailer-consumer channel. For the last ten years the farmers are selling surplus wheat to government pocurement agency under which the State Government purchase huge quantity of foodgrains at primary wholesale markets and sells/ them through fair price shops in cities at a fixed price.

A major quantity of the marketable surplus of food grains, is sold by farmer-sellers in their respective villages at a much lower price than they can obtain in the wholesale market. This type of sale generally takes place when the cultivator is in debt. Majority of low-income cultivators remain in the clutch of old *Zamindars, Sahukars* and contractors who purchase their grains in their respective village. In the field study it was observed that the farmers of 30% of the villages selltheir produce in the village (Fig.2). On the other hand the intinerant traders or beoparies also move from village to village for collecting agricultural produce from farmers at comparatively reduced price. In the Patha area the intinerant traders purchase surplus foodgrains only from 15 villages. Village-trader deal in his individual capacity. He usually collects the produce from the villages and brings it to the wholesales markets. Local landlord, especially the medium size landholders, also sell their surplus produce directly to the village traders or to in traders in the towns.

FIG. 15.2

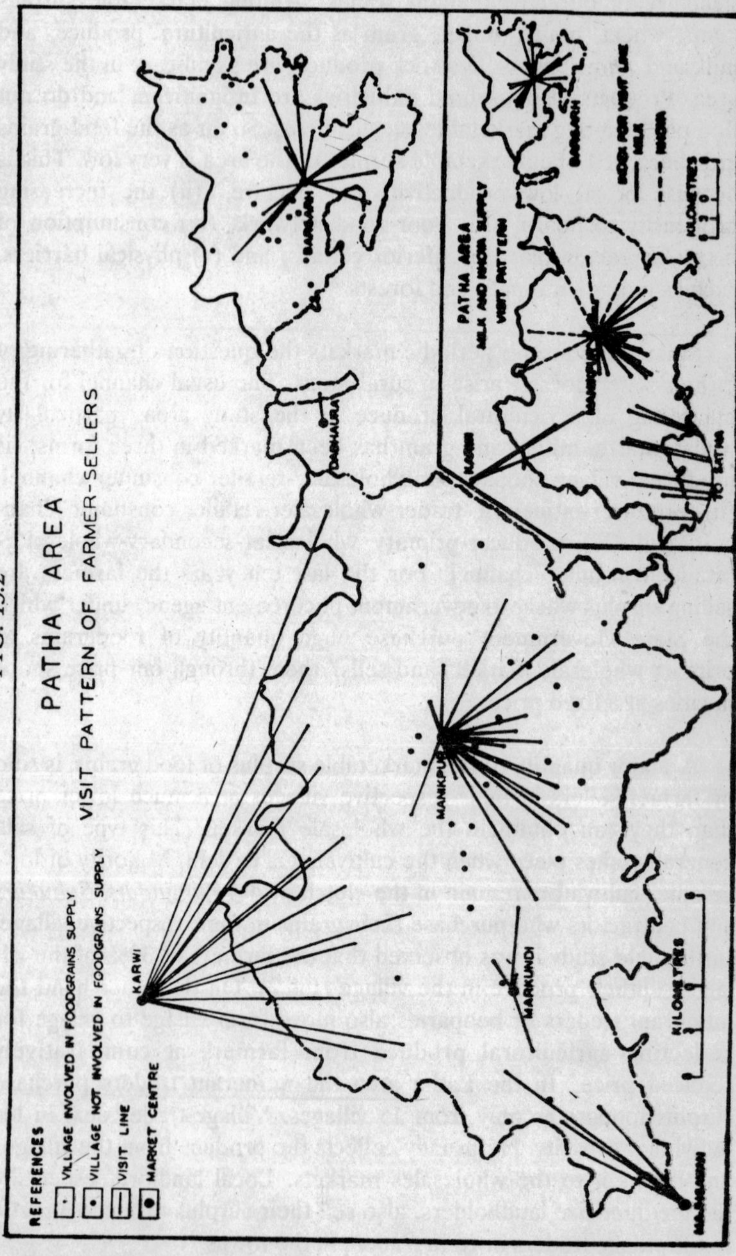
PATHA AREA
VISIT PATTERN OF FARMER-SELLERS
REFERENCES
VILLAGE INVOLVED IN FOODGRAINS SUPPLY
VILLAGE NOT INVOLVED IN FOODGRAINS SUPPLY
VISIT LINE
MARKET CENTRE
KARWI
MANIKPUR
MARKUNDI
BARGARH
KILOMETRES
PATHA AREA
MILK AND KHOA SUPPLY
VISIT PATTERN
MANIKPUR
BARGARH
KARWI
MILK
KHOA
KILOMETRES

Though a major portion of agricultural produce is disposed of at village level, a small quantity of the produce finds a place in the market. There are only three market centres, i.e. Manikpur, Bargarh and Markundi which entertain the farmer-sellers of 19, 14 & 4 villages respectively (Fig.2). Farmer-sellers of these villages sell their surplus grains directly in the markets. The farmer-sellers of border villages visit market centres located out side the study area. Karwi, an important town of Bundelkhand and a *tahsil* headquarters is situated at a distance of 15 km. from the northern border of the Patha area and entertains the farmer-sellers of 13 villages mostly of northern and north-western parts. Majhgawan and Dabhaura markets, both situated along Allahabad-Jabalpur railway line in M.P., receive foodgrains from the farmer-sellers of 4 and 1 villages respectively of the study area. The maximum distance covered by a farmer-seller comes to 20 km. Fig.2 clearly shows the visit patterns of the farmer-sellers.

The main animal products in the study area are milk, *khoya,* curd, *ghee,* and animal skin. Milk and khoya are the only two marketable surplus items. The consumption of fluid milk is generally confined to the area of its production. Though the production of milk is not encouraging yet the villagers supply the surplus milk to nearby towns and service centres or sell to the middlemen who usually purchase milk in bulk quantity from different villages and sell in towns at high price. There is no organized agency to purchase surplus milk at a resonable price. The village level data collected with the help of schedules reveal that 67 villages supply milk where as some of the milkmen in 6 villages prepare *khoya* which they sell in Manikpur town (Fig. 2). The data also reveal that middlemen collect milk from 50% of the 67 milk surplus villages and carry it by trains to Satna and Allahabad where it is sold to retailers and consumers residing in towns. This intermediary system is a granite wall between the dairy plant and producers and the system exploits both of them (Bakshi, 1979 p.20). With the help of space preference data the visit patterns of milk supplies have been shown in Fig. 2 which depicts that milk sellers of 11 villages sell their surplus milk out side of the study area, particularly at Karwi and Satna towns while the milk sellers of 31 villages are associated with Manikpur and Bargarh service centres.

MARKETING PROBLEMS

Communications from the field to the village and from village to the *mandi* are often extremely poor and defective in backward regions like the one under study. There is also a lack of feeder roads connecting villages to market towns and nearest railway stations so that produce cannot advantageously be transported to *mandis.* Due to very low accessibility to all weather roads majority of villages remain detached not only from development programmes but also from the facilities of *mandis* and markets. Majority of the villages come in the zone of passive interaction on account of very low intensity of goods and traffic flow. In the present set up of rural transport network, villagers are compelled to travel, some times, more than 10 km. distance on foot for the transaction of their surplus produce at market centres and thus loose their time and energy. Villagers become victim of itinerant traders, middlemen and local merchants on account of poor transport facilities.

The Patha area also lacks the optimal spatial integration and functional coordination of settlements due to the absence of periodic markets. The absence of periodic markets compells the farmer-sellers to dispose of their surplus agricultural produce to local merchants and to itinerant traders.

Besides poor transport facilities and absence of periodic markets, there is a lack of any kind of collective organization among producers. Thus it is common to find that the producers of grains and milk as a class are being exploited by the traders. The farmer, in general, sells his produce at an unfavourable place and at an unfavourable time and usually he gets very unfavourable terms (N.P. Committee Report, 1948). Because of poverty, indebtness and unsatisfactory nature of communication, the produce of this region is sold soon after the harvest when there is a glut in the market. The farmers who sometimes mortgage their standing crop on account of loan, do not get the price of the produce and some times they are forced to dispose of the major portion of their produce almost immediately after the harvest in order to return the debt of the local merchant or of the zamindar. There is also the problem of superfluous middlemen who handle the major part of marketable surplus.

The marketing charges payable by the producers are numerous and varied in non-regulated markets and they tend to reduce considerably the return to the producer from the sale of his produce (Memoria, 1976 p-725, 746). The farmer-seller of the study area has to arrange the sale of his produce in the market place and thus he becomes bound to pay commission to the arhtiya or the *dalal* (Broker), weigher and labourers. In most of the villages the storage facilities are poor because of the indigenous methods of storing the foodgrains. The study area does not enjoy warehouse and other storage facilities even in the adjoining big markets and mandis. Lack of information is an other problem as neither villages have contact with the outside areas nor they are in touch with the trend of market prices. They mostly depend on hearsay reports received from the village traders. Moreover, this backward area does not enjoy the facility of banks which could finance loan to farmer-sellers at lower rate against the security of goods.

STRATEGIES FOR IMPROVING THE MARKETING SYSTEM

Improvements in agricultural marketing and its harmonious operation can certainly secure better returns to a farmer and good quality of goods at reasonable prices to the consumers (Behari, 1974). One feature essential to efficient marketing is the development of transport and communication system. Imperfections in marketing structure as also spatial disparties in prices, in many cases, have their origin in deficiencies in the tarnsportation system (Tripathi, 1972). In order to have active interaction between rural areas and market centres an integrated network of transport routes with a high degree of connectivity, some of the forest roads which interconnect main unmetalled roads, should be made open for goods traffic with the coordination of Forest Department and P.W. Department. The State Government should give the highest possible priority to the construction of all-weather feeder roads for facilitating the movement of agricultural produce to *mandis*. Spatial organization to the optimum level cannot be achieved unless a sound net work of periodic markets as well as daily markets is available. All of the seven rural central places, i.e. Kehuniya, Saraiyan, Unchadesh, Murka, Baramuafi, Rukma Khurd and Intwadundela (Fig. 1) must have a periodic market. For this very task the *nyaya panchayats* must be pursuaded to start periodic market at these rural central places.

In order to make marketing more efficient and minimize the problems of storage and warehousing, establishment of market towns is the need of the day. Johnson (1965) has advocated the setting up of market towns for regularising the rural economy. Wilfred (1968) endorsed the role of market towns for commercialization of agriculture. According to him more market towns area necessary to provide farmers with a convenient place to bring their produce and to supply warehouse, processing plants, consumer goods and credit facilities. Most of the defects and malpractices to the advantage of producer-seller can be removed by the excercise of proper control over markets and this could be done by the establishment of regulated markets either by local bodies or under State legislation (Srivastava, 1981). Manikpur must be developed as the main market town for improving the market facilities by setting up a mandi there and connecting it with all weather motorable roads with the rural central places. Cooperative marketing of agricultural and animal produce is also necessary. As some of the cooperative societies are working properly in the study area the primary marketing society should be started to function at the earliest so that it may minimize the malpractices at market centres and remove the intermediary system. However, the establishment of multipurpose farmers service societies which made the farmer free from all botherations of obtaining credit and disposing of the produce and products at a remunerative price, allows the members to concentrate on increasing the farm production. This type of society must be started in the study area to make the farmers free from the clutches of itinerant traders and local contractors.

SIXTEEN

R.S. Dixit

Market Centers of a Backward Economy - Hamirpur District (U.P.): Perspectives on Centrality and Hierarchy

Introduction

One of the most important perspectives of the study of spatial organization of nodes/points includes the orders in which they occur within the study region. This brings us to the questions of gradation and grouping into tiers of size classes, which, in other words is termed as the study of hierarchy. The objective of this paper is to identify the hierarchy of market centres of the study area - the Hamirpur district of the U.P.

THE STUDY AREA

The study area, the Hamirpur district, is one of the southern districts of Uttar Pradesh. The territorial limits of Hamirpur district lie between 25°7 N to 26°7'N lat. and 79°17' E to 80°21 E long. The district has an average length of approximately 96 km from north to south while the average width from west to east is around 90 km. The total area of the district is 7165 km^2 (i.e. 2.43% of U.P.). The northern half of the district is a vast plain, while the southern half is characteristically a plateau area consisting of several hills of the Bundelkhand of Uttar Pradesh (Dixit, 1984).

The administrative setup of the district comprises of 6 *tahsils* namely Maudaha, Kulpahar, Rath, Mahoba and Hamirpur. There are 11 development blocks. The district is predominately an agricultural one and industrially rather. The density of population is 167 persons per km^2 against 377 persons per km^2 that of the state of Uttar Pradesh. There are 11,94,168 persons in all in the district (1981). A total of 78 market centres exist in the district (1983).

METHODOLOGY APPLIED IN THE PRESENT CASE

In India, studies on hierarchy of market centres have been carried out by Singh (1962), Vishwanath (1967), Mukherjee (1968), Sinha and Mandal (1974 pp. 79-84). Saxena (1975), Shrivastava (1976) and Jana (1978 pp. 164-74). Jana has claimed to present a composite hierarchy considering the attendance at a market, the quality and quantity of goods traded, the periodicity of market centres, and other factors (1978, pp.170-71). Shrivastava (1976) has put up a new methodology based on the number of shops and the total shop-openings (SODA method) at the market centres of Naugarh tahsil of Basti district, U.P. Besides, Dixit (1984 a, 1984 b) has also made attempts in this direction.

A study of the parameters which affect the hierarchical structure of market centres within the area is a necessary prelude to a discussion of the technique adopted to determine the hierarchy. This is concerned with the problem of differentiation of market centres into broad classes based on composite/aggregate size of market centres. In order to demonstrate clearly the existence of various hierarchical classes of market centres in the study area, it is imperative to analyse the parameters which affect the order of market centres. It is important to note that the nature of settlement (urban/rural) does effect the aggregate size of market centres as it contributes in a big way towards the importance of a market. In general, villages deal mainly in retailing activities and wholesaling has secondary significance while towns and cities have more complex business activities. Therefore, rural centres are smaller and urban centres, larger.

The following parameters have been chosen to determine the orders of market centres within Hamirpur district:

Total Population

Total population of the centre in which the market is located has an affective bearing on the importance of the market because the larger the market centre, the more complex and varied will be the functions of the market and therefore the higher its attractive power and ambit of interaction.

Population Engaged in Tertiary Activities

In a backward district where markets are mostly periodic, haphazard and disorganized, official data on the number of people engaged in trade and commerce at the market centre were not available. Nevertheless, the Census of India have considered a special category which is an umbrella class and includes the number of people working in the above mentioned occupations. In the absence of precise data this parameter was chosen as a relative indicator of people engaged in trade and commerce.

Estimated Average Attendance

The estimated average attendance on a market day plays an important role in determining the size of a market centre. The congregation of people on a market day is directly related to the level of a market centre.

Marketing Functions

Marketing functions are of two types - wholesale marketing and retail marketing. The centres which carry out wholesale functions are mainly larger because they have the power to attract farmers, manufacturers, dealers in any kind of raw materials, government procurement agencies and the like, to sell or to buy commodities. Smaller market centres, on the other hand, attract lesser people who like to purchase commodities of daily consumption in lesser quantities. Hence, the more varied are the marketing functions the more important is a market, and the higher is its order in the hierarchy.

Major Commodities

The number of important commodities is much greater in larger market centres than in smaller ones where the demands of people are lesser. Wherever the population is larger and more urbanised the demand and supply will be varied. Hence, the greater the types of commodities arriving a market the more will be the tendency of the market to be large.

Periodicity

Smaller market centres are periodic, i.e. they do not meet everyday. Some of them are weekly, some bi-weekly/tri-weekly. The number of market meetings increases generally with the size of the market centre. The centres which have a greater number of permanent shops and daily shopping activities are undoubtedly, larger markets. Thus, the daily market centres are bigger in many ways than the periodic market centres.

Road/Railway Accessibility

Without a good transport network, no region can develop its existing level of markets and marketing. There are numerous examples that the development of transport network has been responsible for giving rise to market centres and other developmental aspects as well. Road transport is more relevant in this case as it is cheaper than the laying of railway lines as well as more penetrative. Markets which have this facility of being better connected to other important markets. rail transport is good for long distance trade. Hence, with the additional benefit of a railway station, or proximity to it, market centre attracts demand and supply of commodities from even outside the region. Thus, it becomes larger and more significant. The additional benefit of higher accesibility is that even perishable commodities reach the market very fast with the result that a supply of fresh vegetables, milk, eggs, and butter becomes an attractive features of a market.

Shop Openings

Another indicator of the significance of a market is the number of shops which remain open during the week, regardless of the periodicity of the market. During market days a large number of itinerant traders, local as well as outsiders, and others, who are temporary local shopkeepers, set up their wares for sale. But there are certain permanent shopkeepers who keep their shops open throughout the week. Here, a formula has been devised (Shrivastava, 1976) to work out an index which would serve as a relevant indicator:

$$SO_n = (PR_n \times 7) - (RP_{nc}) + (T_n + I_n) \ (P)$$

where

SO_n = number of shop openings,
PR_n = number of permanent and/or regular shops
PR_{nc} = number of permanent and/or regular shops in case of weekly closure,
T_n = number of temporary shops,
I_n = number of itinerant shops,
P = number of peak days in case of daily market or periodicity in case of periodic markets.

Areal Overage

Last but not least in importance is the factor of area of the market. At a smaller centre, fewer number of permanent shops lesser temporary and itinerant shopkeepers would not occupy much space to set up their shops as compared to a larger centre to which a larger and more varied congregation is gravitated. Hence, the total space occupied by a market on market days, areal coverage in other words, serves as an important indicator of the size and importance of a market.

The above factors are logical generalizations. A few anomalies do occur in some factor or the other. Therefore, all the factors have been considered simultaneously for each market and a composite picture of each has been drawn up. This was possible by giving weights to each factor and adding up all the weights to determine the centrality of market centres.

The centrality of a market centre has been measured as follows:

$$Ci = \frac{O_s}{M_s} \times 100$$

where,

Ci	=	centrality index
O_s	=	observed score or weight of a market centre.
M_s	=	maximum possible score/weight.

The weightage scheme is given in Table I. The table includes all the relevant parameters and their respective weights.

FIG. 16.1

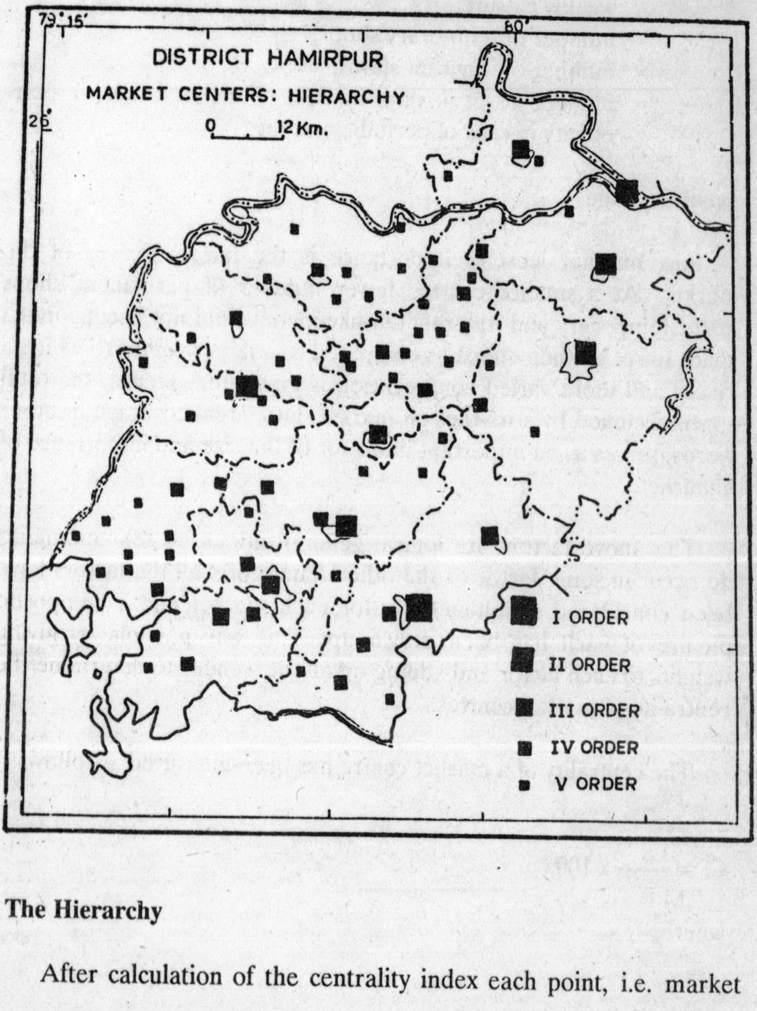

The Hierarchy

After calculation of the centrality index each point, i.e. market centre was plotted on a graph having the rank of it on the x axis and the centrality index on the y axis. The orders of market centres were clearly observed and found as follows:

I Order - Regional Market Centre (Ci above 80)
II Order - Sub-regional Market Centre (Ci 60-80)
III Order - Small urban Market Centre (Ci 40-60)
IV Order - Major Rural Market Centre (Ci 20-40)
V Order - Minor Rural Market Centre (Ci upto 20)

The above orders of market centres of the district Hamirpur have been demonstrated in Fig. 1. It is very significant and worth mention that distinct groups have emerged on Fig. 1 demonstrating tiers of market centres.

While the only first order market centre, Mahoba, is located in Kabrai sub-unit, the five second order market centres are located in the sub-units of Maudaha, Charkhari, Rath, Kurara, and Sumerpur. They are the same as the names of the sub-units except the case of Kurara sub-unit in which the second order market centre is Hamirpur. There are five third order market centres : Kharele, Kulpahar, Jaitpur, Kabrai, and Kurara located in the sub-units of Muskara, Charkhari, Jaitpur, Kabrai,and Kurara. The fourth order market centes which are 17 in number are absent in the sub-units of Rath, and Kurara. There are three each market centres of this order in sub-units of Muskara, Charkhari, and Kabrai; two each in Jaitpur, and Panwari; and one each in Maudaha, Gohand, Sarila, and Sumerpur. In Muskara they are Muskara, Binwar, and Gahrauli, in Charkhari, Rainpur, Gaurahri, and Sungra; while in Kabrai they are Madoba rural, Srinagar, and Sijahari. Mudhari, and Ajnar in Jaitpur; Panwari, and Pipari in Panwari, Geondi in Maudaha; Gohand in Gohand, Sarila in Sarila; and Chhani Buzurg in sumerpur. As regards the fifth order market centres, Muskara has the maximum number (11), followed by Panwari (9), and Sarila (7), Charkhari and Rath have 5 each while Gohand has 4 such centres. Maudaha, Jaitpur, Kabrai, and Kurara have two each while Sumerpur has only one market centre of the fifth order (Fig. 3).

TABLE I : DISTRICT HAMIRPUR : MARKET CENTRES - CENTRALITY WEIGHTAGE SCHEME

Parameter			Class of Parameter	Weight
1.	Total population	Rural :	i) Upto 2,499 persons	0.05
			ii) 2,500 to 4,999	0.10
			iii) 5,000 to 7,499	0.20
			iv) 7,500 and above	0.30
		Urban :	i) Upto 19,999 persons	0.40
			ii) 20,000 to 34,999	0.70
			iii) 35,000 and above	1.00
2.	Population/ Tertiary	Rural :	i) Upto 33 persons	0.05
			ii) 34 to 66	0.10
			iii) 67 to 99	0.20
			iv) 100 and above	0.30
		Urban :	i) Upto 199 persons	0.40
			ii) 200 to 599	0.70
			iii) 600 and above	1.00
3.	Average	Rural :	i) Upto 499 persons	0.05
			ii) 500 to 999	0.10
			iii) 1000 to 4,999	0.20
			iv) 5,000 and above	0.30
		Urban :	i) Upto 19,999 persons	0.40
			ii) 20,00 to 34,999	0.70
			iii) 35,000 and above	1.00
4.	Function/Exchange Orientation Main yard/ Sub-yard	Rural :	i) Retail-popu.upto 3,999	0.05
			ii) 4,000 and above	0.10
			iii) Retail-wholesale. Sub yard	0.30
			iv) Main yard	0.80
		Urban	i) Centres-No yard.	0.25
			ii) Sub yard	0.40
			iii) Main yard	1.00
5.	Commodities	Rural :	i) Upto 2 commodities	0.05
			ii) 3 - 4	0.10
			iii) 5 - 6	0.20
			iv) 7 and above	0.30
		Urban :	i) Centres-local imp.	0.40
			ii) distt. level imp.	0.70
			iii) imp. above distt.	1.00
6.	Shop Openings/ week		i) Upto 249	0.05
			ii) 250 to 499	0.10

			iii) 500 to 999	0.25
			iv) 1000 to 1,999	0.50
			v) 2,000 to 4,999	0.75
			vi) 5,000 and above	1.00
7.	Areal Coverage of Market meeting place		i) Upto 999 m^2	0.05
			ii) 1,000 to 9,999 m^2	0.10
			iii) 10,000 to 19,999 m^2	0.25
			iv) 20,000 to 49,999 m^2	0.50
			v) 50,000 to 99,999 m^2	0.75
			vi) 1,00,000 m^2 and above	1.00
8.	Road Accessibility		i) Centres on road	1.00
			ii) within 2 km	0.75
			iii) 2 km. to 4 km.	0.50
			iv) beyond 4 km.	0.10
9.	Railway Accessibility		i) Centres with Rly. Stn.	1.00
			ii) within 4 km.	0.75
			iii) 4 km. to 8 km.	0.50
			iv) 8 km. to 12 km.	0.25
			v) 12 km. to 16 km.	0.10
			vi) beyond 16 km.	0.00
10.	Periodicity	Rural .	i) Weekly	0.10
			ii) Bi-weekly	0.20
			iii) Tri-weekly	1.40
		Urban :	i) weekly	0.20
			ii) Bi-weekly	0.40
			iii) Daily	1.00

TABLE II : DISTRICT HAMIRPUR : MARKET CENTRES - HIERARCHICAL ORDER

Areal Sub-unit (No. of MCs)	Number of Market Centres in Various Hierarchical Orders				
	I	II	III	IV	V
Maudaha (4)		1		1	2
Muskara (15)			1	3	11
Charkhari (10)		1	1	3	5
Jaitpur (5)			1	2	2
Panwari (11)				2	9
Rath (6)		1			5
Gohand (5)				1	4
Sarila (8)				1	7
Kabrai(7)	1		1	3	2
Kurara (4)		1	1		2
Sumerpur (3)		1		1	1
Total (78)	1	5	5	17	50

Factors Affecting Centrality of Market Centers: Correlation Analysis

Centrality value of a market centre is the index of the total personality of market centre in question. It shows the aggregate size of particular market centres. The computations related to this index are based on various factors which have their bearing on the hierarchy of market centres.

Centrality Index and Attendance on a Market Day

To find out the extent to which the aggregate size of a market centre is affected by the attendance at it, an exercise was done and a scatter diagram was drawn on simple log graph showing centrality index on the Y axis, and the attendance of market on the X axis. The values of all of the 78 market centres were plotted on the graph. Co-efficient of correlation was computed and the values of r, Y and X were also found out (Fig. 2).

The r value of 0.7667 showing that the congregation at a market place is an important indicator of the total size of the market centres.

Centrality index and Shop Opening per Week

The number of shop openings per week of a market centre also greatly affects the hierarchy of a market centres. In case, a market centre has a large number of shop openings per week, it should generally, be a bigger market centre as compared to the one which has a lesser number of shop openings per week. This relationship has been statistically illustrated on a simple log graph (Fig. 3).

The values of r clearly shows that the centrality index is greatly affected by the number of shop openings per week in a market centre. The two are directly related to a considerable extent. The results also show that in the case of th present study area, Hamirpur district, the number of shop openings per week have greater bearing on the centrality index of a market centre in comparison to attendance on a market place or site.

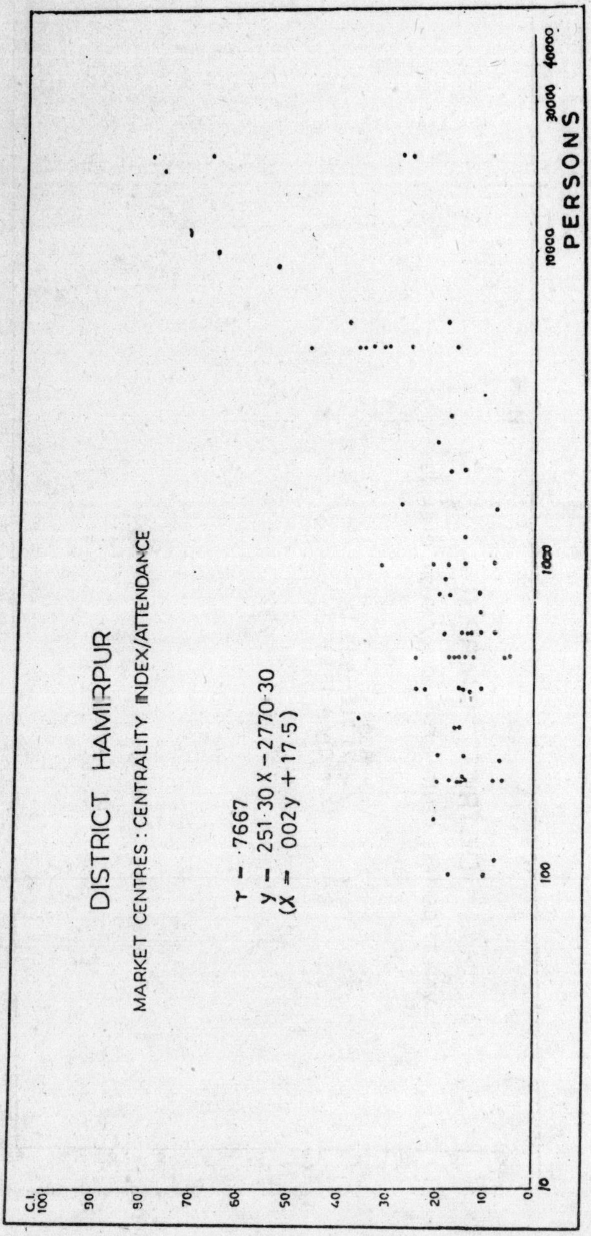
DISTRICT HAMIRPUR
MARKET CENTRES : CENTRALITY INDEX/ATTENDANCE
r = ·7667
y = 251·30 X −2770·30
(X = 002y + 17·5)
C.I.
100
90
80
70
60
50
40
30
20
10
0
10
100
1000
10000
30000
40000
PERSONS

FIG. 16.2

FIG. 16.3

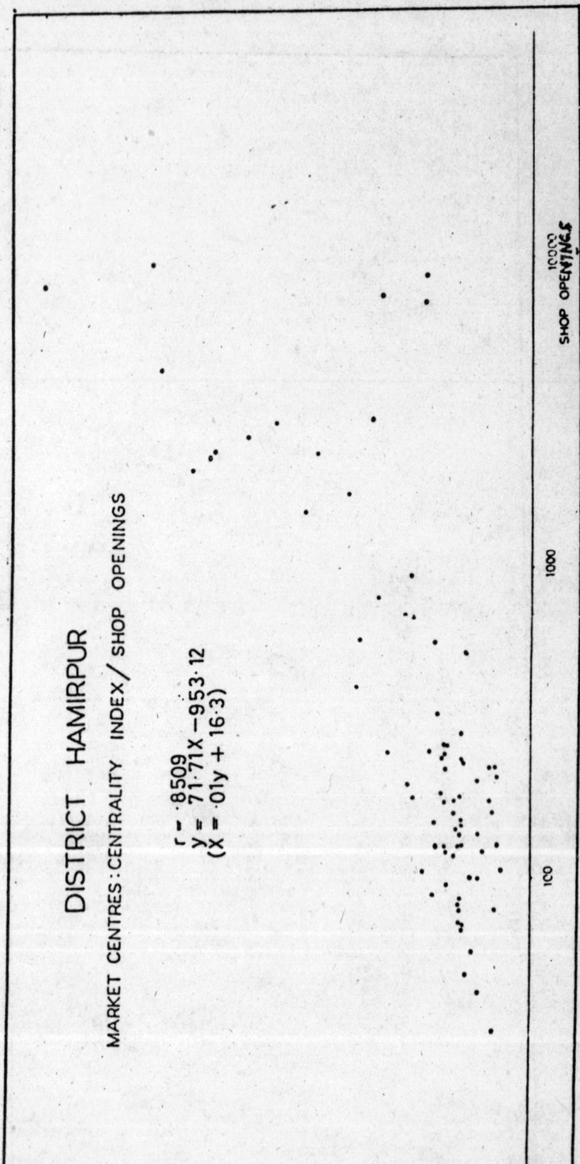
DISTRICT HAMIRPUR
MARKET CENTRES : CENTRALITY INDEX / SHOP OPENINGS
r = ·8509
y = 71·71X −953·12
(X = ·01y + 16·3)
C.I.
SHOP OPENINGS

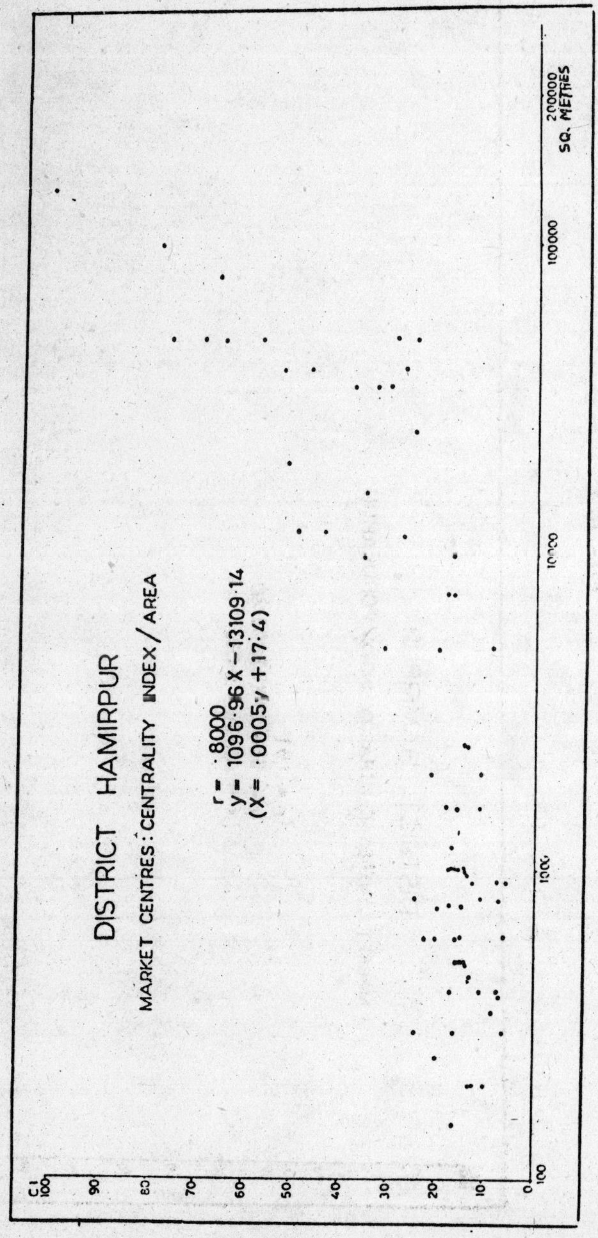
DISTRICT HAMIRPUR
MARKET CENTRES : CENTRALITY INDEX / AREA
r = ·8000
y = 1096·96 X − 13109·14
(X = ·0005 y + 17·4)
C.I
100
90
80
70
60
50
40
30
20
10
0
100
1000
10000
100000
200000
SQ. METRES

FIG. 16.4

FIG. 16.5

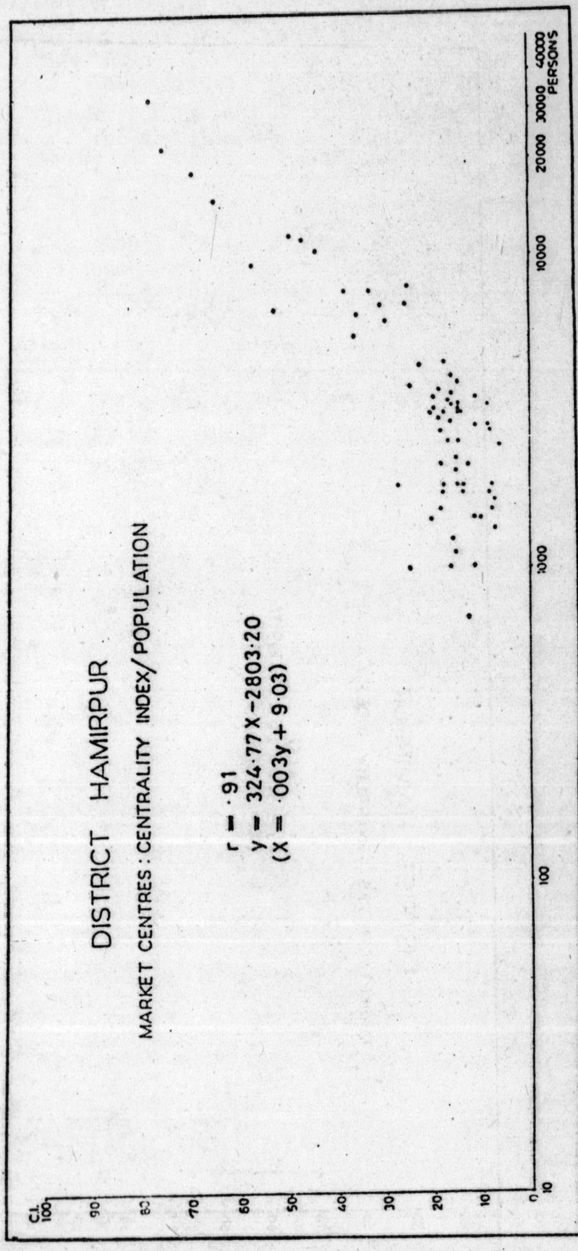
DISTRICT HAMIRPUR
MARKET CENTRES : CENTRALITY INDEX/POPULATION
r = ·91
y = 324·77X −2803·20
(X = ·003y + 9·03)
C.I.
100
90
80
70
60
50
40
30
20
10
0
10
100
1000
10000
20000
30000
40000
PERSONS

Centrality Index and Area of Market site or Place

Generally if a market center is held over a vast area, it generally happens to be a bigger one in comparison to others. A small size market centre would hold its meeting on relatively a small pace.

The co-efficient of correlation of 0.8 (Fig. 4). It shows that the area of a market site or place has a considerable bearing on the centrality index of a market centre in the district.

Centrality Index and Population

Centrality index of a market centre is affected by the population of the concerned market centre. It is a general observation that the importance of a market centre would be relatively more in case the market centre has a large population and vice-versa.

It is evident from the above that the population of a market centre affects the centrality index of the same to a considerable extent. The co-efficient of correlation is as high as 0.91 (Fig. 5), meaning thereby that the population of a market centre is directly related to the centrality index of the same.

The most populous market centres of the area have immense business. It is supported by the cases of Jaitpur, Gohand, and Sarila. Jaitpur is only a rural market centre, but it is a big village (10,308) and therefore, it has the status of a third order market centre while Sarila (6,445) and Gohand (5,519), although urban places, are only fourth order market centres.

An overview of the above correlation analysis shows that although all of the four factors discussed above affect the centrality index of market centres but population has emerged as the strongest factor affecting the centrality index of market centres.

CONCLUSION

The relationship of centrality index with these four factors can be hypothesized in the following form:

That there is a direct relationship and that too to a considerable extent between the centrality index of a market centre and its attendance on a market-day/shop openings per week/spatial coverage of market site or place/population.

SEVENTEEN

D.A. Gedam

Sellers' Travel Behaviour and Periodic Market Cycles in the Wardha Valley of Maharashtra

Introduction

This study has been confined to the northern boundary of the Vidarbha region (10°32' north to 21°37' north latitude, 77°27' east to 79°47' east longitude) in the Maharashtra, respectively(Fig.1). The periodic marketing system has diversified locational patterns, timings, sizes, nature and scales of economic functions. Buyers and sellers are the actors in the system. Market meetings are daily or periodic. Some market-places have permanent and semi-permanent stalls. The market-places have rural or urban location. A few participants, specially, sellers in the market-places are mobile in the region. This mobility helps to create periodic market cycles with the temporal separations, related to locational spacing of periodic market places.

In this paper, the author focusses attention mainly on circulatory pattern of itinerant sellers who operate within an extensive network of periodic market-places. The study of travel pattern of mobile sellers or market cycles reveal their varieties associated with sellers in the region. Different categories of market efficiency have been analysed on the basis of varying proportions of sellers to buyers in sampled periodic market-places.

FIG. 17.1

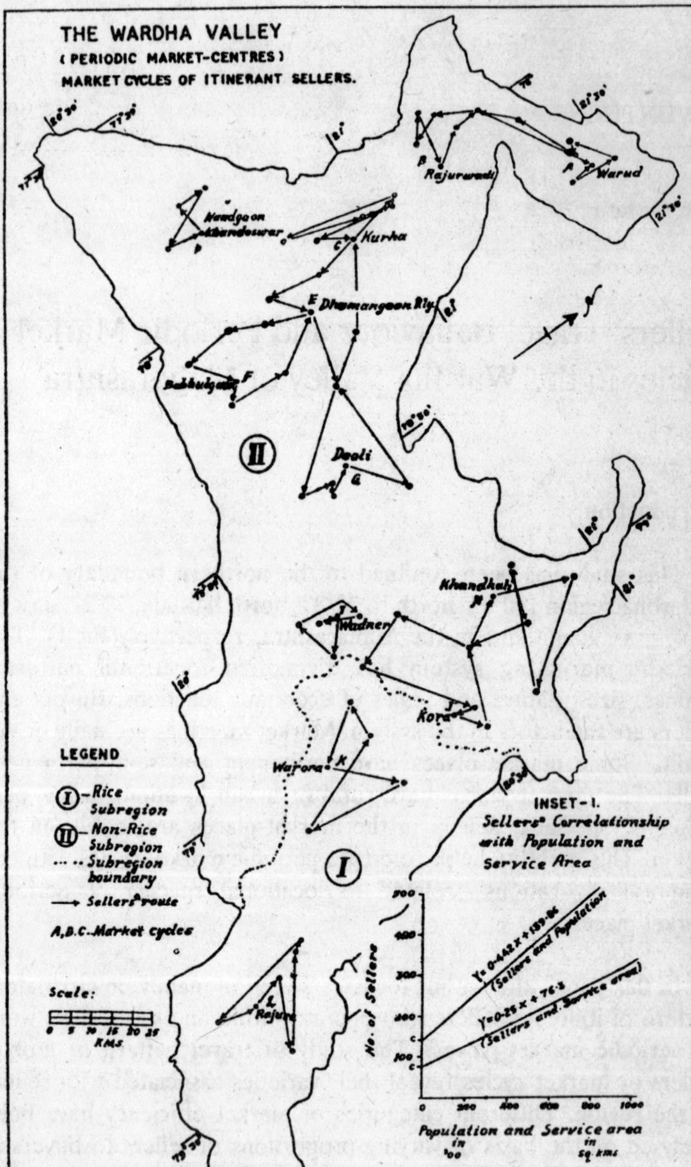
THE WARDHA VALLEY
(PERIODIC MARKET-CENTRES)
MARKET CYCLES OF ITINERANT SELLERS.
Rajurwadi
Warud
Kurha
Dhamangaon Rly.
Babhulgaon
Deoli
Khandhali
Wadner
Kora
Warora
Rajura
LEGEND
I - Rice Subregion
II - Non-Rice Subregion
.... Subregion boundary
→ Sellers' route
A,B,C..Market cycles
Scale:
0 5 10 15 20 25
KMS
INSET-I.
Sellers' Correlationship with Population and Service Area
Y=0.442X+159.86 (Sellers and Population)
Y=0.25X+76.3 (Sellers and Service area)
No. of Sellers
Population and Service area
in '00
in Sq. kms

HYPOTHESES

Market cycles with large population sizes contain large periodic market places and are relatively continuous then those concerned with periodic market-places of smaller populations. The system and network of periodic market-places may persist, if vendors realize that agglomoration of goods and services is profitable at a given place and day/days. Sellers in short duration periodic market places, i.e. *Gujaris*, and morning market centres are engaged in selling for two to three hours and display relatively small total weekly travel time. Our emperical evidence throws light on the increase of assessibility to market places and rise in purchasing power enabling itinerant sellers as well as buyers to make decision for their attendance from a larger choice of sub-set of market centres. It can be argued that if a seller is concerned primarily to minimize movement costs, he will follow circumferential or travelling salemen's route. High transport costs limit the extent of market cycles. The marked increase in number of mobile vendors is found associated with well developed transportation facilities, production of commodities in large quantity and densely populated areas. Correlation of the number of itinerant sellers with population of the connected market nodes including their service areas, is stronger, relatively, than the correlation of the service areas of corresponding market centres of periodic market places in a given market cycle.

THE ROLE OF SELLERS

The problem of participants in the periodic marketing system requires some clarification. Even though the definition of market place refers to "buyers" and "sellers", the question of their identification remains unsolved. Several categories of sellers may be distinguished. The group of participants are found engaged in buying and /or selling in the market-place, farmers and non-farmers (Smith, C.A., 1974). At one extreme there are the sellers who visit one or two periodic market places weekly (or who attend a market-place only once during the market week), and who either cultivate or engage in craft activities during the remainder part of the market week. At the other extreme, there are a number of sellers who move around a network of periodic market-places, returning to their homes each night (Tamaskar, 1983). These categories of sellers are related with such periodic market-places, which are hardly, within a range of three to six kilometres from their home places. Between these two extremes there are mobile sellers who visit each periodic market places in a cycle and who return home at the end of market week. Generally, horizontal exchange is very common feature in the valley, except for specialised commodities, viz., onions, chilly, turmeric, etc., which find out let to nearby large settlements or even outside the region.

In the case of the Wardha Valley, the categories of the sellers can be distinguished as shown in Table-I. The adoption of the part-time/full time distinctions and exclusion of these visit, who are present neither to buy nor to sell in the periodic market-places, provides a useful and simple topology, which is set-forth in the Table-II.

The full-time/part-time distinction is applied to those participants who derive their support primarily from farming and those who have a regular additional non-farming source of income.

TABLE I: SELLERS.

'A'		'B'	
Full-time sellers Non-farmers) Long-distance sellers.		Part-time sellers (Farmers) Short-distance sellers.	
Wholesale sellers of vegetables, spices fruits, etc. (at vigorously active periodic market places)	Itinerant sellerss	Male	Female
		Local sellers	Street sellers
		Hawkers	Peddlers.
Middleman sellers (at vigorously active periodic market places	Only male sellers		

Table-II implies that a substantial number of participants is present in the market place to obtain cash through the sale of goods and services or to obtain or order goods and services. Other purposes can be served by a visit to the market-place, and some people are present in the market-place neither to offer goods and services for sale nor to purchase goods and services. The fact that market places have economic and non-economic functions is accepted without dispute, but the degree of these functions varies from one market place to another. It is appropriate in the present context to consider briefly the economic functions of periodic market place in the Valley.

TABLE II : TOPOLOGY OF MARKET-PLACE PARTICIPANTS.

Participants	Professional/ non-profess-ional sellers To	Reasons for presence in Market-place. To Buy	To buy & Sell.	Sell.
1	2	3	4	5
Full-time farmer	Non-professional	I	II	III
Part-time farmer	Non-professional	IV	V	VI
Non-Farmer	Professional	VII	VIII	IX

(Smith, R.H.T., 1976)

Note- I Purchase of convenience goods, II-Selling for cash, III-Horizontal exchange, IV, V & VI - Purchase of goods for re-sale after processing, VII,VIII & IX - Whole time sellers (rural and urban based).

Periodic market-places broadly perform three economic functions simultaneously : Local exchange, internal trade and central place function (Eighmy, 1972). But in case of the Wardha valley two economic functions are observed simultaneously, *i.e.*, local exchange and internal trade. Local exchange mediates family surplus and deficits (Gedam, 1981). It is based on small-scale division of labour, and requires no more than a subsistence economy. The services available at the market-place are simple. Internal trade at periodic market-places facilitates distribution of commodities of local surplus and this involves participants who play no role in local exchange (Table-I). As internal trade begins to dominate local exchange at a market site, the services performed by the market-place tend to become complex, which is observed in the Valley. The whole transaction involved is that of horizontal trade.

SELLERS' TRAVEL BEHAVIOUR

The analysis of the data shows that a majority of sellers (approximately 80% of the total) sell at a single market-place. Such sellers usually attend one vigorous market-centre in a week where there is sufficient activity to achieve their profit threshold, without further travel. However, at all levels of market-place, there is a good number of sellers who regularly visit from two to seven market-centres. The linking of the market places together in a system is accomplished through the movements of these sellers with their goods.

It is necessary to specify several assumptions, under which the analysis of optional seller travel behaviour proceeds. Firstly, it is assumed that sellers would have complete information about the location and timings of all market places which are within the range of their visitations. Secondly, their objective would always be to find the least-cost set of periodic market places in terms of distance travelled. Thirdly, the routes sellers follow between market-places are always linear. It is impossible for sellers to find a prompt solution to their transport problem, unless they are willing to relocate (that is to exchange their behaviour of choosing a different set of market-centres) or eliminate certain market-days.

The range of travel of itinerant sellers in the Wardha valley varies approximately between 9 to 20 Km. a day, with the round trip totalling upto 40 to 120 Km. throughout the week. They transport their goods etc. by trucks, private buses,state transport service buses, railways and mostly in their own bullock-carts. Itinerant peddlers travel and render services for sharpening tools, cutlery and move mostly on bicycles. Potters use donkeys and some sellers carry their goods on horse backs to the periodic market-centres. Most of the part-time travelling (occasional nonprofessional) sellers in this region return home each night.

Vendors selling seasonal fruits such as melons, water-melons, etc. , may be called seasonal sellers. They raise fruits in the beds of Wardha valley and most of its tributaries (mainly, the Madu and Bembla, the Wenna, etc.) in the summer season. The producers of these fruits are mostly fishermen, who take to this as an additional occupation once in the year. Such vendors are accompanied by members of their families to sell these fruits at the nearest periodic market-centres. A large number of butchers and fishermen sell meat and fish respectively throughout the year, but in the month of *Shravana* (July-August), *Kartika* (October-November) and *Pausa* (January) the sale of fish and meat diminishes due to religious restrictions.

FEMALE SELLERS IN PERIODIC MARKETING SYSTEM

The above theoretical highlights the overall role of the different categories of sellers in periodic marketing system of the Valley. Male and female sellers are the two main categories of the sellers, but the female sellers are found less in number than male sellers (Table-III).

TABLE III : VARIATION IN DISTRIBUTION OF THE MALE/FEMALE SELLERS IN THE VALLEY AND ITS' SUBREGIONS.

Valley		Rice		Non-Rice	
1.		2.		3.	
No.of vendors		No. of vendors		No. of vendors	
Male	Female	Male	Female	Male	Female
25069	1627	6475	681	18324	946
93.90%	6.09%	90.87%	9.13%	95.1%	4.9%

The following conclusions emerge from Table-III:-

1. In the valley as a whole the percentage of the female sellers is markedly less, and

2. the "Rice" sub-region has a greater percentage of female sellers than that of their counterparts in the "Noe-Rice" sub-region.

The Wardha valley has 337 periodic market-places in which the average number of male sellers works out to be 74. The corresponding figures in the "Rice" and "Non-Rice" subregions are 187 and 61 respectively. The Table-IV sets out of corresponding figures for female sellers.

TABLE IV : DISTRIBUTION OF FEMALE VENDORS.

Region/ sub-region.	Total No. of market centres.	No. of market centres with female partici-pation.	No.of market centres without female partici-pation.	Total No. of female sellers.	Average No. of female sellers (Colm.5/3)
1	2	3	4	5	6
Valley	337	135	202	1627	12
Rice	36	26	10	681	26
Non-Rice	301	10p	192	946	09

Table-IV reveals that the average number of female sellers in the "Rice" sub-region of the Valley is greater than that in the "Non-Rice" sub-region, because the female vendors are large in number in marketing activities in the "Rice" sub-region. This can be attributed to their relatively extensive participation in the collection of fire-woods, gum, honey, wild-fruits and other commodities in forested tracts and brought by them to sell in neighbouring periodic market-places in large quantity. These female sellers visit at the most two periodic market-places in a week which are within the range of three to six kilometers from their residence. Not all female traders are mobile. Female vendor, who belongs to the *Gond* tribe starts to the market centres between 9.00 to 10.00 A.M., and procures, hardly Rs.6/- to 10/- from sales of fire-wood for which she has to walk three to six Km distance on foot to the neighbouring periodic market-places. These female sellers get back to their homes before dusk on the same day.

ITINERANT SELLERS AND MARKET CYCLES

Itinerant sellers are found to attend several successive periodic market centres within a week and serve a large number of buyers than those who visit a single periodic market-place. The flow of goods and sellers in a periodic marketing system are conditioned by the market schedules. On a certain day, the movement of sellers and products is predominantly in one direction, while on the consecutive day the focus of activity shifts to another periodic market-place. The mobile vendor has a number of alternative of itinerary in the valley.

TABLE V : THE RELATIVE DISTANCE OF TRAVELLING SELLERS' ROUTE THROUGH SAMPLED NETWORK OF PERIODIC MARKET-CYCLES.

Sl. No.	Market code No.	Home place of itinerant seller.	Straight line aggregated distance (Km.)	Average distance of sampled cycle (Km.)	Per day average distance within the cycle (Km.)	Average of aggregate day distance of sampled cycles(km)	Departure (6-7)	Standard deviation of column 6.	Aggregate length of sampled marked cycle in individual	Average No. of days in sampled market cycle.
1	2	3	4	5	6	7	8	9	10	11
1.	3	Warud	94.00	82.00	13.40	14.10	-0.7	3.18	7	6
2.	33	Rajurwadi	55.00	82.00	9.20	14.10	-4.9	3.18	6	6
3.	89	Deoli	88.00	82.00	14.70	14.10	0.6	3.18	6	6
4.	131	Kurha	89.00	82.00	14.80	14.10	0.7	3.18	6	6
5.	146	Dhamangaon Rly.	91.00	82.00	15.20	14.10	1.1	3.18	6	6
6.	176	Nandgaon Khandeshwar	42.00	82.00	10.50	14.10	-3.6	3.18	4	6
7.	225	Babhulgaon	84.00	82.00	12.00	14.10	-2.1	3.18	7	6
8.	263	Wadner	50.00	82.00	10.00	14.10	-4.1	3.18	5	6
9.	278	Kandhali	120.00	82.00	20.00	14.10	5.9	3.18	6	6
10.	281	Kora	93.00	82.00	15.50	14.10	1.4	3.18	6	6
11.	310	Warora	95.00	82.00	19.00	14.10	4.9	3.18	6	6
12.	337	Rajura	88.00	82.00	14.70	14.10	0.6	3.18	6	6

It is possible for mobile seller to select a specific periodic market cycle at least partly because he perceives it as corresponding to some integration which already exists amongst the adjacent market-places. This seems to be one implication of "market cycles" which is defined as composed of a complete and integration of market-places held over four-day to seven-day periods' in this region.

It has been observed in the valley that in a market ring sellers and buyers have no uniform activity patterns, not all periodic market centres meet just during a market week, not all market centres are of equal activity and not all goods are ubiquitous chain of a series of market nodes generated by a given market calender where some orderly correlationship between the itinerant sellers and the total population of its service area is in evidence. In other words, market-places within a specific period, where direct relationship between the itinerant sellers with the total population and their service areas can be witnessed.

Table-V spotlights that mobile sellers in this valley visit 4 to 7 periodic market-places through various periodic market cycles. Periodic market circuits of seven days bring bring out a very close relationship with improved and fast development transportation technology to neighbouring significant periodic market centres in the same cycle. There is a solitary instance of a four - day market cycle of which Nandgaon Khandeshwar (Code No. 176) (Fig. 1) is one of the components, because itinerant sellers have not been able to perceive to attain relatively more than the expected profit threshold by visiting more than four periodic market-centres, commensuate with the labour and time involved. The value of standard deviation from average distance of each day, *i.e.,* 3.18 explicates per day average distance travelled and actual distance travelled by these vendors in the network of market cycles.

The itinerant sellers of non-perishable commodities sell in a week for 4 to 7 days, and cover an extensive service area of market cycle and serve large population therein. The degree of influence of the mobile sellers bearing on services areas and population served therein manifests a marked variation in the market cycles of the periodic marketing systems, as revealed in Table-VI. Table-VI sets-forth the aggregate areas, covered by itinerant sellers within selected

TABLE VI : ITINERANT SELLERS AND THEIR INTENSITY OF INFLUENCE IN PERIODIC MARKET CYCLES.

	Service Area				Population				Coefficient of variations.		
Home place sampled market centre of itinerant sellers.	Service areas in Km^2	Average service area in Km^2	Departure (2-3)	Standard divia-tion (of col-umn2)	Population in service area (Figure in '000').	Average popula-tion (Figures in'000')	Departure (6-7)	Standard diviation (of column 6).	Service area (V value)	Popula-tion (V value	
1	2	3	4	5	6	7	8	9	10	1	
1. Warud	958.25	'	318.08	'	399	'	181	'			
2. Rajurwadi	730.36	'	90.19	'	60	'	-158	'			
3. Deoli	626.75	'	-13.42	'	240	'	22	'			
4. Kurha	523.17	'	-117.00	'	124	'	-94	'			
5. Dhamangaon Railway.	541.17	'	-99.88	'	308	'	90	'			
6. Nandgaon	272.46	'	-367.71	'	173	'	-45	'			
Khandeshwar		640.17		186.39		218		134.77	29.12%	61.82	
7. Babhulgaon	704.41	'	-306.06	'		'	-58	'			
8. Wadner	334.11	'	-306.06	'	174	'	-44	'			
9. Kandhali	761.42	'	121.25	'	78	'	-140	'			
10. Kora	782.15	'	141.98	'	73	'	-145	'			
11. Warora	691.51	'	51.34	'	509	'	291	'			
12. Rajura	756.26	'	116.09	'	319	'	101	'			

market cycles. The aggregate area covered by individual market cycles ranges from 272.46 Sq.Kms. to 958.25 Sq.Kms. and population numbers from 6000 to 509000 in a week. The lower value of coefficient of variation, i.e. 29.12% highlights that overall service areas approximate to the mean than that of population in sampled periodic market cycle for it itinerant sellers.

The following discussion and Inset-1 (Fig.1) are useful to confirm the above theoretical conclusion. The values of coefficient correlation of population with itinerant sellers and service areas with the latter, are 0.53 and 0.41 respectively. In the periodic market the trend of relationship between population with sellers and service areas with sellers is shown with the help of regression lines as inserted in Inset-1 (Fig.1). These statistical values bring out a clear-cut direct relationship of aggregate population served in market cycles and sellers involved in the same cycles and of the service areas and sellers involved in them. The former variable have a close mutual relation, than the latter variables.

Travelling sellers by definition have itinerries, who choose subsets of market-places to visit in the market cycle (Shrivastava, V.K., 1978). The existence of linked market cycles is relatively large in number. They have been evidenced in areas of dense population. High instances of the existence of linked market rings are seen (Fig.1 A to C, F to H & J). These linked market cycles touch each other at some market nodes from where mobile sellers converge and then diverge into adjacent market cycles.

Table-VII shows that the maximum duration of rest in periodic market cycles does not exceed three days. It brings out that Warud and Babhulgaon , *i.e.*, home bases of itinerant sellers, lie on seven-day market cycles. These market cycles occuring on each successive day of a market calender, have been called, "Perfect Periodic Market Cycle". Even in a perfect market cycle intinerant sellers come back to their homes atleast once a week. A relatively small number of mobile vendors participate in this category of marketing activities (Fig.1) exemplifies an instance of three rest days, *i.e.* Sunday, Wednesday and Friday in a week.

TABLE VII : REST DAYS OF ITINERANT SELLERS IN SEVEN-DAYS MARKET CYCLES

Sr. No.	Market code No.	Market-Cycle with home base at	The duration of market cycle	No.of days/ days	Rest day/ day/days
1	2	3	4	5	6
1.	3	Warud	7	-	-
2.	33	Rajurwadi	6	1	Monday
3.	89	Deoli	6	1	Saturday
4.	131	Kurha	6	1	Saturday
5.	146	Dhamangaon-Railway	6	1	Wednesday
6.	176	Nandgaon Khandeshwar	4	3	Sunday Wednesday & Friday.
7.	225	Babaulgaon	7	7	-
8.	263	Wander	5	2	Saturday & Monday
9.	278	Kandhali	6	1	Friday
10.	281	Kora	6	1	Wednesday
11.	310	Warora	5	2	Saturday & Tuesday
12.	337	Rajura	6	1	Thursday

MARKETING EFFICIENCY:

The concept of marketing efficiency is based on the observed strength of sellers being able to fulfil the supply of normal requirements of commodities, available generally for sale at individual periodic market-places to the observed number of buyers. The expected number of sellers at different periodic market of buyers reported by their respective organising authorities. It has been observed that on an average the ratio between buyers and sellers is 10:1 . The expected number of sellers at a market-place has been matched against the observed number of sellers at it. The correspondance of these two categories of sellers has been designed as balanced marketing efficiency. The excess of observed number of seller over the expected number of sellers and deficiency of observed numbers of sellers below their expected numbers are called overbalanced marketing efficiency and underbalanced marketing efficiency, respectively. Under-balanced marketing efficiency puts sellers to undue and heavy strain to render their services to their patrons, while overbalanced marketing efficiency exposes sellers to battle for buyers, resulting perhaps, in buyer's market due to heavy competition among sellers. Goods and services may be available at relatively cheap prices at market places with overbalanced marketing efficiency. According to percentage of different categories, specially overbalanced and underbalanced of marketing efficiency, it has been observed that these two categories equally share the marketing system in the Valley. It has been concluded tentatively that in underdeveloped region the balanced category of marketing efficiency is relatively low.

CONCLUSION

In the Wardha valley, 'simple peasant or traditional marketing system' is met with. Two groups of participants are found engaged in buying and / or selling. It has been found that the number of mobile vendors is small in number than those of the other categories of sellers throughout the Valley, where peasants also sell their surplus. The large scale production of onion, chilly, turmeric and pumpkin by the progressive farmers is purchased by the middlemen at periodic market-centres. Most of the peasant sellers export directly these commodities by trucks and also export though wholesale sellers to outside regions, Specially, Andhra-Pradesh and adjoining parts of the valley, *i.e.* Nagpur, Amravati, Yavatmal, Multai, etc. The travelling sellers who move around a network of periodic market cycles have been able to perceive to attain the expected profit-threshold. Linked market cycles (Fig.1) are correlated with the length of market calender in which the itinerant vendors return to frequent to adjacent sub-set of market-placed. Four instances of discrete market cycles (Fig.1-D, I,K and L) are separated from each other. In general, the periodic market cycles are complex because of the number of ways in which they are diversified by petty peasant sellers, female sellers, buyers and others.

EIGHTEEN

Vishwa Nath, Jata Shankar and Triyugi Nath

Consumer - Behaviour in North Awadh Plain

Regional Personality

North Awadh Plain (26°53'N to 28°53'N lat and 79°37'E to 81°24'E long covers as area of 24040.6 km^2 with a population of 77.7 million in 1981. The density of population is 323 person/Km^2. 61% of the total population belongs to scheduled and backward caste which are socially and economically backward. 94.7% of the working population depend on agriculture for its livelihood. There are 722 market centres in the study region. Daily and bi-weekly markets are the only means for satisfying the needs of the local people.

It has been noted that farmers use nearest market centres for meeting their requirements. The consumers are aware about the market locations and market days in their surrounding area and they make their choices according to their level of knowledge. It is only on special occasions that the consumers travel distant market centre for meeting the requirement of their social, cultural, religious and administrative needs (Skinner, 1964).

It is a well known fact that consumers wish to earn maximum profit in minimum effort. The consumer behaviour pattern in Indian context has been studied by Tamaskar (1979). Saxena (1975), Shrivastava (1978), and Vishwanath (1975) etc. The study of these marketing geographers reflect that in developed countries consumer prefer higher market centres for the requirement of a higher needs and special quality goods. Consumer mobility is restricted due to low per capita income limited needs and low accessibility of market centres. Higher order goods trickle down to middle and lower order market centres from higher order market centres. High order goods are thus also available at lower order market centres in undeveloped countries (Shrivastava, 1976).

It has been observed that consumer mobility is influenced not only by economic factors but also by socio-cultural and religious factors (Shrivastava, 1977).

The study of the consumer behaviour in the study region has been attempted in view of the indigenous characteristics mentioned above.

The information about consumer behaviour has been collected by personal interviews from 20% of the consumer's present at a market on the market day. Market centres have been selected on the basis of random sampling. In this context informations about their home, village, its distance and direction from market centres, their purpose of visiting the markets, goods purchased by them etc. have been collected. Four essential goods like vegetable, *kirana,* food grain and cloth have been particularly selected as these are the most preferred goods of the people of this region.

Consumer - Behaviour

As mentioned earlier main factors governing the consumer behaviour in the region are poverty of people, low purchasing power and accessibility of market centres. In addition socio-cultural factors and religious attitude also influence the behaviour of people. In the study area periodic markets are held in the afternoon with brusque selling in the middle hours. The behaviour pattern has been analysed mainly in context of mobility and means of communication used by the consumers.

Mean (average) Moving Capacity

The average distance travelled by the consumers is based on the distance upto which the consumer can go to the market centres by available means of transportation and can come back to his village in a day. Christaller (1966) has assumed this distance to be 4 km. In Indian conditions Walter Neale (1965) determined this distance as 6 km. and Shrivastava (1976) found out an average distance of 5 km. in eastern U.P.

FIG. 18.1

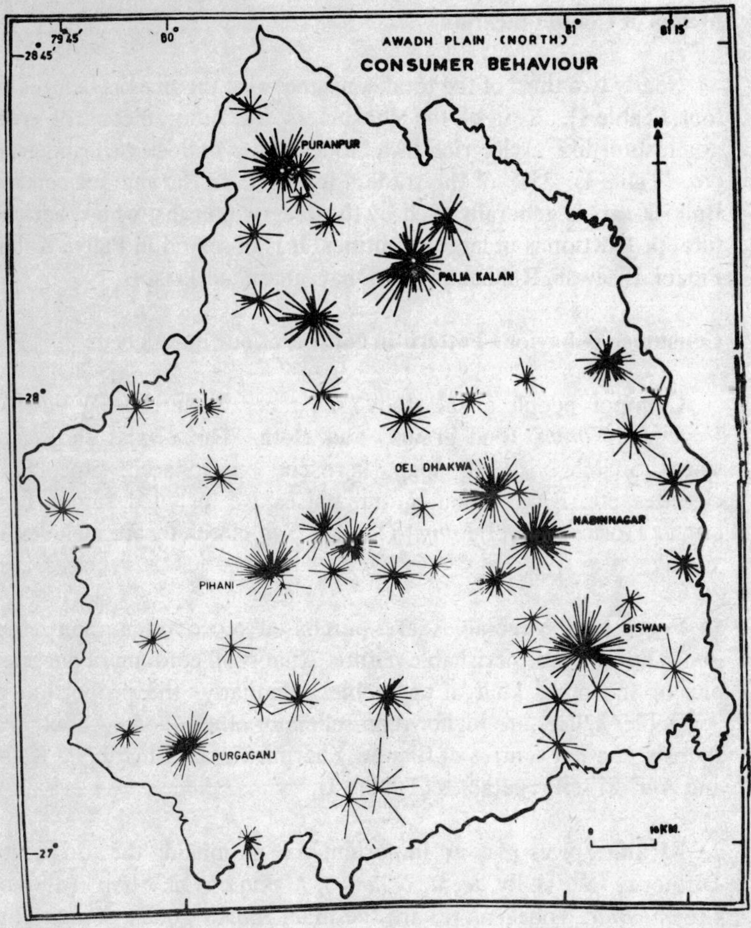

Majority of the consumers of the North Awadh Plain visit the market centres on foot due to the lack of means of transportation (Table-I). The average distance travelled in the study area is 5 km.

which is similar to eastern U.P. findings. It is also observed that the the frequency of consumer decrease with increasing distance from market centres (Fig.1. It has been observed in the case of Bisawan, Sherpur Kalan, Neri, Ahirori, Khutar and Bhatpurwa market centres.

Means of Communication

Nearly two third of the total consumer visit the market centres on foot (Table-I). Rest of the consumers use other means of communication like cycle, rickshwa, tonga, bus, bullock-cart and train etc. (Table-I). 25% of the traders use cycle in the market centres. Bullock-cart is generally used by those agriculturalist whose agricultural production is in large quantities. It is observed in Paliya Kalan, Pihani, Bisawan, Rakhauna and Dhaurahara markets.

Consumer Behaviour Pattern in context of our main goods

Common people of the study area generally purchase goods like Vegetable,*Kirana,* food grains, and cloth. The *Kirana* shops sell spices, match box, oil, soap, kerosene oil, tobacco, pipe, *Bidi*, cigrettee etc. Rice, wheat, gram, pulses are included among food grains. Hosiery, towel, *Lungi*, Dhoti & *Sari* cloth etc. are included in 'cloth'.

1. **Vegetables** Vegetables are purchased more often than other goods due to their perishable nature. Almost all consumers purchase one or the other kind of vegetables. Similarly, the proportion of vegetables sellers are higher than sellers of other goods. About 70% shops at market centres of Biswan, Sherpur Kalan, Bhatpurwa Kalan and Ahirori sell vegetables (Table - I).

2. **Kirana** Spices play an important role in making the food testy. Turmeric, salt, chilly, *Jeera*, *Dhaniya*, *Manihari* Oil. Soap, Tale and Cream, *Bidi*. Tobacco etc. are the main *Kirana* goods. *Kirana* consumers are also found in majority in the market centres, next to consumers of vegetables. More-than 75% of the total consumers come to purchase *Kirana* at Bhatpurwa Kalan and Neri market centres.

TABLE I : CONSUMER - TRADER'S BEHAVIOUR PATTERN (IN %)

Sl. No.	Market Centres	Purchasing & Selling Commodity				Means of transportation		
		Vegetable	Kirana	Food-Grains	Cloths	On Foot	Bi-Cycle	Bus train
1.	Biswan	72.5	62.3	19.3	23.5	50.0	38.0	12.0
2.	Khutar	87.2	66.6	10.5	11.7	60.0	35.0	5.0
3.	Sherpur	78.9	65.0	16.0	20.0	78.0	22.0	-
4.	Bhatpurwa Kalan	88.5	78.1	17.2	3.5	65.0	35.0	-
5.	Unchauliya	57.8	65.3	11.3	13.4	77.0	25.0	8.0
6.	Neri	82.4	75.4	15.4	17.3	72.0	22.0	6.0
7.	Navin Nagar	63.7	52.4	10.6	11.2	88.0	12.0	-
8.	Ambarpur	53.4	61.3	8.5	2.7	91.7	8.3	-
9.	Kaudha	65.6	49.4	9.2	18.2	80.0	16.0	4.0
10.	Ahirori	85.6	59.5	25.3	21.3	60.0	40.0	-
11.	Bhagawant Nagar	59.2	45.7	7.5	13.0	54.0	14.0	2.0
12.	Purena	58.3	54.3	5.6	9.0	80.0	12.5	7.5
13.	Birsinghpur	79.1	67.2	17.0	21.2	75.5	24.5	-

Source: Field Study, 1980-81.

3. **Food Grain** The low income group and agricultural labourers do not produce food grains for the own need. They purchase food grains from these market centres. In the study region 40% of the shops in Pihani and Bhira sell food grain. Labourers fulfill their needs in these market centres. The average distance travelled by the food grain consumer is less than the average distance. It is due to the weight of the goods purchased. About 20% of the total consumers come to purchase food grains in Ahirori and Biswan market centres in the study region (Table-I).

4. **Cloth** Cloth are one of the essential needs of man most of the persons purchase cloth according to their economic status. Cloth shops are less in number than other shops in these market centres. However, people move longer distance for cloths. In Biswan, Sherpur Kalan and Birsingpur markets a distance of 10 km. and above has been total the study regions (Table-I).

Conclusion

In this way consumer behaviour is generally influenced by distance. Distance is based upon the facilities of means of transportation. The fore going analysis leads to the conclusion that consumer behaviour pattern is also influenced by the mode of transport, quality, and availability of goods in the market area region. Bicycle plays an important role in the means of transport used by the consumers because it is means of vehicle of the poor people.

NINETEEN

H.O.Srivastava and
K.N.Tiwari

The Nature of Market Area Regions in Saryupar Plain

The aim of this paper is to illustrate the characteristics of tributary areas served by market centres in the Saryupar plain of Uttar Pradesh (India). The study region is a part of the middle Ganga plain. Bordering Nepal, the study area extends from 26°5' to 28°30' north latitude and 80°57' to 84°9' east longitude. Covering an area of 33.2 thousand Km^2. Saryupar plain encompasses five districts of Uttar Pradesh, i.e., Bahraich, Gonda, Basti Gorakhpur and Deoria. from west to east respectively. On the eastern side it borders Bihar. Of the total population of 12.8 million (1981), 95% is rural. The density of population is 387 persons/km^2. It is predominently an agricultural area where 89% of the total work foce is engaged in agriculture. The region possesses 19,294 villages and 18 town. Of the 1228 market centres of the region 56.7% are weekly, 35% bi-weekly, 0.7% tri-weekly and 7.6% of them are daily markets.

This paper has been divided into three parts. In the first part the bases of demarcation of market area regions have been outlined. The second part briefly deals with the methodology and the nature of market area regions has been discussed in the last part.

BASES OF DEMARCATION

It is hypothesised that the hierarchy of market centres influences the extent of the tributary are commanded by a market. Higher order market centres provide a wide variety of goods and [1] services and.

therefore, attract consumers from far and wide. Their tributary areas are also large. Market areas of subsequently lower order centres are nested within the market areas of their higher order counter parts(Huff, 1962). It may thus be said that the hierarchy of market centres also coincides with the hierarchy of market area regions.

Besides the hierarchy of market centres, consumer behaviour also forms one of the bases of demarcation of market area regions. It is universally recognised that consumer visit market centres more frequently for goods of daily needs, i.e., vegetables, spices, meat, edible oils, fuels, tobacco etc. They also prefer to buy such goods from nearby centres. Only for the purchase of higher order goods, i.e. clothes, ornaments, electrical goods, medicines, ceremonial goods etc., they would like to travel longer distances (Christaller, 1966). In this way the range of consumer movement is smaller in case of goods of daily needs and larger in case of goods of higher order. In the case of the study region which is predominently rural, the former characteristics may be called normal characteristic. It is because only on special occassions the farmers may like to visit distant market centres.

Periodicity of rural markets is also one of the factors influencing the demarcation of market area regions. Market areas of daily markets are smaller because they provide opportunity of exchange everyday. The consumers can visit them more frequently. On the other hand, market areas of weekly or bi-weekly markets are larger because they provide exchange opportunity only once or twice a week. Consumers from a wider range would like to make use of the opportunity of exchange on fixed days and time of the week. This also provides the necessary threshold for the continuance of periodic markets. Periodic markets are also arranged in market cycles so that exchange opportunities on different days of the week are available for contiguous areas. However, the market areas of daily and periodic markets vary in extent according to their status in the hierarchy.

METHODOLOGY

After discussing the bases of demarcation of market area regions. attention may now be focussed briefly on the methodology adopted.

FIG. 19.1

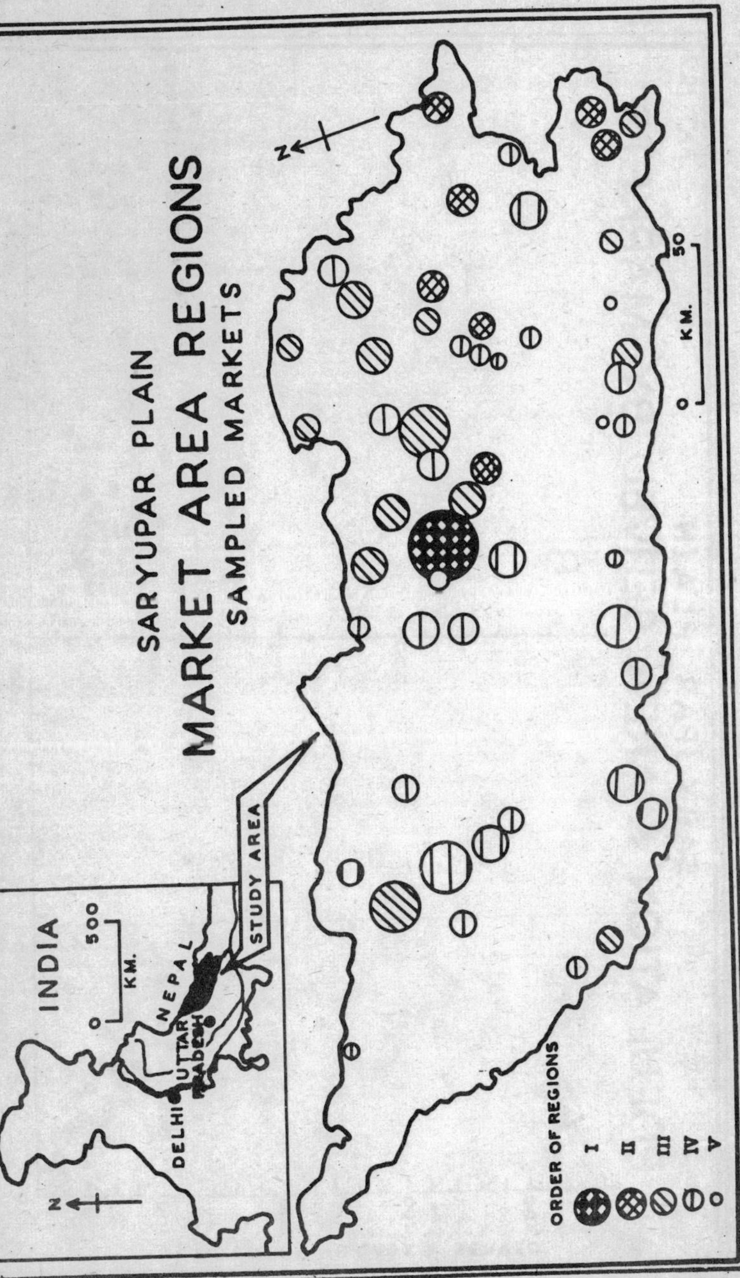
SARYUPAR PLAIN
MARKET AREA REGIONS
SAMPLED MARKETS
INDIA
0 500
KM.
NEPAL
UTTAR PRADESH
DELHI
STUDY AREA
N
0 50
KM.
ORDER OF REGIONS
I
II
III
IV
V

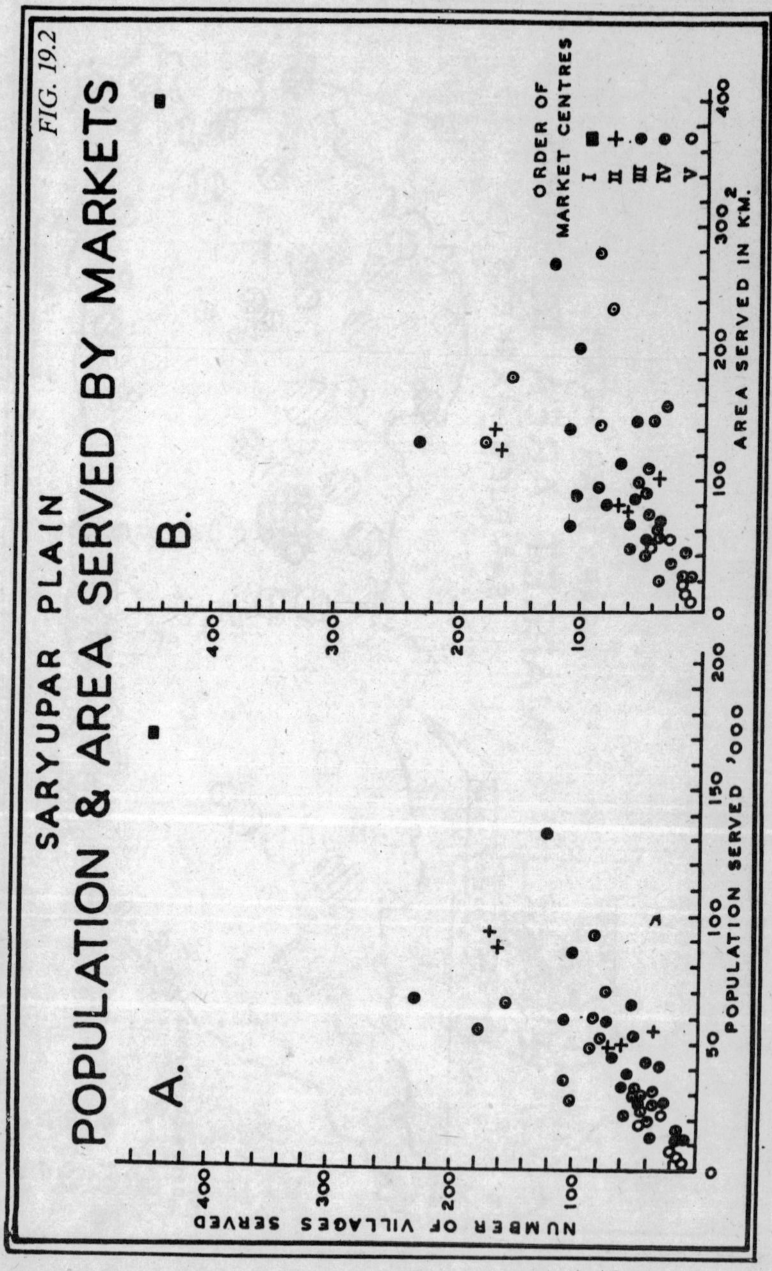
FIG. 19.2
SARYUPAR PLAIN
POPULATION & AREA SERVED BY MARKETS
A.
B.
NUMBER OF VILLAGES SERVED
POPULATION SERVED '000
AREA SERVED IN KM.2
ORDER OF MARKET CENTRES
I
II
III
IV
V

Empirical work on market area regions is based on the sample survey of 10% market centres of the Saryupar Plain. Average and maximum distances from which the consumers visit the respective market places have been worked out. The distances travelled are larger in case of higher order centres and smaller for lower order ones. For example at Bansi, the market centres of highlight order, average and maximum distances are 11.0 km. and 40.0 km. respectively, whereas they are 1.5 km. and 3.0 km. respectively in case of a lowest order market centre Deoria (Table-I).It is also noted that distance travelled by consumers are larger in the western part of the region than in the eastern part. It is mainly due to comparatively low density of population and larger inter-market distances.

Following an earlier attempt (Shrivastava, 1975) consumer behaviour lines were drawn towards each market centres from the place of origin of2Xthe consumers. Thereafter, on each of the sampled markets, circles were drawn according to the average range from where the respective markets draw their consumers. The number of villages, their area and population served by each of the sampled markets were also enumerated. The results were mapped (Fig. 1) and graphed (Fig. 2). The following characteristics of market areas may be noted.

TABLE I : SARYUPAR PLAIN MINIMUM AND MAXIMUM RANGES OF SELECTED SAMPLED MARKETS

	Market Centre	Minimum Range Km.	Maximum Range Km.
1.	Bansi - DP	11.00	40.00
2.	Salempur - D	5.5	16.5
3.	Bhatpar Rani - DP	5.0	15.0
4.	Shoharatgarh - DP	6.5	11.0
5.	Anand Nagar - DPT	8.0	52.0
6.	Siswa Bazar - DT	8.0	21.0
7.	Bhinga - DP	10.5	21.5
8.	Rudhauli - P	10.0	18.5
9.	Sekhui - P	4.0	13.0
10.	Deoria - P	1.5	3.0

D - Daily market,
P - Periodic market,
T - Town.

THE NATURE OF MARKET AREAS

It may generally be noted that market areas of higher order centres and the number of villages and population served by them are larger (Figs. 1 & 2) as compared to market areas of lower order centres.

The market area of the highest order centre, i.e., Bansi, is 400 $Km.^2$ It serves 445 villages with a population of 1.7 lakh. Bansi provides a large variety of goods and services and tops in case of number of shop openings (Shrivastava, 1976) also. It is located in an area of higher density of population and was once the capital of the earstwhile Bansi state. It is a focal point of road transport and, lying on the bank of river Rapti, it was once a river port also.

Market areas of second order centres are also extensive. For example market area and number of villages served by Salempur, a road-railway junction also, are 150 $Km.^2$ and 170 respectively. Mehandawal serves an area of 125 $Km.^2$ of 163 villages. It may be noted that the market area served by third order centres is expected to be even smaller but it is not so in the study region. Anand Nagar and Siswa Bazar are third order market centres. The population and area served by them is comparatively larger but the number of villages served by them is smaller. Both are road-railway junctions. The size of settlements in the western *Tarai* belt in which they lie is larger hence the number of villages served by them is smaller. A similar apparently abnormal trend is noted in areas where due to smaller size of settlements the number of villages served exceeds over the expected limit.

Anomaly in the extent of market area regions is noted in case of fourth and fifth order market centres due to variations in inter-market distances. Market areas of lowest order centres are very small due to lower shop openings, lack of accessibility and lower population density.

CONCLUSION

The above discussion shows that in Saryupar Plain there are some exceptions to the norms of relationship between extent of market area, population and number of villages served. Factors behind these exceptions, which are found in a few typical areas, are sparsely distributed population, low density, scattered nature of settlements and variation in inter-market distances. These factors influence the range of market areas. Such exceptions are notable in the western part of the region (Fig.1). Extent of market areas has also been influenced by the availability of means of transport. Historical factors also have their say in influences the size of the market areas. Because of momentum of early start these centres command larger market areas inspite of their lower hierarchical status. Similar deviations are noted elsewhere also (Tamaskar, 1966; Barnum, 1966 and Wood, 1974).

NOTE

1. Basti district has been fifurcated into two districts the other being siddhanagar with headquarters at Naugarh.

TWENTY

Ram Surat and
Nirankar Lal

Commercial Characteristics of Agricultural Mandis in Eastern Uttar Pradesh

Introduction

Eastern Uttar Pradesh is one of the backward areas of the country. Its economy depends on agriculture. The whole sale agricultural markets established by the government, known as *mandi*, play a vital role in the exchange of agricultural products. The paper attempts to high light some of the commercial characteristics of the *mandi* centres.

Eastern Uttar Pradesh extends between 23° 51' N lat. to 28° 23' n lat. and 81° 5D' E long to 84° 45' e long. It covers an area of 85.8 thousand km^2 which is nearly 29% of the area of Uttar Pradesh. Fifteen districts of the state area included in eastern U.P. The total population of the study area was 4.15 million which is equal to 37% of the total population of Uttar Pradesh. There are 59 main agricultural *mandis* and 115 sub-*mandis* in the study area. The distribution pattern is nearly uniform.

The aims and objects of *mandi* centres

Agricultural *mandis* are established with a view to provide the farmers an opportunity to sell their produce at the rates supported by the government. After gradation of the produce the *mandi* committee arranges for correct weighing of the produce and on the spot payment through arranges for correct weighing of the produce and on the spot payment through the banks. The *mandi* committee ensures fair terms of trade between the producers and the buyers. It also provides facility for innovation diffusion related to high yielding varieties of seeds, fertilizers, pesticides etc. The rates of grading, weighting, loading, un-loading are limited to 1.7% of the total value of the produce of the farmer. Besides, public utility services are also available at *mandi* centres.

Commercial characteristics

The importance of a *mandi* centre is evaluated in terms of the quantity of arrivals handled by it. The arrival of agricultural produce is divided into two parts, i.e. primary arrival and secondary arrival. The primary arrival is one which is brought by the farmers directly to the *mandi*. The secondary arrival consists of produce exchanged among the *mandi* centres. This shows that these agricultural markets can handle produce imported from areas out-side the study region.

The 59 *mandi* centre handled nearly 15 *lakh* metric tonnes agricultural produce during 1979-80. This was equal to 16.5% of the produce handled by all the *mandi* centres of U.P. It may be worth mentioning that eastern U.P. comprises of 23% of the total *mandi* centres of U.P. as a whole. Out of the total produce handled 70.5% was classified as primary arrivals (Table-I). In the next year (1980-81) an increase of 15.7% was noted. This increase was less than the increase (23%) of the produce handled by all the *mandi* centres of U.P. The spatial pattern of increase was random. However, the increasing amount of agricultural produce handled by *mandi* centres shows that the farmers are increasing their production and are being benefitted by the plans to develop agriculture.

A further analysis of arrival patterns shows that primary arrivals are nearly double of the amount of the secondary arrivals (Fig. 1). It is because the area consists of a majority of farmers and many of them are availing this facility of disposing of their goods. The north eastern district of Gorakhpur contributed most in the primary arrivals, where as the eastern most district of Ballia received more secondary arrivals than primary arrivals. It is also seen that it is the frequency of *mandi* centres which matters in so far as the amount handled by them is considered. For example Pratapgarh district has

Table I : EASTERN UTTAR PARDESH: STRUCTURE OF ARIVALS OF MANDIS CENTRES - 1979-82. (*LAKH* METRIC TONNES)

Year	Primary Arrivals			Secondary Arrivals			Total Arrival		Total Arrival of U. P.	
	Qty.	%	Increase %	Qty.	%	Increase %	Qty.	Increase %	Qty.	Increase %
1979-80	10.39	70.5	-	4.34	29.5	-	14.73	-	88.96	-
1980-81	11.39	66.8	9.7	5.66	33.2	30.2	17.05	15.7	106.47	19.6
1981-82	13.49	72.9	18.4	4.99	27.1	11.7	18.49	8.4	112.19	5.4

Source : Agriculture Produce Committee, U.P., Quarterly Bulletin, October, 1982.

FIG. 20.1

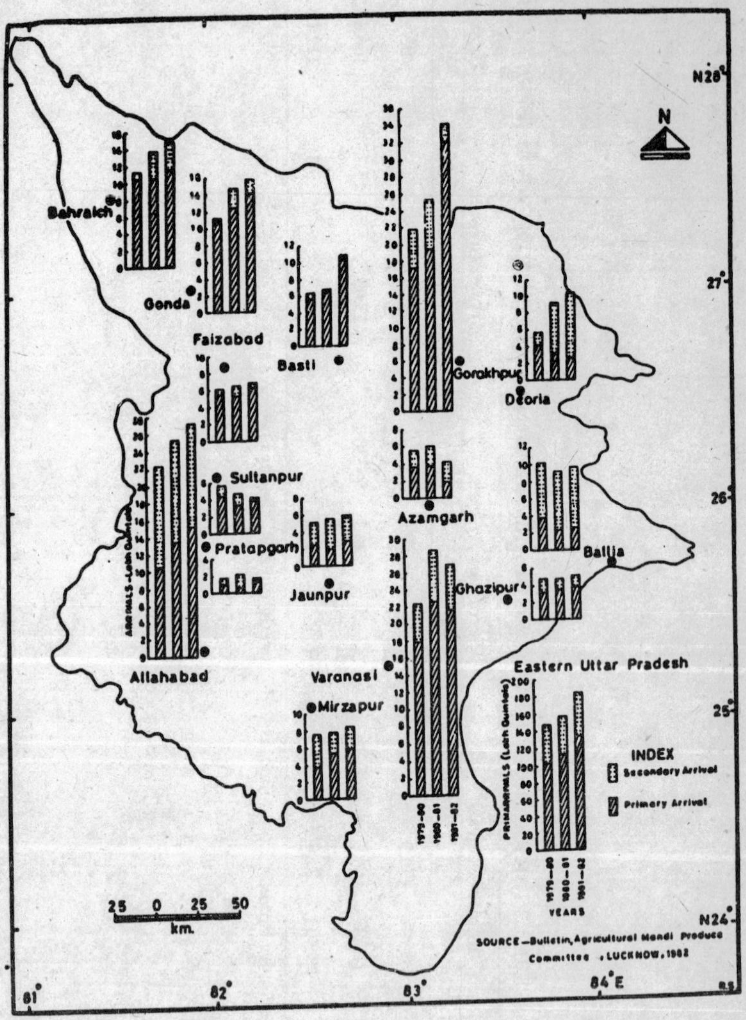
N
N28°
27°
26°
25°
N24°
81°
82°
83°
84°E
Bahraich
Gonda
Faizabad
Basti
Gorakhpur
Deoria
Sultanpur
Pratapgarh
Jaunpur
Azamgarh
Ballia
Ghazipur
Allahabad
Varanasi
Mirzapur
Eastern Uttar Pradesh
ARRIVALS—Lakh Quintals
1979—80
1980—81
1981—82
YEARS
INDEX
Secondary Arrival
Primary Arrival
25 0 25 50
km.
SOURCE—Bulletin, Agricultural Mandi Produce Committee, LUCKNOW, 1982

least number of *mandi* centres and its contribution is also very small. The flood prone areas handle more secondary arrivals. It is evident in case of Ballia district where secondary arrivals are three times of the primary arrivals. It may thus be hypothesised that the *mandi* centres function to reduce the imbalances in food grain production.

The three districts of Gorakhpur, Varanasi and Allahabad handle 50% of the total amount of primary arrivals. The Saryupar Plain districts of Bahraich, Gonda, Basti, Gorakhpur and Deoria handle more primary arrivals. The three major *mandi* centres combined handle 45% of the total commerce of the region. These *mandi* centres are well connected with transport routes. Allahabad and Varanasi, (Gorakhpur recently) are connected with states like Bihar, M.P., Haryana and Punjab directly. These powerful *mandi* centres overlap the trade areas of smaller *mandi* centres around them. Such *mandi* centres are Pratapgarh, Sultanpur, Azamgarh and Jaunpur etc.

The Quantum of Trade

The analysis of the quantum of trade shows that primary and secondary arrivals are directly related in the region. Some *mandi* centres handle more secondary arrivals than primary ones. In such *mandis* the relation is indirect.

The Structure of goods

The commercial characteristics of *mandi* centres can also be explained through the structure of goods dealt by these centres. It may be pointed out that these markets sell goods specified by the government. There are 112 such items. These may be grouped under major heads like wheat, rice, pulses, oil seeds, fibres, spices, grass and fooder etc. Among garden produce vegetables and fruits are included. Besides animal products like milk, cream, *khoya*, leather, bones, hornes, and forest produce like gum, firewood, timber, *tendu* leaves, *lac*, catechu etc. are also sold.

The sources of income

Major part of the income of the *mandi* centres comes from taxes.

These taxes are levied on the buyers @ 1% of the value of goods purchased by them. No taxes are levied on producer farmers. A part of the income is yielded by other sources like licence fees etc.

In 1979-80 the total income of the mandi centres of the study area was Rs. 2.2 crores which was 15.5% of the total *mandi* income of U.P. This increased to 3.02 crores in the following year and Rs. 3.36 crores in 1981-82. This was equal to 17% of the total state income from this source. Nearly 88% of this income was obtained through primary arrivals. The three main *mandi* centres, i.e. Allahabad, Varanasi and Gorakhpur account for 45% of the total income from *mandi* centres of eastern U.P.

It may thus be observed that the *mandi* income is gradually rising. Its spatial distribution, of course, is not uniform. It is due to changes in the volume of arrival of goods.

Conclusion

It may thus be concluded that agricultural *mandi* centres are a form of public intervention in the distribution system of agricultural produce. Though such produce are specific but they include a wide variety of produce. It is also observed that the public participation with *mandi* centres is increasing and the income so obtained by the farmers is being invested (in part) in agriculture which leads to more production. This chain of increasing income and increasing capacity to invest can lead to the development of the area in general.

TWENTY ONE

Mahatam Prasad and
Bhagwan Deo

Identification of Central Places : A Case Study of Campierganj Development Block (Pharenda Tahsil, Gorakhpur District)

Central places play a vital role in the process of development. Central places are those settlement which fulfill the socio-economic and politico-cultural necessities and supply services and commodities to their surrounding area. In such studies, it would be of practical importance to make use of field data. The aim of this paper is to identify central places in Campierganj Development *Block* using field data.

STUDY AREA

Campierganj Development Block (26°55' - 27°7'N Lat. & 83°12' 23'30' E. Long.) a sub-division of Pharenda *Tahsil* of Gorakhpur district, Uttar Pradesh, encomposes an area of 235.3 Km^2. with a population of 87487 (1971) and density of 372 persons/km.^{2} This area, as a part of the *Tarai* region of U.P., and is situated between two perennial rivers, i.e. the Rapti in the west and the Rohin in the east. Agriculture is the main occupation of the area. More than 80% of the people of the area are engaged in agricultural activities. The main crops of the area are wheat, banana, sugarcane, groundnut and paddy. Industrial activities are very few. Thus, this area characterises a backward economy.

METHODS OF IDENTIFYING THE CENTRAL PLACES

Since Christaller's (1933) classic study, several approaches have

Table I : Facilities Available Within the Settlements of Campierganj Block

S.No.	Name of Settlements	Type of facilities	Total number of facilities	Population (1971)	Rank
1.	Peppeganj (Sahabaganj)	35	612	5146	1
2.	Campierganj (Chaumukha)	35	283	2563	2
3.	Machhaligaon	16	65	2021	3
4.	Ramchaura	13	52	1263	4
5.	Baurabari	13	39	1562	5
6.	Ram Nagar Kevtalia	13	21	1813	6
7.	Inderpur	13	20	2906	7
8.	Laxmipur	11	25	995	8
9.	Rajpur	10	24	2072	9
10.	Mohnag	10	18	1477	10
11.	Mohd.pur urf Jungle Babban	9	30	244	11
12.	Suras	9	23	1820	12
13.	Mahawankhor	9	19	1008	13
14.	Makhanaha	9	13	1743	14
15.	Nawapar	8	21	1669	15
16.	Basantpur	8	20	3158	16
17.	Jungle Jhajhwa	8	19	900	17
18.	Kuin	8	9	488	18
19.	Algatpur	7	17	1182	19
20.	Karahia	7	11	189	20
21.	Aktahwa	6	20	774	21
22.	Jungle Bihuli	6	11	2633	22
23.	Jungle Aghi	6	10	2475	23
24.	Mohammadpur urf Hagana	6	10	1562	24
25.	Sheopur Karmaha	6	10	1067	25
26.	Madwapur	6	9	686	26
27.	Sarpatha	6	8	2214	27
28.	Karim nagar	5	8	1346	28
29.	Seolahia	5	7	1055	29
30.	Alinabad	5	7	443	30
31.	Loharpurawa	5	6	2579	31
32.	Bajahi	5	6	500	32
33.	Kunjal Garh	5	6	359	33
34.	Badshahpur	5	5	760	34
35.	Baratgara	4	9	3009	35
36.	Piprabari	4	8	576	36
37.	Bharawalia	4	7	1408	37
38.	Bagahibhari	4	7	932	38
39.	Mohd.pur	4	7	500	39
40.	Gopalganj urf Harnampur	4	5	1970	40
41.	Alamchak	4	5	1137	41
42.	Ramawapur	4	5	777	42
43.	Sonatikar	4	54	246	43
44.	Laxmipur	3	12	1481	44
45.	Bishnupur	3	8	498	45
46.	Amawa urf Amghat	3	8	186	46

47. Janakpur	3	5	1530	47
48. Jhawankot	3	5	654	48
49. Kalyanpur	3	4	2111	49
50. Parasia Bujurg	3	3	1073	50
51. Bajaha	3	3	566	51
52. Campiernagar	2	9	596	52
53. Banbhagalpur	2	5	912	53
54. Bargadahi	2	4	1846	54
55. Deorwa	2	4	59	55
56. Dharampur	2	2	2030	56
57. Madhawapur	2	2	1146	57
58. Aligarh	2	2	1319	58
59. Parsa	1	5	324	59
60. Chandipur	1	3	517	60
61 Tendua Bishambharpur	1	2	1770	61
62 Baijnathpur	1	2	804	62
63. Gulaharia	1	1	991	63
64. Chauri	1	1	972	64
65. Karmahwa	0	0	497	65
66. Khokhari	0	0	399	66
67 Khiria	0	0	166	67
68. Amarha	0	0	145	68
69. Dharmadih	0	0	71	69
70. Barhia	0	0	40	70
71. Sekhul	0	0	25	71

Source : Based on field survey, 1985.

been developed and various techniques have been used by geographers to identify the hierarchy of central place system in different regions, which have been critically reviewed by Davies (1966, pp. 51-65). A number of geographers have made attempts to study the functional characteristics of service centres and define their class-system (Sen, L.K. 1971, Shrivastava, V.K. 1976, Singh J. 1979). This paper makes use of a hitherto uncommon method in an attempt to identify and select the central places. It is based on the actual movement of people for availing goods and services to central places. This information has been obtained through personal field work.

The present study is thus based on primary data collected in the field. During data collection all the 71 revenue villages have been taken into consideration. Two questionnaire were used for this purpose. One of them was related to amenities in settlements and the other was related to the movement of people for purchase of central goods. Random sampling was used in selecting the families interviewed at different villages. Samples were taken from each status group of families such as high, middle and low income groups. They were asked as to which centre did they usually visit to avail the goods and services they need. Thus, information was collected from one thousand families. One an average, 15 family heads from each village were thus taken into account.

SCALOGRAM METHOD

On the basis of collected data a scalogram has been made, which represents the types and number of infrastructural facilities. Settlement were then ranked according to the preference of (i) type of amenities, (ii) number of units, and (iii) population (Table I). According to scalogram it appears that only 64 settlements possess amentities. Peppeganj is first while Chauri stands 64th in ranking order.

SOCIOGRAM METHOD

The sociogram method is supposed to show graphically the pattern of interaction or inter-dependence by the movement of people between settlements for selected facilities. This pattern can be shown on maps on the basis of preference for central places, by arrows showing the actual connection of villages to central places. In other words, arrows are the indicator of people's perception of a central place. The thickness of arrows shows the intensity of use of a central place. It was found that only 32 settlements interact with various central places. (Table-II, Fig. 1)

Comparing both the methods some salient features in the rank order of settlements emerge. Scalogram shows that 64 villages possess amenities as mentioned above, but sociogram represents that people go to avail facilities only to 32 settlements. It is very necessary to know about the reason why people do not go to avail the facilities to the rest of the settlements. The study reveals that these settlements have very ordinary facilities which are few in numbers and types. Most of them are of ubiquitous nature such as primary school. People get these facilities very easily either in the settlements where they are inhabited or from those settlements which are rather more

FIG. 21.1

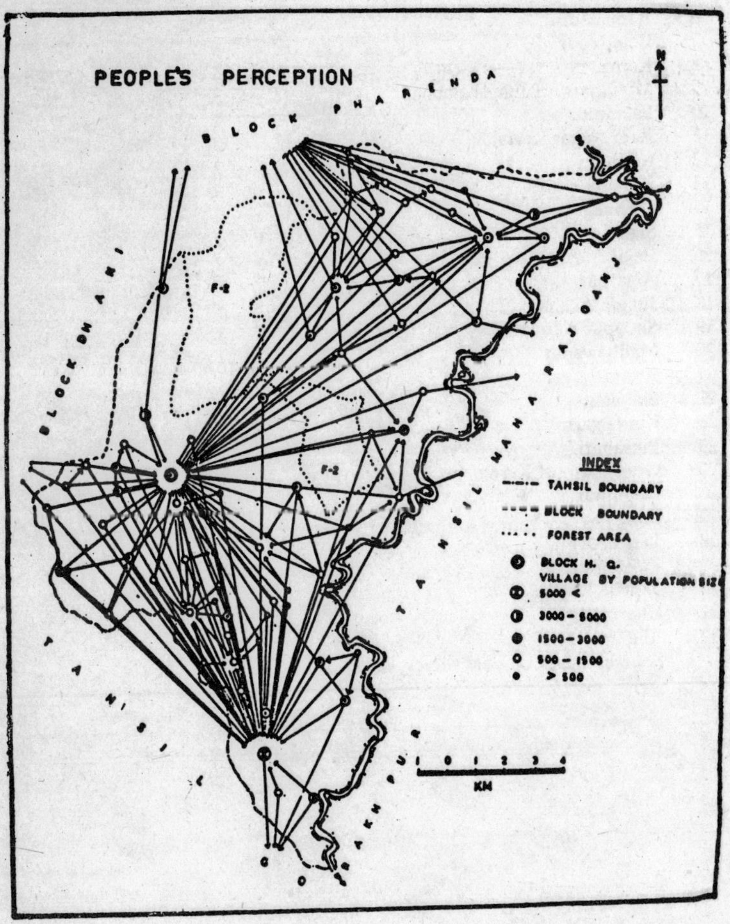
PEOPLE'S PERCEPTION
BLOCK PHARENDA
BLOCK DHANI
TAHSIL MAHARAJGANJ
TAHSIL GORAKHPUR
F-2
F-2
INDEX
TAHSIL BOUNDARY
BLOCK BOUNDARY
FOREST AREA
BLOCK H. Q.
VILLAGE BY POPULATION SIZE
5000 <
3000 - 5000
1500 - 3000
500 - 1500
> 500
0 1 2 3 4
KM

Table II : PEOPLE'S PERCEPTION IN EMERGING CENTRES OF CAMPERGANG BLOCK

Sl. No.	Name of settlement	No. of arrows	Rank
1.	Campierganj	58	1
2.	Peppeganj	44	2
3.	Machhaligaon	10	3
4.	Inderpur	8	4
5.	Mahawan Khor	8	5
6.	Ramchaura	7	6
7.	Bhaurabari	6	7
8.	Kuin	6	8
9.	Mohd.pur urf Jungle Babban	5	9
10.	Laxmipur	4	10
11.	Ram Nagar Kevtalia	3	11
12.	Nawapar	3	12
13.	Karahia	3	13
14.	Mohnag	2	14
15.	Suras	2	15
16.	Bajahi	2	16
17.	Algatpur	1	17
18.	Jungle Agahi	1	18
19.	Sheopur Karmaha	1	19
20.	Madhawapur	1	20
21.	Karim Nagar	1	21
22.	Sheolahia	1	22
23.	Kunjalgarh	1	23
24.	Piprabari	1	24
25.	Gopalganj urf Karnampur	1	25
26.	Laxmipur	1	26
27.	Janakpur	1	27
28.	Jhawakot	1	28
29.	Kalyanpur	1	29
30.	Parasia Bujurg	1	30
31.	Dharmpur	1	31
32.	Aligarh	1	32

Source : based on field survey, 1985.

important than the rest of the settlements. Ranking order of settlements according to sociogram is not just the same as scalogram. For Example, according to scalogram Peppeganj stands first, Campierganj second and Ramchaura fourth. According to sociogram Campierganj tops over Peppeganj and Ramchaura occupies the sixth rank.

It has been made clear above that though some settlements have amenities yet people do not go there to avail them. Thus, it is noteworthy that only the existence of amenities in a settlement may not be the criterion for identification of central place. People's perception is rather an important criterion. According to sociogram method important centres are Campierganj, Peppeganj, Machhaligaon, Inderpur, Mahavan Khor, Ramchaura, Bhawarabari, Laxmipur, Kuin, Mohammadpur urf Jungle Babban. Ram Nagar Kevtalia, Navapur, and Karahia having three or more than three arrows. Among these centres which are able to be as central places and their hierarchical order is identified by Bisection method.

BISECTION METHOD

The bisection method has been used to identify on a map the high, middle or lower order central places by geometrically dividing the space on the basis of some knowledge or ranking of central places. It is based on the assumption that the lower order central places are expecpted to develop in the middle of higher level central places. If one or two of the most important centres in the *block* proper and in the neighbouring *block* are known, it is possible to except lower level centres around the bisection line it will be decided on the basis of (i) people's perception, (ii) type of amenities, and (iii) number of amenities respectively. This methods makes it possible to identify most important central place in the study area. According to bisection method Peppeganj is most important central place. This central place lies mid-way between Gorakhpur and Pharenda (Fig.2A). Again the central places of same order as Peppeganj are searched out in the neighbouring area. These centres are Gorakhpur, Khalilabad, Mehdawal, Maharajganj, Pharenda, Siswa Bazar and Pipraich. Campierganj stands in second order according to bisection line drawn on the basis of two higher order centres of Peppeganj and Pharenda. Ramchaura has a higher rank but it left

FIG. 21.2 (A & B)

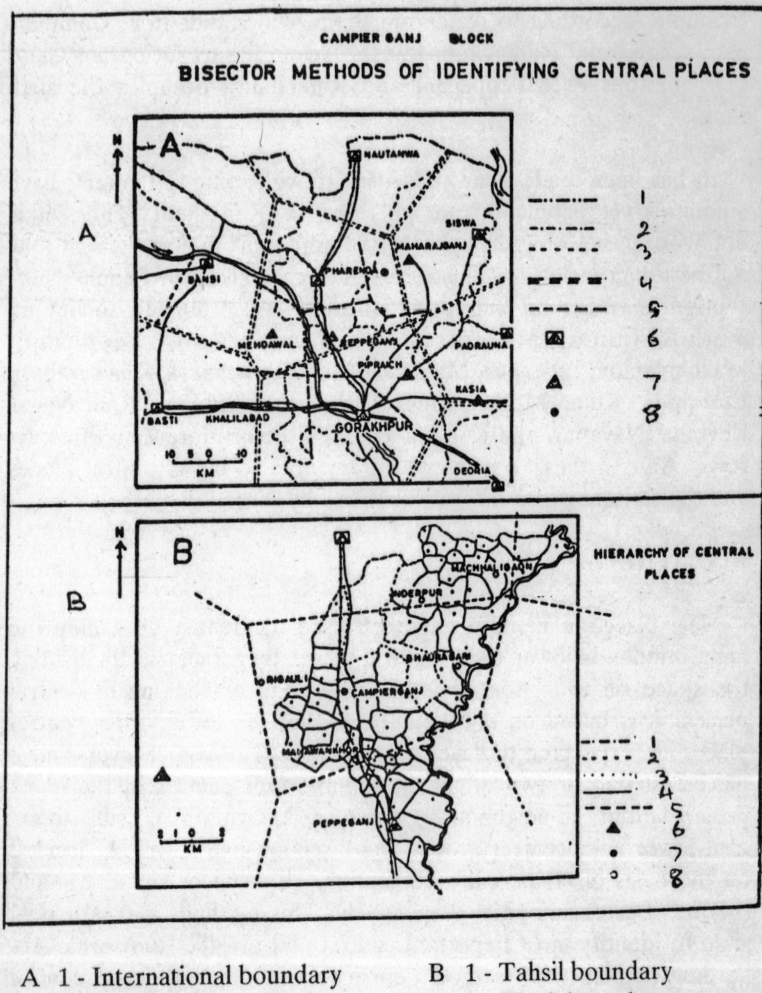

A
1 - International boundary
2 - District boundary
3 - Tahsil boundary
4 - Bisection line for top centre
5 - Bisection line for sub-centre
6 - Fixed top centre
7 - Identified sub-centre
8 - Lowest sub-centre

B
1 - Tahsil boundary
2 - Block boundary
3 - Forest area
4 - Village boundary
5 - Bisection line
6 - First order centre
7 - Second order centre
8 - Third order centre

out as it is just near Campierganj the most important centre of the study region. The third level centre of the study area are Machhaligaon, Inderpur, Mahawan Khor and Bhawarabari (Fig.2B).

Thus, using all the afore-said methods the central places of the study area are listed below (Table-III).

TABLE-III : HIERARCHY OF CENTRAL PLACES IN CAMPIERGANJ DEVELOPMENT BLOCK

Rank order	Name of the central place	People's perception (no.of-arrows)	Types of ameni-ties	No. of amini-ties	Popula-tion (1971)
I	Peppeganj	44	35	612	5146
II	Campierganj	58	35	283	2568
III	i. Machhaligaon	10	16	53	2021
	ii. Inderpur	8	13	20	2906
	iii. Mahavan Khor	8	9	23	1008
	iv. Bhawarabari	6	13	39	1562

Findings

The study brings out the following findings:

(1) For identification of central places people's perception is more important than the number and type of establishment of amenities in a settlement,

(2) It is not necessary that the most important centre has its locations in the central part of the study area. For example Peppeganj as a first order centre has its peripheral location in reference of study area.

Acknowledgements:

The authors are thankful to Dr. V.K. Shrivastava, Department of Geography, University of Gorakhpur, for suggesting this method and giving useful suggestions in the preparation of this paper.

TWENTY TWO

E. Swaminathan

Market Centres and their Hierarchy in Coimbatore Region-Tamil Nadu

Introduction

Market centres are concerned with either collection of goods from or the distribution of goods and services to the people living in the surrounding areas or beyond (Yeates and Garner, 1971). These market centres perform various types of commercial and service activities. The commercial and service activities performed by these centres vary with each other depending upon their location, population size and purchasing power of the people in the surrounding area. The variation in the offering of services (functions) results into the hierarchy of market centres.

In the present study an attempt has been made to study the nature of commercial and service activities performed by various market centres and to identify their hierarchy in Coimbatore region. The structural relationship exhibited by these market centres is also attempted.

Study Area

The study confines to Coimbatore region spread over an area of 756.14 km^2. This region has a population of one million. There are 58 market centres in all and Coimbatore city is in the centre of this region.

Data Base

The study is based on secondary and primary data. The secondary data were collected from the records of the commercial tax offices and Block Development Offices in this region. The data so collected was verified during the field survey. All together 76 commercial and service activities were selected for establishing the hierarchy of market centres.

Technique employed

Factor analysis with principal component solution has been employed for the grouping of the variables and to discover the underlying dimensions. Secondly the cluster analysis (Numerical Taxonomy) technique was employed for grouping of the market centres into different levels of hierarchy on the basis of the similarity that exist among the market centres in terms of the commercial activities performed by them. It may be stated that 57 market centres out of 58 in the study were subject to the above said analysis leaving Coimbatore city. The correlation technique was applied to bring-out the association between population and functions and functional establishments.

Results and Discussion

It has to be stated that 74 commercial and service activities were first subject to Pearson's product moment correlation in order to assess the similarity between them. The inter-correlation Matrix (74x74) was subjected to principal component analysis with varimax solution. Altogether, this has resulted into 14 factors, accounting for 89.16% of the total variance as exhibited by 74 functions in 57 market centres in the study area.

The first component has the highest eigen value of 28.12 which accounts for a maximum variance of 38.13%. The second component with an eigen value of 8.22 accounts for a total variance of 11.11%. The eigen values of third and fourth components are 5.83 and 4.73 respectively and they account for a variance of 7.89% and 6.4% respectively. The eigen value of the fifth component is 3.29 and the total variance explained by this component is 4.46%. This shows the diminishing significance of these components. The variation between the market centres as contained by the 74 variables can be easily contributed to 14 components. The factor loading matrix (74 x 74) shows the correlation of each of the 74 variables with the degree of association between the variables and the components.

TABLE I : SHOWING THE FACTOR LOADING OF THE PRINCIPAL COMPONENT I

S.No.	Nature of the activity	Factor Loading
1.	Fancy goods	96
2.	Non-agricultural credit society	96
3.	Photo studio	93
4.	Scrap iron	88
5.	Vegetable shop	84
6.	Typing institute	83
7.	High School	81
8.	Jaggary	81
9.	Agricultural crediet society	75
10.	Furniture	75
11.	Bank	75
12.	Automobile spare parts	73
13.	college	72
14.	Drug store	71
15.	Cycle and spares	70
16.	Cattle feed shop	69
17.	Printing press	69
18.	Provision shop	66
19.	Middle school	65
20.	Petrol filling station	62
21.	Tea shop	58
22.	Electrical goods shop	55
23.	Foot-wear shop	53
24.	Vessel shop	52
25.	Sanitary ware	50
26.	Cloth shop	49
27.	Handicrafts	46
28.	Bakery	46
29.	Kerosene shop	45
30.	Sweet shop	44
31.	Rubber, Leather & Plastic goods	40

Decimal points are omitted. Factor loading greater than 70 is considered for factor representation of the variable.

The factor loading matrix was subjected the 'varimax rotation' and it has resulted in the high loadings of variables on one factor. In order to show the hierarchy of commercial and service activities the factor loading matrix has been constructed. The lower limit of the

TABLE II : SHOWING FACTOR LOADING FOR THE PRINCIPAL COMPONENT II

Sr.No.	Primary variable	Factor Loading
1.	Agro-service	94
2.	Chicory	88
3.	Nursing home	87
4.	Flour mill	83
5.	Cotton yarn	81
6.	Engineering machinery	79
7.	Firewood shop	69
8.	Hotel	63
9.	Primary school	63
10.	Handicrafts	63
11.	Cinema Theatre	62
12.	Rice mill	62
13.	Library and Reading room	59
14.	Crackers	59
15.	Oil mill	59
16.	Footwear shop	53
17.	Bakery	53
18.	Sweet shop	51

TABLE III : SHOWING THE FACTOR LOADING FOR THE PRINCIPAL COMPONENT III

Sr.No.	Primary Variable	Factor Loading
1.	Metal shop	94
2.	Agricultural implements	89
3.	Rubber, Leather & Plastic goods	85
4.	Cotton seed and cake	82
5.	Electrical goods	78
6.	Cloth	70
7.	Petty Shops	69
8.	Co-operative stores	69
9.	chemicals	66
10.	Printing press	64
11.	coffee works	63
12.	Handicrafts	59
13.	Ration shops	55
14.	Automobile spare parts	53
15.	Furniture shop	45
16.	Hotel	40

factor loading considered here is 0.40. The activities which are having a factor loading of 0.70 is considered pure and undimensional. On the basis of factor loading pattern it has been considered that the first seven components representing seven levels of hierarchy of activities. These seven component account for 74.85% of the total variance.

TABLE IV : SHOWING FACTOR LOADING FOR THE PRINCIPAL COMPONENT IV

Sr.No.	Primary Variable	Factor Loading
1.	Books and stationery	90
2.	Foodgrains and pulses	85
3.	Petty shop	59
4.	Fertilizer shop	56
5.	Sugar	45
6.	Chemicals	45
7.	Health centre	43
8.	Hotel	40

TABLE V : SHOWING THE FACTOR LOADING OF THE PRINCIPAL COMPONENT V

Sr.No.	Primary Variable	Factor Loading
1.	Wet grinding	93
2.	Drug store	58
3.	Tea shop	49
4.	Tile and timber	48
5.	Fertilizer shop	43
6.	Cement and cement pipes	42
7.	Rice mill	41

TABLE VI : SHOWING THE FACTOR LOADING OF THE PRINCIPAL COMPONENT VI

Sr.No.	Primary Variable	Factor Loading
1.	Coconut	78
2.	College	51

TABLE VII: SHOWING THE FACTOR LOADINGS OF THE PRINCIPAL COMPONENT VII

Sr.No.	Primary Variable	Factor Loadings
1.	Tile and Timber	78
2.	Health centre	76
3.	General Goods shop	73
4.	Kerosene	72
5.	Hardware	68
6.	Crackers	58
7.	Hospital	55
8.	Cement and Cement pipe	54
9.	Hotel	51
10.	Cinema/Theatre	50
11.	Radio sales	49
12.	Firewood	41
13.	Footwear	40

Table I shows the high factor loading on some of the commercial and service functions. The highest loadings are associated with personal functions (fancy goods, photo studio) followed by financial (non-agricultural credit society, bank, agricultural credit society), educational commercial typing institute, high school, college) and retail functions (vegetable shop, jaggery, furniture, automobile spare parts, cycle and spare parts shop). These activities are normally found in higher order market centres. Since, the first component accounts for the largest proportion of the total variance (38.12%), it is considered as the most important basic dimension of variation in the market centres in the study area.

The pattern of factor loading for the second component is shown in table II and it reveals that high loadings are associated with retail and health facilities. These services are generally found in the lower order market centres.

The third component (Table III) shows high loadings associated with retail activities. The fourth component (Table-IV) also shows that it is highly associated with variables (functions) relating to retail activities. The fifth component (Table V) shows that high loading variables in this component are associated with personal service. The sixth component which component which accounts for 3.36% of the total variance and is associated with retail activities. The seven component (Table VII) is associated with health and retail activities.

From the results discussed earlier it becomes evident that there are seven levels of hierarchy of functions. In the first level of hierarchy there are ten variables that are highly loaded. These facilities are found in centres where the population is more than 20,000. Therefore, it may be concluded that these functions are higher order functions.

In the case of second level functional hierarchy the functions are found in those centres where the population is ranging between 10,000 - 15,000. Agro-service is the only exception in this level because it is found in a centre where the population is 40,000.

FIG. 22.1

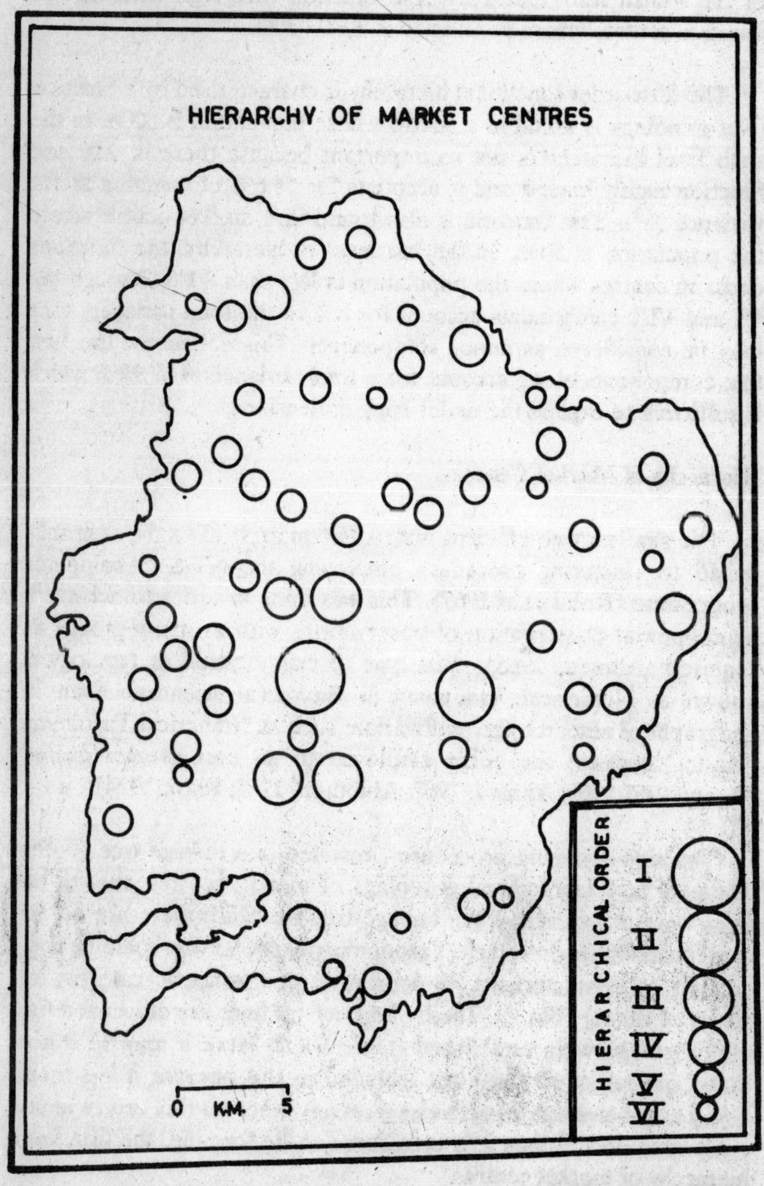
HIERARCHY OF MARKET CENTRES
0 KM. 5
HIERARCHICAL ORDER
I
II
III
IV
V
VI

In the third level functional hierarchy, the functions with high loadings are found in centres where the population is 5,000 to 8,000. In the fourth level hierarchy, the function with high loadings are found in centres whose population is 3000 - 5000.

The fifth order functional hierarchy is characterised by a function (wet grinding) is found in a centre whose population is 5000. In the sixth level hierarchy is not so important because there is only one function highly loaded and it accounts for 56.6% of common factor variance (h^2). This function is also found in a market centre where the population is 5000. In the last level of hierarchy, the functions occur in centres where the population is less than 3000. Though the VI and VIII components account for 6% of the total variance, they may be considered as minor components. This is because the first five components along account for a total variance of 67.98% which is sufficient to explain the under-lying dimensions.

Hierarchy of Market Centres

The similarity co-efficient matrix (D^2 matrix) (57 x 57) was subjected to clustering procedure employing the NT-SYS computer programme (Rohlf et.al 1967). This was done in order to achieve a near optimal classification of observations with as many groups as required (Ahmed, 1965). This type of classification or typology is known as Numerical Taxonomy in Biological sciences. Even in geographical research the multivariate such as Numerical Taxonomy (cluster analysis) are being employed to an ever greater degree (Berry, 1958,1967; Ahmed, 1967; Abiodum, 1969; Knox, 1974).

The step grouping procedure , resulted in a linkage tree (fig.2). Then to have hierarchical groupings of market centres, the cut-off lines were drawn across the linkage tru. Beacause there are no accepted standards on values (Taxonomic distances) that could be considered as characteristics or indicative of taxonomic category or status of cluster (Fig. 2). Totally four cut-off lines are drawn and five major groups were established (table VIII). Here it may be stated that Coimbatore city was not included in this because it has more commercial and service activities than any other market centre in the study area and further it is considered to be forming, the first level hierarchy of market centres.

FIG. 22.2

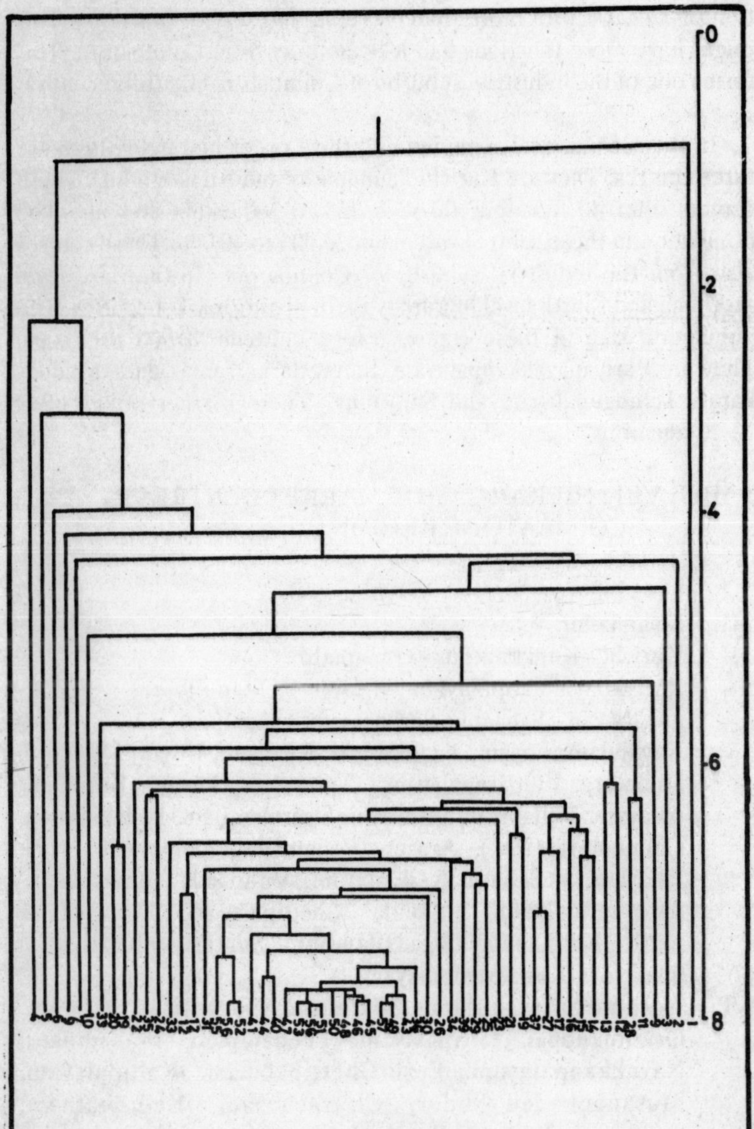

Singanallure is in the second level of market centres hierarchy eventhough it comes in the first level of grouping. This has a population of 1,12,206 with more than 60 retail and service functions. This might have more functions had it been away from Coimbatore. This forms one of the industrial suburbs of Coimbatore city (till recently).

In the second level grouping and third order hierarchy there are three centres. They are Kurichi, Ganapathy and Kuniamuthur. These centres offer 40 functions through 225 to 300 establishments. The population in these centres vary from 20,000 to 40,000. These centres also from the industrial suburbs of Coimbatore. In the third level grouping and fourth level hierarchy there are six market centres. The population size of these centres range between 10,000 to 20,000. They are Periyanayakkanpalayam, Sulur, Sarkarsamakulam, Madukkarai, Telungupalayam and Sanyanur. These market centes offer 30-40 functions.

TABLE VIII : HIERARCHY OF MARKET CENTRES IN COIMBATORE REGION

I	Coimbatore
II	Singanallur
III	Kurichi - Kuniamuthur - Ganapathi
IV	Periyanayakkanpalayam - Sulur - Madukkarai - Telungupalayam - Sanganur-Sarkarasamakulam.
V	Kavundampalayam, Vilankurichi, Kalapatti, Irugur, Vellalore, Gudalur, Kumarapalayam, Tudiyalur, Perur, Kurudampalayam, Vellakinar, Vadavalli, Veerakeralam, Pallapalayam, Coimbatore (NM), Arasur, Vellamadai, Pannimedai, N.N. Palayam, Vedapatti, Rasipalayam, Virapandi, Othaikalmandabam, Iddikarai, Ettimadai, Chettipalayam, chinnavedampatti, Kannapalayam, Nilambur, Sarvarnampatti, Titlipalayam, Kondayampalayam,
VI	Agraharasamakulam, Malaimuchanpatti, Pattanam, Orathukuppai, Giripalayam, Peedampalli, Maliampatti, Nayakkanpalayam, Peru-Chettipalayam, Kallipalayam, Muthugoundan Pudur, Chitrachavadi, Keoranatham, Somayampalayam, Vellanipatti.

In the fourth level grouping and fifth order hierarchy there are 32 market centres. These centres provide 10 to 25 functions. The population size of these centres vary from 6000-10,000.

In the last level grouping and sixth order hierarchy there are fourteen centres. The population size of these market centres very from 1000-5000. The number of functions offered in these centres vary from 2 to 9. And these centres offer such function as primary school, post office and petty sops which are lower order functions.

Structural relationships with hierarchy of market centres

As market centres increase in their population they are expected to show an increased in the number of activities (functions) and increase in the functional establishments. Similarly when there is an increase in the functions offered in the market centres there is also a positive increase in the functional establishments. (Berry and Garrison, 1958, Barnum 1966, Strafford, 1963). The relationship between the variables have been assessed on the basis of Pearson's product moment correlation. The correlation co-efficient computed between population and functions is 0.715 which is significant at 0.01 level. This shows that there is a positive relationship between population and functions found in the market centres in Coimbatore region.

There exists a positive and significant relationship between population and functional establishments. Because the correlation co-efficient computed between them is 0.825 and there exists a linearity. The correlation co-efficient computed between functions and functional establishments in the market centres in the study area is 0.978. This shows a high positive association between functions and functional establishment in the market centres.

Conclusion

In the present investigation the hierarchy functions has been identified. They show seven levels. On the basis of cluster analysis the hierarchy of market centres have been established. These market centres fall into six levels of hierarchy on the basis of functions performed by them. The market centres also exhibit all the structural relationship identified in the earlier studies. The hierarchy can be used as a tool for planning development of Coimbatore region.

TWENTY THREE

Venu Trivedi

Hierarchy of Service Centres of Indore District (Madhya Pradesh)

Indore District is situated in the south-west of Madhya Pradesh. It extends from 22°' N to 23°5' N lat. and from 75°25, E to 76°15' E long. Covering an area of 3546.75 Km^2 (Table-I). Indore district consists of 4 *tahsils* and an equal number of Development *Blocks*.

TABLE I. AREA AND POPULATION OF INDORE DISTRICT.

S.No.	Tahsil/Development Block	Area Km^2	Population (1981)
1.	Depalpur	1022.25	1,32,644
2.	Indore	958.43	9,70,410
3.	Mhow	804.51	1,93,829
4.	Sanwer	761.56	1,12,590
	Total Indore District	3546.75	14,09,473

Regional Personality

Indore District is situated on the Malwa Plateau, the average height being 548m. A.S.L. It experiences a typical *monsoon* type of climate. Chambal and Kshipra are the main rivers which drain the area. Black cotton soils predominate. Nearly one-fourth of the total area of the district is under forests.

The population of the district was 14.1 million in 1981. Indore, the district headquarters is a million city. The region of study is well served by railway lines and roads both and has direct connections with Bombay, Agra, Delhi, Vadodara and other big cities of Madhya

Pradesh. Mhow (77537), Depalpur (8343) and Sanwar (7946) are other towns of the district.

The region

The object of the present study is to assess the services provided by settlements and to identify their hierarchy. Indore district has predominently an agrarian economy but due to its central location, it has become an important industrial, cultural, educational and administrative centre of western Madhya Pradesh.

The total number of villages in Indore district is 654. Only those settlements have been included in the present study whose population exceeds 1000 (Table-II).

TABLE II : CLASSIFICATION OF THE SETTLEMENTS OF THE INDORE DISTRICT

Sl. No.	Tahsil	1000-2000	2000-3000	3000-4000	4000-8000	Above 8000
1.	Depalpur	23	1	1	1	2
2.	Indore	22	6	3	5	2
3.	Mhow	15	5	2	4	1
4.	Sanwer	13	8	-	1	-

Bases for identifying the settlement hierarchy

Normally the hierarchy of service centres is determined by (i) threshold population, and (ii) centrality, which is determined by goods and services the settlement provides. Population is not the only criteria for all services which a settlement provides. A settlement with a large population may not necessarily provide a large number of services. For example Bada Bangarda (4114) and Shivni (3602) are small towns but each of them provides only two services. Therefore, the number of services provided by a settlement have been taken as the base to determine its hierarchy (Table-III). They have been grouped in to six categories.

TABLE III. SERVICES INCLUDED IN THE STUDY

S.No.	Service
A.	**Educational** 1. Primary School, 2. Middle School, 3. Higher Secondary, 4. College/Technical, University.
B.	**Health** 6. Primary Health Centre, 7. Sub-Health Centre, 8. Family Planning Centre, 9. Veterinary Hospital, 10. Medical Research Centre.
C.	**Administrative** 11. Gram Panchayat, 12. Police *Chowky*, 13. Police Station, 14. *Block* Head Quarters, 15. Tahsil Head Quarters, 16. District Head Quarters, 17. commissioner Head Quarters.
D.	**Communication** 18. Post Office, 19. Post/Telegraph, 20. Telephone, 21. Head Post Office.
E.	**Trade & commerce** 22. Weekly Market, 23. Cooperative Bank, 24. Commercial Bank.
F.	**Transport** 25. Pucca Road, 26. Railway Station, 27. Bus Stand, 28. Aerodrome.

The information regarding above services have been collected from the District Statistical Office and from the *Block* Development Office, Indore, and for data related to the travelling pattern the *Patwaries* and other responsible persons were contacted. In determining the hierarchy of service centres two methods have been adopted.

The population needed to maintain any service or function is called the threshold population. For example the minimum population for a primary school in Kalibillod of the study area is 1003. This may be called the threshold population for primary school. The comparative score of a service is calculated by dividing the threshold population of a service by the threshold population of the primary school or the smallest service.

The hierarchy of services

The hierarchy of services has been identified by using functional score and comparative score methods.

It should be borne in mind that the availability of the services is more important than its number in a settlement. Bhatt (1976, p.45) has calculated functional score of the services with the help of the following formula:-

$$Wi = \frac{N}{Fi}$$

Where,

Wi = The score of that specific function
N = The total number of settlements
Fi = The number of settlements where the services are available.

For example the total number of higher secondary schools in the study area is 28 and the total number of settlements is 115. Therefore, the functional score of higher secondary schools is:-

$$\frac{115}{28} = 4.10.$$

for calculation of the comparative score of each service,primary school is considered to be the smallest service and has been taken as the base. The following formula has been used to calculate the comparative score

$$\text{Comparative Score} = \frac{\text{Score of any specific service}}{\text{Score of the primary school.}}$$

For example the functional score of the primary health centre is 7.66, therefore, the comparative score of the primary health centre will be

$$\frac{7.66}{1.0} = 7.66$$

The functional and comparative scores thus arrived are given in Table-IV.

TABLE IV : FUNCTIONAL AND COMPARATIVE SCORE OF SERVICES OF INDORE DISTRICT

S. No.	Services	Settlements where the function exist	Functional Score	Comparative Score
1.	Primary School	115	1.00	1.00
2.	Middle School	69	1.19	1.19
3.	Gram Panchayat	92	1.25	1.25
4.	Pucca Road	92	1.25	1.25
5.	Post Office	77	1.49	1.49
6.	Bus Stand	66	1.74	1.74
7.	Veterinary Hospital	38	3.02	3.02
8.	Co-operative Bank	35	3.28	3.28
9	Commercial Bank	35	3.28	3.28
10.	Sub-Health Centre	32	3.59	3.59
11.	Higher Secondary School	28	4.10	4.10
12.	Weekly Market	27	4.25	4.25
13.	Family Planning Centre	18	6.38	6.38
14.	Primary Health Centre	15	7.66	7.66
15.	Post & Telegraph	13	8.84	8.84
16.	Railway Station	13	8.84	8.84
17.	Police Station	12	9.58	9.58
18.	Telephone	08	14.37	14.37
19.	Police Chowky	04	28.75	28.75
20.	Block Headquarters	04	28.75	28.75
21.	Tahsil Headquarters	04	28.75	28.75
22.	College/Technical	03	38.33	38.33
23.	University	01	115.00	115.00
24.	Medical Research Centre	01	115.00	115.00
25.	Head Post Office	01	115.00	115.00
26.	District Headquarter	01	115.00	115.00
27.	Commissioner Headquarter	01	115.00	115.00
28.	Aerodrome	01	115.00	115.00

According to Table-IV services can be classified into three categories :-

1.	Lower rank services	1.0 to 4.25
2.	Middle rank services	6.38 to 14.37
3.	Higher rank services	28.75 to 115.00

The hierarchy of settlements

The hierarchy of the settlements has been identical with the help of the following two methods :-

1. Scalogram
2. Functional score.

The well known the scalogram technique (Fig.1) in determining the hierarchy of the services has been used. Under this the services have been arranged in the increasing order.

The services of each settlement have been recorded for obtaining the functional score. For example the functional score of different services of Bicholi Mardana is exhibited in Table-V.

TABLE V. FUNCTIONAL SCORE OF BICHOLI MARDANA

Settlement	Available Services	Comparative score
Bicholi Mardana	Primary School	1.00
	Middle School	1.19
	Veterinary Hospital	3.02
	Gram Panchayat	1.25
	Post Office	1.49
	Co-operative Bank	3.28
	Pucca Road	1.25
	Bus stand	1.74
	Total	14.22

Thus the functional score of the services in Bicholi Mardana is 14.22. A semi-log graph has been prepared to indicate the hierarchy of the services. On the basis of this graph the settlements have been classified into five groups (Fig.2).

Group I: Under this group settlements which have a functional score of more than 800 have been included. The number of such settlements is only.

Group II: Under this group settlements which have a functional score between 200 to 800 have been included. In the present work no settlement has been included under this group.

Group III: Under this group such settlements have been taken which have a functional score between 100 to 200. There are three such settlements.

Group IV: Under this group those settlements are included which have a functional score between 20 to 100. There are 29 such settlements in the present study.

Group V: Under this group settlements having a functional score between 1 to 20 are included. Their number is 82 in the study region.

A semi-log graph has been prepared for settlement hierarchy on the basis of the functional score and the population of the settlements (Fig.2). According to this semi-log graph the following classification of the settlements has been made (Table-VI).

TABLE VI : CLASSIFICATION OF THE SERVICE CENTRES OF INDORE DISTRICT

Sl. No.	Functional Score		Number
1.	Below 20	Central village	82
2.	20 - 100	Service Centres	29
3.	100 - 200	Market Centres	03
4.	200 - 800	Growth points	-
5.	Above 800	Growth centres	01

All 115 settlements of Indore district are listed below according to their hierarchical grade -

Growth Centre : Indore

Market Centres : (1) Mhos, (2) Depalpur, (3) Sanwar.

Service Centres : (1) Rau, (2) Manglia, (3) Manpur, (4) Gautampura, (5) Betma, (6) Hatod, (7) Budhaniyapanth, (8) Barlai Sagor, (9) Budhi Barlai, (10) Tillor Khurd, (11) Harsola, (12) Kampel, (13) Choral, (14) Khudel Bujurg, (15) Simrol, (16) Ajnod, (17) Datoda, (18) Dakachya, (19) Solsinda, (20) Hasalpur, (21) Khurdi, (22) Bahirampur, (23) Kudana, (24) Kanadia, (25)

Rangwasa, (26) Kodariya, (27) Girota, (28) Gwali Palasia, (29) Bhatkhedi.

Central Villages : (1) Ataheda, (2) Guran, (3) Palia Haidar, (4) Rala Mandal, (5) Gokalpur, (6) Rangwasa Khurd, (7) Dudhiya, (8) Dannad, (9) Jamli, (10) Palda, (11) Badgonda, (12) Bicholi Mardana, (13) Umariya Khurd, (14) Men, (15) Chhadoda, (16) Joshi Gurania, (17) Ambachandan, (18) Potlod, (19) Kachhalia, (20) Pigdamber, (21) Umriya, (22) Bisnawada, (23) Neori, (24) Kelod, (25) Machal, (26) Samlya Chau, (27) Kadwat Khurd, (28)

FIG. 23.2

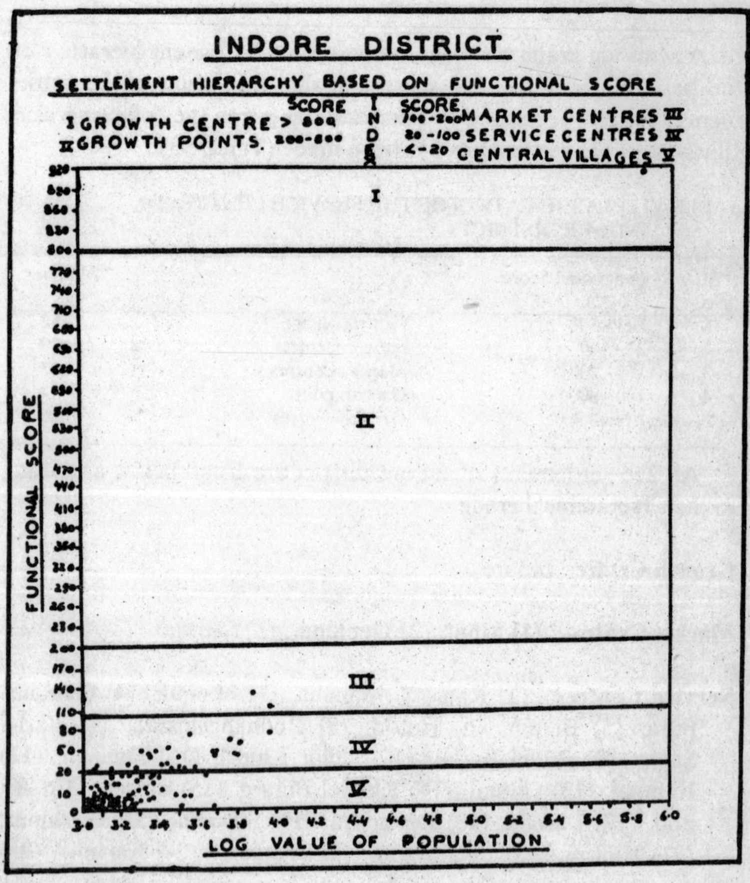

Kankriya Pal, (29) Talawali ?Chanda, (30) Sanawadiya, (31) Piwdai, (32) Piplda, (33) Murkheda, (34) Kamalpura, (35) Jamburdi Hapsi, (36) Bawdhiya Khurd, (37) Banedia, (38) Badodia Khan, (39) Chander, (40) Darmat, (41) Tillor Bujurg, (42) Bicholi Hapsi, (43) Sagdod, (44) Nagpur, (45) Kelod Kartal, (46) Daulatabad, (47) Yeshwant Nagar, (48) Tihi, (49) Kali Billod, (50) Chordia, (51) Arrangpura, (52) Lasudia Mori, (53) Bank, (54) Chota Bangarda, (55) Badhana, (56) Kadwali Bujurg, (57) Bhil Badoli, (58) Sinhasa, (59) Pedmi, (60) Nenod, (61) Kaji Palasiya, (62) Jalodia Gyan, (63) Sunala, (64) Morod, (65) Dharawala, (66) Sonvay, (67) Methwada, (68) Palasia, (69) Kalmer, (70) Darji Karadia, (71) Memand, (72) Neo Guradia, (73) Nihalpur Mandi, (74) Mudla Nayata, (75) Asrawad Khurd, (76) Shiwani, (77) Chandan Khedi, (78) Bada Bangarda, (79) Puwarda Dai, (80) Farkoda, (81) Kankriya, (82) Talawali.

Thus, Indore is the only growth centre in the present study where all higher order services are available (Fig.3). People from far off areas visit Indore for their higher order services. The functional score of Indore is 899.69. In the hierarchical order, the settlements included are Mhow, Depalpur and Sanwer, whose functional score is less than 200. A large gap of 700 may be noted between two successive grades of hierarchy.

Now the three groups of the services of the study area may be explained as given in Table-VII.

TABLE VII. RANKING OF THE SERVICES.

Lower Order Services	Middle Order Services	Higher Order Services
Primary School	Family Planning Centre	Police station
Middle School	Primary Health Centre	Block Headquarters
Gram Panchayat	Post & Telegraph	Tahsil Headquarters
Pucca Road	Railway Station	College/Technical
Post Office	Police Chowki	University
Bus Stand	Telephone	Medical Research Centre
Veterinary Hospital		Head Post Office
Cooperative Bank		District Headquarters
Commercial Bank		Commissionary Headquarters
Sub-Health Centre		Aerodrome
Higher Secondary School		
Weekly Market.		

FIG. 23.3

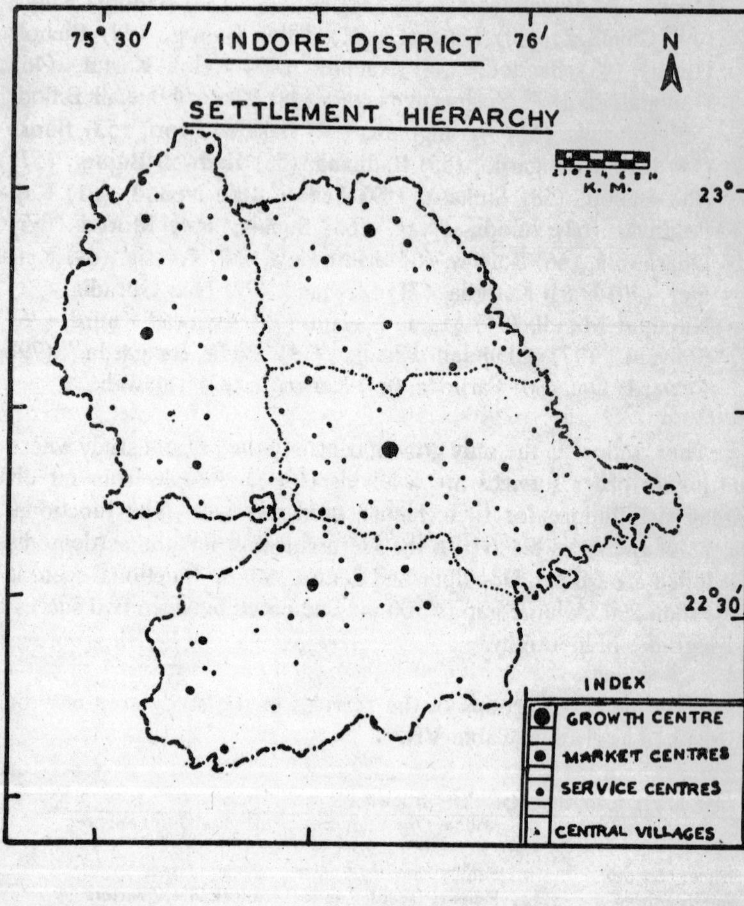

Conclusion

From the above study it is obvious that in the area of study, Indore is the only growth centre, having a number of services. If the growth rate remains the same, Indore will attract many more facilities to become a giant urban centre. The surrounding parts of Indore will never be benefitted and there will be a marked disparity in the economic development of Indore and its surroundings.

TWENTY FOUR

H. Lal and
H.R. Yadav

Development of Commercial Activities in Gorakhpur City

Introduction

Gorakhpur, the divisional headquarters and symbolically the regional capital of the SaryuparPlain, is situated at the confluence of rivers Rapti and Rohin at 26° 45' N lat. and 83° 22' E long. in the northeastern part of Utter Pradesh in India. It is about 270 Km north-east of lucknow, the State Capital and 210 Km north of Varanasi. If a straight line is drawn between Kathmandu and Varanasi, the city lies in between Its connection with Nepal is through Sonauli (102 Km.) to the north. The average height of the city is 120 m. A.S.L. .Constant shifting of the Rapti has shaped the internal structure of the city in different stages. Presently, the city is bound by the Ajawania Nala (Rohin) to the west and by Rapti river (which touches its southern corner) to the south. Further, Ramgarh Tal dominates the physical landscape to the southern side. Kusumhi Forest marks its eastern extremity. Part of its northern frontier is marked by Chilua Tal formed by river Rohin. Floods have also been significant in shaping the morphology of Gorakhpur. It is only with the help of embankments in the western and southern parts that the city could be saved to some extent from the floods. Some of the localities are still in-undated during the rains as they are sufficiently at a low elevation. Situated as it is near Nepal (an inland country which needs outlet) and the Tarai region of the Himalayas on the one hand and the densely populated agricultural tract of the middle Ganga Plain on the other, it serves as a natural gateway to the

Nepalian and *Tarai* goods to the plains in the south and south east. Moreover, it enjoyed for a long time the locational advantage of being located on an inland water route - the Rapti, through which it had a direct connection with Calcutta. Hence its situation is endowed with potential nodality which made large traffic flow possible to and from the city.

The convergence of several routes from the surrounding fertile land helped in providing the basic needs of the city and it has also affected the general layout of the city. Till the advent of the railway line, Rapti was an important waterway for the transport of men and material and hence had a significant bearing on the city's growth as a centre of trade. But at present due to the railways and roadways, the riverborne trade has greatly declined.

This paper studies the evolution and spatio-temporal aspects of the business or commercial activities of the city of Gorakhpur

Historical Evolution of Commercial Activities[1]

The old city was situated north of the present railway line. From the time of the first settlement around the nucleus of the Gorakhnath Temple until the close of the eighteenth century, Gorakhpur passed through a more or less similar phase of development. Under the *Nawabs* of *Avadh* this city remained a military centre and as such, it afforded protection to the traders and the merchants. Hence the city also developed the function of trade and commerce which gradually made it an important business centre of the *Saryupar* Plain. During this period Gorakhpur had two important market centres. As the city was divided into two physical parts by the central water course, one market on either side was developed. These markets were :-

i) The *Urdu Bazar* or the *Chowk,* was situated near the fort, south of the then water course. Being the main market place, it was the focus of main routes linking different parts of the southern city.
ii) The *Alinagar Bazar* was situated north of the water course. This was also the focus of the main routes connecting different parts of the northern parts of the city.

There were seven grain markets scattered in different parts of the city and forming the nuclei of different business areas. There was one cloth market at Captainganj Mohalla. The preponderance of grain markets indicates the agricultural character of the surrounding areas. Most of them were either street markets or were held in closed compounds (*Ahatas*).

By the middle of the nineteenth century its nodality was fairly well established and it helped Gorakhpur in serving as a pivot for the entire trade of the *Saryupar Plain* including the bordering districts of Bihar and Nepal. A considerable trade in cloth, sugar and salt had grown up and export trade in food-grains had also increased.

The introduction of the railways in 1885 brought the modern phase of development of the city. Most of the railway lines connecting Gorakhpur with other important centres of U.P. and Bihar were completed during the first quarter of the present century. The city became the headquarters of the Oudh Tirhut Railways (O.T.Rly.) and regional roadways transport centre by the time of the Independence. In this way the cultural and commercial contact of the city with the *Saryupar* plain and other adjacent towns increased considerable due to the railways and the roadways.

After the Independence

After the Independence the city has made great stride. The selection of Gorakhpur as the headquarters of N.E.Railways has added multidimensional development to the commercial activities of the city. Further, several industries including a major fertilizer factory have been established. The old ones have expanded considerably giving the city an industrial look. Locomotive workshop of the railways and textiles - powerloom form the next important industries in the city. It may be noted that handloom weaving has been an old industry of this city. The handloom products are famous as they use better designs and are of good quality. At present there are more than ten thousand handlooms and several small powerlooms are also operating here. Among other industries the noted ones are engineering, paper-printing, soft drinks, tobacco, chemicals and dyes, glass-work and ice factories etc. Medium sized industries have sprang-up in the industrial estate in the north on Pipiganj and some in the east on Deoria-road. Gradually Gorakhpur is getting industrially mcre importance also.

So far as the educational functions are concerned, the city has grown considerably. It has an University, an Engineering College, a Medical College alongwith scores of degree colleges and industrial technical institutes within its limit.

Thus Gorakhpur performs many industrial and educational functions and has shown a sharp increase in its population during the recent past. The decade 1961-71 had marked increase of 28.1%. While in last decade the population growth was about 25.3%. The commercial hubs of the medieval period *Urdu* Bazar and Alinagar have now been linked with each other by a series of commercial establishments and new centres like Golghar etc. have sprang up recently.

The area covered by commercial establishments in the city was only 35 ha in 1961 (only 1.2% of the developed land). In 1971 it became 9.2% (36 ha) of the total area of the town. (Fig-1) A field survey conducted in 1985 reveals that more than 18% of the total area of the city was under this category of landuse. It may thus be seen that the area covered by this land use has just doubled within last one and a half decade.

The area covered by commercial establishments in the city was only 35 ha in 1961 (only 1.2% of the developed land). In 1971 it became 9.2% (36 ha) of the total area of the town. (Fig-1) A field survey conducted in 1985 reveals that more than 18% of the total area of the city was under this category of landuse. It may thus be seen that the area covered by this land use has just doubled within last one and a half decade.

According to Table-I, 18.39% of total workers were engaged in trade and commerce in 1971. In Turkmanpur, persons engaged in this category was the highest (1179 persons) while in Jatepur it was the lowest (only 158 persons). Rahmatnagar, Maya Bazar, Urdu Bazar and Railway Colony had more than 1000 persons engaged in trade and commerce.

FIG. 24.1

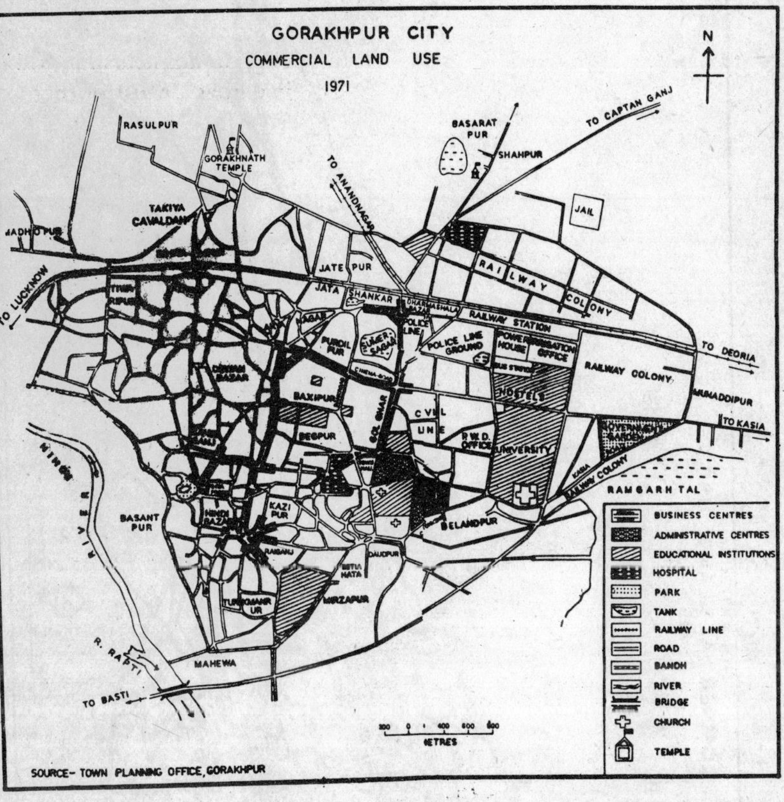

The density of persons engaged in trade and commerce was highest in the Urdu Bazar (1252 persons km^2) and lowest in Jatepur (67 km^2). Average density for the whole town was 288 /km^2.

The existing Commercial Structure

The existing commercial structure has been depicted through field work. Each retail establishment was plotted individually and symbolically on a large scale road map of Gorakhpur. Accordingly thirty three shopping centres have been marked on the map (Fig.2 & Table-II)

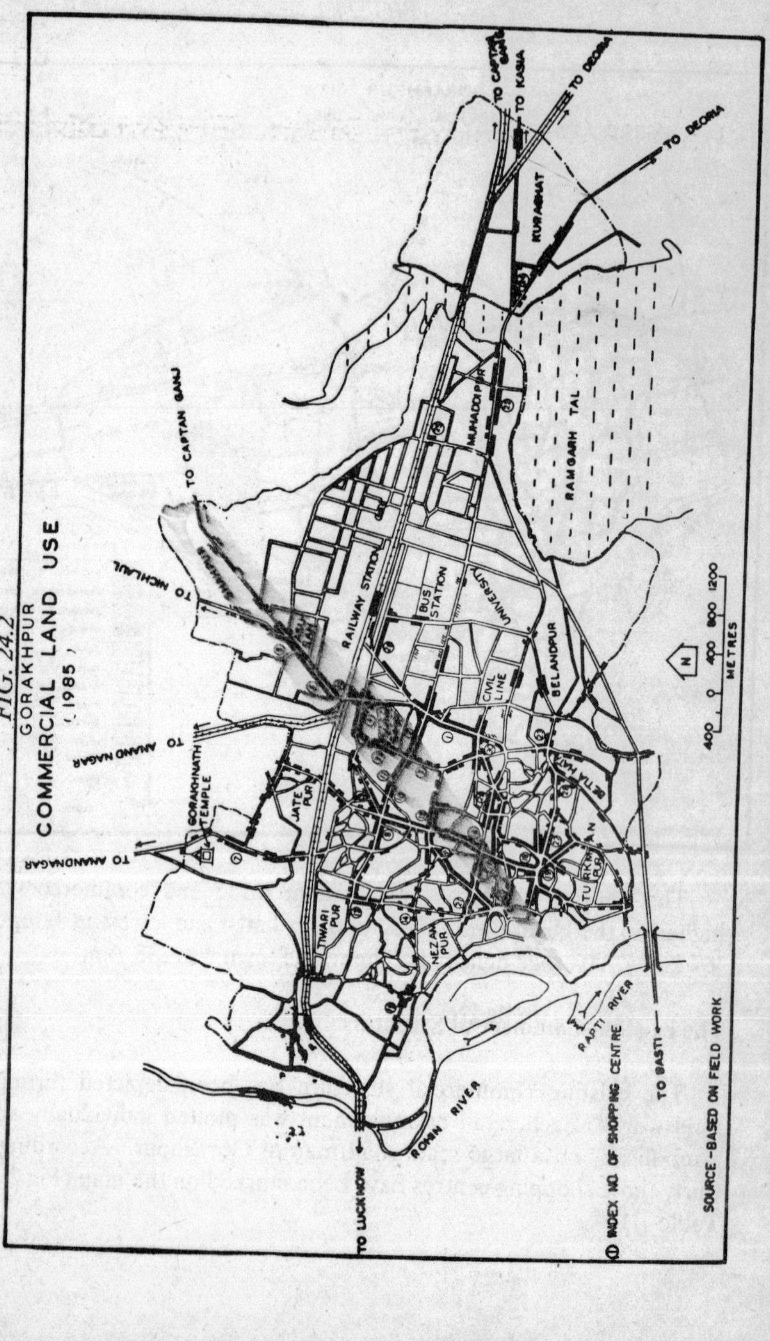

FIG. 24.2
GORAKHPUR
COMMERCIAL LAND USE
(1985)

Out of the 8166 establishments in the city, 6466 (79.2%) are concentrated in the thirty three commercial centres and the rest of the units are distributed in other parts of the city and along diffeıent roads in a scattered form. They do not form any compact-belt or nucleus of business.

Table I : TRADE AMD COMMERCIAL ACTIVITIES IN GORAKHPUR BY WARDS (1971)

Wards	Area Km^2	Total workers		Trade &Commerce		Commerial Area Km^2
		No.	Density/km^2	No.	Density/km^2	
1.	5.21	5217	1001	546	105	0.013
2.	2.06	3884	1885	605	294	0.013
3.	1.08	4002	3705	1075	995	0.03
4.	1.17	4437	3792	874	747	0.005
5.	0.98	2198	2242	529	540	0.028
6.	2.03	4043	1992	1002	494	0.041
7.	0.93	1882	2024	476	512	0.004
8.	1.55	2142	1382	569	367	0.0113
9.	0.94	3139	3339	1177	1252	0.039
10.	1.47	4246	2888	1179	802	0.0062
11.	1.08	4064	3763	769	712	0.007
12.	4.34	6828	1573	1038	239	0.041
13.	2.35	6852	2916	158	67	0.0318
14.	5.23	4000	765	528	101	0.0041
15.	8.43	4000	474	685	81	0.0799
City	38.85	60934	1568	11210	288	0.357

Source: Calculated on the basis of cenus data and records of Town and Country Planning Deptt. Gorakhpur.

It is obvious from Table- I that different retail centres are characterized by a large variation in the number of shopping unite as well as in the number of retail functions (Table - II). However, it is important to note that while a large number of functions are present in almost all larger markets, their intensity greatly varies.

The survey reveals that the maximum number of shops, i.e. 440, is found in Golghar market and the minimum is in *Ghasi katra* (28). There are only three markets - Golghar, Buxipur and Sahabganj, where number of shops is more than 400. Number of shops ranging between 200 - 400 are found in Dharmshala, Urdu Bazar, Maya Bazar, Kundraghat, Station Road, Alinagar, Gorakhnath road, Asuran Chowk, Pandey Hata, Cinema road and Mohaddipur. Remaining eighteen shopping centres have the concentration of less than 200 shops.

Table II : RETAIL CENTRES IDENTIFIED IN GORAKHPUR AND THEIR CHARACTERISTICS

S. No.	Name of Retail centre	Number of shops.	No. of functional types	Area in m^2	Area per shops m^2	% units in the city total
1.	Golghar	440	37	713.47	1.62	5.4
2.	Cinema Road	225	34	334.44	1.48	2.8
3.	Bank Road	117	24	100.33	0.83	1.4
4.	Dharmashala	385	43	312.14	0.76	4.7
5.	Asuranchauk	251	34	367.88	0.55	3.1
6.	Engineering Gate	178	16	156.07	0.84	2.2
7.	Gorakhnath Road	278	33	334.44	1.21	3.4
8.	Alinagar	289	30	289.84	1.02	3.5
9.	Hazaripur	109	25	211.81	1.85	1.3
10.	Dilezakpur	76	22	100.33	1.30	0.9
11.	Purdilpur	32	16	66.88	2.04	0.4
12.	Baxipur	417	40	535.10	1.30	5.1
13.	Zafra Bazar	148	29	278.7	1.86	1.8
14.	Ghasi Katra	28	13	66.88	2.41	0.3
15.	Ilahibag	54	19	211.81	3.91	0.7
16.	Nakhas chauk	138	31	412.47	2.97	1.7
17.	Retichauk	187	31	390.18	2.06	2.3
18.	Urdu Bazar	374	37	724.62	1.85	4.6
19.	Pandey Hata	251	18	278.7	1.11	3.1
20.	Gita Press	97	18	200.66	2.04	1.2
21.	Sahebganj	424	25	713.47	1.67	5.2
22.	Mohaddipur	204	34	401.32	1.86	2.5
23.	Betia Hata	111	16	200.66	1.78	1.4
24.	Kundraghat	301	33	390.18	1.30	3.7
25.	Charphatak	144	21	39.0	0.28	1.8
26.	Station Road	296	26	133.77	0.46	3.6
27.	Raiganj	79	21	167.22	2.13	0.9
28.	Alahdadpur	92	27	189.51	2.04	1.1
29.	Maya Bazar	319	40	624.28	1.85	3.9
30.	Town Hall	187	30	334.44	1.77	2.3
31.	Chaurahia Gola	32	7	89.18	2.78	0.4
32.	Dharmshala Vegetable market	102	6	33.44	0.32	1.3
33.	Sumer Sagar Road	101	25	167.22	1.67	1.2
	Rest of Gorakhpur	1700	53	1594.16	0.92	20.8
	Gorakhpur	8166	53	11164.72		100.0

Source: Personal survey by H.R.Yadav, in 1984-85.

So far as functional types are concerned Dharmshala stands first with 43 types of shops while Golghar, Urdu Bazar and Maya Bazar consist of more than 35 types of functions each and rank next in order. Minimum number of functions can be seen in Chaurahia Gola, a grain market and Dharmshala vegetable market only.

So far as the area covered by shopping centres is concerned, Golghar, Urdu Bazar and Shahebganj have more than 540 m^2area while Charphatak and Dharmshala vegetable market have minimum coverage. Chaurahiagola, GhasiKatra and Purdilpur have less than 75m^2 to 540m^2 area.

The area of per shops differs from one shopping centre to another. Highest size (3.91m^2) is in Ilahibag and lowest (0.28m^2) is in Charphatak. Shopping centres having large extension and lesser number of shops have bigger size, of shops. On the other hand those centres with minimum extension but having more shops have smaller size of shops (tableII).

The distribution of shops dealing with food materials is common to all markets. There are specialized markets which deal with almost exclusively in these goods. The wholesale and retail function of cereals and pulses is highly concentrated in Shahabganj (49.52%), and Chaurahia Gola (84.4%)in south-western part of the city. Shahebganj (24%), Betiahata Crossing (52.2%) Charphatak (51.4%,) Dharmshala (52%) are famous for vegetables. Wholesale and retail both activities are found in Shahabganj Subzi *mandi* but others are related to retailing only. On *Thawai-ka-pul* shops of meat and fish are found. Same is the case of Dharmshala avegetable market also. It is remarkable that the wholesale function includes retail transaction also. The purely retail shops in food articles are more equitably distributed. Some grocers can be seen in every market.

Pandeyhata is famous for textiles (53.8%) in the south western part of the city. Here retail and wholesale both the functions are found. Although, handloom clothes are sold in Gorakhnath, Golghar, Urdu Bazar but Geeta Press Road is the leading centre (40.2%) and Golghar (15,2%) are specialized markets.

Shops dealing in general merchandize are found all over the city but the \Urdu Bazar (12.8%) is the leading market followed by Golghar (5.7%). On the otherhand, engineering works and automobile repairs (15.2%) are concentrated on station road. Other large concentration of different specialized goods are jewellery in Urdu Bazar (17,9%), Medicine in Townhall (21.4%)and Bhalotia Market (60%). Buxipur specializes in books and stationeries (12.4%).

Conclusion

Thus the retail structure of Gorakhpur has developed gradually and systemetically. In 1971 commercial activities were limited to Sahebganj, Urdu Bazar, Alinagar, Retti and Nakhas Chowk, Cinema Road, Dharmshala and Golghar-townhall only. But after about one and a half decades the pattern has become different. Commercial activities expanded throughout all the existing shopping centres. Due to this, some new shopping concentrations have emerged. These are Asuran Chauk, Gorakhnath Road Bank, Road, Maya Bazar, Betia hata etc. The development of the commercial activities in Gorakhpur city has maintained a continuity along with the development of the city. It shows a linear development along both or one side of the road. Further, it will serve as an important service centre to the rich agricultural region of the *Tarai* area of U.P. and Bihar and more so of Nepal also.

NOTE

1. Based on District Gazetteers, Gorakhpur.

TWENTY FIVE

V.N. Lal

Commercial Activities in a Small Town: A Case Study of Bachhrawan Town in Uttar Pradesh

The paper discusses the role of commercial activities in the morphology of Bachhrawan Town Area of Rai Bareli District of Uttar Pradesh, India.

Study Area

Bachhrawan town lies (26° 28' N. Latitude and 81° 7'; E' longitude) in Rai Bareli District of Uttar Pradesh. It is located 32 Kms. away from its district headquarter and 50 Km. away from State's capital, Lucknow. More or less the study area has a mid-way location on Rai Bareli-Lucknow road. It is connected by a railway line as well, which runs parallel to the road. The study area is connected by a pucca road to Mahrajganj (tahsil headquarter) to the south eastern side, with Mauranwan (in district Unnao) of the western side, with Haidargarh to the north-western side and with Gurubakshaganj to the south-western direction. The study area has social amenities like education, health, police station, post and telegraph, electricity, development block headquarters etc. It was declared Town area as late as in 1935.

Agriculture is the basic economy of the surrounding area Paddy and wheat are grown as main crops. Besides these, small millets and barley are also grown.

Bachhrawan is a morning market. Market hours are spread between 8.00 A.M. to 6 P.M. Surrounding markets in the neighbouring area open in the afternoon on their respective market days. This is the main reason which attracts the people to visit Bachhrawan for commercial needs. 'Khanakharia' (multi purpose horse driven vehicle) are the main means of transportation of the rural people. Few buses are also available but they are not used for regular business trips.

Methodology

The present paper is based on primary and secondary sources of data. Field survey was conducted to collect data for the number of type of shops, their openings, structure etc. Market visitors were interviewed on market days in July, 1985.

Spatio-Temporal Location

Bachhrawan is a daily-cum-periodic market, the periodic market being held on Tuesday and Friday. Its market days are sychronised with Rani khera (Wednesday and Saturday) to the north, Thureni (Tuesday and Sunday) to the south-east, kundanganj (Wednesday and Saturday, the south west, Rampur Sudauli (Tuesday and Saturday) to north west and Sahrgon (Thursday and Sunday) to north. All these surrounding markets are located within a radius of about 10 km. from this market but for Sahngo market, which is nearly 20 km. away from Bachhrawan.

Commercial Morphology and Structure

Towns are shaped by institutions of different types such as social, economic, governmental, religious and cultural etc. These are associated with various types of landuses and with the complex intra-city flow of goods and people which make up the spatial organisation of urban morphology (Davis 1972,pp 59-82)

The town's commercial morphology covers the area of main market and other marketing sub-centres which more of less perform commercial activities.It may be noted that the expansion of commercial area is not only the result of the demand of neighbourhood population but also a result of low land values (Singh & Lal, 1983,

.pp 1-25).

Bachhrawan is a square shaped market place. The commercial activities are concentrated in the south-western portion of the study area specially on the both sides of roads. It is interesting to note that governmental offices, police-station, educational institutions and medical dispensary are located close to the commercial area mainly on Lucknow-Rai Bareli road. Residential areas are found mostly to the north eastern part of the bachhrawan town. Bus stand is located on the Lucknow road in western side. Extreme western and eastern parts are devoted to agricultural land use.

The bachhrawan commercial area has been divided into four subdivisions which are are follows:-

1. North market & Kuti
2. Bandh Tola
3. Uttar & Dakshin Bazar
4. Lucknow road side market

There are a total number of 528 shops in the study area. Of these, 70% consist of durable goods and rest constitute service type of shops. The durable goods consist of cloth, kirana, foodgrains, general stores, jewellery, machinery etc. Out of 528 shops 52 shops sell cloth whereas 30 sell medicines, 28 jewellery, etc. Among the service shops, pan (betel leaves) shops top the list (44) followed by 29 shops of tailors, 23 shops of confectionaries, 22 units of cobbers and 15 units of hair cutting saloon. It is interesting to note that most service shops are held on open ground i.e. cobblers, hair cutting saloon, cycle repairing etc. Gumti type of wooden structured shops can be usually seen in the study area which occupy either side of the road. It exhibits increasing demand for business land use of the area.

More than one third of the total shops are centralised in the north market area whereas 'Uttar' & 'Dakshin' Bazar and Lucknow road side markets area combined possess nearly half of the total shops of the study area. This forms the main commercial area of Bachhrawan.

The commercial nodes may be described separately as follows:

Table I : STRUCTURE OF SHOPS IN BACHHRAWAN 1985

S.No.	Sub division of Commercial centre	Number of shops
1.	North Market & Kuti	207
2.	Bandh Tola	35
3.	Uttar Dakshin Bazar	126
4.	Lucknow road side market	125
5.	Others	35
	Total	528

1. **North Market & Kuti**

This is the main commercial area of Bachhrawan. It is worthy of note that nearly half of the total number of shops of cloth, iron, tailoring and machinery of the study area are centralised in this commercial node (Table-1). It constitutes nearly 30% of the total shops at the study area. Table-2 reveals that nearly every type of shops are found here. Cloth shops are more numerous than any other type of shops. It may be noted that nearly 8% of all the tailoring units are attached to the cloth shops which is very natural, shops like parchun, general store and jewellery are also in a large number in the area.

2. **Bandh Tola :**

This is the eastern extension of the north market area where 35shops (table-1)are found. There are specialised type of shops in this tola. More or less nearly every type of shops can be seen here, cycles, dispensary, iron, parchun shops are mostly noted. Service type of shops predominate in this area.

3. **Uttar & Dakshin Bazar**

There are 126 business establishement in this zone. These constitute nearly 24%of the total business establishment at the study area. Nearly 50% business of parchun is controlled by this sub-commercial area. Cloth, parchun, general store and jewellery business are taking place. In addition this area commands nearly 1/3 business of cloth, kirana and general stores. This is the potential area of the commercial uses.

4. **Lucknow road-side market**

This is the best located commercial zone being located on the main road runs from Rai Bareli to Lucknow. The shops have proliferated in this area due to the location of educational facilities, bus stops, offices etc. During the market day, the road side area is encroached by temporary shops/businessmen which creates traffic jam during peak market hours. Nearly 125 additional shops are visible during market day. Medical stores also centralized here (Table-I). Specialized services like hotels, restaurants etc. are also found. They serve the needs of outside visitors.

Consumer frequency

It may be noted that the study area is visited by 1500-2000 persons each day. However, on market days, the number swells up to 2500-3500 persons. The marketing hours are confined from 8.00 A.M. to 6.30 P.M. This is the only market which is open on all the week days in general and on the market day in particular. The surrounding rural markets open in afternoon hours on their respective market days. Cycles and 'Kharkharia' are the means of rural transportation. Nearly 650 cycles and 85 'Kharkharia' have been noted on the market days.

On the market day nearly 80% visitors come here for commercial purposes and the rest come for other reasons. Most of the consumers (70%) prefer to visit the study area because of the availability of goods and services at cheaper rates.

Commercial Mechanism

Bachhrawan is the only commercial centre between Rai Bareli and Lucknow which are the main supply centres for the neighbourhood market centres area. Ranikhera, Thureni, Kundanganj, Pashchim gaon, Rajaman, Rampur sudauli and Sahango periodic markets depend on Bachhrawan market for collection of goods and services. Thus Bachhrawan is the main supplier of goods and services to the surrounding sub commercial centres. Whole-sale commission agents (Arhatias) operate in this area. They have specialised in whole-sale and 'Semi-whole sale' trade and effect to the commercial activities. Octroi Tax system also prevails in the study area.

Catchment Area

The catchment area of the particular goods and services are different, i.e. jewellery pirchasers come nearly 20 to 25 km. away from the study area. Consumers of cloth, Kirana, Kerosene oil, usually come with in the radius of 7-12 km. from the Bachhrawan market. In this way the range of goods and services are quite different from each other. In general the tentative limit of catchment area of this commercial centre is within a radius of about 15 km. The tentative limits are Nigoha in the west, Hydergarh in the north Parirakala in the north-east, Pahnasa in the east, Kundanganj in the south and Pashchimgaon in the north.

TABAL II : AREA AND POPULATION SERVED, 1971

Radius km.	No. of Village	Area km	Population (000)
0 to 4	17	73.10	24.90
4 to 8	33	134.24	33.91
8 to 12	52	196.30	53.00
Total	102	403.65	111.81

Bachhrawan market serves about 102 villages in an area of 404 km.^{2} (Table -II) The effective market area covers a radius of 12km.

Conclusion

It is concluded that Bachhrawan market has a nodal location on the road which runs from Rail Bareli to Lucknow. The absence of other markets has made it more important. It supplies the goods and services to the population of the surrounding rural area. Wholesaling has also developed in this market along with retailing. The merchants of this market visit Lucknow for their supply of goods and commodities.

The future propects of this town are good. It can develop as a whole-sale commercial market because it is located in a region where others markets are absent. This town are good. It can develop as a whole-sale commercial market because it is located in a region where others markets are absent. This is the only market which opens all over day on the market days and the other surrounding sub-market open for half day in the afternoon.

TWENTY SIX

S.C. Bansal

Market Activities and Morphology of a Periodic Market Centre - A Case Study of Chutmalpur of District Saharanpur

Periodic market centres play an important role in the growth, development and planning of rural economy. It is the main focal point for commercial activities of most peasant societies, and it retains considerable importance for the trade of specialized products in many of the most advanced economies. In addition to that it plays an important socio-economic role. Market place trade is frequently linked with other forms of commerce.

Chutmalpur is a small medium-size village of Saharanpur District. It is lies on 29° 53' N latitude and 77° 47' E longtitude. It is situated at a distance of 23 km. north-east of Saharanpur City 23 Km north-west of Roorkee Town and 12 km. south of Beharigarh. It functions as a great thoroughfare and controls the road traffic between the plains and the hills. Despite the natural barrier of the Bhabar tract, Chhutmalpur has made tremendous progress in trade and commercial activities with the introduction of transport facilities.

Origin and Evolution

This market came into existance during the 1940-50 decade when a few cattle herders came here and settled. After the Independence it was inhabited by refugees from Pakistan. With the introduction of bus services on this route, this village attracted the concentration of shops. After sometimes a weekly market became a regular feature of every Sunday. Within a span of only thirty years this centre has become a leading weekly market of the district. It has become an entrepot of agricultural and forest products. It has shown a rapid increase in population since the 1951. Nearly 2350 persons have been added in its population during the last three decades. It has a sub-post office, telephone office, telegraph centre, two banks, one picture hall, bus depot and an Inter college etc.

Chhutmalpur is one of the the leading periodic markets of the district. It is held on every Sunday. It has both retail and wholesale dealings. It has 372 permanent establishments dealing in various commodities, Nearly 48.9% of the establishments provide services. All these shops are located along the triangle formed by Dehra Dun Saharanpur Roorkee roads. Saharanpur Road is exerting more influence on the development of trade activities. Dehradun road has attracted industrial goods. This area supplies raw materials like wood to 18 saw mills of this road. Shops dealing in general merchandise, parchun. tea, fruit, betel, hotel, agricultural implements are in good number. This centre has six petrol pumps, giving evidence of its importance as a junction of roads. Service establishments are 154 in number which provide bicycle and car repair, medical, hair dressing, radio and watch repair, blacksmith services etc. especially to the residents of neighbouring villages. The presence of these shops at this village confirms the fact presence of these shops at this trade centre.

It is observed that there is much development of trade and commerce along the Saharanpur and Dehra Dun Roads, Saharanpur Road is getting more incentive, because of its link with Saharanpur, a district headquarter. Dehradun Road has specialised in shops dealing mainly with forest products

Market Morphology

Chhutmalpur's morphology resembles the C.B.D. of towns. It has the concentration of vegetable shops on a vast ground located on the western side of Saharnpur road. Food grains shops are found predominantly at the exit/entry points of all main roads leading to the periodic market area. Shops dealing in spices are concentrated mainly on the road surrounding the bus stand.Cloth shops are aggregated on the western margins of Saharnpur road. The development of such aggregations seems to be affected by the following fac-

tors:
(i) The nature of sale goods, (ii) the source of supply area of the commodity, (iii) the value of articles sold by these shops, (iv) the space needed by the shops (v) the accessibility of the shops in reference to means of transport, and (vi) the demand of the commodity.

i. Service units like those of cobbler. blacksmith, carpenter, hair dresser are found in the central part of the market. Shops dealing in kirana spices or in other non-agricultural commodities are found mostly in the interior part of the market area.

ii. The roadside shops reveal affonity to the area to which they are directly connected, Dehradun road in Chhutmalpur market has the concentration of establishments related to the processing of wood as this road is directly connected with the wood producing villages of Bhabar and Shiwalik regions.

iii. If the comodity is valuable and needs less space, then the shops of such commodity ate concentrated in the central part of the market. The jewellery shops have shown such type of development Shrivsastava. V.K. 1983).

iv. Certain commodities require more space, so the shops dealing in such commodities are generally concentrated in either in open spaces or on the outskirts of the periodic market space. vegetable, Gur, Khandsari shops come in this category.

v. The mode of transport also affects the location of shops in the periodic market. Shops dealing in bulky materials are generally concentrated on the fringe area directly connected to the supply areas. vegetables, food grains, wood timber are generally brought by bullock carts and trucks from villages and are located at the periphery of market area.

Chhutmalpur market helds nearly 880 shops on market days. Shops remain open from morning to evening (Table I).

TABLE I : NO. & TYPE OF SHOPS

Type of Shops	No.		
(a) Agricultural products shops	246		
i. Fruit had vegetables	125		
ii. Foodgrains	96		
iii. Ground nuts	22		
iv. Others	03		
(b) Service shops	88	(c) Consumer shops	266
Shoe repair	59	cloth	125
Gold smith	12	Kirana	102
Tailor,Hair dress	17	Utensils	11
washerman etc.		Books/stationery	28
(d) Industrial shops	81	(e) Luxury & other	
Fresh products, wood	22	goods shops	199
Bank shoe shop	35	Tobacco spices	146
others	24	Betel, Supari	
		(Betelnut) others	37
Total shops = 880			

This study reveals that Chhutmalpur is a growing periodic market of the area. The nature of goods shown that this market serves the surrounding area as a central place. Its strengthening will contribute to the development of its dependent area.

Theme III

Rural - Urban Linkages and Development

TWENTY SEVEN

Agnes K.Musyaki and
R.A. Obudho

The Role of Periodic Market Systems in Spatial Development: A Case Study of Machakos District, Kenya

Machakos District of Kenya is one of the forty four regions that the kenya government has decided to make as major planning unit. This is in order to discourage centralized planning and encourage planning at the grass roots. Machakos District has long been know as one of the problem districts. In every two years out of ten, a major drought and a lack of adequate food supply has plagued this area. Government efforts to eradicate this problem include projects that geared high food production. However, in order to see that these efforts to benefit the rural residents, an efficient food distribution system is vital. A system organised around the already important channel for food distribution - the rural periodic markets, would benefit the majority of the people.

This paper therefore, analyses the contemporary rural periodic marketing system in Machakos District, Kenya. A hierarchy of the market system is identified and a methodology developed based on field data collected over a period of two years, 1982-1983. Six variables are considered and the sum of their Z-scores constitute an index of market importance. The variables analysed include (a) population density, (b) market turnover, (c) agricultural potential, (d) accessibility, (e) size of town, and (f) the size of stalls at the market.Based on this information a four level hierarchy of the 45 identified markets is identified. This hierarchy is different from the government documented hierarchy of settlements. The market ring is also analyzed since it affects food distribution. The spatio-temporal integration of the markets is also studied. The overall pattern of market distribution is compared to the population distribution.

This is followed by the analysis of the actual movement of foodstuffs - only maize, beans, pigeon peas, fruits and vegetables. Some of the ideas in Alan Hay and R.H.T. Smith's theory of "Internal Trade" will be tested to the case of Machakos. Machakos District markets play a great role in both internal and local trade. The internal trade model identifies two main processes. Firstly, is the bulking process which involves the accumulation, starting with the rural producer of a small quantity of foodstuffs until the consignment size is too large for any further accumulation. At this point an exchange takes place which is accompanied by a change in the size of the consignments. The second is the bulk-breaking or distribution process. This process begins with the limiting consigments being broken down into smaller and smaller parts until the consumer is finally reached. An increase in the units and values at various stages of the processes show certain intrinsic features of the economy of Machakos District and those of developing countries in general. Possible solutions to the problems resulting from this study are explored and discussed.The main problem to be solved being how to use the best spatial structure of the rural periodic marketing system to provide everybody in the district with adequate food supplies all the time so that death and malnutrition is wiped out from this district. A concept of spatial closure is discussed and given as one way this problem can be solved. Other solutions require the restructuring of the spatial economic structures. The specific questions and which form the basis for this study can be summarized to include the following :-

(a) The contemporary and functional system of markets in Machakos District;

(b) The relationship between the volume of consignments of food and the number of stages involved in the exchange processes from producer to consumer;

(c) The extent to which trade activities and functions are hierarchically arranged; and

(d) Finally, the deficiencies in the flows of information and transportation and market facilities required in order for traders to adjust to difference in supply and demand conditions at the different bulking and distribution points so as to maximize their net returns and minimize net losses.

TWENTY EIGHT

D.K. Singh and
J.K. Routray

Rural Market-Potential as a Measure in Regional Development

Introduction

With the growing consciousness of a unified humanitarian approach to commercial economic activities, the world governments are bound to take measure of narrowing up of the gap between the 'rich urban' and 'poor rural' space organisation in immediate future.

The complex system of man's space organisation of gainful commercial economic activities though has transcended the simple and subsistence village economy system, its production base is predominantly in the countryside. The foundation of the structure of commercial activities is composed of a network of three areal components - (i) production space, (ii)marketing nodes, and (iii) transport and communication links-with the string of dancing these components controlled from a key-board of man-environment relationship and interaction. The rural marketing potential in this concern of human drama of commercial economic activity, so far almost unnoticed, is in fact a strong concept to recon with for assessing the quantum of regional development in order to specify both interregional and intra-regional disparities.

It is with this hypothesis that this paper seeks to spell out the concept of 'rural marketing potential' and then to suggest a space-interaction potential model with a perception component for the two variables of inter-marketing nodal distances and market-mass for the rural marketing process in understanding the magnitude of both inter and intra regional development and disparities. This, it is hoped, may help in indicating the process of developmental gap in space organisation. In order to transfer the subsistence economy of the countryside into a gainful commercial economy (necessary for the regional development) goods must not only be transported from the areas of production to those of consumption, but they also must be transferred from the hands of producers, by collection and subsequent distribution, into the hands of consumers and 'this is the function of marketing' which is a major factor in the changing economic aspect of rural areas (Applebaum, 1954).

The process of regional development

The process of regional development is a complex one. The levels of development achieved by any regional unit is the composite picture of a large number of physical, cultural socio-economic and infrastructural variables. The reflection of the total development is a two way process: sometimes originates from within the regional unit (internal) and sometimes flows from outside (external) but the most logical and common process is the cross product of both. The internal process depends on the available resources endowment and other development potential factors. The development potential component includes population potential (in term of quality and quantity), resource potential (land, mineral, water, forest etc.) and infrastructure potential. The external process which seeks to create development is universalised through industrial, trade and commercial activities. The possibility of getting industrialised to every unit of space is no doubt a difficult task but is contrast to this trade and commercial activities are very common and really important next to agrarian activities in rural areas. Market being the focal point of trade and commercial functions and the point of maximum interaction with the immediate surrounding areas, thus creates scope and provides facilities for the geographic concentration of activities. The geographic concentration further leads to development. The status of market with diversified marketing activities measured in a composite form to reflect the regional personality in terms of development of the immediate region under uniform rural-cum-agrarian set up. The annual volume of transaction in marketing, trade and commercial activities by the service area population can speak about the status of living of those rural population and directly and indirectly expresses the process of *micro rural development*.

There are many statistical techniques available and applied to measure the regional/rural development achieved by different units of space by preparing composite indices of physical, cultural, socio-economic and infrastructure variables. The comparative picture thus tells about the pattern of spatial development. However the alternative approach of measuring development is suggested through marketing potential.

Market Potential Model

Market potential of a market centre can be considered as an index of intensity of possible spatial interaction between producers, consumers and markets. This market potential at a market place 'i' is presented below with the analogy of the demographic potential models as:

$$V_i = \sum_{J=1}^{n} (m_j/d_{ij})$$

Where V_i = the total marketing potential of the i th marketing centre

M_j = mass of the market centre 'j'

d_{ij} = Distance between tow market centres i and j

In this case the mass may be the total income generated at the market place or may be the composite index of the marketing functional activities.

The domestic market potential of any identified market centre as per Hammond and M Cullah (1974) is as follows:

$$M_i = \sum_{j=1}^{n} (P_j a_j / d_{ij})$$

Where M_i = Domestic market potential of centre 'i',

P_j = Population of each market sub region/subzone

a_j = per capita income of the region,

d_{ij} = Distance between centres i and J.

Here the market potential is purely considered on local level and therefore, better known as 'domestic market potential' where the exports are not counted.

In the present statistical set up of our country, the availability of per capita income data at local level (even at the district level) is not at all possible, hence Sharma, Routray and Singh (1984) pp. 45-64) suggested a different mass as compared to Hommond and Mc Cullah. The mass of the market place may be taken in the following two different ways:-

a) Composite index of the marketing function present in the market centre;
b) the product of population and the composite index of the marketing functions.

Mathematically the marketing potential model of Sharma, Routray and Singh is presented below:-

(i) $$M_i = \sum_{j=1}^{n} (C_j / d_{ij})$$

(2) $$M_i = \sum_{j=1}^{n} (C_j P_j / d_{ij})$$

Where M_i = Market potential of the market centre 'i'
C_i = Composite index of marketing activities,
P_j = Population of the j th centre,
d_{ij} = Distance between i and j.

and $C_j = \sum_{i=1}^{n} (W_i X_{ij})$ (j=1...m)
Where C_j = Composite index of marketing activities of the j th centre
W_i = Weight of the i th marketing function
X_{ij} = Value of the i th function (number of establishment or shops under i th function at the j th market centre

The market potential model of Hammond and Mc Cullah has got limited use and application in Indian context as because the income data per market centre is not available. However Mohanty and Singh (1980) has applied this particular model for the study of domestic market potential of the Lower Mahanadi-Brahmani Basin in Orissa. Similarly the work of Sharma, Routray and Singh is the modified form of Hammond and Mc Cullah where income is dropped and marketing functions are duly weighted in the model. These studies are concerned with the hierarchy of market centres and identification of marketing regions. These models are no doubt the basic ones and provide enough scope to rethink and to reuse as a measure/indicator of regional development.

The model here suggested in its first place tries to recognise the rural market centres based on periodicity of marketing activities as suggested by Shrivastava (1984, pp. 40-44). According to this all the rural market places may be classified into three groups of identity: (i) Permanent, (ii). Temporary or periodic market places, and, (iii) Daily cum-periodic market places,.

The present model is based on the following assumptions:-

(a) The quantum and varieties of marketing activities are the function of percapita annual income and the number of persons in the service area of the concerned marketing centre.

(b) The per capita annual volume of transaction per market limiting to the specified service area is the reflection of the proportionate per capita annual income and thus can speak about the living status of the population and further about the pattern of development in the service area if it is compared to other market centres and marketing areas.

Under the above consideration the suggested model is a partial modification of the usual market-potential model in order to measure the potential more realistically than the earlier models of direct consideration of market mass distance as the two variable.

In measuring the regional development the rural market-potential index is derived as given below:

$$Mv_i = \frac{X_j . a_j . b_{ij}}{d_{ij}}$$

$$i = i.........n$$
$$j = 1.........m$$

Where Mv_i = Rural market potential of tl. narket centre,

X_j = Per capita annual volume of transaction in the concerned market centre 'j' (X is obtained dividing the annual volume of transaction in rupees from all commercial establishments of the market centre j by p which is the total population of the concerned marketing service area, i.e. the service area of 'j' can be determined by collecting information regarding the movement of population from surrounding village those who depend on that particular market centre for commercial activities).

a_j = Multiplier for the category/periodicity of market centre,

d_{ij} = Actual shortest road distance between the centre i and j,

b_{ij} = The transport efficiency co-efficient pedestrian/motorised between i and J.

Conclusion

The market potential index thus derived and by superimposition over the administrative map (at block or district level) of any region will certainly indicate the pattern emerged out of development indices derived by any standard technique will be similar with the development pattern as derived by market potential indices.

TWENTY NINE

K.D. Sharma

Non-Convergence of Central Functions and Rural Under Development: A Himalayan Paradigm

Introduction

The process of socio-economic development in any area is closely related to the characterstics of its homogenous and nodal region. The former relates to the homogeniuty among economic properties, the latter to the spatial functional organisation in terms of the provision of functional requirements and their location‑l hierarchies.

The nodal region and the conceptual formulates related to it have received considerable attention of geographers and planners. This interest has been generated by an increasing realisation of the possibilities of integration of existing as well as planned functions in all their complexities of interaction and locational hierarchies which are needed to promote the growth and diffusion of the process of regional development. This is intended to be achieved by allocating to proper locations the functions that are expected to meet the socio-economic requirements of a community in a region. These functions are of two types : those comprising the various components of retail trade; and the government sponsored public welfare functions. The former is performed at some of the market centres which are located in different types of settlements, the latter operate through such institutional services as medical, education and postal centres.

The locational segregation of lower order functions belonging to the same hierarchial level results in the operation of these functions. as one system so as to achieve a greater homogeniuty in the spatial organisation of lower order nodes, to promote concentration of services in a large number of centres, to help them grow into multifunctional centres and to further strengthen the functional interaction between the nodes and their functional areas.

In a mountainous region, characterised by rugged topography and subsistence agriculture, the basic network of rural central places evolves due to the operation of the forces of *laissez-faire* economy and the regional social and cultural influences. As a result of the nature of the evolutionary process by which central goods and services get concentrated, the settlements offering these assumes great importance as traditional centres. This importance is often further strengthened by the local religions and cultural functions performed by these centres and inevitably these centres exist and function as representatives of the areas of their location and reflect as well as promote the process of development in the area.

It is only logical that such places should offer the best sites for the location of institutional and public welfare services so that the two sets of functions operate in spatial conjunction. The divergent location of these is likely to promote their functioning as independent, parallel systems, increase the number of interaction movements and may ultimately result in the under-utilisation of some of these. Any or all of the perceived consequences would defeat the basic purpose for which the location of these services was planned and created.

OBJECTIVES

This paper is an attempt to study the spatial organisation of an area where the retail-trade and public welfare institutional functions do not converge locationally. The paper also addresses the consequences of such a pattern. For this purpose, the example have been drawn from Rohru *tahsil* of Simla district in Himachal Pradesh. The *tahsil* had an area of approximately 222 km^2 and a population of 75236 persons in 1981. It had 168 villages and only one town, Rohru, with a population of 2335 persons. The example cited in this paper pertain to 23 villages and a population of approximately 13000 persons.

The following example of the consequences of divergent location are cited:

1. **Gajiani**

Gajiani is a village with a population of 373 persons and an area of 171 ha. The approach to this village is narrow foot paths. The nearest town, Rohru, is located 22 km. from this village. The village has been the headquarters of a *ghori*, a revenue sub-unit of *pargana*, before and during the British period. It administrative status promoted the concentration of commercial activity and at the time of the conduct of field work in August 1984, the village offered tea leaves, salt, soap, kerosene oil, match-boxes, P.V.C. shoes, combs, cigarettes and provisions. These commodities were being purchased from Gajiani by the residents of 10 adjoining villages. In addition Gajiani has middle school which draws pupils from these villages. The population served by this rural market is 4341 persons. On an average a person travels 3.5 Km. to visit Gajiani where as the maximum and minimum distances travelled to it are 8.0 and 0.5 Km. respectively.

However, the only medical facility for the region served by Gajiani is located at Tikri, which has a population of 446 persons and an area of 113 ha. It is located 2 Kilometres west of Gajiani and is served by another market which also has medical, educational and postal facilities. As far as the utilisation of medical services is concerned, all the settlements served Gajiani, and Gajiani itself, depend upon Tikri. Thus the medical service area for these villages is centred at Tikri. It comprises of 16 villages and a population of 7051 persons. The maximum and minimum distances travelled are 10.0 and 0.5 Km. respectively. The average distance travelled works out to be 4.0 Km.

An entirely different pattern is identified for the utilisation of postal services. The only post-office serving all the settlements in the commercial and education catchment areas of Gajiani is at Pekha village (population 729 persons, are 262 ha) located 2 Kilometres east of Gajiani (Fig.1). It also has a primary school drawing pupils

FIG. 29.1

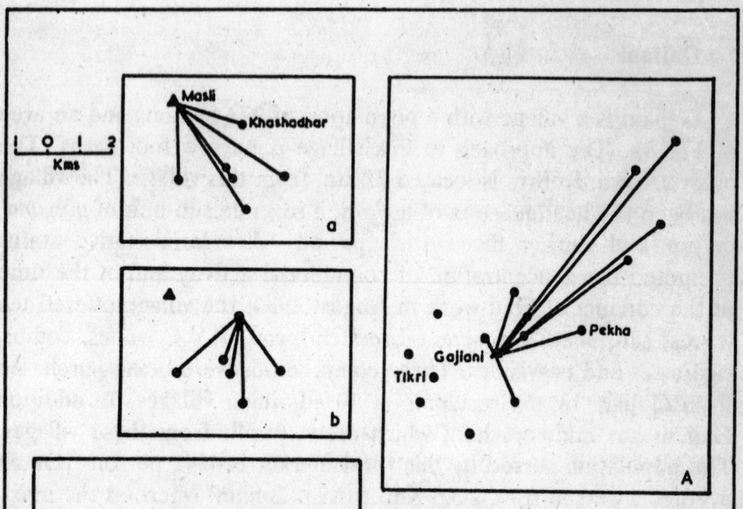

Fig. I Travel Patterns for Non-Convergent Central Functions Travel Patterns for market (A,a); dispensary (B,b); and post-office (C).

from 4 villages. The village does not perform any commercial functions. Thus the inhabitants of the villages served by Gajiani have to go to Pekha to obtain postal facility for which the average distance travelled is 3.3 Km. and the maximum and minimum distances are 6.0 and 1.5 Km. respectively. Only eight villages with a population of 2569 persons utilise this facility.

2. Masli

A similar pattern of location and utilisation of central functions has been indentified at Masli, another rural market centre in the region (Fig.1).

A comparison of the attributed of utilisation of central functions and services at these places fails to bring out the basic problem related to divergent location particularly in terms of the distance travelled by the consumers.

TABLE I: SERVICE AREA ATTRIBUTES POPULATION, NUMBER OF VILLAGES SERVED, AVERAGE AND MAXIMUM AND MINIMUM DISTANCE TRAVELLED
(ARRANGED VERTICALLY)

	Trade	Medical	Postal
	4341	7051	2569
1. Gajiani	(10)	(16)	(8)
	3.5Km.	4.0	3.3Km.
	(8.0-0.5 km.)	(10.0-0.5)	(6.0-1.5 Km.)
	8554	4200	-
	(6)	(5)	-
2. Masli	3.0 Km.	2.0 Km.	-
	(4.0-2.0 Km.)	(2.5-1.0 Km.)	-

Source : Computed from data collected in the field.

The minimization of distance travelled has been recognised as the basic determinant of the consumers travel pattern. This aspect assumes greater importance in a mountainous subsistence agricultural region such as Rohru in which almost all movements are pedestrian (Table-I). The divergent locations of different central functions result, not only in a simple increase in the distance covered, but in travelling the same distance in different directions (Fig.1). Thus for example, a person travelling to Gajiani to purchase something walks 3.5 Km on an average and covers an additional 3.3 Km in a different direction to get to Pekha to make use of postal facility. In actual travel the distance are far more.

Such locational arrangements nullify the objectives of 'minimization of distance' and 'the multi-purpose market trip' pattern of consumer travel behaviour. In addition, such locations prevent the emergence of locational specialisation in the service centre, and do not conform to what may be termed as the *laissez-faire* landscape. In reality, instead of one nodal-functional region, a number of functional regions with different nodes emerge in the same area. These regions can be referred to as the regions of *laissez-faire* landscape, and the public welfare institutional landscape. Since the two are not coextensive, one of these is underutilised. The *laissez-faire* system, being more closely integrated at the grass-roots level does not suffer. The under-utilisation of the institutional services defeats the very purpose of their establishment.

Field enquiries in these villages revealed that the medical and postal facilities are being actually under-utilised due to the extra time and distance involved.

The reasons for the emergence of each non-convergent locations can be listed as administrative decisions based purely on statistical information not revealing the ground reality, and political consideration. It is suggested that there should be some utilisation evaluation after institutional services are established at a location and if it is not possible to remove the functional imbalances through relocation of services, these should be repeated in other central places.

Conclusion

The locational convergence of retail trade and public welfare institutional services, such as educational, medical and postal, can promote greater homogenity in the spatial organisation of lower order service centres, promote concentration of services in a large number of centres and strengthen the functional interaction between the nodes and their functional areas.

The rationale for the selection of suitable locations and the subsequent establishment of public welfare institutions should take into consideration the existing pattern of central places which are basically retail trade centres centres and have evolved through the operation of the forces of laissez-faire economy through historical time. Their importance as traditional centres of retail trade produces a functional spatial organisation suitable to the specific socio-economic requirements of the region.This is particularly true of the lower order rural central places located in mountainous regions characterised by subsistence agriculture economy.

The superimposition of the public welfare landscape on the already existing *laissez-faire* landscape should ideally promote and strengthen a homogenous and mutually sustaining functioning of the two. The selection of sub-optimal locations for the establishment of institutional services leads to independent functioning of the two systems of services and their functional areas.

The divergent location of nodes performing different services of the same hierarchical order results in the under-utilisation of some of them. In this process, the institutional service suffer more because of their superimposed nature and recent establishment. In addition, the initiative provided by retail trade functions for travelling to such nodes is also eliminated.

It is suggested that such functional gaps and imbalances should be removed either through relocation of such services, and if this is not possible, through a restructuring of the pattern of location of these services.

general establishment of rural market [illegible] should [illegible] on the existing pattern of [illegible] trade centres [illegible] of the process of [illegible] importance as traditional central [illegible] a functional spatial organisation suitable to the [illegible] economic requirements of the [illegible] central places [illegible].

The [illegible] land [illegible].

[illegible]

[illegible]

THIRTY

Jai Prakash Rai and
Ram Nayan Rai

Planning of Growth Centres for Micro-Level Development: A Case Study of Lower Son Basin

Introduction

Experience over the years has shown that river basin planning is still viable not only from ecological point of view but also from the point of view of resources management and planning of infrastructure. This paper attempts to establish this concept taking the case study of a part of the Son river basin, i.e. the Lower Son Basin.

The Lower Son Basin extends between 23°34' N lat. to 24°46' N lat., 83°12' E Long to 85°6' E long. It covers an area of 14.8 thousands Km.^{2} with a a population of 40.6 lakh. In shape it looks like a measuring flask. Its average length is 240 Km. (north-south). Average width is 40 Km. in the northern part and 120 Km. in the southern part. Phyiographically, the northern half is a plain, the rest being a pleateau.

Theoretical background

Attempts have been made to propose development strategy of different areas based on central place and growth centre concepts. An example is the study on Miryalguda Taluka, (Sen, L.K., 1971). But the fusion of the two classical theories has not been successfully attempted. This dialemma of research in developing countries has been discussed by Bronger (1977 pp.245-50) where in he noted a gab between the empirical evidences and theoretical norms adopted.

Barbara Harriss (1976 pp.39-48), on the other hand, observes that the conceptual base adopted as a basis for planning and none bothers about the gap between the villages and the towns (Shrivastava, V.K., 1980 pp.195-206). This situation calls for cautions use of such concepts.

Growth centres are expected to fulfil the following objectives:-

1. Growth centres enhance the capacity to benefit from innovations.
2. Growth centres accellerate the pace of economic development of the region they serve.
3. Growth centres utilise the infrastructural facilities available in a region.
4. The distribution system of an area is regulated by them.
5. They help in diffusing the development inputs in problem areas.

These objective have been kept in mind in the planning of growth centres in the Lower Son Basin. The basis of such planning depends on the hierarchy of central places starting from *hats* to small towns.

The existing situation

There are ten growth points in the Lower Son Basin. Among them Arrah, Sasaram. Dehri, Dinapur-Nizamat, Daltonganj, Garhwa etc. are important. The population of these centres ranges between 10 to 50 thousand. All these centres are towns and perform functions like industry, trade, transport and services. Engineering industry (Sasaram), Cement manufacturing (Dehri & Japla), Aluminium utensils (Daltonganj), Bata Shoe Company Chemical industry (Dinapur) are some of the examples of industrial base these towns have been recokned as growth centres (Fig. 1).

Further, 40 market centres of the region have been indentified as service centres. Obra, Maner, Vishrampur, Barun, Mohammadganj, Arwal, Bhandaria are some of them. These market centres posses cottage industries and are open to year round traffic.

FIG. 30.1

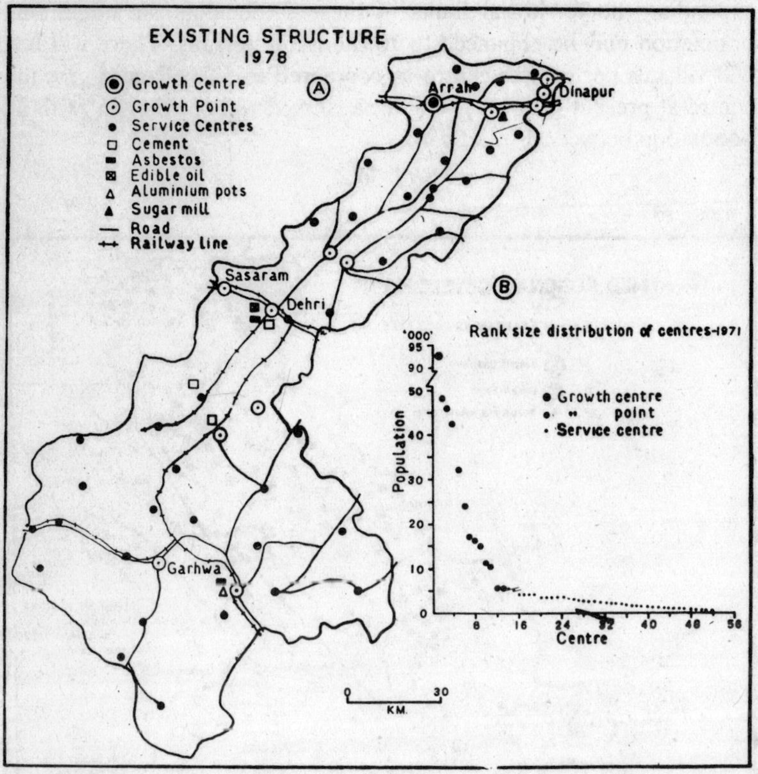

It has been seen that every growth point serves 523 villages and 3 to 5 *lakh* population (Table-I). The area per centre comes to 1500Km^2. Each service centre serves 130 villages, 1 *lakh* population and an area of 370 Km^2. This is beyond the capacity of the centres concerned, which indirectly means that the region lacks growth points and service centres.

The proposed scheme

Taking into account the regional imbalances in the distribution of towns, their functions, infrastructure etc. (Rai, J.P., 1982), it has been proposed to promote 10 additional growth points (a total of 20) in the region. The average population of the settlements functioning as growth points can vary between 5 to 50 thousand. By expanding the territorial limits of these settlements the minimum population may be enhanced to 10 thousand persons. There will be 260 villages per growth centre as compared to 523 villages/ growth centre at present (Table-I). The area served will be 750 Km^2 with a population between 1 to 2 *Lakh*.

FIG. 30.2

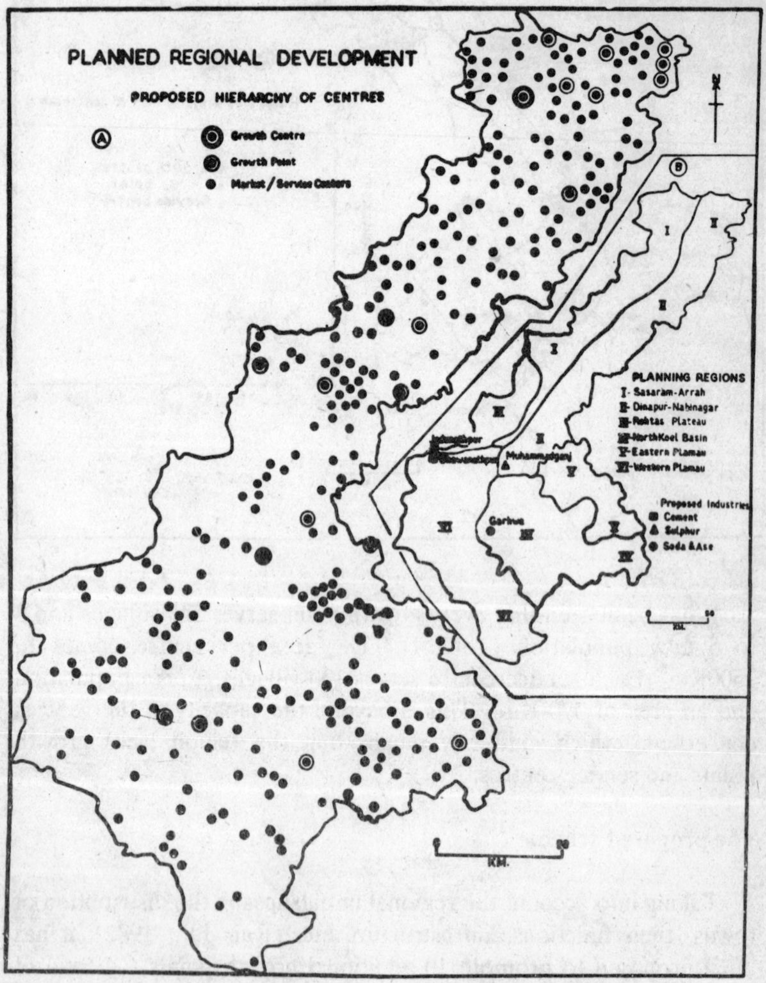

TABLE I : GROWTH CENTRES FOR MICRO-LEVEL DEVELOPMENT

	Existing			Proposed		
	Growth centre	Growth point	Service centre	Growth centre	Growth point	Service centre
Number	1	102	40	1	20	320
Village	5230	523	130	5230	260	16
Population	3697000	3697000	92425	3697000	184850	11550
Area (Km2)	14830	1500	370	14830	750	46
Average population of centres	100000	10000to50000	5000tc100000	100000	5000to50000	5000

Further a total of 320 service centres have been proposed (Fig.2). All these settlements possess the minimum functions of a rural market. Rural market centres evolve with the socio-economic needs of the population they serve (Udhaw Ram, 1982). Markets are intimately related with the means of transport and provide suitable sites for the initiation of industries etc. Such centres may, therefore, grow as service centres. Each service centre will support 16 villages with an average population of 12 thousand and an average area of 50 Km^2. As the average walking distance of the rural population in this area is 6 to 7 Km. (Rai, J.P., 1982) the service centres may serve the population efficiently.

In order to sustain the above system and to improve their efficiency for providing developmental inputs, other infra-structural elements like irrigation facilities, transport, complementary industries, agricultural machinery and industries etc. may be provided. Also the population may be decentralised by creating employment opportunities. The following schemes oriented towards territorial justice (Shrivastava, V.K. , & Rai, J.P., 1981 pp.251-57) may be implemented:-

a Planning of agriculture on an additional 21% of the culturable waste land available in the area.

b Environmentally sound small scale irrigation scheme should be initiated.

c The maximum land holding limit should be reduced from 8 ha at present to 4 ha in the near future.

d The distribution system of agricultural inputs like HYV seeds, agricultural implements, fertilizers, pesticides should be streamlined,

e Industries like asbestos, soda-ash cement etc. should be added in the southern plateau region where an industrial base already exists.

f Cottage and small scale industries based on carpet weaving, handloom, agricultural machinery, bakery etc. should be developed in the northern plain areas.

g The population from the northern part (density 476/Km^2) should be checked by decentralising the people to move to the south (density 169/KM^2) by creating employment opportunities.

h And lastly, the means and modes of transport should also be improved and modernised.

Micro-Planning regions

The Lower Son Basin may, therefore, be divided into the following micro-planning regions-

i Western Son region (Plain)
ii Eastern Son region (Plain)
iii Rohtas Plateau region
iv Eastern Palamu plateau region
v Western Plamu plateau region
vi North Koel basin.

THIRTY ONE

Asmah Ahmad

Rural-Urban Migration: A Challenge to Development?

Introduction

Since independence in 1957, the Malaysian Government has instituted a rigorous social and economic development programme. At the vary beginning rural development was emphasized with the aim of increasing the income earning capacity and quality to life of the rural poor. The major programmes included agricultural development by means of improved organization, co-operation and provision of infrastructure especially rural roads and irrigation; the latter to enable double-cropping of paddy as well as the improvement of social and community services in the rural areas. Although the rural development strategy was firmly rooted in the subsistence padi economy which aimed at eventual self-sufficiency, what was clearly augmented was output and not planters' income. In the face of rising world production and falling rice prices, Malaysian rice industry suffered in which by mid 1960s Malaysian padi output managed to satisfy only about 60 percent of domestic consumption (Rudner, in Lim, 1975 : 82). Hence up to 1965, Malaysian rural development strategy did not succeed in generating substantial improvement in the rural subsistence economy.

A shift in emphasis was detected in the First Malaysia Plan (1966 - 70) whereby producers' income and not merely sectoral output became the object of rural policy. Likewise a shift was also made towards concentrating on crops yielding the highest marginal revenue product, notably rubber. Besides efforts were also concentrated in building agricultural education and research, rubber replanting and new land development (FMP 1966 - 70: 105). This resulted in a fairly satisfactory rate of economic development in terms of production and income. The gross domestic product grew at an average rate of 6 per cent per annum in real terms which was above the targeted rate of 4.9 per cent. However, the problems of poverty, unemployment and economic imbalance among the ethnic groups still remained unsolved which the 1969 riots brought yet another shift in the government development policy with the inception of the New Economic Policy (NEP) in the Second Malaysia Plan (1971 - 75). The former is a socio-economic policy designed to achieve national unity through the two-pronged objectives of poverty eradication and restructuring of society. The NEP was conceived to stretch over a period of 20 years. It is the outcome of the second strategy that is going to be the focus of the present paper.

In Peninsular Malaysia, rural to rural migration has been the major form of migration pattern since mid - 1960s which accounted for nearly 45 per cent of the total internal migration during the inter-censal period of 1970 - 80 (Department of Statistics, 1983 : 77). This was in part due to rural development and the development of land schemes in the various states, particularly Pahang. Although the drift of rural dwellers to urban areas only constituted 16 per cent of all migration over the same period of time, such drift to big towns and cities was seen to be on the increase. Katiman (1982) has shown that towns with 75,000 persons and above had experienced an increase in population by 28.1 per cent in 1980 over that of the 1970 figure. Out of this growth, 51.7 per cent were from net in-migration. That big towns (with population of 100,000 and above) are experiencing a rapid growth is also shown by the increase in their numbers from 2 in 1947 to 11 in 1980 with an increase in terms of inhabitants from 365,000 persons to 2.9 millions; an increase of 724 percent over a span of 33 years (adapted from Katiman, 1983: 7, 10). From the ethnic viewpoints, more Malays have come to big urban areas. This is seen to be more pronounced after the evolution of the NEP in 1971. Its second "two-pronged strategy', that is reducing and eliminating the identification of race with geographical location, saw the deliberate policy of the government in encouraging the migration of rural Malays to urban areas. The move, that is, urbanizing the

Malays is seen to be means of correcting the racial imbalance one so often sees in Malaysian towns. This pattern of mobility (mainly labour mobility) from rural to urban areas has become a quandary in itself. Migration is encouraged on the one hand, in order to restructure society but on the other hand, it created strings of repercussions in the sending areas although not without its rewards.

In the light of the above background, this paper is written with the aim of highlighting the effects of rural-urban migration, both social and economic, on the out-migrants but more particularly on the sending areas and the rural-based families left behind. The question of whether or not migration challenges rural development will then be discussed.

The Study

This study is drawn from part of village studies conducted by the author in 1981, in an identified poverty district, Baling, in the northwest of Peninsular Malaysia (Figure 1). It has a total area of 1,502 km^2 and a population of 107,926 persons in the last 1980 census as compared to a population of 104,118 persons in the 1970 census. The majority of the population are Malays comprising 77 per cent and residing mainly in the villages. About 2 per cent of the population are 'Others' who are mainly of Thai descendents. The Chinese and the Indians made up almost equally the rest of the population.

In the study, a questionnaire survey was carried out in nine villages with a total of 476 heads of households. The villages are of varying distances (by road) from the chief urban centre, Baling. They are also of varying degrees of accessibility and endowment as well as of varying sizes (Figure 1).

For the purpose of the study, out-migrants are taken as those individuals who are absent from their respective villages at the time of the survey. However, in order to differentiate between the recent and the 'older' movers, they were grouped according to the length of their absence from the village. By doing this it was found that only 10 percent of them had moved less than a year, 50 per cent between 1 and 4 years and the rest for a much longer period.

FIG. 31.1

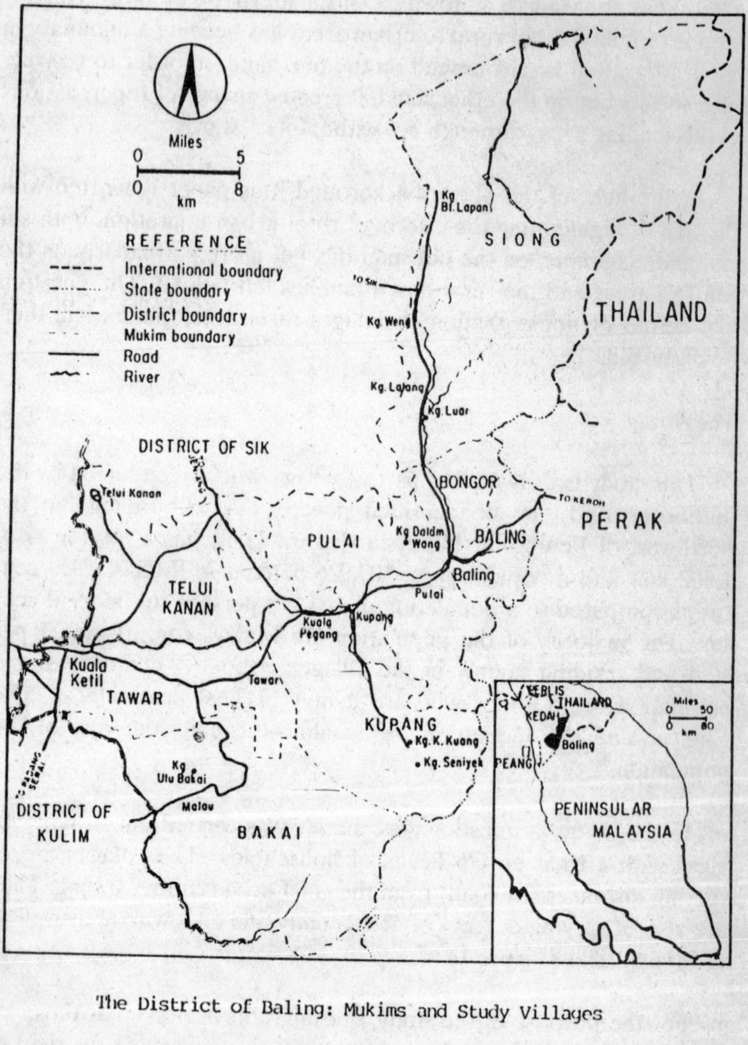

The District of Baling: Mukims and Study Villages

There is also a need to differentiate the migration experience of heads of households from that of their dependents. Migration of the former has occurred sometimes in the past and among some may reoccur in the future. Migration of household heads' children, on the other hand, has been, is and will be taking place. It appears to be an on-going process and will probably remain so for as long as there is imbalance in the country's social and economic development. Migration will proceed when the place utility of an alternative area is deemed better-of (Wolpert, 1965) or when there appears a positive differential in expected income between two places (Todaro, 1969).

The Findings

Adult members of households were found to form the bulk of the out-migrants, accounting for 99 per cent, while the rest was made up of female heads' spouses. Only 8 per cent of household heads used to leave their villages before, mainly in search of better job opportunities outside. In contrast, at least 30 per cent of their dependents aged 16 years and above were absent at the time of the survey for various reasons mainly in pursuit of economic betterment, 80 per cent among the males and 21.3 percent among the females) with marriage coming second in importance 13.8 per cent among the males and 72.4 per cent among the females) and studying third (about 6 per cent each).

Out-migration : Some Background Features

i. Characteristics

The regularity in the pattern of migration differentials do appear to exist in the study area. Migration of adult members of households was found to be highly selective of sex and age with an overwhelming majority being male in the 21 to 30 years age bracket (Figure 2a). Female migrants appear to be younger than male migrants (Figure 2b). Seventy-two per cent of female adults who had migrated were below 26 years old as compared to 50 percent in case of male adults. They, however, shared a common feature, in that, the absence of age group 21 - 25 years was highest in both cases.

That migration is characteristically more pronounced among individuals with certain educational background is also apparent here. Those with more years of schooling were found to be more migratory than those with fewer. The secondary school leavers were found to constitute a high proportion (65 per cent) of the migration

FIG. 31.2 (A to F)

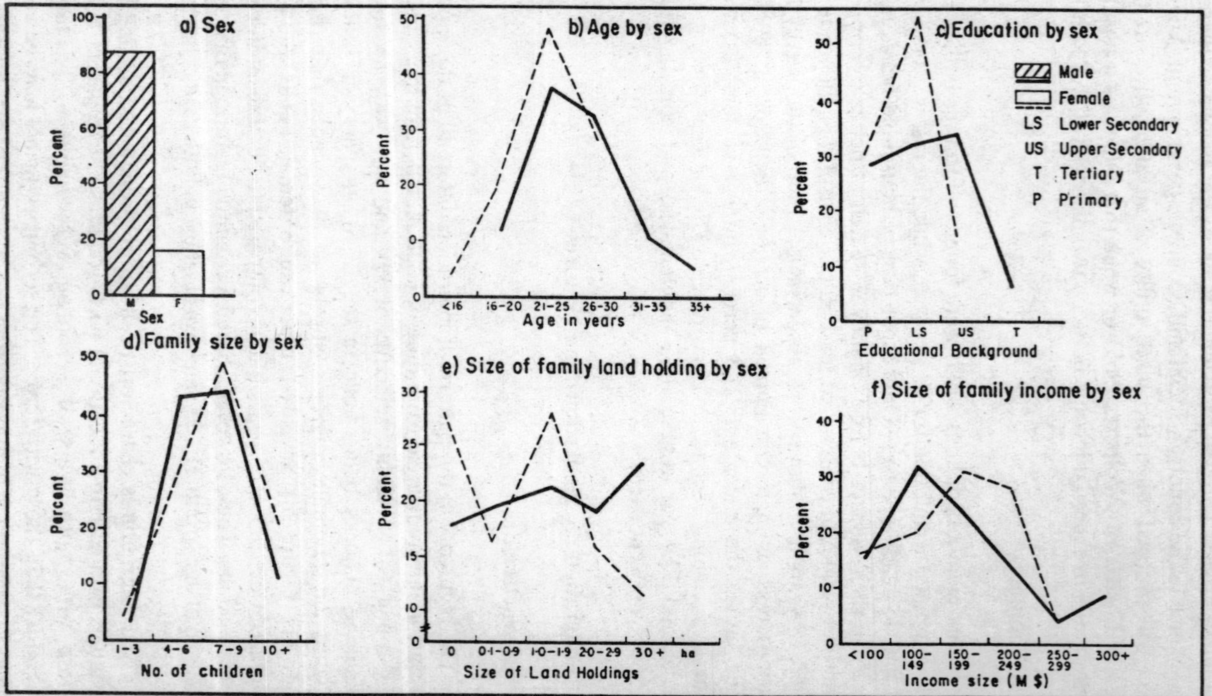

Background Characteristics of Migrants, 1981.

stream as compared to those with only primary education. Almost all those with tertiary education mainly from technical colleges and universities were found working in Kuala Lumpur, the capital city. While the upper secondary school leavers formed a slight majority among the male migrants, the female migrants were mainly characterized by those with lower secondary education (Figure 2c). One of the reasons for this was that, most of the girls who went for secondary schooling die not manage to proceed toO-level after Form 3 examination.Both social and economic factors (such as back of motivation, big family and financial difficulty) were among the reasons for the high rate of failure and drop out.

Social background of migrating adults is also found to show a distinct pattern. For this purpose, social background is seen in the form of family size arising from the number of siblings that a migrant has. A family is taken to be small when it comprises between 1 - 3 children; medium-sized when it is between 4 - 6 children and large when it has 7 or more children. Analysis showed that the migrant were mostly from a large family background with more than half of them having a family of 7 or more. Besides other personal reasons, the desire to break away from familial and economic constraints of a large family triggers the movement among the move adventurous. The desire to break away from hardship and to help support the family had resulted in the migration of female adults. This was particularly apparent when 68 per cent of migrating female adultls were found to be from the large and the very large family background (Figure 2d). Many of these girls either worked in factories or 'offered' themselves as domestic helpers.

Analysis of economic backgrounds of migrants in terms of family income size and size of land owned by the parents revealed that they were generally poor and almost landless. About three-quarters of them were from families whose income were below MS250 per month, that is below the poverty line household income of MS250 per month in 1981 used in the study. Three-fifths of them were also from families whose land assets were less than 2 ha each. Out of this, one-third was landless or at least one-fifth of all the migrants was from landless background. That female migrants were from among the relatively poorer group and with relatively limited land assets were clearly shown again in the findings (figure 2e and 2f). Females are generally less migratory than males. However, circumstances of hard living in the village coupled with virtually non-existent rural opportunities made it such that those with education had to find job opportunities outside in order to help alleviate the hardship of the family. The fact that financial aids from town help relieved family budgets was admitted by the parents whose daughters were working outside the village. While female migrants featured a generally difficult economic background, among the males, however, there was tendency of increasing migration with increasing size of family land and income (Figure 2e and 2f). The importance of this observation reflects that individuals with large financial resources would tend to be more migratory as they can survive longer while searching for the elusive urban jobs(Todaro, 1981). On the whole they seem to come from all socio-economic strata with the majority being poor in common with most rural inhabitants.

ii. **Destinations**

Migration streams in developing countries more often than not are biased in nature as a result of unbalanced job opportunities available between rural and urban areas. Such regularity could also be observed in the study are when a bout 80 per cent of the economically motivated migration were found to end up mainly in large towns and metropolitan areas. Among the destinations, Kuala Lumpur is the single largest recipient of all migrants from Baling, accounting for at least one-quarter of them (Figure 3). As the hub of the country, the main industrial, commercial and administrative activities are concentrated in Kuala Lumpur. These factors have thus attracted aspiring youths to seek the relatively greater job opportunities in the city. Nonetheless, job seekers are found wherever employment opportunities are created. Thus when two major construction projects, that is, the western link of the East-West Highway and the Temenggor Dam, were opened up in Grik (a northern town/District in the neighbouring State of Perak) it had become a popular destination among the migrants. About one-quarter of those who had migrated to other states was found to be concentrated in Grik alone while the rest were scattered in smaller numbers in various other states.

FIG. 31.3

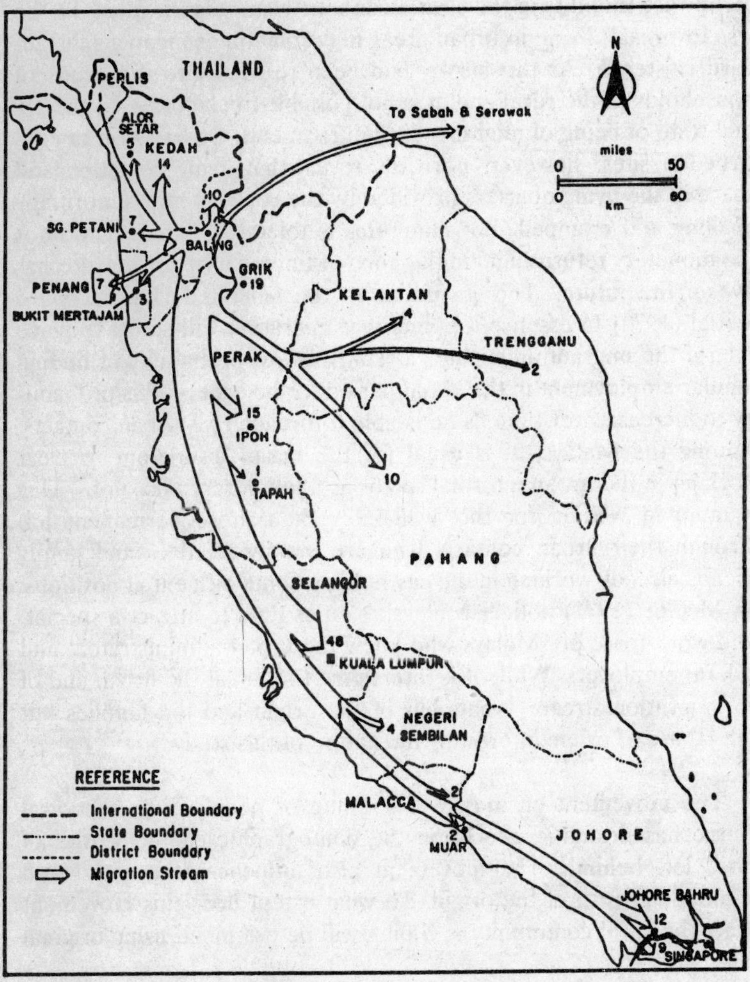

Destinations of Migrants from Baling, 1981.

Out - migration : The Effects

The effects of out-migration are many and varied. To the

migrants, as rational men, it is the avenue to acquire better economic returns and among the more successful (with high income) an upward mobility in the socio-economic class stratification. To the less fortunate, living in urban areas may sometimes mean a substandard existence. As this survey had been restricted to the heads of households at the rural end, it is not possible to elaborate on the actual state of being of migrants at the urban end. Observation in construction sites, however, normally reveal that living condition and space in the living quarters provided by the contractors are normally apalling and cramped. For many this is tolerated in anticipation of the monetary returns, and in the hope of finding a better job alternative in the future. This is similar to the amended Harris-Todaro model (1970) In essence it points that migration will still take place even if the migrant anticipates a relatively low probability of finding regular employment in the initial period for he expects this probability to increase over time as he is able to broaden his urban contacts. Among the Malays, it is usual for the urban in-migrant to treat working in the urban informal sector as a temporary measure. This is done in waiting for the availability of a more permanent job through their urban contacts who are mainly relatives and family friends already working in the city holding some influential positions. As McGee (1971) notices Mulaysia's cities tend to attract a specialized work force of \Malays who knew the urban administrators and federal employers. While it is interesting to look at the urban end of the migration stream, whats left of the origin and the families left behind are of prime interest by the nature of this study.

The movement en masse of a group of people from the rural source has dramatic effects on the demographic characteristics of those left behind. The movement also influences the social and economic growth of the origin. To what extent does this movement affect the rural community in Baling will be examined using original date.

(i) **Demographic Consequences**

Since rural-urban migartion is selective of certain characteristics, it affects the composition of the population in both sending and receiving areas. Generally, out-migration areas lose a disproportionate percentage of the younger and better educated population.

Our data supports this observation too as discussed in earlier section. At least 95 percent of the migrants were below the age of 36 years. This reduces their proportion in the total population as shown by the marked middle indention to the population pyramid as shown in Figure 4a as compared to the more even slope of Figure 4b. As migration is more pronounced among males than females, it has also affected the sex ratio of the population concerned. The sex ratio (number of males per 100 females) for the age group 15 - 39 was found to be 84 as compared to 97 for Peninsular Malaysia in 1980. The respective sex ratio for the whole population were 97 and 100.

This age-specific out-migration tends to reduce the population growth rate in the area. The disproportionate removal of the population of family-formation ages can directly reduce the number of births. As can be seen from Figure 4, the base of pyramid (a) for Baling is narrower than the broad base of pyramid (b) for peninsular Malaysia as a whole. Analysis of the mortality rates among children aged 0 - 4 years from 1977 - 1980 in Baling showed a decreasing trend for the various child mortality rates.[1] Considering the number of children below the age of 5 who died during the last 5 years was relatively small, the reduction of the population aged 0 - 4 was thus mainly the result of falling birthrate. Assuming that the population is stable, the declining birthrate is found to have reduced the number of births by 15 per cent in the last 5 years.

Out-migration can also affect the socio-demographic characteristics of the rural areas. For instance, the relatively young out-migrants also comprise the better educated section of the population. About 75 per cent of them were found to have at least a lower secondary education. None of the tertiary educated, with the exception of a few in the teaching profession, stayed back. their out-bound movement thus resulted in a brain-drain for the society left behind. Any hope for a more educated, modern and productive farming society would not materialize. The remaining society would remain very much the same in outlook and would be further incapacitated with ageing.

This brings us to the issue of dependency ratio (ratio of persons 0 - 14 and over 60 to those of 15 - 59 age group). The loss of a disproportionate percentage of the younger population can result in an increase in the proportion of the total population economically pen-

FIG. 31.4

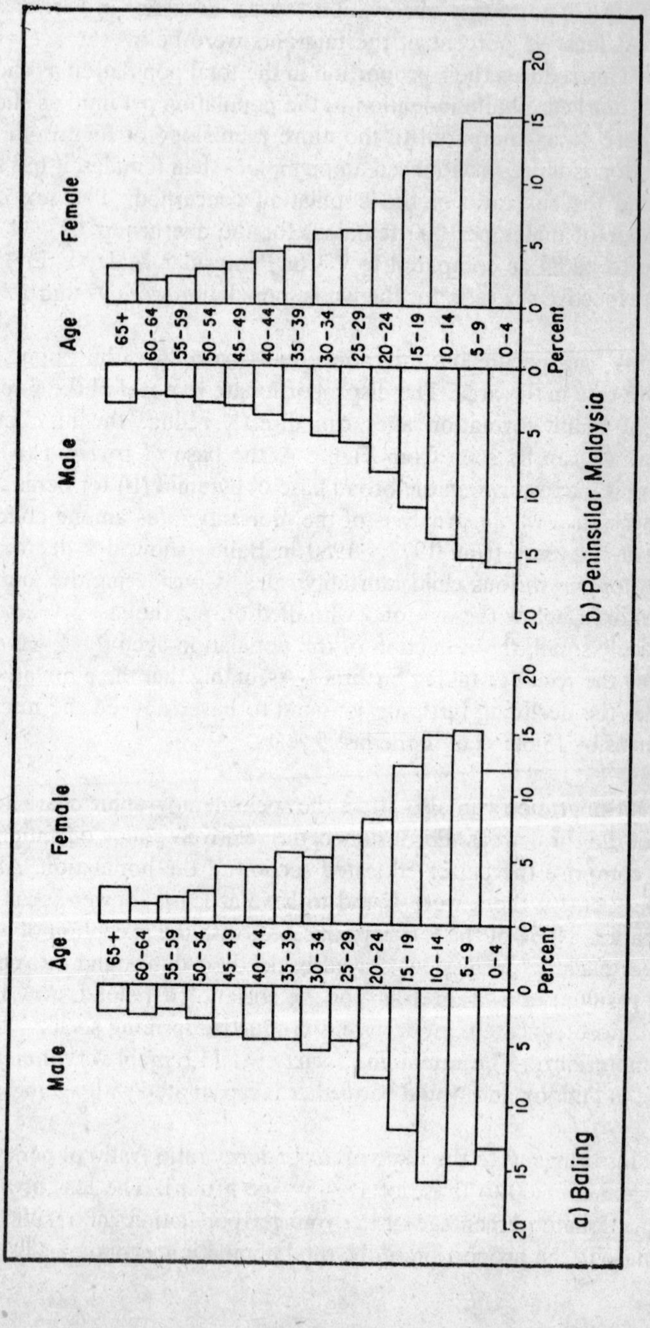

The Relative Age-Sex Structure of Baling and Peninsular Malaysia.

dant as the relative share of the productive workers is reduced. In order to measure this effect of out-migration, the ratios for the periods 'before' and 'after' migration had taken place were calculated. The result showed that the dependency ratio had increased slightly from 0.73 to 0.92 after migration. As not all the adults were economically active and fully employed, especially in the 15 - 19 age group (for a majority of them was still schooling and looking for jobs), and if they were taken as dependents, the dependency ratio was seen to increase from 0.92 to 1.5.

(ii) **Economic Consequences**

The reduction in the share of productive workers can also affect the amount of labour required to work in the fields and farms. A frequently made claim is that the loss of able-bodied men from the rural areas results in the reduction of the total agricultural productivity and in a general deterioration of the local agricultural system (IL0, 1960; Skinner, 1965). In these studies, the authors have noted a decline in agricultural productivity in rural areas experiencing heavy out-migration. In our study, the reduction in total agricultural products is measured in terms of the area of land left either partially or fully unutilized as a result of labour shortage. It was found that at least 54 ha of padi land in the study area was left idle. Although the main reason cited for this idleness was lack of water, shortage of young labourers to work in the paddy fields due to out-migration was also mentioned. With regard to the rubber land, 48 ha were found to have been left idle involving 12.8 per cent of the relatively more productive rubber land (with matured and old trees). Out of those who had idle rubber land 96.5 per cent ascribed its cuase to lack of manpower especially young labour. Most of these landowners were in the older age groups of 55 years and above and hence require younger men to help undertake the more rigourous nature of rubber tapping. Out-migration of the young labour stock had reduced total rubber output by 13 percent (assuming output per unit area is constant) and that of rice output by a smaller fraction.

That shortage of manpower acts as a constraint to increase in agricultural production and yield was also acknowledged by the landowners. About two-third of them admitted that they face manpower problems in their effort to increase their agricultural productivity.

Out of these, about 45 percent ranked its priority as third most important after land and capital. Other rankings were, Priority 1 (13.9percent);Priority 2 (21.7percent); Priority 4 (13.9percent) and Priority 5 (7.2percent).The deficient number of young labour force can become one of the contributary factors in perpetuating poverty among the villagers.

Although out-migration of young men can affect the productivity levels of agriculture, the rural-urban linkage created is not without advantages.One of the economic benefits of out-migration is the return of money and resources by the migrants to their respective home areas. Literature on this urban-to-rural remittances and its related aspects are exhaustive.[2] They cover about the extent of these remittances, the determinants of such financial flows and the use made in the rural areas of the money received. The flows normally involved not less than 10 percent and some as high as 69 percent of the income earned by the migrants.

The existence of monetary flows from migrants to their rural home areas is also evident in our survey. It was found that out of the 18 percent of the household heads with side incomes 57 percent received them in the form of remittances sent by the children from outside. About 68 percent of them received these remittances monthly, the amount varied from MS50 to Ms200 with an average of MS50 per month. At least MS36,000 in cash per year flowed into the area accounting fro not less than 5 percent of the area's yearly cash income. The value of the out-migrants' remittances would be more considering that among the relatively well-paid, contributions to parents sometimes take the form of buying conspicuous goods viz, furniture etc. There were also known cases who contributed a lump sum averaging about MS400 at a time for such undertakings as repairing of house,building of wells and latrines etc. At least 37 percent of the migrants sent money home or gave to their parents on their occasional visits home.However, half of them remitted less than MS500 per year.

It is not the intention of this paper to dwell on the determinants of the flows. It is suffice to mention that from the study it was found that the nature of the job secured or acquired, the amount of pay that goes with it and the extent of personal commitment that determine the extent,frequency and regularity of financial flows from migration receiving to migration sending areas.What is more important here is the question of what then are the income generating effects of these remittances to the rural recipients? Stark (1976) claims that remittances represent a significant means for removing supply constraints to improved productivity in agriculture. Lipton (1976), from his survey of available literature, lists in order of importance four priorities that appear to govern rural use of remittances.These priorities are:

i pay of debts and provide education for sons;
ii purchase of consumption goods to meet everyday needs;
iii education of younger siblings; and ivinvestment.

He estimates the second priority absorbs about 90 percent of remittances received. Also some of the investment takes the form of capital transfer rather than capital formation.

Table I : DISTRIBUTION OF USE OF INREMIITANCES MADE BY THE RURAL RECIPIENTS (M=61)

	Type of Use	%
	Basic consumption	68.9
	Consumption & Children Schooling	13.1
	Consumption & Saving	18.0
i.	Repair of housing	(27.3)
ii.	Journey for pilgrimage	(45.5)
iii.	Payment for bired Labour	(18.2)
iv.	'Air agriculture'	(9.0)
		100.0

Figures in parentheses show the ultimate use of savings made by the recipients.

The use of inremittances as an addition to purchase consumer goods to meet everyday needs is also significant in our survey, at least two-third of the recipients used the money for purchasing daily consumption alone (Table 1), Other additional uses were to finance children's schooling and savings. almost half of the saving was, however, made with the intention of financing the pilgrimage to Mecca. Among the Malays, especially in a traditional society, performance a pilgrimage has become a life-long ambition only with its performance will the five tenets of Islam been fulfilled. A person who has become a 'Haj' (having performed the pilgrimage) is also highly respected in traditional society With limited funds saving represents a means to achieving the spiritual goal. Savings were also used in repairing and completing of houses. This is almost similar to what was found by Visaria (1986) in India, when cash remittances reduced the need for farmers to sell all small surpluses and enabled them to generate saving. However,the saving was invested, not in agriculture, but in better housing which seemed to be a more immediate need.Only only about a quarter of the savings was directly used to finance agriculture, mainly for payment of hired labour in rice farming. To some part of the remittances was used to promote agriculture generally such as the purchase of implements, seeds, fertilizer and weedicides. But their proportion was small.

Although not mentioned in the responses, we have found that the relatively bigger savers often act as 'capital' source for the needy. In times when a farmer needs to raise a large amount of cash immediately, he will normally go to the better-off retired farmers (often those with considerable remittances from children) to sell his land or 'offer'his padi land for hire as are payment to the money loaned. The amount ofthe loan will depreciate about MS173 per hectar per crop cultivated. The agreement will terminate until such time when all the loan is paid either all by way of depreciation or when he is able to raise the cash to settle the balance. Normally the farmer-debtor will try to settle the loan quickly as possible but the creditor is assured of at least one crop.Indirectly this can be considered as an involuntary or unconscious way of capital formation on the part of the creditor but a capital transfer for the debtor.

Is Migration A Challenge To Development?

So far we have seen the various aspects of rural-urban migration viz its features and impacts, the latter pertaining to the rural end. we now come to the crucial issue of the paper, that is, how does rural-urban linkages through migration challenge rural development? Development in its final analysis can be equated as positive change.But change itself can work both ways. The preceding discussion saw how a planned strategy ended up in a paradoxical dilemma.

It can not be denied that migration tends to bring some positive changes to particular rural families especially among those affected and in receipt of remittances.It was noted from the survey that remittances had brought about certain physical changes in the villages especially in terms of better housing and the improvement of the general well -being of the family left behind. Besides,migration has also affected the social set-up of the rural-based families.In the villages, the religious and the wealthy are normally those who are highly respected by the villagers. With modernization, a new type of wealth has been given respect in the society. An individual is highly respected by the number of successful children he has.

Successful children do not only boost family prestige, they also bring to the village a blend of outside money, knowledge and attitudes. In their study of two centres in Nigeria, Orubulaye and Caldwell (as cited in Caldwell,1976) found that wells and latrines had been provided for individual houses almost solely by educated children working in distant places. Such similarity was also found in the study area. Knowledge of the area has shown us that the building of individual 'pour and flush' toilet system in two ofthe villages before the introduction of compulsory building of toilet facilities with the provision of 'community' gravity-feed water supply was mainly the initiation of educated and working children. Wells built in house compounds were also provided by the children through their monetary contribution. They were also the ones who were responsible to the improvement of their parents' house. AS most of them maintained close link with their villages by making at least 2 visits a year to their respective families, ideas of modernization can be transmitted to the village through them. On the other hand, benefits received by particular families tend to reinforce their social structure and hence perpetuate inequalities amongst households in the villages.

As a whole our data shows that very little of the remittances is used directly as investment for rural development.. This is similar to some of the findings by other authors. From a review of a large number of village studies, Connell et.al (1976), found that remittances have little potential for generating change in the village. Similarly, Amin(1974) also emphasized that remittances are too small a sum to have any positive impact on the village. Due to this, the area of out-migration will continue to be poor and without modern facilities. Samad (1982) in the survey of three villages in Negri Sembilan also found that wealth flows from the destination, in some respect, benefit the village and in another, do not bring much change to the village condition.

In our study, remittances are seen to serve as a means of maintaining the rural based families or as a repayment of a social debt arising from past assistance received from the families. The magnitude of the social debt is determined by the degree of poverty of the rural-based families, the amount of money invested by the family in the migrant and the amount of the income earned by the family. Given that recipients are primarily parents and village elders, it is not surprising that most of the money remitted is used for increased consumption, education and better housing.

The fact that very little of the inremittances is used to increase agricultural productivity (as seen earlier in Table 1)negates the notion that the loss of young labour from the rural areas can be compensated or replaced by the monetary flows from them to be used in hiring other labour in their stead.The latter would also be difficult to materialize .One reason is that not only is there other more immediate needs such as physical survival to take care of; other labour, on the other hand, are also hard to come by. Although the 'pull-push' theory may still hold true in explaining out-migration, other abetting factor that can promote the chain of movement is the legacy ofcolonial education system which emphasized a clerical-type learning rather than technical training needed to create an efficient peasantry.This has led to the preference for non-farm jobs to toiling the soil among the young.

Asmah (1983) in another part of the same study had shown that the income of the population in the area had worsen over the years. Despite using the same total household income of MS250 per month as used by the Indentification and coordination Unit (ICU) of the Prime Minister's Department in 1978 and by including the non-cash income to ours, it was found that the ICU's figures,, 65.5 percent incidence of poverty for Baling was comparatively lower than our finding of 76.1 percent. This could imply two things, either our villages are in the relatively poorer area in the District, or that the extent of poverty has increased during the span of the three year period between the two studies. However our sampling method for the study villages, personal observation and knowledge of the area had shown that our choice was not biased thus eliminating the first implication leaving us to verify the second.

To imply that the income of the villagers had deteriorated called for an examination of their income-generating activities particularly among the peasants who were subjected to external market fluctuations. More than three-quarters of the villagers were found to have relied directly on the production of the rubber and pady as their main source of income (in cash and in kind) with a major proportion of the rest relying on monthly wages and salaries. While the incomes of the latter were more stable and tended to increase with time (through annual increment), peasants' incomes on the other hand, relied heavily on the prices of commodities which were highly flexible. Commodity prices for both padi and rubber over the period were seen to be favourable. The increase in price subsidy for pady, however, did not affect the peasants in our study area as they only grew padi for subsistence. The average price of smallholder rubber (unsmoked sheet grade iii) also improved from MS1.35 per kg in 1978 to MS!76 per kg in 1980. If this was the case one would aspect that peasants' rubber incomes would improve simultaneously. But they did not.

One particular reason for the failure of rising commodity prices to improve farmers' incomes, was the reduction in the total rubber output or productivity brought about by a general deterioration ofthe local agricultural system. It was found that 65 percent of the rubber land in the area were either old hence of low productivity or still immature and unproductive. AS such peasants' rubber output had been reduced by at least one-half due to old and unproductive trees. A complementary factor leading to the general low agricultural output produced by the peasants is the phenomenon of land being left 'idle'. One of the reasons behind the idleness of land in the area was the lack of able-bodied manpower as a result of out-migration as discussed in the earlier section. AS a consequence, peasants' total rubber output was further reduced by at least one-tenth.

Lack of young labour, besides age and capital, was also found to be a deterrent factor to such undertakings as personal replanting of old rubber plots. The financial problem faced by rubber small holders in undertaking replanting was often related to the labour problem since lack of labour compelled the samllholders to use contractors to fell their holdings; and in many cases contractors demanded a down-payment beforehand. They could overcome this problem by applying for replanting assistance from the Rubber Industry Smallholders' Development Authority (RISDA). Unfortunately the majority could not benefit from either RISDA's replanting grant or subsidy scheme because their land had no legal titles which were necessary before aids could be given, as they originated from illegal opening up of land gazetted under Reserves

Conclusion

This paper has shown that rural-urban linkages through out-migration of rural youth and urban remittances have brought about unbalanced effect to the village. While urban remittances are beneficial to certain rural household , their existence does not lead to an increase in the agricultural productivity of the origin.In fact, the rural area was seen to shoulder greater responsibility and being faced with more problems, demographically, socially and economically.

The encouragement of migration to urban areas as a measure of overcoming a certain problem as deemed necessary by the policy makers may appear viable, but the possibility that it may inflict a far reaching effect should not be dismissed. This is especially so when development is biased towards the more advanced, urban sectors while trusting in backwash effects to convey development into the rural economy , the latter would also be faced with other intricate problems.

NOTES

1. Decrease in mortality rates among children aged 0-4 years in Baling from 1977 - 80 were as follows :

   Neo-natal mortality rate - from 34.0 to 23.8 deaths per 1,000 livebirths infant mortality rate - from 30.9 to 30.8 deaths per 1,000 livebiraths Toddler mortality rate - from 4.3 to 3.5 deaths per 1,000 population 1 - 4 years.
2. Among the list are Caldwell, 1969; Anderson, 1972; 1974; Mohammad, Butcher and Gotsch, 1973; Johnson and Whitelaw, 1974; Stark, 1976; Rampel and Lobdell, 1978 to name a few.

THIRTY TWO

Hetty Verhagen and
P. Parthasarathy Rao[1]

Marketing of Commercial-Farm Inputs in Semi-Arid Tropical India

Introduction

In the Semi-Arid Tropics (SAT) of India most farmers are using very limited amounts of commercial inputs, especially in non-irrigated areas. The use of commercial farm inputs in India is relatively recent. After 1966, high-yielding-varieties became popular and trade in fertilizer, pesticides and seeds became more important.

The main purpose of this study is a. to describe the channels through which fertilizer, pesticides and seeds flow from the manufacturers to the farmers, and b. to find out whether there are constraints in these supply channels which are responsible for the low input use.

The paper is divided into two sections. The first section deals with the description of the marketing channels for deals with the description of the marketing channels for fertilizers, pesticides and seeds, government policy concerning these inputs is also briefly discussed. The existing problems in the delivery system of these inputs are highlighted as observed during the course of this study at the All-India level. In the second section the extent of utilization of commercial inputs at farm level in three villages in three different zones of the SAT India are compared. The problems faced by the farmers in procuring the inputs are analyzed.

Description of Channels

In the fertilizer trade three different channels can be distinguished (1) private, (2) Cooperative, and (3) government channel. Fertilizers have been declared as an essential commodity and since 1967 Government intervention is more and prices are fixed by the government. The government channel in fertilizer trade grows in importance during times of scarce. Fertilizer supplies. The functioning of the fertilizer market is hampered by some problems arising due to market control. There are problems of transport and storage owing to seasonal demand of fertilizers. The government allocation policy based on demand forecast creates imbalances in supply and demand leading to speculative fertilizer prices. The fertilizer pricing system has led to huge government subsidy. The distribution margins in fertilizer trade are low and hence dealers resort to some malpractices.

Government intervention in pesticide trade is less as pesticides have not been declared essential commodity, Four different channels can be distinguished (1) Private, (2) Cooperative, (3) State Government channel, and (4) National Government Channel. In the seed trade quality control is important. There is not enough knowledge of he market and proper coordination is required between the different organizations dealing in seeds.

Utilization of commercial inputs at Farm level

The three villages-- Shirapur, Kanzara (Maharashtra state) and Aurepalle (Andhra Pradesh)--considered in this study are part of ICRISATs village level study. It is found that in all the three villages fertilizer use on non irrigated land is low. Among the non irrigated crops HYV sorghum and cotton receive some fertilizers in kanzara. The value of pesticide use per hectare is low in all the villages, except for commercial crops in Kanzara village. In all the villages farmers generally go to the nearest town to buy inputs. Most of the farmers in Kanzara village buy their fertilizer from Cooperative Societies unlike in Aurepalle where farmers go to private shops. In all the villages farmers reported some shortages particularly on complex fertilizers. Prices of fertilizers fluctuate with private dealers;
but cooperative societies and government godowns charge the

government fixed prices. In all the villages farmers buy pesticides mostly from the private shops. There is no major shortage on pesticide supply in these villages.

Commercial input use in Indian agriculture is relatively recent. Prior to 1940, fertilizer use was negligible and was confined to plantation and commercial crops. Widespread use of pesticide in the Indian agriculture started around 1948, after the Bengal famine, which brought into the light the importance of pesticide in the field of agriculture. However, the quantities used was negligible. A new agricultural strategy in 1966 saw the introduction of high yielding varieties (HYV) of seeds first for wheat and then for rice and other coarse cereals. Compared to the traditional method of cultivation, in the new agricultural strategy crops were found to be more responsive to fertilizer and to be also more susceptible to pest infestation.

With the increase in area under HYV of food crops there was a considerable increase in the demand for both fertilizers and pesticides. The new strategy envisaged massive imports as well as expansion of domestic fertilizer and pesticide production capacity. In Table-I, the increase in the use of fertilizer pesticide and HYV-seeds over time is shown together with imports. This process led to 'monetarization' of the Indian agricultural sector. Farmers started growing crops for the market and consequently came into closer contact with commercial farm inputs. In the changed environment the marketing channels for commercial farm inputs gained importance. Timely supply of adequate quantities of different types of fertilizer and pesticides, availability of transport and storage facilities, reasonable prices and government policies became the focus of discussion since they determined the proper use of available inputs.

Nearly two-thirds of India's cropped land falls in the semi-arid zone of which less than one-third has well-developed irrigatiion resources. The non-irrigated semi-arid tropics (SAT) cover nearly 42% of India's cropped area and 65% of that in the Indian SAT. This area is mainly spread over Madhya Pradesh, Maharashtra, Gujarat, eastern Rajasthan, central Andhra Pradesh and Karnataka as can be seen in Figure 1. From the figure we find that fertilizer use and extent of irrigation are closely relate.

Thus commercial input use in not equally spread throughout India both in terms of area covered and quantities used. It is important to determine the cause of the difference between optimal and actual input use. Risk aversion, lack of knowledge, lack of labour, money and credit constraints, or lack of labour, money and credit constraints, or lack of timely availability are seen as main reasons for non-optimal input use.

In this study we investigate how far the functioning of the input market is a constraint for farmers in obtaining the commercial inputs such as fertilizer, pesticides and seeds particularly in semi-arid areas of India.

FIG. 32.1

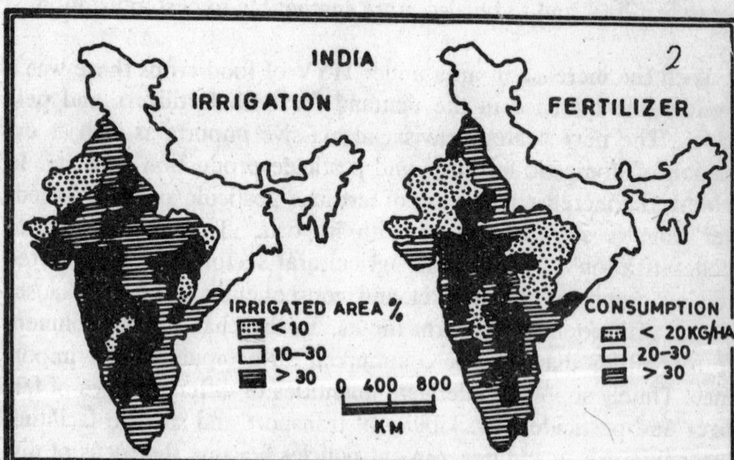

The aim of this study is to:

A. Describe how markets for inputs are operating in India.
B. To identify which of the inputs are facing constraints of what types.

In the first section of this study the functioning of the fertilizer, pesticide and seed market in India is described. While discussing the channels for these inputs government policies on pricing, subsidy, allocation, imports, promotion, etc. are highlighted. The existing problems in the delivery system of these inputs are discussed with a view to improving the efficiency of the existing marketing channels so farmers will have better access to these inputs.

In the second section the extent of utilization of commercial inputs at farm level in three villages of three different zones of the SAT India are analyzed.

TABLE I : PRODUCTION AND IMPORTS OF FERTILIZERS, PESTICIDES AND CERTIFIED/ QUALITY SEEDS IN INDIA OVER TIME

	Fertilizer		Pesticides		Certified/quality Seeds	
	Consumption N+P+K 000 tonnes	Imports N+P+K 000 tonnes	Production 000 tonnes	Imports 000 tonnes	Production 000 tonnes	Imports
1955-65	130.8	na	na	na	na	-
1965-66	784.6	na	13.9	12.1	na	-
1975-76	2893.7	1635.0	34.3	15.3	na	-
1980-81	5516.0	2759.0	43.3	4.3	218.6	-
1981-82	6067.0	2042.0	48.7	3.7	241.8	-
1982-83	6418.0	1131.7	na	na	366.1	-
1983-84	7710.0	1355.7	na	na	512.7	-
1984-85	8374.0*	3597.3*	58.4*	1.1*	705.6*	-

* Estimated figures; na = applicable
Source: various reports

The Fertilizer Marketing

The Structure of the Fertilizer Marketing Channels

Currently fertilizers are marketed through three different channels the private channel, the governmental channel and the cooperative channel. Fertilizer is handled by private companies in the private channel. In the governmental channel the fertilizer is sold from government godowns at taluka or block level and in the cooperative channel cooperative societies at various levels are distributing fertilizer through retail outlets Figure 2. The importance of the three channels differs from region to region as seen from the number of sales points for the different channels in Table-II. In the eastern and southern states the private channel is very strong.

FIG. 32.2

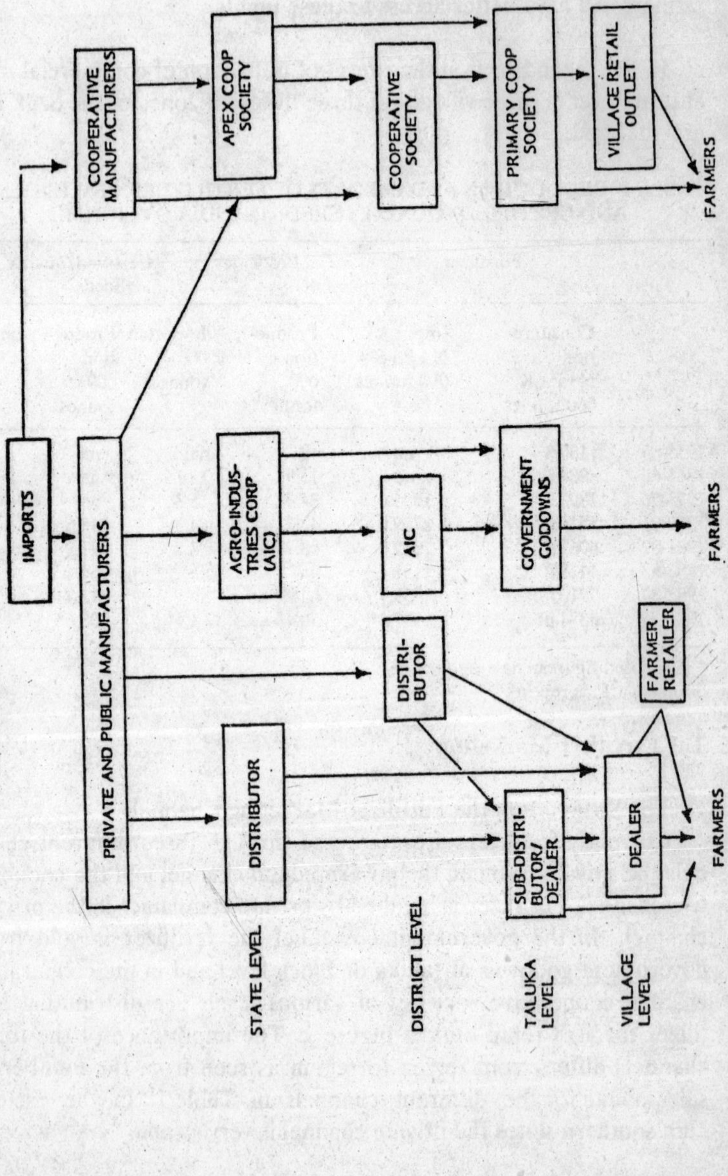

Market channels for fertilizers.

TABLE II : THE NUMBER OF FERTILISER SALES POINTS, CROPPED AREA SERVICED AND CONSUMPTION PER SALE POINT IN DIFFERENT REGIONS OF INDIA (AS ON 31-3-1984)

Region	Coop. and other institutional agencies		Private outlets		Total sales	Gross cropped points	$N+P_2O_5+K_2O$ consumption area/sale points (ha)	consumption per sale point (tonnes)	$N+P_2O_5+K_2$ per unit of cropped area (ha)
	No.	Percent	No.	Percent					
Central	18939	53	16600	47	35539	1980	68.8	34.6	
East	6013	16	32064	84	38077	966	24.2	24.3	
North	8158	61	5213	39	13371	1221	119.9	98.1	
South	11981	30	28296	70	40277	842	54.6	64.8	
West	10188	55	8365	45	18553	1900	70.3	37.0	
All India	55279	38	90538	62	145817	1325	59.6	44.9	

Source: 'Fertilizer Statistics' 1983-84. Fertilizer Association of India.

In the northern states of India where dealers have to cope with many logistical problems the cooperative and government channels are important. These figures for different states in India are given in Appendix Table-I.

The gross cropped area per sale point is 1325 ha on average. It is around 1900 ha in central and western India and only 842 ha in southern India. The N+P O +K O consumption per sale point is 59.6 tonne on the average and varies from 120 tonne in northern India to 24 tonnes in eastern India.

The Private Channel

In the private channel fertilizer flows from private and public manufacturers through distributors at wholesale level and dealers, sub-dealers and farmers-retailers at retail level to the farmers. All the prices and margins are fixed by the government.

The fertilizer is sold to the distributor at the wholesale price, that means consumer price minus distribution margin.

The manufacturers as well as the distributors give off-season rebate and quantity rebates for several products. The rebates differ from product to product and situation to situation,. It would be interesting to know that 23 different fertilizers pass through the distribution network. They consist of stright as well as complex fertilizers. The productwise distribution pattern differs from state to state depending upon cropping pattern and soil type.

Most of the distributors, dealers and farmers prefer to buy fertilizer on credit. There should be sufficient distribution credit for fertilizer trade to buy and stock fertilizers before the season and production credit for the farmers to purchase them. The main sources of credit for distributors are commercial banks and the fertilizer manufacturers.

For farmers the sources of credit are commercial banks, cooperative banks, government loans, local moneylenders and friends or relatives.

The Government Channel

In the government channel fertilizer is sold to the farmers in government godowns at taluka or block level. The importance of this channel varies from state to state dependent on the interest and the managing capacity of the people in charge and on the need for public fertilizer sale because of lack of private traders dealing in fertilizer.

The government channel is also important because the private channels are mostly concentrated near the rail lines and are not spread in the interior areas.The recent government policy to introduce block delivery system whereby transport charges are paid upto the block level is aimed to overcome this shortcoming in the present distribution network.

The government channel grown in importance during ties of scarce fertilizer supplies. Under such circumstances every farmer is only allowed to buy a fixed quantity of fertilizer depending on his cultivated area.

The Cooperative Channel

Cooperative societies at State, district, taluka, block and village level are set up to take care of the farmers, interest, There are cooperative societies for marketing, storage, processing and financing. Some of them deal with only one aspect and others deal with more than one., It was the government policy to encourage cooperatives in the distribution of fertilizers. There are a few fertilizer units in the cooperative sector also. Since cooperatives handled several activities like lending, purchase of farm output etc. this was a right step. In case of a cooperative marketing society which handles crop output as well as inputs, farmers can buy fertilizer on credit and repay after harvesting with their produce. In other cases farmers can get loans from cooperative banks, The size of the loan depends upon the land they own. In most of the cases 2/3 of the loan is in cash and 1/3 is in kind that means for 1/3 of the loan they can banks charge 12%interest a year, while commercial banks charge 15 to 18% interest.

The committee on fertilizers in 1965 felt that the cooperatives lacked marketing experience, and owing to inadequate distribution margin, fertilizer distribution has in many cases been a monetary drag on the cooperative system. It thus did not want to overburden the cooperatives, and hence suggested a multi-agency approach for fertilizer distribution system.

However, cooperatives still constitute an important outlet for fertilizers with about 45% of the total fertilizers consumed being distributed by this channel, Table-III.

Government regulations of fertilizer trade

The Indian government intervened in the fertilizer market to encourage its more widespread production and use. Fertilizers were declared essential commodities through the Essential Commodities Act/Fertilizer Control Order in 1967. This implies that allocation of fertilizers, quantity to be imported, and all the prices and distribution margins in the fertilizer trade are fixed by the government. All distributors and dealers in fertilizer are obliged to have a licence to sell fertilizer which is issued by the District Director of Agriculture. The government also has lain down some strict quality control measures under Fertilizer Control Order for all the indigenously manufactured products., Government officials check quality of products in the field by taking samples at dealer outlets and storage points. In case of proven malpractices the persons responsible lose their license and are condemned.

Allocation policy

The imported as well as the indigenous fertilizer is allocated by the government in biannual zonal conferences. These meetings are attended by experts of the Ministry of Agriculture, the Ministry of Fertilizer and Chemicals, representatives of fertilizer manufacturers of the FAI owned departments of Agriculture of the different States in the zone,. While making the allocation plan, care has to be taken that one region is not dependent on the supplier only and one manufacturer should not be dependent on the fertilizer consumption of one region only. There should be enough competition among the different manufacturers of important inputs.

Table III : DISTRIBUTION OF FERTILIZERS BY COOPERATIVE SOCIETIES IN INDIA FROM 1978-79 TO 1983-84.

Years	Total consumption NPK ('000 tonnes)	Fertilizers sold by cooperative societies NPK ('000 tonnes)	% of total consumption
1978-79	5117	2150	42.0
1979-80	5265	2350	44.7
1980-81	5516	2530	45.9
1981-82	6067	2867	47.3
1982-83	6387	3016	47.2
1983-84	7792	3375*	43.3*

Source : AnnualReport 1983-84, National Cooperative Development Corporation.

* Estimated.

Fertilizer Pricing System

Fertilizer prices are controlled by the government since 1944. The prices of statutorily controlled fertilizers have not been revised for the last two years since June 29, 1983. when they were brought down from the 1981 prices,. This has led to an increase in government subsidy., The trends in fertilizer prices during the last two decades reveals that these have been consistently kept at fairly low levels. Table-IV illustrates this trend for urea from 1979 onwards.

The fertilizer pricing system in. India has evolved round two broad objectives to induce increased consumption of fertilizer which (apart from other inputs) in turn, enables increased foodgrain production and at the same time encourages growth and efficiency in the Fertilizer Industry to meet the increasing demand. The Government of India introduced the Retention Price Scheme (RPS) for nitrogenous fertilizer in November 1977 and for complex fertilizer and TSP in February 1979 based on the recommendation of the committee.

Distribution margins

Not only the consumer price and retention price is fixed by the government but the distribution margin as well. The distribution margins and prices for urea from 1956 till 1983 are given in Table-V.

The governmennt allows a higher margin for cooperative societies since 1981. The distribution margin in Rs/tonne has increased during this period but the margin as a percentage of the consumer price shows a slight decline

Shortage and Transportation

The fertilizer companies are patronising the public warehouses who are providing a package of services at known costs throughout the country. The public warehouses are run by the Central Warehouse Corporation and the State Warehouse corporation. Fertilizer is transported from the factories to the warehouses in the different states mostly by rail. Seventy per cent of the fertilizer transport (in tonnes/km) goes by rail, 28% by road and 2% by water.

Storage and Transportation

The fertilizer companies are patronising the public warehouses who are providing a package of services at known costs throughout the country. The public warehouses are run by the Central Warehouse Corporation and the State Warehouse Corporations. Fertilizer is transported from the factories to the warehouses in the different states mostly by rail. Seventy per cent of the fertilizer transport (in tonnes/km) goes by rail, 28% by road and 2% by water.

The Government of India reimburses the manufacturers the transport costs from the factory to the warehouse. Transport costs are pooled for price equalization policies. In the early stages of fertilizer use it is good to equalize transport costs so that farmers far price equalization policies. In the early stages of fertilizer use it is good to equalize transport costs so that farmers far from manufacturing centres are not at a disadvantage. The recently introduced Block Delivery System where transport costs are reimbursed upto the block level is to encourage retail outlets in interior areas also.

The transport costs from the distributor to the dealers is not subsidized by the government. Sometimes, the distributor pays it partly or completely but mostly the dealer is responsible for these costs. In most of the cases the farmers transport the fertilizer by bullock cart or by bicycle to his farm.

TABLE IV : THE AVERAGE COST OF IMPORTED UREA AT THE FARM GATE, THE AVERAGE COSTS OF INDIGENOUS UREA (AVERAGE RETENTION PRICE PLUS EQUATED FREIGHT) AND THE MAXIMUM SALE PRICE EFFECTIVE FROM VARIOUS DATES.

Year	Average cost Rs/tonne of Imported urea	Indigenous urea	Max.sale price Rs/tonne	Effective from
1979-80	2194	1848	1450	10-3-79
1980-81	2731	2016	2000	08-6-80
1981-82	3026	2541	2350	11-7-81
1982-83	2768	2909	2150	29-6-83

Source : Pratap Narayan, 'Dynamics of price and subsidies in fertilizers -- Indian experience. Fertilizer News, Vol. 8, No. 8, p.21.

Promotion

Fertilizers use in India is still low and many farmers use far less than the recommended doses. Many farmers are not fully aware of the advantage of fertilizer use, so promotion is a very important means to raise fertilizer consumption and increase the agricultural output. The burden of fertilizer promotion invariably falls on the government although it is the joint responsibility of manufacturer, and distributor. Private manufacturers may not be in a position to take initiative on their own.

Promotion is done by the Ministry of Agriculture through village extension workers and by the fertilizer manufacturers. All the public cooperatives as well as the private manufacturers do have an intensive fertilizer promotion program., The Ministry of Agriculture reimburses the expenses they make on the extension programs. These promotion measures should be understood by the farmers and should not only created an awareness in them but also induce a desire to use fertilizers. Simple and easy to follow messages should be putforth. The promotion programs consist of: posters; video films; radio programs; newspaper advertisement, farmers meetings, field days; crop seminars;

supply of minikits; village adoption programs; district adoption programs.

Table V : THE DISTRIBUTION MARGIN FOR UREA FERTILIZER.

Effective from	Distribution margin (Rs/tonnes)	Urea Price (Rs/tonnes)	Margin as % of urea price
1-2-1966	70	680	10.3
1-4-1967	80	840	9.6
1-4-1968	80	860	9.4
17-4-1969	80	946	8.5
9-3-1971	80	923	8.7
17-3-1972	80	959	8.4
1-10-1973	80	1050	7.7
1-6-1974	80	2000	4.0
18-7-1975	115	1850	6.3
16-3-1976	115	1750	6.6
8-2-1977	115	1650	7.0
12-10-1977	115	1550	7.5
10-3-1979	115	1450	8.0
8-6-1980	115	2000	5.8
11-7-1981	115	2350	4.9
13-11-1981	140* 120**	2350	6.0 5.1
20-5-1983	150* 130**	2350	6.4 5.5
29-6-1983	150* 130**	2150	7.0 6.0

Source : Naryana, B.L., Fertilizer Distribution Margins Fertilizer Marketing News, Vol.16, No. 10.

* For institutional agencies. ** For private dealers.

Evaluation of Fertilizer Trade

Fertilizer marketing as can be seen is a complex problem involving price regulation, efficient use of transport network to keep down costs and to provide fertilizers at same cost to distant places also, keeping a watch on storage costs to minimize wastage on space, and finally fertilizer promotion activities. To requlate and control a market satisfactorily without using the price mechanism is very difficult especially is a huge and diverse country like India. There are many difficulties at all levels in the marketing channels.

Seasonal demand of fertilizers

Although fertilizer production is regular throughout the year the consumption is not. Most of the farmers buy the fertilizer just before application because they do not have cash or do not get credit to buy fertilizer in advance. Farmers also do not have storage facilities and under dry land conditions the level of fertilizer use largely depends on the rainfall received just before sowing,. The peaks in the fertilizer consumption causes lost of problems because of lack of sufficient transport and storage facilities.

Demand Forecast and Allocation Policy

The government allocation policy between states leads to pockets of scarcity or surplus thus generating black market prices. Forecasting fertilizer demand is crucial since imports are based of the forecast of demand. Any substantial deviation from the actual offtake leads to shortages of glut in the fertilizer market. It is for all fertilizers or for a particular type. This leads to the problem of shortages within a state and fertilizers are transported from low consumption districts to high consumption districts at premium prices.

Pricing System

The Retention Price Scheme (RPS) is a drag on the government exchequer since government has to maintain inefficient units by subsidizing their production. In recent years the government subsidy on fertilizers has been increasing. In 1982-83 the total subsidy on imported and domestic fertilizer was Rs. 6480 million. During the last two decades the consumer prices of fertilizer have been consistently kept at fairly low levels while this may be good the better off farmers take advantage of this rather than the small farmers.

Inspite of such huge subsidies the paddy/urea price ratio is very low in India (0.52), which means fertilizer prices are still high from farmers point of view. The fertilizer subsidy scheme is very costly and it can cause problems in the future.

Distribution Margins

The margins for fertilizer trade in India are very low which stimulate malpractices in the private channel. The consumer prices of fertilizer are fixed by the government but in time of shortages prices will rise on the black market. In times of surplus prices will be lower than the government fixed prices. Distributors and dealers sometimes create a shortage to raise the prices artificially. Another malpractice common in the private channel is that the bags are damaged on purpose and contain less than the original quantity. Fertilizer is sold in 40 or 50 kg bags only but in some villages dealers sell small quantities ranging from 5 to 30 kgs. The prices they ask in such cases are higher than the government fixed prices.

Promotion and extension

Promotion and information on fertilizer use are very important to raise fertilizer consumption and increase the agricultural output.

The farmers come in direct contact with dealers (retail outlets) and not with the manufacturers or distributors. Hence, it would be ideal if every dealer is in a position to give proper advice to farmers on fertilizer use. However, the situation is different, most dealers have little technical knowledge about fertilizer use and farmers generally cannot trust their advice. Dealer training programmes on agricultural input use should be taken up on a priority basis.

Farmers Choice of Direction Channel

The decision in which of the three channels a farmer buys fertilizers is based on many considerations. Normally, farmers buy fertilizer in the nearest shop but reasons to go to other shops can be numerous, for instance, lower prices, better terms for credit, better availability, special relationship with a dealer etc. Government godowns mostly have limited stock and farmers are not always able to buy the type of fertilizer they prefer.

In the private channel the prices fluctuate slightly with the demand but in cooperative societies fertilizer is always sold at the government fixed prices. In times of shortages farmers prefer to buy fertilizer at the cooperative society and in times of surplus they prefer private dealers because the price is less. Sometimes farmers are forced by cooperative societies to buy a type of fertilizer which is in surplus when they; want to buy another type of fertilizer which is in shortage.

Pesticide Marketing

In the new agriculture technology based on HYVs pesticides play an important role. Cotton, rice and vege tables together accounted for about 80% of the total pesticides used in Indian agriculture (Table V1). Although pesticide consumption in India is increasing along with production, India uses only 3% of the worlds consumption of pesticides. India consumes only 450 gms per ha which is very low compared to 10,800 in Japan and 1,500 in USA and 1870 gm/ha in Europe (In 1965 pesticide use in India was only 77 gm/ha).

The maximum amount of formulated pesticides in India are used in the southern states of India which are more prone to pest attack. The northern states which have relatively colder climate, pesticide use is low. Exact figures are difficult to obtain. Table VII shows the retail value of pesticides marketed in India in 1980. Andhra Pradesh, Gujarat and Tamil Nadu head the list. In Andhra Pradesh cash crops like cotton and tobacco and cereals like rice may be responsible for high consumption.

India now-a-days is almost self-sufficient in the manufacture of pesticides. Finished products are formulated from technical grade material which is locally manufactured, only 5% of the material are imported, but it comprises some 15 different compounds.

Marketing Channels

Figure 3 shows four marketing channels through which pesticide provided by manufacturers and formulators are supplied to the farmers. The retail outlets for pesticides are similar to those for fertilizers. However, not all fertilizer dealers deal in pesticides and vice versa. The number of pesticide outlets are also less compared to fertilizer depots. Cooperatives have increasingly taken up the distribution of pesticide but the private channel is still the most important distribution channel. In 1983, there were 9,500 selling points in the public sector against a total of 71,000 selling points. Thus about 80% of distribution points are on private sector, 20% with cooperatives and state departments.

FIG. 32.3

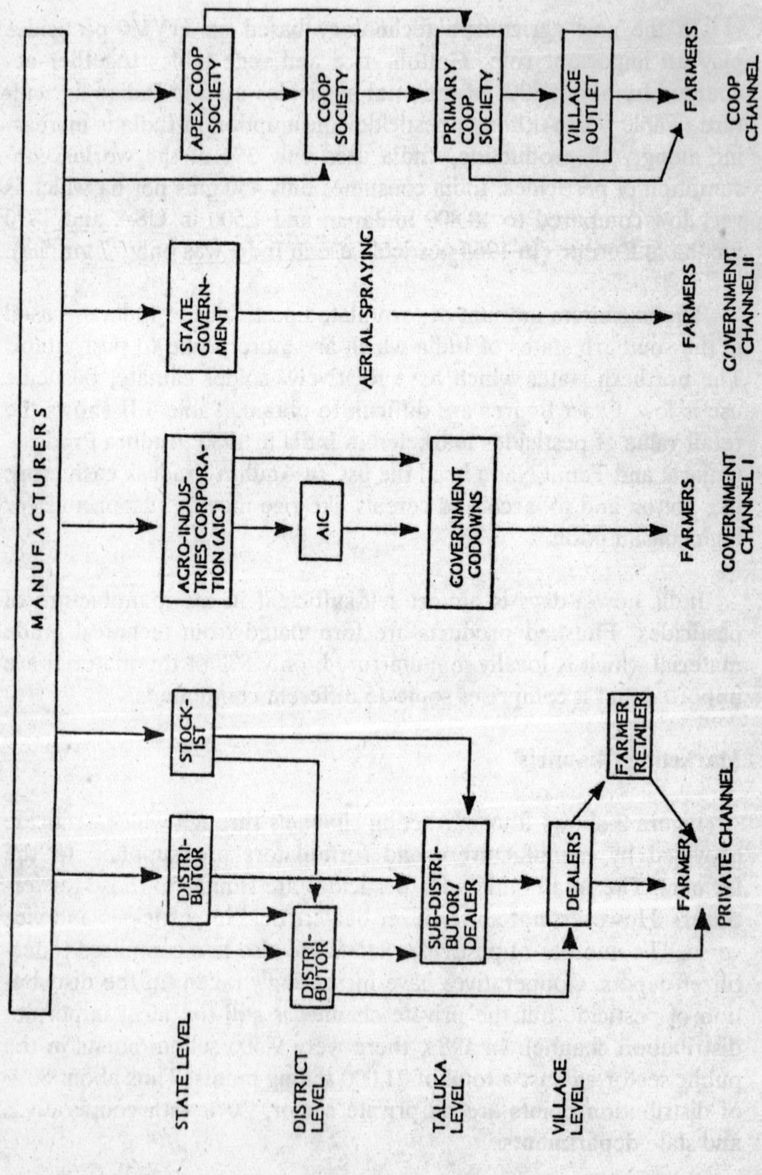
MANUFACTURERS
APEX COOP SOCIETY
COOP SOCIETY
PRIMARY COOP SOCIETY
VILLAGE OUTLET
FARMERS
COOP CHANNEL
STATE GOVERN-MENT
AERIAL SPRAYING
FARMERS
GOVERNMENT CHANNEL II
AGRO-INDUS-TRIES CORPORA-TION (AIC)
AIC
GOVERNMENT GODOWNS
FARMERS
GOVERNMENT CHANNEL I
STOCK-IST
DISTRI-BUTOR
DISTRI-BUTOR
SUB-DISTRI-BUTOR/ DEALER
DEALERS
FARMER RETAILER
FARMERS
PRIVATE CHANNEL
STATE LEVEL
DISTRICT LEVEL
TALUKA LEVEL
VILLAGE LEVEL

Table VI : PESTICIDE USAGE PER CROP IN INDIA, 1980. [RETAIL VALUE (FARM-GATE) IN MILLION RUPEES]

Crop	Ratail value (million Rs)	Percentage
Cotton	1390	40.5
Rice	1020	29.5
Vegetables	390	11.4
Sugarcane	190	5.6
Pulses & oilseeds	150	4.4
Plantation	150	4.4
Others	140	4.2
Total	3430[1]	100.0

Source : Banerjee, A.K., "Outlook for Pesticides : Lessons from Abroad," Pesticides Annual, 1980-81, p.5

1. The corresponding first point sales value in the same year, i.e. from producers/formulators to distributors/stockists was Rs. 2.820 million.

The Private Channel

In the private channel pesticide flows from the manufacturers through distributors or stockists, sub-distributors, dealers and farmers-retailers to the farmers. This is very much similar to the marketing of any other consumer product except that it is subject to some special rules and regulations. Private companies have repre-sentatives at district-level who get in contact with distributors to book orders and give information about the use of the pesticides. Multinational companies for instance do not allow the distributors to sell the same products of different brand names.

Government channel I

The manufacturers sell pesticides in bulk with rebates to the government at state levels. The products are sold in mobile sales offices or local government depots supervised by the District Director of Agriculture. There are nearly 6 to 7 thousand depots managed by different state governments. Manufacturers are willing to sell certain quantities of products to the government because it acts as an indirect promotion for their product. Farmers have more confidence in brand names and products sold in the government godowns. Consumer prices in this channel is about 15% less than the private channel.

Table VII : VALUE OF PESTICIDE MARKATED IN INDIA, 1980.
[RETAIL VALUE (FARM-GATE) IN MILLION RUPEES]

State	Retail value (million Rs)	Percentage of total Indian market
Andhra Pradesh	500	14.6
Gujarat	450	13.0
Tamil Nadu	400	11.7
Maharashtra	300	8.8
Punjab	270	8.0
Uttar Pradesh	210	6.0
West Bengal	200	5.8
Haryana and Delhi	180	5.3
Karnataka	150	4.4
Bihar	100	2.9
Subtotal	2760	80.5
Others	670	19.5
Total	3430[1]	100.0

Source : Benerjee, A.K., "Outlook for Pesticides : Lessons from Abroad," Pesticides Annual, 1980-81, p.5.

1. The corresponding first point sales value in same year, i.e. from producers/formulators to distributors/stockists was Rs. 2820 million.

Government Channel II

This channel provides plant protection through aerial spraying. The government buys plant protection products for tobacco, sugar-cane and cotton in bulk. The products are sprayed through helicopters as aerial spray and the farmers pay about Rs. 10 to 20 per ha which is added as a cess to their land taxes.

Government regulations in pesticide trade

The government has taken several policy measures for the development of the pesticide industry in India. This industry is open to large houses and foreign majority companies. Priority is accorded to this industry for the import of raw materials and intermediates which are not indigenously available. In order to sustain the formulation industry, pesticides in pure form are allowed to be imported. The import of pesticides which are indigenously manufactured is banned. However, in the cases where the cost of indigenous production is high or inadequate to meet the demand, import of pesticide is permitted.

Quality control is an important aspect in pesticide marketing. It is aimed to check adulteration and sub-standard products. Five regional pesticide testing laboratories have been set up for Quality Control besides various other laboratories at state level. It is governed by Indian standards specification.

Promotion

To "use" the right type of pesticides at the right time in a proper way needs a lot of knowledge. The pesticide industry does not give enough information and quidance to pesticide users, but all the manufacturers do have a promotion program of posters, crop folders, demonstrations, video films, radio programs, newspaper advertisement and stands on fairs.

Promotion of pesticide use and user's training is also done by the village extension workers of the Ministry of Agriculture. Promotion of agro-pesticide use should be of the informative kind. Farmers need simple information on such a complicated subject.

Problems in Pesticide Trade

In the pesticide trade government intervention in the form of rules and regulation are less, as compared to fertilizer trade. The market is mainly controlled by the pricing mechanism. Although the trade regulations for pesticides are simple, there are difficulties at all levels in these channels.

Under the existing policy, technical grade pesticide manufacturers are required to make available 50% of their production to n0n-associated formulators but the prices at which such supplies are made are not economical for the formulators.

The times till new pesticides are approved by the registration committee is a problem to the manufacturers because they cannot sell the new product for at least two years. Another problem for the manufacturers is that power, water and raw materials are not always available in sufficient quantities.

The demand for pesticides is difficult to predict and dealers sometimes cannot sell the products before the expiry date passes. If the same product is in shortage some time later dealers will try to sell the old products to farmers if they have some.

Sometimes it is difficult for farmers to get reliable information on proper pesticide use, because government godowns are far away, farmers cannot get in touch with the village extension workers and the advice of private dealers is not correct.

The quality of the products is also a problem because it varies and farmers lose confidence in pesticide use. In 1983-84 1,072 pesticide samples were analyzed by the Central Insecticides Laboratory of which 25.1% were not satisfactory.

Seed Marketing

India's seed industry was little developed until the mid-sixties when as a consequence of plant breeding breakthrough, HYVs and hybrids emerged that were significantly superior to the traditional varieties and required seed processing on scientific lines. The production of certified/quality seed from 1980 in India for some crop group is shown in Table VIII. The total seed production has doubled during the last four years.

In 1963, the National Seeds Corporation (NSC) was established by the government of India to promote the seed industry from production through to marketing and to establish a system of quality control. Although the NSC is not meant to be a agency for the production and distribution of quality seeds by 1974/75 it had become the largest producer accounting for 73,000 tonnes of seed, representing about 50% of indigenous production. In 1974, the National Seed Programme (NSP) was taken up to develop a broad-based, decentralised network of seed production, processing, storage and marketing agencies. The NSP established State Seeds Corporation

(SSC) and took over the production role which NSC had hitherto performed. It was not contemplated that every state corporation would become self-sufficient in respect of the total needs of the state, and in any case this is not sound because this might not be the economically either.

Before a variety can be multiplied as certified seed it has to be notified and licenced by the State Variety Release Committee (SVRC) and the Central Variety Release Committee (CVRC).

Private seed companies produce certified seeds as well as truthfully labelled seeds (also called quality seed). Truthfully labelled seed (quality seed) are varieties which are not notified and licenced by the government. The brand name is used as a guarantee for the quality.

The Seed Marketing Channels

In the seed trade separate channels are not easy to distinguish as can be seen in Figure 4. Private distributors and dealers get the supplies from the NSC, the different SSC's or private seed companies. The cooperative societies purchase seed from the NSC and the SSC only. The NSC and the SSC have their own sale counters at taluka level. The quantity sold through these sale counters is not much. However, they function as a check-point for prices and quality for farmers.

In the government godowns only certified seed produced by the NSC or SSC is sold. The Andhra Pradesh State Seeds Corporation for instance sells 60% of its production to agro industries corporation, 30% to the NSC' 10% to private dealers and 1% through their own sales counters.

Government godowns -- NSC and SSC -- do not provide credit facilities to farmers. Cooperative societies mostly do give credit to farmers for buying seed and the credit facilities given by private dealers depend on the relationship between trader and farmer.

FIG. 32.4

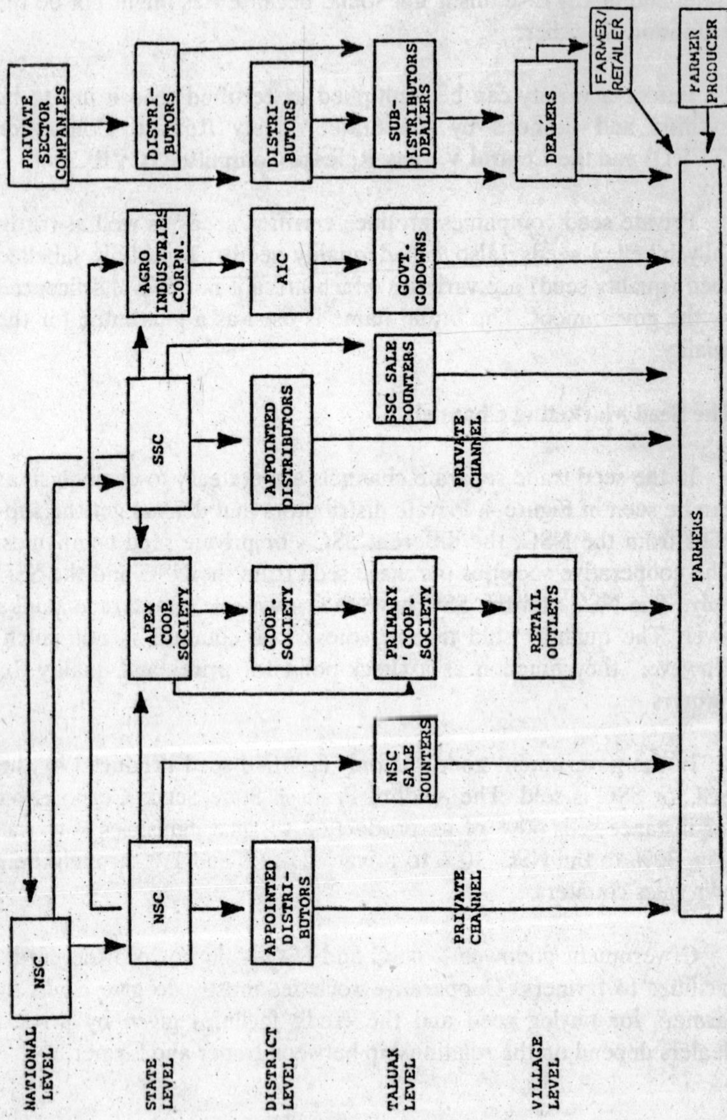

Market channels for seeds.

TABLE VIII : PRODUCTION OF CERTIFIED/QUALITY SEEDS IN INDIA. ('000 TONNES)

	1980-81	1981-82	1982-83	1983-84
Cereals	187.4	201.3	292.9	372.6
Pulses	10.2	11.9	20.7	55.4
Oilseeds	1.4	4.4	16.5	85.7
Fibres	7.0	9.6	13.5	28.7
Potato	11.8	13.4	20.0	33.9
Others	0.8	1.2	2.5	6.0
Grand total	218.6	241.8	366.1	512.7

Source : Lakshmi Roy, "The New Green Dimension of the Seventh Plan", The Economic Times, August 14, 1985.

Government regulations in the seed trade

Generally the government regulations in the seed trade are less. Certified seed produced by NSC or SSCs has to be from varieties notified and licensed by the CVRC.

Certified seed has to be sold in sealed bags and the label should mention the germination ratio and date of production. Private companies are allowed to sell all the varieties they want to and do not have to sell it in sealed bags.

The government came out with the Seed Control Act in 1983 declaring seed to be an essential commodity and requiring compulsory registration of dealers, imposing price control etc. However, the operation of the order has been stayed by various courts. The issue is now pending before the Supreme Court.

Promotion

Most farmers are aware of the fact that quality seed is necessary for attaining higher levels of productivity. Still much information has to be given to farmers on the optimal quantities and varieties they should use. The NSC and SSC have some promotion programs, they train village, extension workers, have posters, crop folders demonstrations, video films, and newspaper advertisement. Private breeders do have a promotion program on the above lines and mainly propagate their brand name.

Evaluation of the Seed Trade

Farmers mostly use their own seed or buy seed from other farmers. If the farmer decides to buy seeds from other sources he generally prefers to buy seed from a local dealer because they

-sell seed in unsealed bags so the farmer can look at it and judge the quality;
-they sometimes provide credit facilities;
-the shops are mostly nearly;
-they sell uncertified seed at lower prices.

The NSC and SSC dealers do not provide credit to dealers and this is an important reason for dealers to buy seeds from private breeders.

The quality of the seed sold is not always satisfactory. Seed is a living product and has to be handled and stored with care. Storage facilities in consuming areas are not always adequate.

Sometimes the germination is too low or adulteration has taken place. After seed is declared an essential commodity malpractices can be prevented more easily.

The seed industry in India has to cope with many difficulties. There is hardly any coordination between the different organizations. There is not enough knowledge of the market, the preference for varieties differ from place to place and change over time rapidly.

Situation on Commercial input Marketing in Three Villages in Sat India

In the previous section the functioning of the input markets for fertilizer, pesticides, and seeds was described at the all-India level. In this section, the utilization of commercial inputs at farm level in three different villages in the SAT India are compared. Individual farmer's use and access to fertilizer, pesticides, and seeds are studied.

The three village considered in this study are part of ICRISAT

Village Level Studies being conducted since 1975 in 6 village in 3 major agroclimatic zones of India. In each of these villages, data from 40 households (10 each from landless labor, small, medium, and large-farm categories) were monitored by resident investigators on all aspects of farming including input, output details. Shirapur, in Sholapur district (Maharashtra), is characterized by low and unstable rainfall, and is dominated by post-rainy season cropping of mainly coarse cereals and pulses on medium-deep Vertisols. Kanzara, in Akola district (Maharashtra state) has similar soils, stable and somewhat higher rainfall, very little irrigation, and fairly high area under nonirrigated, commercial crops like cotton, hybrid sorghum. Aurepalle in Mahbubnagar district (Andhra Pradesh), state has red soils, high irrigation, low rainfall and relatively smaller holdings. The cropping pattern is dominated by paddy. For the present study on input markets extra information is gathered by means of interviews with farmers using fertilizer and other inputs. Input dealers in the vicinity of these villages (including neighbouring towns if any) were also interviewed.

The nearest market town for farmers in Aurepalle village is Amangal which is 10 km away. Farmers in Shirapur go to another village, Mohol 10 kms away, and Kanzara farmers go to Murtizapur town which is also 10 kms away. In all the three villages farmers transport their produce mostly by bullock carts and inputs also by bullock carts, bicycle or bus.

When the mean values (for all farmers in 1983-84) of the fertilizer use on irrigated and non-irrigated areas are compared, Table IX we find that the use of fertilizer on non-irrigated land is low in all the villages. In Kanzara village farmers use some fertilizer on non-irrigated land particularly for crops like HYV sorghum and wheat. In Shirapur, the use of fertilizer on non-irrigated as well as irrigated land is negligible. The value of the seed used per ha is higher on irrigated land. The Kanzara farmers invest more money on seeds as compared with the other two villages. The value of the pesticide use per hectare is low in all the three villages on irrigated as well as unirrigated land. In Kanzara village pesticides are mainly used on cotton and chillies.

Table IX : THE VALUE OF FERTILIZERS, PESTICIDES, SEEDS AND TOTAL INPUT VALUE IN RS/HA IN STUDY VILLAGES IN THE YEAR 1983-84.

	Aurepalle		Shirapur		Kanzara	
	Irri-gated	Not-irri-gated	Irri-gated	Not-irri-gated	Irri-gated	Not-Irri-gated
Fertilizers	558.96	17.21	65.09	0.48	429.18	148.46
Pesticides	13.49	10.69	6.98	1.30	126.46	5.53
Seeds	190.79	38.52	129.09	28.84	434.94	85.68
Total inputs	2919.80	477.46	2519.96	358.81	2112.02	899.32
Output	5947.4	1070.51	1875.89	732.02	4411.39	1923.35

Farmers access to fertilizer

Most of the farmers in Aurepalle village buy their fertilizers from private shops in Amangal. In Shirapur village there are only 6 farmers who bought fertilizer regularly during the last three years out of 30 VLS respondent farmers. They go to private shops in Mohol or in Sholapur which is 22 kms away from Shirapur.

In Kanzara village 18 out of 23 respondents usually buy fertilizer in a cooperative society in Murtizapur and 5 farmers mostly go to private shops in Murtizapur.

One-third of the respondents in Aurepalle sometimes face supply constraints on complex fertilizer like 28:28:0 (three farmers) and 14:35:14. The dealers in fertilizer in Mahbubnagar district (Mahbubnagar, Jedcherla, Kalwakurty, etc.) problems in getting sufficient supplies of complex fertilizer like 17:17:17, and 28:28:0.

In Shirapur there was one farmer who had difficulties with getting the complex fertilizers 19:19:19 and 15:15:0 in August and September. Dealers in fertilizer in Sholapur and Mohol do not face any problems in the fertilizer supply in their region.

Sixteen out of 23 respondents in Kanzara village have problems with buying the type of fertilizer they want on time. Shortages exist on the complex fertilizer 18:18:10 and 20:20:0 at sowing time in June and on Urea in August/September. Dealers in Murtizapur and Akola admit that there are sometimes shortages on these fertilizers.

In the current year the private traders in Murtizapur did not have any stock of 18:18:10 and only a limited stock of 20:20:0. Private traders were selling Urea at the government fixed prices. Farmers who wanted to buy complex fertilizer at the cooperative society in Murtizapur were forced to buy one bag of Urea for every two bags of complex fertilizer.

Small farmers in Aurepalle sometimes buy fertilizer in quantities less than one bag from private traders or other farmers. The price per kg is 5 to 10 per cent higher in that case.

According to most of the respondents who buy fertilizer more than once during a year, the fertilizer prices fluctuate during the year. At times of shortages private dealers charge more than the government fixed prices and in times of surplus prices are slightly less. The cooperative societies as well as the government godowns always charge the government fixed prices. In Amangal the types of fertilizer the farmers prefer are not available.

In Table X the difference between the government fixed prices (+sales taxes) and the mean price the farmers actually paid for some important fertilizers are shown. The Table shows that most of the time the farmers pay more than the government fixed prices. The deferences between the actual and the government fixed prices change from year to year depending on supply and demand situation. Unfortunately, these price differences cannot be compared between the three villages because the pattern of fertilizer use is not the same. The difference between the fixed prices and the mean actual prices in 1983-84 is lower than in the other years for most fertilizers in the villages. Farmers in Kanzara in 1983-84 on an average paid even less than government fixed prices because there was an extra government subsidy on fertilizer, used for irrigated summer groundnut. In Aurepalle the price difference in 1983-84 was lower than in the previous years, despite higher consumption levels. This could be because of better supply position.

Farmers in Aurepalle on an average pay more for fertilizer than farmers in Kanzara. Most of the farmers in Kanzara prefer to buy fertilizer from the cooperative society where prices are always at the level fixed by the government. Farmers in Aurepalle usually buy fertilizer from private shops.

In a research on the use of fertilizer and organic manure done in 1980 , in the three study villages, reasons for farmers not using fertilizer at all or not using the recommended dose was elicited. The main reasons for farmers not using fertilizer are non-availability of credit and lack of irrigation facilities. Nonavailability of credit was mentioned as the most important reason by farmers in Aurepalle and Kanzara for not using the recommended dose. Lack of awareness of recommended dose and inadequate irrigation facilities are also important reasons for not using recommended dose.

Situation on pesticide marketing

Farmers in Aurepalle buy pesticides mostly from private shops in Amangal. Two respondent farmers buy pesticides directly from moneylenders in the village. In Kanazara farmers mostly buy pesticides in private shops and 4 respondents usually go to the cooperative society in Murtizapur. Only 6 of the VLS respondents in Shirapur sometimes applied pesticides, they buy it in private shops in Mohol and Sholapur.

In Aurepalle there are sometimes shortages on Rogor and Sevimol. Roger is mainly used on pigeonpea for Heliothis pod borer control and Sevimol for semi-loopers (Achoajanta) control which reduce the castor yields. In times of serious attack from semi-loopers on castor the availability of Sevimol and sprayers cause many problems. Prices of this pesticide rises by 10 to 15% and sometimes old stocks are sold to the farmers. In normal circumstances the availability of sprayers cause no problems in Aurepalle. Some farmers have their own sprayer, some borrow it from other farmers or moneylenders and others have to hire it for Rs. 5 to Rs. 6 per day.

In Shirapur farmers do not have problems with the availability of pesticides nor sprayers. Farmers who apply pesticides have their own sprayer or borrow it from other farmers.

Table X : DIFFERENCE BETWEEN GOVERNMENT FIXED PRICE AND ACTUALPRICE OF FERTILIZERS PAID BY FARMERS EXPRESSED AS PERCENT TO GOVERNMENT PRICE IN RECENT YEARS IN STUDY VILLAGES.

	1981-82	1982-83	1983-84
Aurepalle			
Urea	9.1	9.1	0.20
DAP	5.3	5.9	-4.0
17:17:17	7.0	8.2	5.0
14:35:14	-	1.2	6.9
28:28:0	4.3	5.7	0
Shirapur			
Urea	6.5	9.3	2.3
DAP	-	-	-8.7**
15:15:15	7.7	3.6	-5.1**
18:18:0	0.8	2.0	-2.0**
Kanzara			
Urea	4.7	8.4	-2.8**
15:15:15	7.7	3.6	-5.1**
18:18:0	0.8	2.0	-2.0**
ANP	8.2	7.3	-10.0**

* Data on one purchase of 50 kg.
** Subsidy on Irrigated Summer Groundnut.

Pesticide supply in Kanzara village is not a real problem although farmers sometimes have to wait for a few days to obtain the pesticide they want to apply. There are enough sprayers in the village.

Situation on Seed

In all the three villages farmers mostly use their own seed. They also buy seed from other farmers and quality or certified HYV seeds from private shops. In Kanzara 20% of the respondents preferred to purchase the sorghum variety CSH-9 in the cooperative society.

In Aurepalle it is common that farmers borrow seeds from other farmers or moneylenders. If farmers borrow paddy or castor seeds they have to give 150% produce back after harvest. For sorghum, millet, pigeonpea and horsegram, farmers have to give 200% produce back after harvest. Borrowing seed from other farmers is not prevalent in Shirapur and Kanzara.

Farmers never have problems in getting enough quantity of the certified quality seed of varieties they prefer in the shops. Sometimes they are not satisfied with the quality of the seed, the germination is not good or adulateration has taken place. This year for instance 1'3 of the respondents in Aurepalle were not satisfied with the certified Aruna Castor seed they had purchased.

Source of Information

Farmers in all the three villages get information and advice on fertilizer and pesticide use mostly from progressive farmers in the village, from their money lender or sometimes from the village or taluka shopkeepers. Only one farmer in Aurepalle goes to the government extension service in Amangal for advice. ICRISAT experiments and ICRISAT investigators in the villages were also mentioned as sources of information.

All the farmers relay on their own experience as far as decisions on seeds are concerned. After seeing a successful new variety with progressive farmers they may decide to try it themselves the next season.

Farmers in Aurepalle, and Kanzara were complaining about the village extension workers. They seldom visit the villages and farmers can hardly get in contact with them. Shirapur is also rarely visited by village extension workers.

Conclusion

If the government wants to prevent malpractices in fertilizer trade which effect the farmers they have to raise the distribution margin for the private channel so there will be more competition and less malpractices. The government allocation policy of fertilizer needs to be critically evaluated. How far the market forces of supply and demand will do a better job of allocation should be considered. For pesticides and seeds quality control measures should be followed strictly. Proper information on the use of these inputs should be given to farmers. Private dealers trading in commercial inputs should be trained for this purpose.

NOTE

1. The authors would like to thank Drs. M. von Oppen, N.V. Narasimham and Mr. K.V. Subba Rao for their valuable suggestions during the course of the study.

THIRTY THREE

S.S. Verma

Urbanization and Regional Development in Rohilkhand Plain U.P

Urbanization is being accepted as an essential part of economic development as well as an important index of regional progress and prosperity of human society (Verma, 1979). The paper attempts to discuss the regional development in Rohilkhand Plain in the same context.

Study Area

Rohilkhand plain (27° 25' N to 29° 55' lat. and 77° 55' E to 80° 28' E long) is the north central part of the Upper Ganga Plain lying between the Ganga river in west and south. In the east 150 m controur line and in the north 300 m contour lines seperate it from *Avadh* Plain and U.P. Himalayas respectively. The region so defined incorporates within its boundary the divisions of Moradabad (Bijnor, Moradabad and Rampur districts), Bareilly (Budaun, Bareilly, Pilobhit and Shahjahanpur districts) and Kichha, Sitargang, Khatima *tahsils* and southern part of Haldwani and Kashipur *tahsils* of Nainital district of Kumaon Division.

The study are is comparatively more urbanized part of U.P. where 23.7% of the total population is urban in comparison to 18% of U.P.

Indicators of the Level of Urbanization

Various attempts have been made to find out an index of urbanization to explain the regional disparity in urban process and pattern.

Taking into consideration this view, an attempt has been made in this study to synthesise every possible dimensions of urban process and pattern. Consequently, the indicators pertaining to both descriptive and normative aspects have been selected. Two components of urbanization, i.e. (A) Urban accretion, and (B) Spatial organization of urban centres are chosen for the present study as suggested by Kundu (1980).

A. Urban Accretion

This component has been comprehended with the help of six indicators, i.e. (i) percentage of urban to total population; (ii) percentage of rural population (U/R); (iii) urban growth during 1901-81; (iv) urban growth during 1971-81; (v) average size of Urban centres (U/N) and (vi) urban density (U/A).

B. Spatial Organization

Five indicators are chosen in this component, i.e. (i) Average number of urban centres (n/A) (ii) Average connectivity (Total number of transport lines terminating in towns of a region divided by the total number of urban centres), (iii) Catchment co-efficient (calculated with the help of formula $\frac{2}{r} \times \frac{n}{AP}$ where 'r' is the hypothetical radius of a *tahsil* which may be determined by the formula 7/22 x area of *tahsil*, n is the number of centres, and AP is actual parametre of *tahsil*; (iv) Accessbility is taken as the ratio between the population served by the urban centres and the total population. To calculate the urban population served, the zones of service area of every urban centre is drawn on the map proposing the radius of service zone for towns of class I, II & III, IV and V & VI as 20, 16, 12 and 8 Km. respecuively. The areas out side the urban service zone are measured and are multiplied by the rural density to obtain the unserved population. After subtracting this population from the total, the urban population served and the percentage of total population may be calculated; (v) Urban concentration (this index is derived using the formula (*Dij*)/n were Dij is the distance of ith low in jth *tahsil* from the nearest town and 'n' is the number of the town of the *tahsil*.

Indicators to Measure the Level of Regional Development

In the present study thirty one socio-economic indicators of various sectors have been chosen.

A. **Agricultural Sector**

(i) percentage of net sown to total area (ii) percentage of double cropped area to total area, (iii) percentage of area under commercial crops to net sown area, (iv) percentages or irrigated land to net sown are, (v) percapita agricultural production, (vi) per hectare fertilizer consumption, and (vii) no. of tractors per *lakh* hactare of net sown area.

B. **Industrial Sector**

(i) Industrial units per thousand population, (ii) percentage of industrial worker to total worker, (iii) out put per unit, and (iv) percapita industrial production.

C. **Educational Sector**

No of (i) Primary Schools, (ii) Junior high schools, (iii) High schools and inter colleges per *lakh* population, (iv) percentage of literate persons, and (v) percentage of literate females.

D. **Health Sector**

Number of (i) primary health centres, (ii) allopathic dispensaries, (iii) Child welfare centres, (iv) Family planning centres, and (v) Number of hospital beds per *lakh* population.

E. **Transport and Communication Sector**

Length of (i) Road and (ii) Railway line per 100 Km^2 area, (iii) Percentage of village under three km. distance from any metalled road, (iv) No. of railway stations per 100 Km^2, (v) No. of Post Offices, and (vi) number of telegraph offices per *lakh* population.

F. **Others**

(i) No. of banks branches per *lakh* population (ii) Percentage of electrified villages, (iii) No. of biogas plants, and (iv) seed and fertilizer stores per *lakh* of population.

Methodology

The taxomomic method has been used to obtain the composite index of urbanization as well as regional development in the present study as suggested by Singh with some modifications. It can be outlined as follows.

A matrix representing the region (1,2.... R) in the column and the group of indicators (1,2.... m) in the row is constructed. The matrix should be replaced by a new matrix placing the standerdized value of each indicators in the same column. The composite index is obtained by using the following formula.

$$C.I = \sqrt{\sum_{J=1}^{R} (Zij-Zoj)^2}$$

Where,

	C.I.	is the composite index for jth region.
	Zil	is the standardised value of indicator for jth region
and	Zoj	is the highest value of standardised score of the jth region.

Lastly to find out the coefficient of composite index, the following formula is used:

$$ccj = 1 - \frac{\sum_{J=1}^{R} Cij}{Co}$$

Where,

CCi is coefficient of composite index of jth region

Cij is composite index of jth region.

and Co is the constant which can be found out by using the formula

Co = CI + 2 SIC

(Where CI and SIC is the mean and SD of composite index respectively.

FIG. 33.1

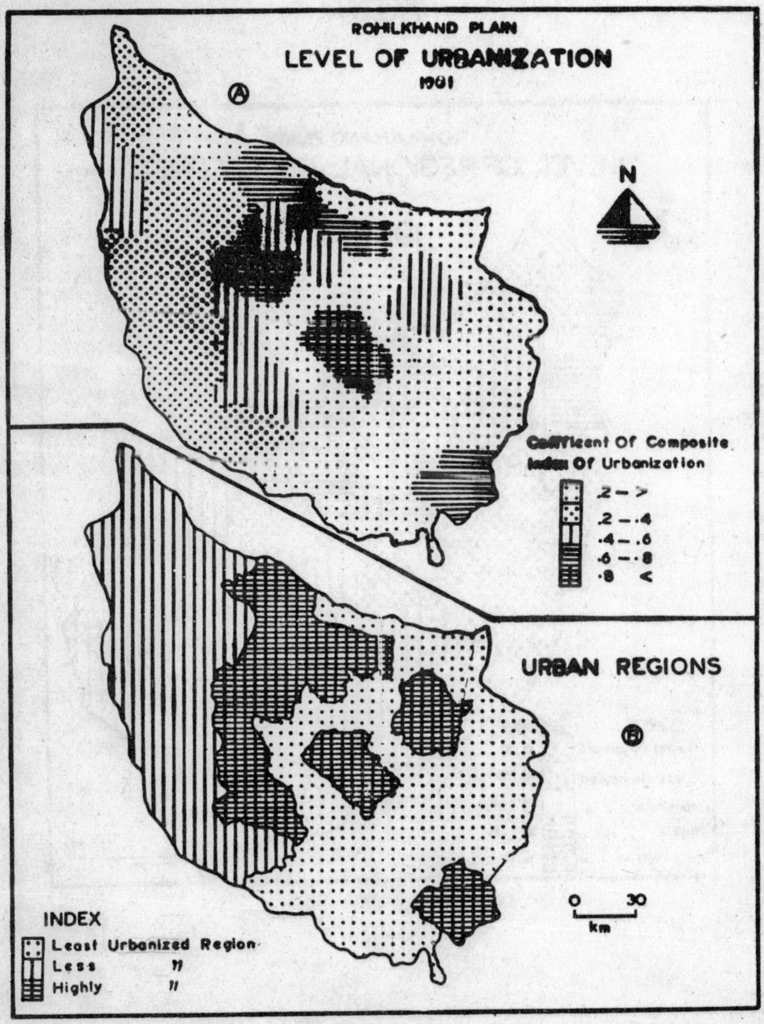

The coefficient of composite index in the the normal condition is positive and ranges for 0 to 1. The higher the coefficient the more the level of development.

Level of urbanization in the study area

The level of urbanization in the form of coefficient of composite index of urbanization is shown in figure 1 A.

FIG. 33.2

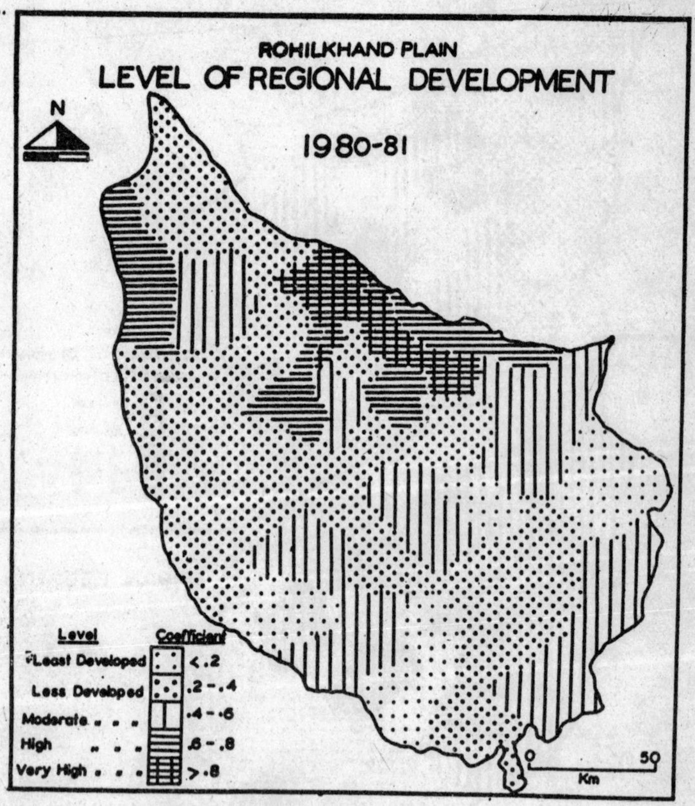

A marked regional disparity in the level of urbanization is visible from the figures and three urban regions of different levels of urbanization can be easily identified (Fig. 1 B). Urbanization is high in the central part of the region, whereas western part is less urbanized and eastern part experienced least urbanization.

Level of Regional Development

Figure-2 presents a cross section of the level of development. The core of developed area lies along the *Tarai* region of Bijnore, Dhampur, Kashipur, Kichha and Haldwani *tahsil*. There is an abrupt gap between high and very low level of development. Moderately developed areas are not contiguous. A larger are a of Rohilkhand Plain remains backward.

The relationships

To find out the degree and direction of correspondence among the relationship of the components of regional development and the level of urbanization, the correlation coefficient is calculated with the help of Pearson's Product Moment coefficient of correlation (r) method.

The correlation between urbanization and the level of agricultural development is statistically insignificant (+0.22) while industrialization level shows a very significant correlation (+0.70) with urbanization. Total educational development indicated a moderate correlation (+0.38) while the development of health services is least correlated (+0.22) (Fig.3). Integrated development of transport and communication has a moderate correlation +0.5 with urbanization which is also a significant one.

The correlation between level of urbanization and regional development is more significant (+0.66). In respect of regional development, the level of urbanization emerges as the most important explanatory variable in the study region. It may be said that urbanization is a pre-requisite and very important infrastructure for the regional development.

FIG. 33.3

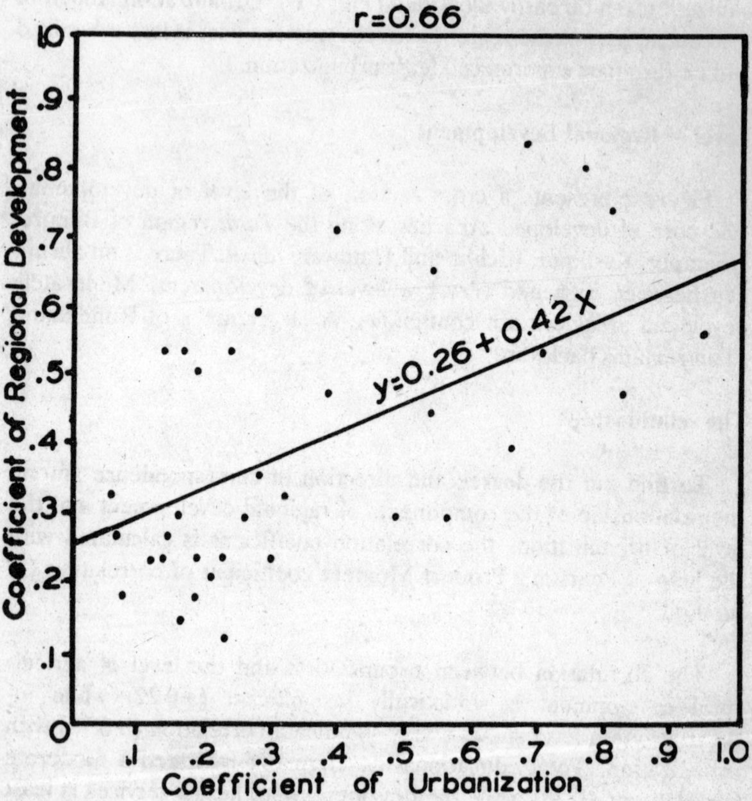

Conclusion

It may thus be summarized that urbanization and regional development have significant correlation. Urbanization thus emerges one of the strong measures for regional development.

Theme IV

Rural Development : Issues, Strategies and Planning Policy

THIRTY FOUR

Nazrul Islam and
Islam Nazem

The Role of Upazila Centres in Rural Development in Bangladesh: A Preliminary Investigation[1]

Introduction

Bangladesh has experienced several models of development since the end of the British colonial rule, both during its phase as part of Pakistan (1947-71) and also as an independent country since 1971. The results of such development activities have not been very very encouraging. Inspite of some evidence of growth at certain brief stages, the cumulative effect has been rather depressing. Overall economic condition has deteriorated, particularly distressing is the fact that gaps between urban and rural areas as well as between groups people have widened.

There are probably many reasons for the failure in achieving desired objectives of development planning in Bangladesh. Each successive government (and there have been many since 1947 or even since 1971) tried to blame its predecessors for failures and for creating new problems. Each then experimented with a new model of development. The latest model has been initiated by the present government soon after it came to power in March, 1982. The model adopted is one of decentralized development and administration and is known as the *Upazila* (sub-district) system. According to this model, major authorities for development planning and implementation have now been taken down from the national or the district level to the present 460 Upazilas. The *Upazila* has in reality replaced the earlier *Thana* level and has an average population of 190,000 and an average area of 260 Km^2.)

FIG. 34.1

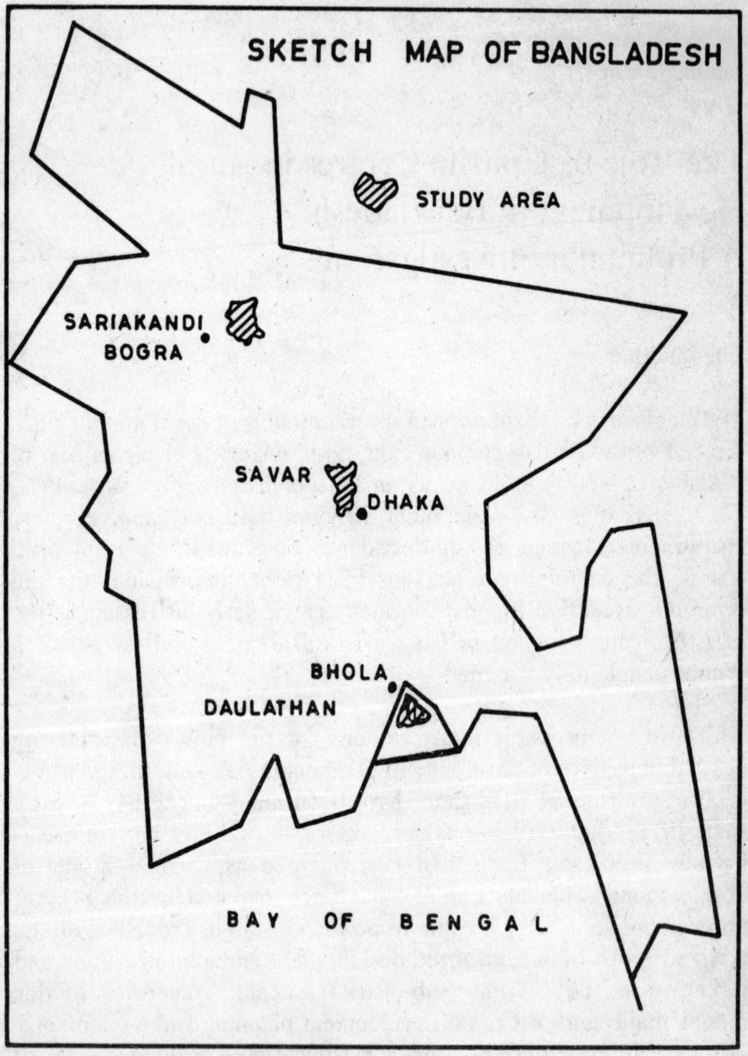

The system also ensures much greater participation of the people, since the principal decision making authority is now an elected body known as the *Upazila Parishad* headed by an elected representative, the Chairman. The bureaucrats and the professionals are theoretically required to respect decisions taken by the Chairman and his Parishad. This is the first time that people's representative would be the principal decision makers in development administration at the local-regional level in the country.

In their search for an alternative development strategy, the formulators of the *Upazila* system had also identified the problem of lack of a spatial dimension in development and were sufficiently convinced that the small urban centre had a great role to play in implementing the decentralized development model in general and in rural development in particular. Thus a major thrust of the decentralized policy has been to develop the *Upazila* centres as focal points of administrative, industrial, commercial and cultural activities so that the common people in rural areas have easy access to necessary services. The Census Commission of Bangladesh has designated all *Upazila* centres as urban places although nearly 400 of these centres were no more than rural market centres when such a change of status was made in 1982. Due to this change the level of urbanization in Bangladesh was raised to 15.2 per cent (1981) from a probable 11 per cent if population of only formerly designated urban areas (municipalities) were considered. The idea of upgrading such a large number of rural service centres into urban places was not totally new, since the concept of fostering 'growth centres' was already introduced both during the First Year Plan (1973-78) and the Second Five Year Plan (1980-85) in which there was a proposal for planned development of 1,200 growth centres in the country.[2] The *Upazila* system, however, settled for a reasonably smaller number of such centres, only one in each *Upazila*.[3]

Objective, Method and Study Areas

The main objective of the present paper is to provide some idea about role of *Upazila* centres in rural development in Bangladesh. Specifically, it attempts to see, (i) what functions and services are available at the *Upazila* centres as opposed to other rural market centres in the *Upazila*, and more important, (ii) who in the rural areas have the real access to these functions and services, or in other words, does the *Upazila* centre actually benefit the majority rural population, the poor?

The study on which this paper is based was restricted to only three *Upazilas*, Savar, Sariakandi and Daulatkhan. These were selected from three different regions of Bangladesh (Fig.1). The selection of these *Upazilas* was also based on their location in relation to other urban centres. Thus Savar in the Centre region (or Dhaka Division) is located close to a metropolitan centre (Dhaka), Sariakandi in the Northern region (or Rajshahi Division) close to a medium sized town (Bogra) and Daulatkhan in the Southern region (or Khulna and Chittagong Divisions near a small town (Bhola). Moreover, all three centres belong to *Upazilas* which started functioning in 1982, so that the *Upazila* system has been operational for sometime when the study was undertaken in mid-1985.

TABLE-I : CRITERIA FOR CLASSIFICATION OF THE RESPONDENTS

Socio-economic Status Group	Land holding (Acre)	Approx. annual income (Taka)*	Major Occup-ation Type	Social Status
High	8.0 or more	30,100 +	Large land owner	Local leader, Upper class
Middle	0.5-7.99	5,001-30,000	Farmer, teacher, govt. employee	Educated, Middle class
Low	less than 0.5	-5,000	Farm and other labour fisherman, others	Working class

* 1 US$ = approximately 25 Taka in mid-1985

Investigation on the functional characteristics of the *Upazila* centres and their role on rural development were conducted at two levels, (i) at the centre itself, and (ii) in two villages in each *Upazila*, one located close to the centre and the other away from the centre. While the surveys at the centre consisted of examination of official documents, discussions with officials and observation, investigation at the village level consisted of interviews with the people using a checklist rather than questionnaires. All surveys were personally conducted by one of the two authors of this paper.) 84 respondents were selected from three villages representing three major socio-economic groups which were determined on the basis of land holding, annual income, occupation and social status as shown in Table.1.

The distribution of respondents by *Upazila*, Village and socio-economic status is shown in Table II

TABLE-II: DISTRIBUTION OF RESPONDENTDS BY *UPAZILA*, VILLAGE AND SOCIO-ECONOMIC STATUS

Socio-economic Status	Daulatkhan			Sariakandi			Savar			All *Upazila*		
	A	B	T	A	B	T	A	B	T	A	B	T
High	3	3	6	3	3	6	2	1	3	8	7	15
Middle	9	7	16	7	6	13	5	5	10	21	18	39
Low	6	7	13	5	6	11	3	3	6	14	16	30
Total	18	17	35	15	15	30	10	9	19	43	41	84

A = A village close to *Upazila* Centre.
B = A village remote from *Upazila* Centre.
T = Total (A + B) respondents.

All three study *Upazila* are nearly the same size in terms of area when rivers are included but their land area vary from 116 Km^2 in Daulatkhan to 315 Km^2 for Sariakandi. In terms of population they vary from 139,000 in Daulatkhan to 262,000 in Savar; the highest density of population is found in Daulatkhan with 3,098 persons per square mile of land are (Table-III).

TABLE III Area and Population of study *Upazila*

Item	Daulatkhan	Sariakandi	Savar
Area (including river) Km^2	266	348	278
Land area (Km^2)	116	315	271
Population ('000)	139	177	262
Population Density	3,098	1,448	2,494

Source: Bangladesh Bureau of Statistics, Govt. of Bangladesh, *Upazila Statistics*, Vol. 1, 1985.

FIG. 34.2

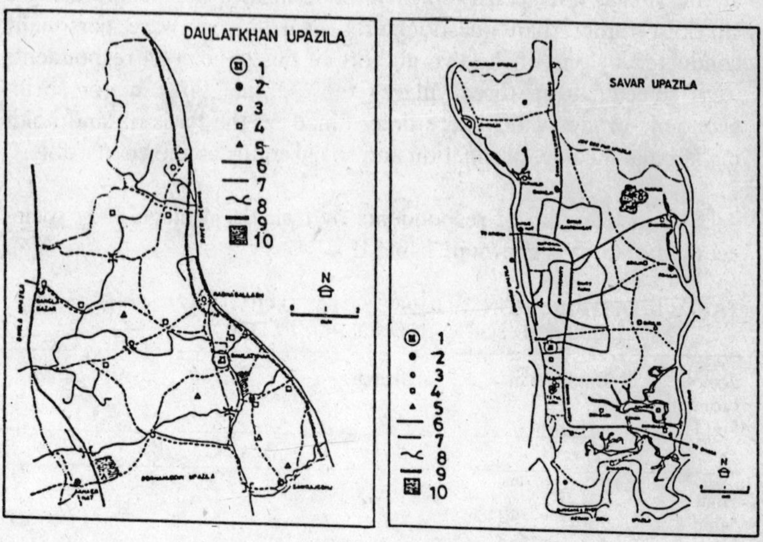

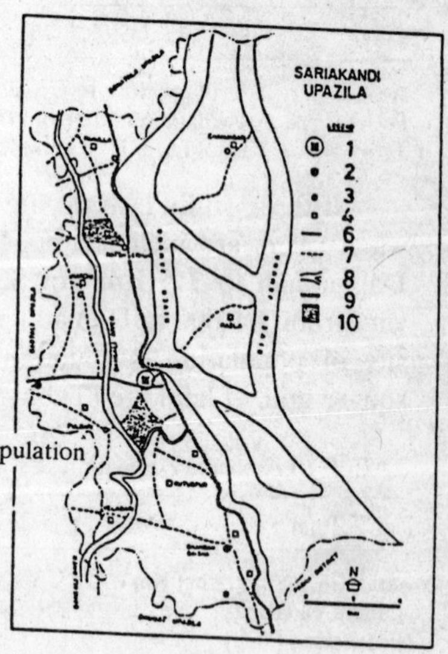

1 - Upzila centre
2 - Rural market centre with residential population
3 - Ruts; *hat*
4 - Union Parishad office
5 - Cyclone shelter
6 - Metalled roads
7 - Unmetalled motorable roads
8 - Waterways
9 - Embankment
10- Study village

TABLE IV : UPAZILA CENTRES AND MAJOR RURAL MARKET CENTRES AND THEIR POPULATION, NUMBER OF SHOPS AND ESTABLISHMENTS AND AVAILABILITY OF SERVICES

Name of Upsila and Rural Markets Centres	Approximate Size dential Population	Number of Retail and shops Industries and other Establishments	SERVICES																	
			Bazar Committee	Post Office	Telephone	Electricity	Govt. Godown	Cold Storage	Hospital	Health Centre	Cinema Hall	General Workshops	Automobile Workshops	News Paper	Bus Service	College	Secondary School	Primary School	Kinder garden	Community Centre
Savar																				
Savar Bazar	8,000	2,500	X	X	X	X	X	X	X	X	X	X	X	X	X	X	X	X		
Amin Bazar	3,000	260	X	X		X				X				X	X		X	X		
Birulia	1,500	60		X		X								X			X	X		
Shimulia	1,000	60		X		X								X			X	X		
Nayarhat	1,000	50		X	X	X								X			X	X		
DAULATKHAN																				
Daulatkhan	3,000	220	X	X	X	X	X		X	X	X			X	X	X	X	X	X	X
Kheerlat	1,200	250	X	X					X						X		X	X		
Bengla Bazar	800	100		X		X								X			X	X		
Guptaganj	1,000	120	X	X		X												X		
Swaraj-	500	50		X						X							X	X		
SARIAKANDI																				
Sariakandi	2,500	200		X	X	X	X		X	X				X		X	X	X	X	X
Chandanbaisha	2,000	160		X						X							X	X		
Phulbaria	1,200	50		X		X				X	X						X	X		

Each of the three Upazilas has several other rural market centres (Fig. 2). In each case, the *Upazila* centre has the largest residential population compared to the other centres in the *Upazila*, and except in Daulatkhan, also the largest number of establishments (Table-IV). In any case, population in any of these three centres is very small, the highest being only 8,000, for Savar. All three *Upazila* Centres are fairly centrally located within the *Upazila*.

The Role of the Upazila Centres: Services Available

Both in terms of residential population and number of establishments, the *Upazila* centres are clearly of higher order compared to the other rural market centres (numbering 7 to 10) in the three *Upazilas* studied. The *Upazila* centres in each of the three *Upazilas* lead other centres in terms of availability of a variety of service facilities as evident from Table -IV. Some of the higher order facilities like college education, government go-down, community Centres, cold storage facilities,or a modern educational facility like kindergartens, are available only at the *Upazila* centre level (some of these facilities are not necessarily at all three *Upazila* centres). Some lower order services like primary or secondary education and postal facilities are available in nearly all rural centres. Electricity and newspapers have also reached most of the markets.

The *Upazila* centre, of course, are distinguished by the presence of a large number of different developmental, administrative and judicial functions (Table V) offered by the various government departments. Most of these functions naturally cannot be found in the other rural centres in the Upazila. All three *Upazila* centres however, do not enjoy the equal number of these functions as yet. Savar, which is located closest to Dhaka, the capital city, has nearly all the functions listed in the table, while the other two lack in some of functions. It is expected that over time all *Upazila* centres would have nearly the same set of functions.

Although most of developmental and administrative functions used to be offered from these centres even before the implementation of the *Upazila* system, several functions were introduced only after the system was established. These are judiciary and planning related functions. A modern educational facility like kindergartens have also been introduced with the inception of the *Upazila* level officials, The *Upazila* centres have also been provided with community centres for socio-economic gatherings.

The Role of the Upazila Centres: Services Received and Services Demanded

The *Upazila* system has been introduced to decentralize development and the Upazila centres were created to make services easily accessible to the rural people. But it has become obvious from the present study that although physical distance is an important variable in determining access to services, it is by no means the most important variable. Rather, socio-economic factors play a very important role in getting access to services.

It is quite clear from Table VI that the *Upazila* centre is an attractive place for the people of high socio-economic status, but not necessarily so for the low status groups of villages. Distance makes no difference for the high status groups in their decision to visit the *Upazila* centres to get services and goods, while it makes only litter difference for the low status groups. Few among the poor have good reasons to visit the centre even when the poor live farther from the centre, very few of them visit the *Upazila* centre. The very few who visit, interestingly do so not for their own purpose but to accompany the high-status people of their village to assist them in carrying their produces on purchases.

Table-VI makes the position further clear. Of those who do visit the *Upazila* centre, the majority of the higher status group do so almost daily. The frequency of their visits are indeed rare, For their small essential purchases they visit the nearest rural market.

The reasons for visiting the centres are also related to the social status (Table VIII), The higher status people would have reasons to perform official work, to buy agricultural inputs or to go for banking services. The poor may go sell their little produces. But the reasons for not visiting the centres are more associated with the poor. The typical reasons are listed in Table IX Lack of purchasing power, inappropriate services, difficulty in getting real access to the services without proper connections are the general reasons. Thus the table

TABLE V : *UPAZILA* LEVEL DEVELOPMENT AND ADMINISTRATIVE FUNCTIONS AND SERVICES
(Provided by specific departments of the Government)

Functions & Services*	Daulat khan	Saria Kandi	Savar
PLANNING			
1. Planning Section	X	X	X
2. Statistical Section	X	X	X
3. Committee for Evaluation of Projects	X	X	X
4. Development Coordination-Committee	X	X	X
AGRICULTURE			
5. Agricultural Extension Services: distribution and supply of inputs and impliments	X	X	X
6. Swanirvor Programme	X		X
7. Irrigation Services	X	X	X
8. Food for Works Programme	X	X	X
9. Pisciculture	X	X	X
10. Forestry	X	X	X
11. Livestock	X	X	X
12. Ideal Farms (for demonstration)	X		X
PHYSICAL INFRA-STRUCTURE			
13. Building and Construction	X	X	X
14. Roads and Highways			X
15. Railway			
16. Water Development Projects/ BW TA etc.		X	
17. Power	X	X	X
18. Telecommunication	X	X	X
19. Public Health Engineering	X	X	X
PHYSICAL INFRA-STRUCTURE			
20. Education	X	X	X
21. Health	X	X	X
22. Family Planning	X	X	X
23. Manpower Development		X	X
24. Labour Welfare			
25. Social Welfare	X	X	X
26. Publicity and Press			
27. Women's Welfare	X	X	X
28. Cultural Affairs	X	X	X

29. Rural Work Programme	X	X	X
30. Thana Irrigation Programme	X	X	X
31. Cooperative	X	X	X
32. Rural Credit	X	X	X
33. Bangladesh Rural Development	X	X	X
RELIEF AND REHABILITATION			
34. Relief and Rehabilitation Function	X	X	X
35. Loan Distribution	X	X	X
36. Committee for Flood and Natural Calamities	X	X	X
INDUSTRY AND FINANCE			
37. Banking Services	X	X	X
38. BSCIC Industrial Estate			X
39. Small and Cottage Industry	X		X
40. Other Industry			X
ADMINISTRATIVE FUNCTIONS			
41. General Administration	X	X	X
42. Magistracy	X	X	X
43. Judiciary	X	X	X
44. Treasury	X	X	X
45. Audit	X	X	X
46. Record Maintenance	X	X	X
47. Registration of Births and Deaths	X	X	X
48. Police and Other Civil Defence Services	X	X	X

* All functions upto 40 are development oriented while those between 41 to 48 are administrative in nature.

shows that majority of the people who do not visit the Upazila centre think that they are not influential enough to get the services, or the facilities they need are not available, or going to get services would only mean more difficulties.

On more detail investigation, it became quite clear that the real service the poor expect is not any goods or inputs, but opportunity for employment and for avenues to increase their income (Table X). On the other hand, the well-off members of the rural community also seem to have unfulfilled needs. They stress on having timely distribution of agricultural inputs, proper distribution of school text books, or facilities to set up industries (Table X).

It was also apparent during the survey that many villages, specially those of the lower socio-economic status and those of distant villages, were not fully aware of some of the services that actually were available at the centre although they had need for these. An information gap between the centres and some members of the rural community do exist even more than two years after the introductions of the *Upazila* system.

Conclusions

This preliminary investigation of three *Upazilas* has shown that the *Upazila* centres have not been very effective in serving the interest of the rural poor although these centres seem to be significantly attractive to the rural rich. The nature of services available at these centres are more appropriate to the needs of people with land or other productive units. Even access to social services like educational or medical facilities are easier and more relevant for the rural elite than for the poor.

TABLE VI: WHETHER VILLAGERS VISIT THE *UPAZILA* CENTRES FOR SERVICES AND GOODS

Socio-economic groups by study villages		Yes		No		Total	
		f	%	f	%	f	%
	A*	8	100.0	0		8	100.0
High	B	7	100.0	0		7	100.0
n = 15	T	15	100.0	0		15	100.0
	A	17	80.9	4	19.4	21	100.0
Middle class	B	10	55.5	8	45.5	18	100.0
n = 39	T	27	69.2	12	30.8	39	100.0
	A	8	57.2	6	48.8	14	100.0
Low	B	3	18.7	13	81.3	16	100.0
n = 30	T	11	36.7	17	63.3	30	100.0
	A	33	76.7	10	23.3	43	100.0
Total	B	20	48.8	21	51.2	41	100.0
N = 84	T	53	63.0	31	36.9	84	100.0

* A = A village close to *Upazila* Centre.
B = A village remote from *Upazila* Centre.
T = Total of village A and B

TABLE VII : FREQUENCY OF VISIT TO *UPAZILA* CENTRES BY SOCIO-ECONOMIC GROUP AND DISTANCE FACTOR

Socio-economic groups groups by study villages		Frequency of visit (in percent)				Total
		Almost every day	Once in a weak	Once in a month	Very rarely	
	A(8)	75.0	25.0	-	-	100
High	B(17)	42.8	28.5	-	-	100
n = 15	T(15)	60.0	26.6	13.3	-	100
	A(14)	35.7	35.7	21.4	7.1	100
Middle	B(13)	23.0	38.4	23.0	15.3	100
n = 27	T(27)	29.6	37.0	22.2	11.0	100
	A(5)	20.0	40.0	20.0	20.0	100
Low	B(6)	-	16.6	33.3	50.0	100
n = 11	T(11)	9.0	27.2	27.2	36.3	100
	A(27)	44.4	33.3	14.8	7.4	100
Grand Total	B(26)	23.0	30.7	26.9	19.2	100
n = 53	T(53)	33.9	32.0	20.7	13.2	100

A = Village close to *Upazila* Centre.
B = Village distant from *Upazila* Centre.
T = Total of village A and B.

TABLE VIII : REASONS WHY THE RESPONDENTS VISITED THE *UPAZILA* CENTRE

n = 53

Purpose of Visit	Frequency	Percent
Official work	20	37.5
Shopping or marketing	18	33.9
To buy agricultural inputs	15	28.3
To attend workplace	13	24.5
For medical and health facilities	10	18.8
Trade and business	10	18.8
Banking and Financial Services (transaction, remittances and loan etc.)	9	16.9
For judicial service	6	11.3
To sale goods	6	11.3
To pay taxes	5	9.5
For agricultural information	5	9.5

TABLE IX : REASONS FOR VISITING *UPAZILA* CENTRES TO GET SERVICE FACILITIES

n = 31

Reasons (as described by respondents)	Frequency	Percent
We are not influential enough to avail the service	18	58.0
The facilities we need are not available	17	54.8
Going for services mean facing more difficulty	17	54.8
Things are very expensive and beyond our affordibility	14	45.2
All the facilities are for the literate people, not for us	11	35.4
We do not get any cooperation from the officers	11	35.4

TABLE X : TYPES AND NATURE OF SERVICES WHICH THE RESPONDENTS STRESS ON HAVING AT *UPAZILA* CENTRE (RESPONSES BELOW 25% ARE EXCLUDED; FIGURES ARE IN PERCENTAGE AND THE ANSWERS ARE IN ORDER OF RANK)

Types and nature of Services	*Upazilas*			
	Daulatkhan n = 35	Sariakandi n = 30	Savar n = 19	Total N = 84
Agricultural facilities i.e. timely distribution of inputs	80	86	63	86
Employment opportunity to raise income	57	80	58	63
Educational facilities i.e. proper distribution of books etc.	60	33	47	45
Health facilities (Medicine Family Planning matters etc.)	31	30	42	32
Facilities to set up industries at Upazila	42	27	26	32
Development of infrastructure (roads, canal, drainage, etc.)	28	27	42	30
Officer should be more cooperative in providing setting services	23	23	36	25

Due to the fact the *Upazila* centres are based on supply oriented viewpoint, the possibility of serving the poor through these centres become rather marginal. These centres may effect some rural development but not necessarily benefiting the poor. Similar situations have been reported for several other Asian countries by Dias (1984).

If the *Upazila* system fails to alleviate poverty or to increase rural incomes, the *Upazila* centres would remain as parasitic urban centres or become centres of exploitation, not unlike the large cities in the country, and whole experiment of decentralized development would be yet another futile exercise. However, a three year period in the life of a major development experiment is rather too short to draw based on a study of rather limited scope. Even then, the visible trends in effects of the *Upazila* system are sufficient signals for its proponents to become more vigilant. If the objectives were meant to be true rural development, the constraints are to be clearly identified and removed as soon as possible. Theoretically, the *Upazila* System has a lot of promise for development in Bangladesh.

NOTE

1. The authors acknowledge financial support of the Canadian International Development Agency (CIDA) in the study. The first author also thanks the AIT/ISS Project for a grant enabling him to present the paper at the International Conference on Geography of Commercial Activities at Gorakhpur, India, 21-23 December, 1985

2. The Government of Bangladesh, *The Second Five Year Plan, 1980-85* (Planning Commision of Bangladesh, 1980)

3. National Physical Planning Project, Rural Growth Centre Planner (Consultant), *Mission Report of Graham Gaston* (Dhaka: Urban Development Directorate, Government of Bangladesh, and UNCHS, 1984).

[illegible]

[illegible]

[illegible]

[illegible]

[illegible]

[illegible]

THIRTY FIVE

Afazlur Rehman

Role of Agro Industrial Crops and Agro - Industries in Rural Development: A Case Study of Budaun District (U.P.)

Nearly 75 per cent of India's population still lives in rural areas. The prosperity of India therefore, lies in the prosperity of its villages. Indian planners, therefore, have been concentrating on various polices of development for growth of rural area since the inception of planning in the country. The well known Community Development programme (1952), Intensive Agricultural District programme (1960-61) and projects covering small Farmers Development Agency, Marginal Farmers and Agricultural Labourers Development, Drought Prone Area programmes, Command Area Development Programme etc. have brought general improvement in the living conditions of the rural population. Despite the over all progress in rural areas, poverty and unemployment are still the predicament of a large number of people in these areas. These programmes were insufficient to reduce rural poverty.

The importance of the agro - industries in the development of the rural areas is widely recognised and needs no emphasis. Their role lies in the fact that they can be started with small amount of capital and owned and established by the villagers. They provide vast employment potential at a comparatively low investment and yield quick returns. The development of agro - industries in rural areas would not only boost up village economy but also reduce time and cost of transportation and distribution.

The study Area

Budaun is one of the backward districts of Uttar pradesh. It lies between 27° 30' and 28° 30' North latitude and 78° 16' and 79 30' East longitude. The district is situated in GangaRamganga Doab in western region of U.P. The Ganga bounds its western and southern boundaries and separates it from Bulandshahar, Aligarh, Etah and Farrukhabad districts. The Ramganga flows on its eastern border and separates it from Shahjahanpur district. It is bounded in the north by Moradabad, Bareilly and Rampur districts. The district covers a surface area of 5206 sq.kms.

Administratively the district is divided into five *tahsils* namely, Gunnaur, Sahaswan, Budaun, Bisauli and Dataganj and further into 18 community Development *Block*. The number of in habitated villages is 1814 and there are 14 only towns.

According to the 1981 census, the total population of the district is 19, 64,00 and the density of population is 3802 km. Little over than State average. The rural population is about 83.8 per cent (16,46000) of the total population. About 86.5 per cent of the working population is engaged in agriculture. It is much higher than the State average of 77.4 per cent. It has been estimated that about 53% of the rural population lies below the poverty line in the district. The share of agriculture and animal husbandry was 97.99 of the total district output in 1978-79 which is the highest in the State from this sector. The per capita net domestic output was only Rs. 351/ in the district against Rs.422/- in the western region and Rs. 359/- in U.P. The percentage of net sown area to total area was 77 in 1980-81 in the district.The intensity of cropping in the district is only 38.5%, and it is lowest in the western U.P., except in Bijnor district. About 60% of the net cropped area is irrigated. The transportation facilities are very poor. The length of metre gauage railway line is only 40 km. It connects only Budaun and Ughani from Bareilly and Agra. The broadgauge line only touches the corners of the district. The road density is only 9.5 km^2 100km. The accessibility of villages surfaced road is an important requisite of rural development. About 50% villages are at a distance of more than 5kms. from the metalled road. The condition of power supply is also very poor in the district.

Objectives of the Study

An attempt has been made to study the following specific objectives:

1. To analyse the rural development schemes of the district;
2. To study the status and spatial distribution pattern of agro - industrial crops;
3. To study the spatial pattern of location of existing agro-industries; and
4. To study the potentiality of agro-industrial crops and future prospects of agro-industries for the development of rural sector.

Data Base:

This paper is based on secondary data collected through various departments/Institutions at central, state and district levels for my doctoral work.

Rural Development Programmes in Budaun District

Since the inception of planned development in India a number of programmes/schemes have been launched by the Government of Uttar pradesh in the rural sector, with a view to bring about a basic change in the agrarian society and improving the lot of rural poor. These main programmes/schemes are such as:

1. Small Farmers Development Agency programme sponsored by the Centre;
2. *Antodaya* programme;
3. Minimum needs programmes;
4. Training to the Rural Youth for Self-employment programme (TRYSEM).
5. *Khadi Gram Udyog* programmes.
6. Land Distribution to Landless, poor.
7. Integrated Rural Development Programme (IRDP).

During the Sixth Five Year Plan all the programmes/schemes have been merged under Integrated Rural Development Programme (IRDP). The IRDP is an approach to achieve all the facilities under an umbrella. The main aim of this programme is to provide the full employment to small and marginal farmer, landless workers and Harijans. Special schemes have been launched under this programme to increase the production and to improve their economic conditions. A number of villages have been adopted by the Central Bank, State Bank of India and Punjab National Bank to provide the loan to rural poors to start the self-employment.

Status of Agro-Industrial Crops

The main agro-industrial crops of the district are oil seeds, pulses, sugarcane, potato and mentha on which the agro-industrial units of the district are based. Onion, opium, chilli, cotton and tobacco are also grown in the district. A brief accounts of main crops are given below:

Oil Seeds:

The groundnut is the main oil seeds of the district which alone comprises 9.83% of the gross cropped area. The fertile parts of *Bhur* tracts of the district are the best suited for the crop. In 1982-83 the area under crop was about 60,714 hectare and production was over 48,693 tonnes.

Toria has second place among the oil seeds in the district. It is an intermediate crop and grown after harvesting maize and before sowing wheat. Thus it is playing the role of increasing crop intensity. The area and production of the crop have increased due to I.O.P. In 1980-81 the area under crop was achieved 9602 against the target of 8000 ha and the production was estimated to be about 6241 tonnes.

The rape and mustard are also important oil seeds of the district. There are grown in *rabi* season. The area and production of rape and mustard has also much increased. In 1980-81 the area under these crops was recorded to be about 7724 ha and production was obtained about 3746 tonnes, which is about double than during 1978-79. But this production is merely 8.5% of Agra district and the per hectare field is also two third of Agra district.

The efforts are being made to increase the area under soyabean and sunflower. The production of seasamum may be much increased as it is sown mixed with bajra, a second rankcrop of the district, by increasing the per hectare yield. High yield varieties of the seed are provided to the farmers. Thus, there is a large scope to increase both the area and the productivity of oil seeds in the district.

Pulses:

The pulses occupy second place among agro-industrial crops covering about 10% of the gross-cropped area of the district. Gram occupies first place among pulses and alone covers about 50% of the total area under pulses. Ambiapur and Dataganj *blocks* are leading producers of gram. Pease, lentil, urad and moong are also grown in the district. The State Intensive Pulses Programme are also being launched in the district to increase the area, production and productivity of pulses.

Sugarcane

The sugarcane is an important cash crop of the district on which not only the economy of the growers depend but also one large scale sugar industry has been established and 14 sulphitation plants and 20 *Khandsari* Units depend on it. It provides the highest employment in the district, About 1300 persons are engaged directly and more than five thousand indirectly in harvesting, loading, etc.

Potato

Budaun occupies fifteenth place in production of potato in U.P. The potato, queen of vegetables, has a commendable industrial value. It is used for manufacturing of starch used principally for the finishing of cloths in the textile industry. In providing employments, potato is a important as sugarcane in the district. There is a much scope to extend both the area and productivity of potato in the district. depending on the extension of cold storages facility in all the *block* and basic quota allocation to the potato growers in near by coldstores.

Opium

Opium is mainly grown by the small farmers of the district. The backward caste *Murao, Lodhe, Chamar* and *Teli* are expert in opium cultivation in the district. It is grown under the license for a fixed acreage by the Norcotics Commissioner of U.P. The farmers are bound to give the full production to the government at the prescribed rate which is based on lower yield lower rate higher yield higher rate.

In 1976-77the opium rate was ranging between Rs. 120 per kg. to 220 per kg. in the state. The average per ha yield is 30 kg. but it up upto 60 kg. per hectare. In addition to this 6 to 8 quintals seed is obtained which contains 50 to 60% edibile oil and 5 to 6 quintals Donda chura per ha which is used in unani and Aryovedic medicines. The present rate of opium seed is ranging Rs. 2000 per quintal in the crop season. Thus, about Rs. 15000 per ha is earned from this crop. It is a highly labour intensive crop because it is collected four times in a season.

Mentha

Mentha is the most suitable crop to the small and marginal farmers which provides cash to them as soon as it is crushed at the oil plant. About Rs. 2250 per ha may be earned by this crop during seven months. This crop is harvested three times after a gap in February and harvested upto September. The per ha yield of mentha gives about 8 kg.oil in first round, 6kg in second and 5kg in third round. The area under crop in the district is only 20 ha. It is grown only in the surrounding villages of Budaun, Ujhani and Asafpur. This crop has not been introduced in other parts of the district due to a lack of crushing plants and the lack of interest of district agricultural department. Mentha oil used in medicines, confectionaries, pests and *pan masala*. India is importing synthetic mentha oil to meet the growing demand.

There is a need to extend the area under mentha and care must be taken by the district agricultural department for the cultivation of this crop as it provides just double the income than that provided by sugar-cane. In addition to this potato may also be grown after this crop in the same year.

The following points emerge from the above descussion.

a. The agro-industrial crops are highly concentrated in the district.
b. Gram and Rape and mustard has shown their wide distribution and 10 to 12 *blocks* are producing more than their average share.
c There is high association in rape gram and sugarcane in more than seven *block*.
d. The contribution of crop area to the gross-cropped area of the *block* is not much relevant to the contribution in production of the district.

State of Agro-Industries

The state of existing agro-industries of the district is discussed as under.

Large Scale Industries

At present there are only three large scale units, sugar mill, one paper mill and one vegetable solvent extraction plant, All the units are located in Ujhani *block*. The two large scale units, the Prem Spinning and Weaving Mill and Strand Board Mill were closed down in 1972. The Kisan Co-operative Sugar Mill and Standard Board Mill are utilising their full capacity but the condition of vegetable industrial complex is very poor as it utilises only one third of its capacity.

Small Scale Industries

The industrial structure of the district is based on small scale agro-industrial units. Cold storage industry is on the top which is not only providing the highest employment but also about 40,000 potato growers directly depend on it. But cold stores are highly centralised as over 70% of the units are located in Ujhani and Jagat *block*. The Sulphitation plants and *Khadsari* industry occupy second place in the district. The edible oil industry occupies third place. *Dal* Rice and

Mentha oil plants have also been set up in the district. The total number of small scale agro-industrial units 107 and they are providing the employment about 3398 persons.

The distribution of small scale agro-industries in the district shows concentration. About one third of the units are located in Jagat *block*, around Budaun city, the district headquarter. Ujhani has second place and covered one fourth units of the district. The main reason of concentration of units in both the blocks are good infrastructural facilities, particularly the railway facility are available only in these two *blocks*. Ujhani is also main agricultural *mandi* of the district. Bisauli block ranks third and twelve units are located there. Only *Khandsari* and cold stores have been established in Amibiopur and Sahaswan *block* and each possesses over five units only. Six *Khandsari* and one mentha plant have also been set up. Wazirganj has six units Usawan, Dataganj and Qadarchowk each have three units and one *Khandsari* unit has been set up in Islamnagar. In seven *blocks* namely, Rajpura Gunnaru, Junawani, Dehagwan located in a contiguous belt in the north Western part of the district, Salarpur, Samrair and Miaon *block* in eastern part of the district, no industry has been started so far inspite of the availability of a good amount of agro-industrial raw materials. The main reason of backwardness is the lack of transfractural facilities, especially the transportation and power facilities.

Potential and Future Prospects of Agro-industries

Budaun district has immense potentiality for future expansion of agro-industries. It has vast resources of agricultural raw material which is exported outside the district. Of the total production only 19% of oil seeds and remaining 29% of sugarcane is utilised by the existing processing units. Most of the oil seeds are exported and cane is utilized in *gur* making. *Dal* Mills are using merely 2.67% of the total pulses production. About 47% of potato is preserved by the cold stores of the district and most of the remaining is exported. There is no preservation unit for onion which is grown on a large scale. An opium unit may also be established. A opium oil seed factory may also be set up.

Vegetables are grown about 13000 ha in the district. A large amount of vegetable in the season is wasted due to a lack of dehydration facility. Before the Independence Budaun was a leading cotton producing district of the country and it was grown on more than 10,000 ha. The press spinning and wearing mill was established in 1939 due to the availability of raw material in the district. If the incentives are provided by the government, the cotton production may be increased.

There is an urgent requirement of cold stores as there is no cold store in eleven en *block* where potato is produced. About 7 *lakh* tonnes of sugar-cane is being utilised in *gur* making. Fifty per cent of this may easily be diverted to sugar mills provided farmers are paid remunerative cane prices within a short time. It could support 4 mini sugar plants with crushing capacity of 500 tonnes per-day. The gur making takes more time to get the field vacant and land is not sown in one season. If these plants are installed about 10,000 ha of land may be re-sown and intensity of cropping may be increased.

The cereals are also produced in abound and in the district. There is no flour mill in the district. The production of wheat is over 45,000 tonnes. Five flour mills may be set up which may provide the raw material to backeries also. A rice mill is also needed in the district. The relaxation is given by the govt. leavy policy on rice mills entrepreneurs may be attracted to establish rice mills.

The district produces more than 38,000 tonnes of maize annually. A dextorse manufacturing plant may be established on the pattern of Haryana and Punjab. It will be worthwhile to note that no industry has been set up in leading maize growing areas of the district namely, Rajpur, Gunnam, Junaman and Dehagwan, Thus, there is an urgent need that a factory may be set up in published for the over all development of this area. It will provide the base to maize growers and they may earn the remunerative prices.

The agricultural by-products are still unutilised which may be used to set up four straw board mills. To utilise this huge potentiality about 121 new agro-industrial units may easily be established which will create the employment opportunities to about 6000 persons.

Conclusion

Budaun is a potential agro-industrial crop producing district of the State. It is unfortunate that vast agricultural resources, which could have played vital role in providing employment and to improve the economy, have been utilised.

THIRTY SIX

S.C. Sharma and
M.L. Sharma

Industrial Planning for Rural Development - A Case Study of Tahsil Tarabganj, District Gonda (Uttar Pradesh)

Introduction

The study area is not endowed with the potentialities for the development of large-scale industries. It is essential to develop medium and small scale industries in the study region to improve the living conditions of the villages. The introduction and encouragement of well chosen village industries in the study area would add to rural welfare in the following ways:-

1. It will reduce unemployment and underemployment considerably.
2. It will provide useful outlet for many of the raw materials and waste materials or agriculture.
3. Then farmers and their family will get an additional source of income which is needed to raise their status and help them tide over difficulties caused by the failure of crops.
4. The products of small industries which utilize the local raw materials and talent do not call for any heavy capital investment.
5. It will establish backward and forward linkages with other sectors to maximise the inter- sectoral pay offs.
6. It will meet the internal demands in particular and external demands in general.
7. It will also attract the flow of labour and capital from bigger areas to smaller services centres and villages.

TABLE 1 : NUMBER OF EXISTING INDUSTRIAL UNITS, (1983).

Sl. No.	Industrial Establishment	No. of Sts. with establish-ment	No. of Units
1.	Oil Expeller	230	485
2.	Flour mill (small size units using grinders)	221	452
3.	Small Size Rice hullers	128	282
4.	Pot making Industry	90	150
5.	Cord Industry	27	60
6.	Kiln Industry	23	25
7.	Crusher Industry	20	22
8.	Saw mills	10	18
9.	Furniture and carpentry	10	15
10.	Babul bark Industry	10	10
11.	Ice Candy	6	7
12.	Cement Grill Industry	6	7
13.	Sericulture unit	6	6
14.	Spices grinding Industry	5	5
15.	Light Engineering works	5	9
16.	Timber Industry	6	7
17.	Candle works	4	6
18.	Repairing of Agricultural Implements	4	7
19.	Lime Industry	4	6
20.	Readymade Garments	4	5
21.	Handloom	0	
22.	Woolen Industry	4 each	
23.	Thread Reeling Inddustry	0	
24.	Bucket Making unit	3 each	
25.	Soap works	0	
26.	Nail Polish works	0	
27.	Stone cutting works	0	
28.	Printing Press	0	
29.	Bakery	2 each	
30.	Battery charging units	0	
31.	Rice mill	2	
32.	Dal mi9ll	0	
33.	Sugar mill	0	
34.	Hair oil making works	1 each	

EXISTING INDUSTRIAL STRUCTURE:

The study region is basically agrarian, therefore, its industrial development has been very slow. There are no large scale industrial units in the area. Only small scale and cottage industries are found. Secondary sector, which includes house-hold industries, manufacturing and construction works, engages 2.14 per cent of the total workers of the region, (Table-1) show that majority of the industrial units of the study area are of small type. For example, all the flour mills are using stone grinders. There is only one rice mill, while small-size rice hullers number 282 and oil expellers number 485. In the same way, small scale agro-based and service industries.

The industrial units of the study area are distributed unevenly. Out of 90 registered units, the highest number (22) is found in Nawabganj and the lowest in Tarabganj (6). The numbers in the case of Colonelganj, Paraspur, Wazirganj and Belsar are 20,20, 14 and 8 respectively.

POTENTIALS FOR INDUSTRIAL DEVELOPMENT

It is clear from the foregoing discussion of the existing industrial structure of the region that secondary sector contributes but quite insignificantly to the economy of the region and it gives employment to only a very small fraction of its population although it possesses sufficient potentialities for future development. The region produces a wide variety of agricultural products and has a sizeable number of live stock which provide a base for many medium and small scale industries in the region. Forests, although they occupy very little area, provide sufficient scope for developing certain industries.

An attempt has been made in forthcoming pages to suggest a suitable planning for the industrial development of the region, which has been discussed under the following heads:-

1. Agro-based Industries.
2. Forest-based Industries.
3. Live stock Resource-based Industries.
4. Other Industries.

AGRO-BASED INDUSTRIES

RICE MILLS

Rice is the main food stuff consumed in the study area. Rice is obtained from paddy by dehusking the same. Rice dehusking activity has assumed the form of an important industry in the region. At present the dehusking facilities range from hand implements to small size rice hullers. The rice hullers are 282 in number and there is only one sheller rice mill. They will require 31725 tonnes paddy per season of 4 months, after which paddy is not available.

TABLE II : PROPOSED RICE MILLS

Details	Production capacity	
	1990 In Tonnes	1995 In Tonnes
1. Total Production of paddy	89,777	1,01,802
2. Paddy required by hullers/ rice mills	31,725	62,846
3. Paddy Reserved for seed (10%)	8,977	10,180
4. Paddy processed by manual labour (20%)	17,954	20,360
5. Paddy available for further processing.	31,121	12,025
6. No. of proposed Rice Mills with the capacity of 5,000 tonnes per year.	6	-
7. No. of proposed Rice Mills with the capacity of 2500 tonnes per year	-	5

It is clear from table-II that about 31121 tonnes of paddy will thus be available for new units in 1990. Six modern rice mills with 5000 tonnes capacity each per year may be set up at Colonelganj Paraspur, Belsar, Nawabganj, Tarabganj and Wazirganj. The region will produce 101802 tonnes of paddy in 1995 making 12025 tonnes of paddy available for further processing, Hence, 5 rice mills with 2500 tonnes capacity each per year may be established at Bhabhua, Mangura, Umari Begamganj, Bahadura and Katra Bhogchand.

RICE BRAN OIL MILL

During the process of dehusking paddy, a powder type of material is obtained which is called rice bran. Rice bran bears oil contents which are extracted in the extraction plant of the rice mill. Thus the rice bran oil is the sub by-product of rice milling industry. Rice milling produces 66 per cent rice, 17 per cent husk, 9 per cent screeming and remaining 8 per cent bran. Bran is processed by oil solvent extraction plants which produces the raw bran oil 15 per cent, de oiled bran 70 per cent and wax and sugar 15 per cent (4).

De-oiled bran is highly nutritive and digestive even for human consumption and mixed with wheat flour, makes good ingredients for biscuits, bread and other confectionary. Rice bran oil can be used for manufacturing washing soap and for splitting fat. Refined oil is edible and is superior to other cooking oils due to lower content of saturated fatty acids in it. The main ingredients of rice sugar are sucrose and glucose. The sugar is edible, rich in B-Vitamins. The wax is suitable for making polishes and emulsifiers (5). Hence, it is suggested to install a rice bran oil plant at Colonelganj upto 1990 and at Nawabganj upto 1995.

PULP AND BOARD FACTORY

Paddy husk may be utilized to manufacture pulp and board. Belsar produces paddy in sufficient quantity in the central position in the region. Hence, It is suggested to establish a pulp and board factory at Belsar, which may also utilize bagasse, i.e. the dry part of sugercane after extracting juice also.

PULSE MILLS

The region will produce 22931 tonnes of pulses in 1990 and 31765 tonnes in 1995. Assuming that at least 40 per cent of it-would be available for milling, it will require 3 dal mills with an installed capacity of 2000 tonnes per year and 5 mini dal mills with an annual capacity of 200 tonnes each in 1990. The former may be set up at Colonelganj, Belsar and Paraspur and the latter at the service centres. In 1995, one additional dal mill is suggested to be established at Wazirganj and 18 mini dal mills at service points.

OIL MILLS

The study area has 485 oil expellers. The region will produce 3895 tonnes of oil-seeds in 1990 and 6641 tonnes in 1995. Keeping in mind the production and the demand, it is proposed to establish oil mills at Colonelganj, Belsar and Paraspur upto 1990 and at Wazirganj, Umari Begamganj, Dumariadeeh and Katra Bhogchand upto 1995.

FLOUR MILLS

The conversion of wheat into flour is one of the simplest mechanical manufacturing operations. The study area exports a considerable quantity of wheat out side the region every year. Maida, atta and suze are the main products of wheat. The total production of wheat is estimated as 1,44,760 tonnes in 1990 (Table-III). If we leave 50 per cent for seed, export and traditional hand grinders, there remains an amount of 72,680 tonnes, of which 65,992 tonnes is required for the present 452 mills (0.4 tonnes each per day). Wheat available for further milling is 6,688 tonnes, for which 45 more small flour milling units with a capacity of about 0.4 tonnes each per day are needed, which may be set up at all the central villages in the study area.

In 1995 , the area will produce 1,63,878 tonnes of wheat. As per table-III still about 9,259 tonnes of wheat will be available for further milling, for which one roller mill with a capacity of 25 tonnes per day to produce maida, suzi etc. may be established at Colonelganj.

TABLE III : PROPOSED FLOUR MILLS

	Details	Production capacity	
		1990 In Tonnes	1995 In Tonnes
1.	Total production of wheat	1,44,760	1,63,878
2.	Wheat not available for milling (10%export 10% seed and 30% for hand grinders.	72,680	81,939
3.	Wheat required by present flour mills (@ 4 quintals or 0.4 tonnes per day)	65,992	72,680
4.	Wheat available for further milling	6,688	9,259
5.	No. of proposed additional small size flour mills with a capacity of 4 tonnes per day.	45	-
6.	No. of proposed roller mills with a capacity of 25 tonnes per day.	-	-1

SUGAR MILLS

Necessary conditions for the cultivation of sugarcane are found in the study area. There is at present one sugar mill at Nawabganj with a crushing capacity of 1,40,000 tonnes per annum (when the crushing season continues for 4 months). The estimated production for 1990 and 1995 respectively is 8,04,112 tonnes and 9,72,144. After subtracting the amount kept for seeding purposes and local consumption in the form of jaggery, the amount available for crushing in the mills comes to 4,02,056 tonnes and 4,86,072 tonnes respectively in 1990 and 1995. Further subtracting the capacity of the present mill, the net amount available comes to 2,62,056 in 1990 and 196072 tonnes in 1995. Hence a new sugar mill may be set up at Colonelganj upto 1990 with a capacity of 1,50,000 tonnes per annum and again at Belsar upto 1995 for the quantity available for further processing at that time.

GUR AND KHANDSARI UNITS

Due to lack of transportation network, the farmers experience very much difficulty in selling their sugarcane to sugar mills. Hence, there is need to establish these units at Paraspur, Tarabganj, Wazirganj and Bhabhua upto 1990 and at Dhanawa, Rangi, Mangura, Paska, Amdahi and Katra Bhogchand upto 1995.

FOOD PROCESSING UNITS

Fruits and vegetables form an important part of our balanced diet. Since these materials are highly perishable hence, they need proper processing for their preservation over a longer period. These products include jams, marmalades and jellies, squashes and juices. Due to the lack of datd and information, it is not possible to suggest a concrete development plan for these industries. one unit is recommended to be established at Nawabganj upto 1990 and one at Belsar upto 1995 as the production of maize is expected to be 62,470 tonnes and 71,454 tonnes respectively.

SEED PROCESSING UNIT

The traditional techniques of farming are changing very fast in the society. Adequate and timely supplies of modern production inputs such as balanced doses of fertilizers, improved and processed seeds and insectisides and fungicides largely determine the success of any agricultural modernisation programme. Hence, it is recommended to install one seed processing unit at Colonelganj upto 1990 and one at Nawabganj upto 1995.

Other agro-based units which have the scope to be developed in the study area, are bakery, papad and potato chips making. These units may be established at every central village of the region.

FOREST - BASED INDUSTRIES

The forest-based industries are an integral part of the vegetative raw material-based industries. The following industries are proposed.

SAW MILLS

The region is predominantly agricultural in nature. There is abundance of raw material in the region. To meet the various wood requirements of the region, it is proposed to install saw mills at every central village.

SILK REELING AND WEAVING UNITS

The study region bears rich potentials for the development of sericulture. This can absorb surplus manpower also. Therefore, silk reeling, spinning and weaving units are proposed to be set-up at Bhabhua, Bhauriganj, Rangi, Mangura, Dumariadeeh, Dhanawa and Katra Bhogchand upto 1990 and at remaining all the central villages up to 1995. Mulberry producing units should be established at the all the central villages.

WOODWOOL AND BABUL BARK UNIT

Babul trees are found in abundance in the study area. Babul-bark is used in the leather tanning industry while woodwool is used in packing of goods. Hence, it is proposed to establish these units at every central village in the region.

ANIMAL - BASED INDUSTRIES

The study area is rich in cattle wealth. Hence, based on livestock resources, a number of industries may be established.

DAIRY UNITS

The study area possesses good prospects for the development of dairying industry. There is a huge demand for milk and milk products, Small scale industry for the production of milk products e.g. milk powder, condensed milk, baby food and butter etc. should be located at Nawabganj and Colonelganj upto 1990 and mini size units at Paraspur, Belsar, Tarabganj and Wazirganj upto 1995.

LEATHER TANNING AND FOOT WEAR MAKING UNITS

The leather tanning industry has a natural incentive for its development. But the modern type of tanneries are lacking in the region due to poverty of the people, the poor conditions of the cattle and unsatisfactory methods of shelling and preservation of hide and skins. The foot wear making has been the traditional occupation of cobblers in the region. But the main problem of them are the shortage of finance, good quality leather and lack of modern equipment and machinery. Hence, it is proposed that modern type of machinery and technical assistance should be provided at every service points in the region. The traditional shoe makers should be given financial help by the rural banks. A tanning training-cum-production centre should be established at Nawabganj, Belsar and Colonelganj, which will collect hides and skins and supply processed hides to the village cobblers.

BONE CRUSHING UNITS

Dry bones of fallen and slaughtered animals are crushed for bone powder manufacturing. This powder can be used as manure and is also utilized in the manufacturing of fertilizers with the present emphasis on the development of agriculture through the use of fertilizers which are costly as well as ill distributed,the demand for bone meal is sure to increase in the region as an alternative to the chemical fertilizers. Hence, it is recommended to install such units at Nawabganj and Colonelganj upto 1990 and at Belsar upto 1995.

OTHER INDUSTRIES

INDUSTRIES RELATED TO AGRICULTURAL IMPLEMENTS

In order to boost up the agricultural production, the demand for improved agricultural implements is increasing in the region. At present there are seven agricultural implements repairing and manufacturing units in the study area. Hence, plants manufacturing improved implements should be established at Nawabganj, Belsar and Colonelganj and repairing work shops at all the central villages. Village artisans like blacksmiths and carpenters be provided accessories from the main plants. They should be trained in modern technical know-how and provided with financial assistance and new tools for manufacturing agricultural implements and other goods.

SOAP MAKING INDUSTRY

Detergents have become an integral item of daily use in the present day society. The main raw materials utilized in soap industry are rice bran oil, *neem*, castor, mahua, linseed and groundnut oils, soda ash and other chemicals etc. Most of the raw materials are found in the study region. Hence, soap making units are proposed at Wazirganj and Colonelganj.

HANDLOOM UNITS

The handloom industry ranks in importance next to agriculture in employment potential. It is well recognized that the handloom sector can provide larger avenues for employment in the rural areas. It is also a labour intensive and capital saving industry. Development of handloom sector has been given a prominent place in the 20 Point Programme. Therefore, liberal financial assistance, modern technology and working space should be provided for their development in the rural areas. It is proposed to establish handloom units at all the service centres and growth points in the study area and regular and adequate supply of yarn at fair price and credit at subsidised rates should be made available at these centres.

READYMADE GARMENTS UNITS

Cloths are the main essential need of the people, so these products are needed everywhere by the society, In order to fulfil the demand of the region, it is recommended to start these units at Colonelganj, Nawabganj, Wazirganj, Belsar, Tarabganj and Paraspur upto 1990 and at all service points upto 1995.

CARPET,DUREE AND WOOLEN PRODUCTS

Carpet, duree and woolen making industry is allied with the handloom industry in the region. This industry uses mostly the rough cotton yarn. Sheepwool is also found in the region. Hence, it is proposed to establish such units at Nawabganj and Colonelganj in the study area.

KILN,LIME AND SURKHI INDUSTRY

Kiln, lime and surkhi making industries are gaining momentum with the rising need of building construction, thus it is a demand based industry. Generally it uses ubiquitous raw material such as thick mud clay. There are 25 kilns at present which are not sufficient to meet the demand of the region, Hence, it is recommended to establish these units at every central village of the study area.

BEE KEEPING UNITS

Bee Keeping is an important occupation by which the farmers can increase their income without any heavy investment. Cross-pollination is needed by many of our Indian crops, which require agents like honey bees., Bee pollination not only enhances the production of the various crops but also improves the quality of seeds and fruits. In the same way farmers can earn money from their own farms and at the same time they can also increase their crop productions both in quality and quantity. Hence, every central village is suggested to develop these bee keeping units in the region.

Other demand-based industries proposed for the study area are jute bags, tat patti, rope industry, ayurvedic medicines, ice candy, candle works, plastic goods, engineering works and paints etc.

CONCLUSION

It is clear from the foregoing discussion that industrial development of the study area depends largely on the agro-industrial sector. That is why the main emphasis has been laid on developing agro-industries which provide scope for viable investments and returns. The main concern has been to suggest the initial strategy for industrial development which can come mainly by way of agricultural development, although suggestions to develop some foot loose industries have also been extended for a balanced and integrated development of the region.

THIRTY SEVEN

S.K. Shukla

Role of Commercial Activities in the Process of Rural Development: A Case Study of Sagar Block (M.P.)

The history of rural development in India can be traced to 1952 when attempt were initiated to achieve all round socio-economic development of villages with the willing co-operation of villagers to lift the centuries old stagment rural economy. Since then various strategies and programmes were formulated on identical.

In the year 1976 a blue print for integrated rural development was prepared. Conceptually I R D P[1] should mean multisectoral development of rural economy by exploiting the local resources, in men material, land and water.to the optimum. It is the intrinsic strength of local commercial activities itself which not only will support the service, the rising standards and sectoral economic activities, but will be in consonance with local enterprise with an intimate knowledge and understanding of local conditions, local needs and local potentialities.

COMMERCIAL ACTIVITIES AND RURAL DEVELOPMENT

Commercial activity is a complex phenomenon encompassing all activities involving the production and trading of goods. The development of commercial activities is vitally linked with the provisions of appropriate communications to all the producing centres in the rural areas, adequate transport links, storage facilities, scientific grading method, credit support and support prices for minimisation of price gap between the producer and consumer.

In the Sagar region (fig-1) varied resources are available, it is necessary to identify new commercial activities and to reorganize the existing one which could effectively be undertaken in rural areas, These are specially related to infra-structural development. Small, cottage and village industries and tertiary sector like processing and marketing of produce, play an important role in the overall economic development of the rural areas.

FIG. 37.1

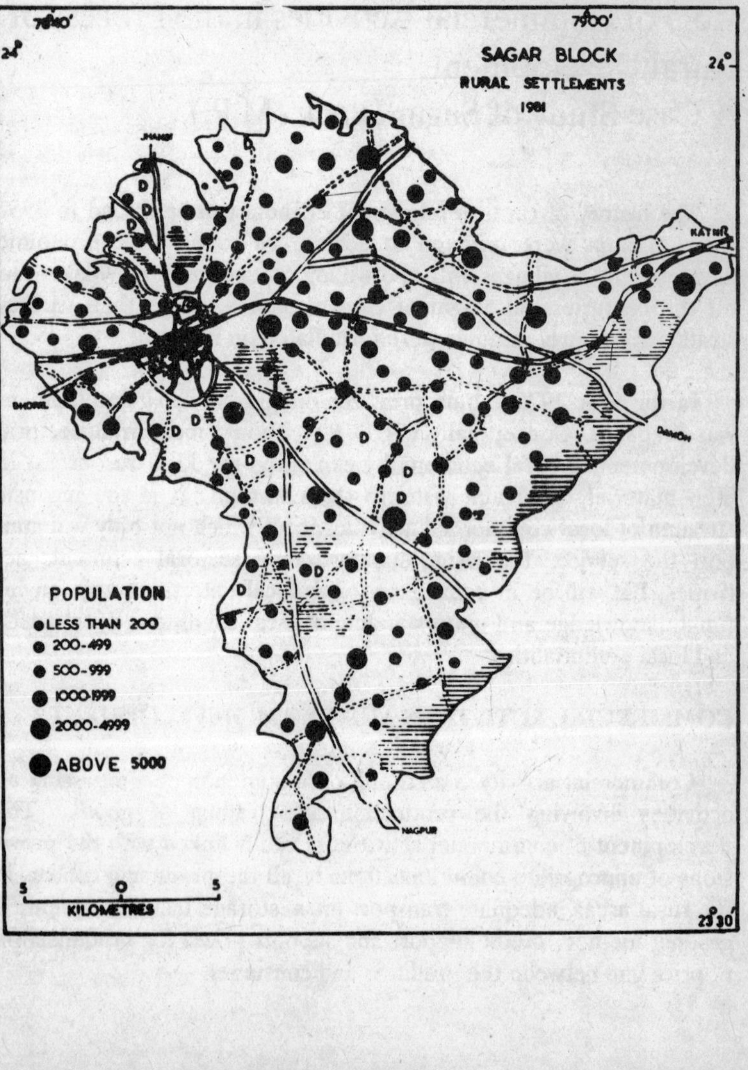

The main object of the IRDP was to develop the three sector of rural economy i.e. agricultural, industrial and tertiary to promote employment and income level of the weaker and needy sections, representing the small, marginal farmers and land-less labourers, which constitute a bulk of unemployment and underemployment in rural areas. In such a system development of commercial activities and marketing assume a special importance.

The Government provides adequate funds under the state plans to ensure the development of necessary infra-structure in the selected block and villages to start with, so that the village and the individual beneficiary oriented programme is adequately supported with the supply of necessary inputs as well as marketing, processing and such other facilities. Unfortunately, in various rural areas, development schemes have mechanically been implemented by the agencies without developing an emotional relationship with the local residents or without understanding their priorities. Sagar region is not an exception to this fact where the various schemes under IRDP have been initiated throughout the region without identifying the villages, availability of local resources and the needs of villagers, and composition of village community. The available funds have been sanctioned to the applicants on uniform basis leaving a number of villages uncovered. The *bolck* agencies under the identification of cluster schemes, conducted the houschold survey in 1984-85 and identified 1246 families below the poverty line (Rs.3500.00 per annum). Out of these 33.5 per cent families belong to the SC/ST. The prevailing disparity between the urban and poor and among the different groups of villagers, is creating a great deal of social tension. This disparity can be reduced only after the problem of landless, marginal and small farmer (major share in agricultural holdings) and artisans, is tackled at the first instance.

It has been observed that the shift in the occupational structure in the rural areas of the region is possible with the development of various commercial activities, Thus, the importance of inter-linking proper arrangements for the growing commercial activities with the implementation of I R D P needs constant emphasis.

AGRICULTURAL DEVELOPMENT

Agriculture plays an important role in the development of rural masses in Sagar region. The region is a predominantly agricultural area. Although a greater part of agricultural activity is devoted to the production of food-grains and a number of commercial crops (Ground nut, Soyabean and linseed) are also produced which are used as raw materials in various agro-based units. Irrigational facilities are limited and only 5.9 per cent of the total, cropped area enjoys the irrigational facilities. Although the region has 4460 irrigation wells with 2110 electric and 980 diesel pumps, even then during summer the region often faces the problems of scarcity of water, even for drinking purposes. During the year 1981-82, the total area under various crops was 51.7 per cent, while 66.4 per cent of the total cropped area was devoted to food crops.

Mixed farming has proved useful specially for small and marginal farmers of the villages like Semrabag, Rajakheri, Kerbana, Bararu, Kaneredeo and Rajuowa lying within the radious of 15 km from Sagar city. The use of high yielding varities of seed and short duration varities of crops have to be made available to the small and marginal farmers of the developing areas like Sagar, to improve the productivity. This is not the end of the problem, unfortunately small farmers are also in a disadvantagous position when compared with big farmers, in purchasing the inputs or in selling of their farm produces for remunerative prices. Small and marginal farmers have no capacity to wait for the time when they could get more remunerative prices, on the other hand, small farmers also have a less bargaining power specially in the areas to which he can offer. This poor condition of sale is further aggravated by his less mobility. Various development programmes have successeed in developing the resource base for agriculture and could enhance and yield rate. But there has been no specific programme for developing the market base to ensure the supply of inputs in time and sale of agricultural produces. Due to this the small and marginal farmers especially have failed to get the desired returns. This has led to the seasonal fluctuations in the hectareage of various crops also.

LIVESTOCK DEVELOPMENT

Next to crops animal husbandry programme has the largest employment potential. The most important feature is that it provides subsidiary occupations and offers gainful employment at the location itself and make better utilisation of female and child labour. Dairying as an activity which has gained considerable popularity among poorer sections of rural community of Sagar region also, it is because of low capital investment, capacity to yield income throughout the year, availability of grass from the adjoining hilly terrain and forest areas which are well suited for fodder cultivation. In the region 15.2 per cent of the area already lying as permanent pastures is also available for grazzing purposes. Similarly 4.3 per cent of the total area lying as fallow land too can be developed for cultivating the improved varities of fodder, to ensure the constant supply of fodder. Being a wheat growing area, supply of straw solves the problem of fodder specially during dry season.

It this context, the milk animal programme has become important as it has employment-cum-increased earning potential for the families of small, marginal farmer and landless labourer. The economic applicability of animal husbandary has been demonstrated excellently well in the villages like Mainpani, Patharia Ahir and Majhgaua where small and marginal farmers along with few landless have a credit of developing a dairy culture in these villages. Still the region has sufficient scope for dairy development and related allied commercial activities if certain problems are tackled.

During the field survey it has been observed that some 51.00 per cent households have only one milk animal, 30.0 per cent two milk animals, 10.5 per cent three milk animals and only 8.5 per cent have more than three milk animals, Most of the marginal farmers and landless laboures have only one milk animal and have to face hardships when the animal is dry for a few months. Among the milk animals buffaloes have a dominating share over cows because of higher yielding capacity.

Intensive programme of livestock, and poultry development certainly can accomodate the unemployed and under employed labour force and can play an important role in the process of rural development.

FORESTRY

The forest has so far been considered a state prerogative. The common impression is that there is very little scope for forestry in farmer's holdings. But the trees can play a very important role by improving the economy of the villagers.

Forests are among the important sources not only for a large variety of products but also provide employment to a sizeable rural population (7.6 per cent of the total area is under forest). Most of the forests occupy the hilly tracts of the region. Among the major commercial forest products, teak is the most outstanding, *Tendu* leaves, *Cheola* leaves, resins, tanning dyes, medicinal plants, essential oils, Khair trees, honey, *lac* and grasses are the important produces.

Forestry is an important source of employment in rural areas encircling the forest belts of Sagar specially in off season and is therefore complementary to the employment in farm production.

There is an increasing demand for industrial wood and fuel wood. The logging operations employ a large number of rural labour besides afforestation operations like cleaning of forest areas, collection of seeds, raising of nursaries, preparations or sites etc.

SECONDARY SECTOR

There is a very close inter-dependence between agriculture and industry. Number of small, cottage and village industries can be setup in the rural areas processing the locally available agricultural, animal and forest produces. These units can be set up with a purpose to meet the local needs rather than developing other area. It is a known fact that industrial and commercial activities along with agriculture can actively participate in the rural development, hence be initiated on an integrated basis.

Cottage and village industries have been accepted as a priority sector in achieving the development of rural areas. Industrial Units processing milk products, Jams, Jellies, Squashes, milling, oil extraction, flour milling, tanning, *bidi* making, saw mills, bricks and roof tile making and making of earthen pots can comfortably be set up in the region. For example processing of ground nuts in villages as per their demand will minimize, the dependence on urban areas for edible oil, on the other hand available initial waste (35% *chilka*) can be used by brick making units as fuel and oil cakes by dairy owners, for which these people are depending on urban units. But these units will need financial assitance, coordination in supply of raw materials, ensured market, and long term administrative protection which are lacking in the region. In addition to this the professional services of people such as cobblers, black-smiths, carpenters, etc, can be improved by upgrading their skills. If the control cloth is provided to the tailors the villagers can have locally made cloths on reasonable cost.

Development of commercial and industrial activities depends much upon the development of the infra-structural facilities such as roads, power and financial institutions. Out of 170 villages, 90 villages (52.9 per cent) are electrified in Sagar block. The process of electrification of villages started from Third Five Year Plan, when only eight villages were electrified. 61.1 per cent of the total electrified villages of Sagar Block has been provided connection during the fifth and Sixth Five Year Plans. Most of the villages above 1000 population are electrified. The existing connections and consumption pattern shows that the domestic connections are very poor in the region. Similarly, the non domestic consumption is also small. Agricultural sector is the largest consumer.

TERTIARY SECTOR

It has been observed that tertiary activities represent by far the most dynamic sector in creating the new employment in the prospecting areas of the developing region. In the rural situation, it will cover trade activities like selling agents for agro-inputs, transport, agents and electricians. Deliberate efforts will have to be made to see the the production of sophisticated goods and services which at present are concentrating in the urban areas are shifted to rural areas.

Rural housing is yet another field in which construction activities can enables the landless labourer to have a suitable subsidiary occupations. On the other hand construction of residential houses, roads, public buildings like schools, hospitals, *Panchyat Bhawan*, markets, storage and warehousing facilities, will help in setting up units or agencies providing constructional material especially from the local areas.

The object of the commercial activities is not only to provide large scale employment to the rural population but also to provide them with a sound self-generating economy something like that which is available in industrial or urban areas. The purpose is also to change the conditions in rural areas which may make it attractive for the villagers to stay instead of migrating to urban centres to become a part of slum. Efforts have to be made to develop growth poles to divert the flow of rural migrants from cities as well from small towns to these growth centres. This will support the decentralisation of industries and help the installation of agro-based, forest based and animal-based industries and related activities in the rural sector.

NOTES

1. Integrated Rural Development Programme.

THIRTY EIGHT

N.K. De and
A.K. Bera

Approaches to Integrated Rural Development - A Block Level Study

Introduction

The integrated rural development means multifaced development of rural economy by exploiting to the optimum the local resources in men, material, land and water. The development is to be made mainly on the basis of local initiative and drive. The goal of integrated rural development is full rural employment. Rural development is often confused with agricultural development. Agricultural development is no doubt basic to not only development of the rural area but also to the development of the industrial sector. But rural development is larger than agricultural development. For this the integration of all economic and social activities necessary for human life like agriculture, cottage industry, infrastructure, transport, labour, wealth, education, housing etc. The interrelation of all these is significant as it implies planning for a given geographical area in all its aspects needed for modernisation and betterment of living (Bhat, L.S. 1976).

Study Area

With a view to study the integrated rural development, Panskura-I *Block*, Midnapur District, West Bengal which lies between 87'44' E to 87'50' E, long. and 22'18' N to 22'30' N latitudes has been taken into consideration (Fig.1).

FIG. 38.1

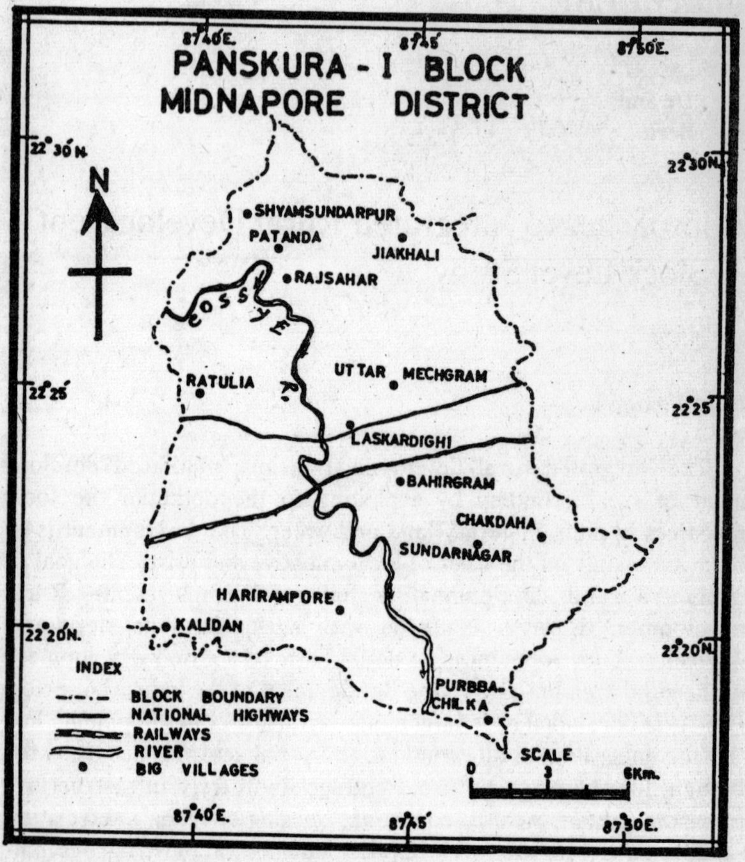

Physical make up

Geologically the area as a whole is composed of alluvium. It is included under the Cossye delta.

The land of Panskura-I *Block* is gently sloping from north-west to south. The north-western part is higher than that of the south which gradually merges with the monotonously flat lands. Local relief varies between 60 Cm. to 80 Cm. The area is drained by the river

Cossye which is flowing from north-west to south of this block and has artificial embankments on both sides.

The climate of the area is *monsoon* type. The rainfall is unequally distributed throughout the year. It is mainly concentrated between June to September, i.e. during the period of south-west *monsoon*. Winter is dry and the amount of rainfall during this period is negligible. The summer is very hot. The area is occasionally affected by the tropical disturbances.

Panskura-I *Block* as a whole is covered by alluvial soils. The alluvial soils are mainly composed of sands, silts and clays brought down by the river. The soils are well drained, leached, dry and coarse in texture. The chemical properties of the soils vary from place to place. In general organic carbon content varies between 0.09-1.05 per cent, $P_2 O_5$ varies between 20.0 to 54.00Kg/ha whereas P^H varies between 5.0 to 7.9 (DE, N.K.,1978).

Socio-economic make up

Out of the 131426 (1981) total population of the block 25539 persons are agricultural labourers. The population pressure on land here is very high (man-land ration is 0.21 in 1981). The density of population is also high i.e. 636 persons Km^2

There are two major communication lines which connect the block with the adjoining areas. The only railway line connecting Howrah and kharagpur as well as the Calcutta - Bombay National highway pass through the area. The National highway and the railway line almost run parallel to each other. The Block Development Programme which is to be seen here is a part of the Intensive District Agricultural Programme (I.D.A.P.). It includes the training of farmers in the use of H.Y.V. of seeds, chemical fertilizers, pesticides and other modern technological aspects of agriculture through the village Level Workers (V.L.W.).

The two types of Banking facilities available in the Block are (a) co-operative Agricultural Marketing Society Ltd, which finance for seeds, fertilizers, pesticides etc.

The Rural electrification programme here is mainly for the operation of shallow tube wells, deep-tube wells, river lift irrigation etc. By this the villagers get ample scope to increase their agricultural production.

General Character of land Use (1981-82)

The general character of land use of the area (1981-82) as derived from the Block Office is as follows (Table - 1)

TABLE 1 : LANDUSE IN 1981-82

	Classification	Area in Hectares	Area in %
1.	Geographical Area	24556	-
2.	Net Cropped Area	16830	68.54
3.	Area sown more than one crop	9296	37.86
4.	Area for non-agricultural uses	6633	27.00
5.	Area under orchard, trees, etc.	928	3.78
6.	Current follows	119	0.48
7.	Permanent Pasture & other grazing land	23	0.10
8.	Others	23	0.10

Source : Panskura - I *Block* Office, Dist. Midnapur.

Out of the total 24556 ha of geographical area of the *block*, 16830 ha i.e. 68.54 per cent in under cultivation, 6534 ha, i.e. 30.68 per cent is devoted to monoculture, 9296 ha i.e. 37.86 per cent in under double/multiple cropping, 928 ha i.e. 3.78 per cent is under orchard and trees and rest of the land is devoted to other purposes, like current follow, pasture, etc.

The area under different types; of agricultural crops cultivated is given in Table II.

The table indicates that the cropping intensity (taking all crops) is 155 per cent. The important cash crops here are Betelvine and Flower. The cultivated are under Betelvine is increasing every year. Huge quantity of the different types of flowers are supplied to Calcutta every day from the block. The other important crops include paddy, vegetables, oil seed, potato, wheat and jute (Chakrabarty,S. 1950).

TABLE II : YEAR - 1981-82

Name of the Crop	Area in hectares	Production in M. Tons.
Aus (Local)	135	189.00
Aus (H.Y.V.)	245	441.00
Aman (Local)	11020	5476.94
Aman (H.Y.V.)	5000	4235.00
Boro (Local	800	1200.00
Boro (H.Y.V.)	2500	4500.00
Wheat	400	1040.00
Kharif Pulses	150	37.50
Rabi Pulses	300	115.00
Oil seeds	560	532.50
Potato	400	3400.00
Jute	360	3600.00(Bale)
Sunhemp	20	100.00
Sugar cane	6	240.00
Bhadoi Flower (Rainy)	100	800.00
Winter Flower	50	90.00
Bhadoi Vegetables	1464	10202.00
Winter Vegetables	1741	17128.00
Summer Vegetables	200	1868.00
Spices	95	80.45
Coconut	50	16.25
Betelvine	8	214.00

$$\text{Cropping Intensity} = \frac{\text{Total area under different crops (Block)}}{\text{Total area under cultivation (Block)}} \times 100$$

= 155%

Source: Panskura - I *Block* Office, District Midnapur.

Proposals for Development

The Proposals for the integrated rural development of the *block* are multifarious. But the most important ones which need immediate attention are as follows:

1. The rapid growth of population results in high pressure on agricultural land. To support these people more cultivable land is needed. The horizontal or spatial extension of cultivable land is more or less impossible in the block. Therefore, emphasis on the vertical extension in the form of intensive agriculture is to be given.

2. Population control and proper education of the people

throughout the block is necessary.

3. Attention for the improvement of the rearing of the domesticated animals (like cows and goats) is necessary.

4. Improvement of the existing fisheries and poultry development programmes.

5. Further improvement in the existing agricultural conditions through modernisation which include proper distribution of seeds, fertilizers, pesticides, management and rotation of crops, irrigation, transport, marketing, cold storage facilities etc.

6. Betelvine from this *block* is despatched to almost all the provinces of the country and even to foreign countries. So plant protection programmes, better yield of the crop and crop research are to be established very soon.

7. Improvement in the existing conditions of flower gardening is a must for the *block*. Because of the lack of adequate knowledge about flowers amongst the growers and the extension workers, the optimum yield is not obtained. So necessary help from the directorate of agriculture, Govt. of West Bengal is desired in this field.

8. There are few small scale/cottage industries like husking machines, oil pressing machines, bakeries, *bidi* making, blacks smithy, pottery, weaving, carpentry, basket making, shoe making, tailoring, printing press, repairing shops, gold and silver smithy, sweet meat shops, etc. etc. Out of these existing industries, repairing shop, tailoring, shoe making, bakeries are suffering much with respect to the supply of raw materials and availability of capitals. Attention is to be given in these aspects.

Conclusions

To achieve the integration of economic and social activities in the block like agriculture, cottage/small scale industry, infrastructure, transport, health, education, etc. the existing essential infrastructure and services of the main centre i.e. Panskura are to be improved along with the other sub-centres (villages) in the *block*. So that greater employment potentials are generated in the entire territory.

In addition, land reforms are needed in the *block*. The proposed agrobased industrialization programmes, however, would open wide dimensions to the surplus labour force spilled over from agricultural sector.

THIRTY NINE

M.P. Tripathi and
Tek Bahadur Gurung.

Impact of Developmental Activities in The Rural Hilly Area of Nepal: A Case Study of Chaurjhahari Tarn in Rukum District.

Introduction

The paper assesses the impact of developmental activities in the rural hilly area of Nepal. The paper is based on field work conducted in 1984. The impact of developmental activities has led to the initiation of central place activities in the study region.

This is an important Tarn in the remote hilly region of Nepal. It is now connected by Air from Kathmandu.

The Study Area

The area under study lies at the confluence of Bheri and Banskhola Rivers to the extreme south-west of Rukum District of Rapti Zone in Mid-Western Development Region (28°0' N to 28° 43' Lat.; 82° 11'E to 82° 15'E long). It has an area of 400 ha. It is a low land plain. The study includes seven villages - Nakhira, Gharigaon, Lamichhane gaon, Tata gaon, Salkhola gaon & Lapuley gaon with a market centre (Fig.1).

Before 1970 there was hill trail connecting Nepalganj to Jumla. People from Dolpa, Rukum, Jajarkot and Sallyan used this route for commercial trips. During 1970 the air service was introduced in and enormous development took place. Since then government offices have been established to change the soico-economic condition of the people. After 1970, a market centre and various offices have been established in Chaurjhahari.

FIG. 39.1

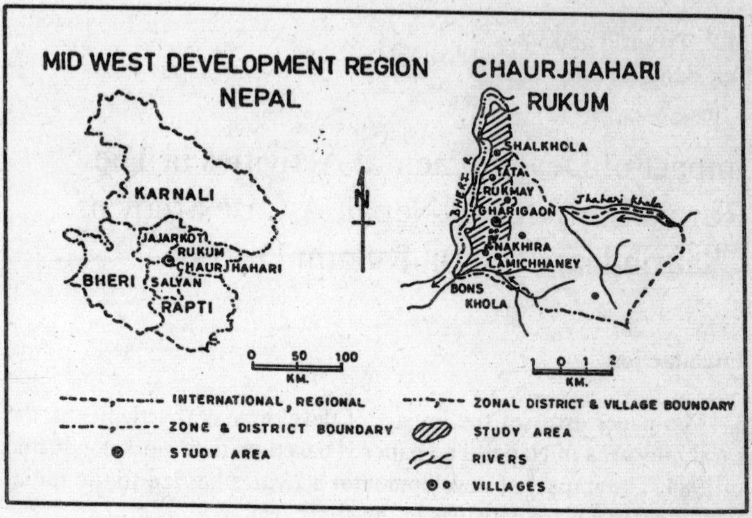

At present due to its locational importance, fertile soil, level land, malaria eradication facilities, social and economic activities, the Tarn has attracted a large number of people from its peripherial zone - Rukum, Jajarkot, Pyuthan and Salyan districts of Rapti Zone.

Methodology

This paper is based on empirical observations. A set of questionnaire was prepared and family heads were interviewed for data collection. Out of total households (34) 26% households were randomly selected. The developmental activities selected for the present study are expansion of irrigation, health and education facilities, establishment of market centre and the provision of air transport.

Impact of Irrigation Facility on Agriculture

Agriculture has been the most important source of living for rural communities in Chaurjhahari. The average size of cultivated land holding is more than half ha (8 *ropani*). Before the completion of Chourjhahari Irrigation canal (19km.) there was no permanent source of water for cultivation and agriculture was solely dependent on the *monsoons*. Due to the uncertainty of the *monsoons* and winter precipitation, the failure of the crop was quite prominent. But now the irrigation facility has reduced this problem and 77% of the cultivated land comes under canal irrigation.

Rice and wheat are the dominant summer and winter crops respectively. Prior to the completion of the irrigation project, 68% of the total cultivated land of the area was used for rice cultivation. 24% and 8% were devoted to maize and millet respectively. In winter 75% of the total winter cultivated land were used for growing wheat whereas 15% and 10% were used for growing pulses and oil seeds respectively. After the completion of irrigation canal the land use pattern has changed. The irrigation facilities have expanded the summer and winter cultivated land resulting in the extension of wheat and rice cultivated land. It has also reduced the dependency on the summer *monsoons* and winter rainfall. Now 75% of the total summer cultivated land comes under rice whereas 21% and 5% come under millets and maize respectively. Decrease in millet and maize cultivated land is mainly because of the extension of the paddy cultivation (Table-I).

TABLE I : CULTIVATION BEFORE AND AFTER IRRIGATION.

	Summer Crops (%)			Winter Crops (%)		
	Rice	Maize	Millet	Wheat	Pulse	Oilseeds
Before	68	24	8	75	15	10
After	74	21	5	80	12	8

Source : Field survey, 1984.

During winter, wheat is the most important crop occupying 88% of the total cultivated land. Similarly, 12% and 8% of the total winter cultivated land comes under pulses and oilseeds respectively.

Though agriculture is of subsistance nature, the production has certainly increased. 18% of the sampled household had surplus production in rice and 1% had a surplus in pulses. These surplus commodities were sold in local market.

The impact of co-operative society in farming is also to be noted. The farmers have been immensely benefitted by the presence of co-operative society which provides help to the farmers in terms of loan, chemical fertilizers, improved seeds and pestisides and insecticides. The main objective of seeds and pestisides and insecticides. The main objective of the co-operative society is to improve the agricultural economy of the farmers. However, in this context a strange situation has emerged for the reasons best known to local authorities. Farmers are provided with financial loans and other facilities. But these loans are not being used properly rather these loans are used on other items. the result is that farmers who do not pay back the loan in time avoid visiting the co-operative society. That is why, only 35% of the sampled households have been found visiting the co-Operative society for necessary help particularly for, chemical, fertilizers, loan to purchase cattle, insecticides and improved seeds.

Since the use of fertilizers has improved the yields, its demand is high. In this respect the co-operative society has failed to meet the required demand of the farmers. That is why chemical fertilizer has been used by only 30% of all the farmers. The rest depend upon cattle manures.

TABLE II : USE OF MANURES FOR CULTIVATION IN CHAURJHAHARI(1984)

No. of Chemical fertilizer user	No. of local manure users	No. of both users	No.of co-operative loan for manure
%	%	%	%
Nil	57	70	29 30 29 35

Source: Field survey, 1984.

Impact of health and education facilities on development

Before 1970 there were no modern health facilities available in Chaurjhahari. The health facility was possible in two and a half hours steep slope walk at Jajarkot. At present there is a health post and two drug stores. Prior to the establishment of health post of Chaurjhahari, 78% people used to visit the local exorcists to cure their sickness, and only 16% used to go to the Jajarkot health post and that too in a case when exorcists failed to cure them. Nearly 6% patients went nowhere because of their belief that sickness would be cured itself.

At present, the superstition of the people on traditional health service has been greatly challenged by the modern health services. Now people go to the junior health assistant in local health post. Beside this the drug stores in the market, also examine local patients. 57% people have consulted junior health assistant of the local health post but still 43% were treated by exorcists. This shows that the local people are gradually leaving their old traditional medical practices (Table-III).

TABLE III : NATURE OF MEDICAL TREATMENT BEFORE AND AFTER THE HEALTH FACILITIES IN CHAURJHAHARI 1984.

Before 1970					
No. of family attended	No. of family exorcist %	No. of family attended to H.P.	%	attended nowhere	%
66	76	14	16	7	8
After 1970					
No. of family attended	No. of family exorcist %	No. of family attended to H.P.	%	attended nowhere	%
38	43	49	57	-	-

Source : field survey, 1984.

Before 1970, there was only a primary school (126 students) in Chaurjhahari. Soon after the establishment of developmental activities, the primary school was raised to the level of a middle school. Another primary school was opened in Nakhira village in 1972. IN 1976 the middle school was again raised to the secondary school level. It may now be raised to Campus level. The number of students was 405 from class I to X (Table IV).

Change in the occupational structure of population

Chaurjhahari is important for agriculture. The main source of living of rural people is mainly based on agriculture. However, after the establishment of developmental activities other opportunities also have become possible for people. The occupational structure of people in Tar has changed. 55% of total population is engaged in agriculture, 2.3% as Government employees, 1.3% shop keepers, 15% students and 26.3% of the total population is found inactive (Table V).

TABLE IV : NUMBER OF STUDENTS IN SCHOOLS IN CHAURJHAHARI TARN.

	Classes									Total
School	1	2	3	4	5	6	7	8	9	10
Sital *Madhyamik Vidyalaya**			70	52	31	35	30	22	39	279
Nakhira *Prathmik Vidhyalaya***			28	21	17	-	-	-	-	- 126
										405

Source: field survey, 1984.
* Middle School; ** Primary School.

TABLE V : OCCUPATIONAL OCCUPATIONAL STRUCTURE IN CHAURJHAHARI

Agriculture		Service		Student		Trade		Infants (inactive)	Plus adults
Nos.	%	No.	%	Nos.	%	No.	%	Nos.	%
296	55	19	2.3	83	15	6	1.3	150	26.3

Source: field survey, 1984.

The impact of market centre on development

As mentioned earlier Chaurjhahari performs the function of a control market for the surrounding hills of Jajarkot, Sallyan and Rukum districts. Prior to the emergence of the established market centre at Chaurjhahari, the local people were entirely dependent upon Nepalganj near the Indian border with Nepal for marketing. The local people used to travel up to Nepalganj, at least twice a year particularly once in summer and the other in winter. But with the establishment of market, the frequency to Nepalganj has been reduced to a great-extent. Most commodities like clothes, kerosene, salt etc. are available in the local market though at a higher price than Nepalganj. Still some people who visit Nepalganj, generally during the winter, (the off-farming season) bring necessary commodities like shoes, kerosene, salt etc. from Nepalganj.

The market constitutes fifty-six buildings and most of them have been used for commercial functions. All the buildings are double storied. The ground floor is being used for commercial activities and the first storey for residential purposes.

Air transport and development activities

Due to the physical space and central location of the Chaurjhahari as air field for STOL plan service was constructed in Makhir in 1971. At the beginning, Chaurjhahari was connected by Kathmandu - Nepalganj route. Later on, the Kathmandu - Chaurjhahari - Nepalganj weekly service was added. The opening of the air service made this place more accessible and its geographical potentialities for concentration of developmental activities were exposed. Soon after the beginning of the air service ~Chaurjhahari Irrigation Project' was launched. Further, owing to its central location, the sub-regional National Trading Corporation was established to distribute commodities for Salyan, Jajarkot, and Rukum districts. Import of commodities for the National Trading was made by the plane service. Again all food-stuffs for distribution to Jajarkot, Salyan and Rukum are transported to Chaurjhahari by plane and this has been responsible for the estab lishment of two go-downs close to the air port. Now due to air linkage and the interaction with Kathmandu, Nepalganj, Surkhet, Dang and Bhairahawa, various sub-district level offices have been established for rural development. The impact of air service in Chaurjhahari is not only seen in the concentration of developmental activities but it has also changed the socio-economic activities of rural people living within Chaurjhari Tarn.

Conclusion

The study area relates to the mid-western developmental region of Nepal which is hilly. However, Chourjhari is a low flat valley occupying a tri-junctional location between Sallyan Jajarkot and Rukum districts. This advantageous site and location in such a remote area have made this place suitable to develop as a central place.

FORTY

Hans-Georg Bohle

Towards New Concepts in Marketing Geography: Polarized Distribution Systems in Third World Countries with Evidence Form South India

Introduction

Stimulated by new debates on development theory such as dependency approaches or mode of production conceptions, geographical research on Third World issues had recently experienced a shift of paradigm.Basically this is a shift away from neoclassical equilibrium models towards conceptions of polarized development. Adequate analytical tools for describing and explaining Third World distribution systems in the context of polarized development, however, have so far not yet been developed by marketing geographers. It is the objective of the present paper to present some empirical evidence and theoretical considerations to this end

Starting from a critical assessment of current theoretical assumptions in marketing geography, the paper will first sketch recent attempts in reformulating them. Some considerations on further rethinking marketing geography will then be added, based on a recent debate in German development sociology on the articulation between different modes of production/distribution in Third World countries. How to transfer such conceptions to the study of marketplace exchange systems will finally be elaborated and illustrated by a case study on fish-marketing in the Cauvery-Delta of Tamil Nadu.

REFORMULATING CENTRAL-PLACE THEORY IN MARKETING CEOGRAPHY

In the first volume of the "Indian Journal of Marketing Geography", the Brazilian geographer Roberto Correa (1983) critically examined and rejected the application of central place theory to the geography of commercial activities in Third World countries. According to his analysis, central place systems appear as historically determined phenomena, which undergo change along with the transformation of overall economic and social systems. Correa argues that the emergence of hierarchically structured, integrated central place systems is linked to the emergence of a comprehensive labour division, which, in turn, is a result of capitalistic penetration and transformation. From this perspective, contemporary central place systems are both a pre-condition and a result of capitalistic development. They represent a territorial structure which secures the reproduction of the rural population and, at the same time, channels profit from the rural hinterland to the metropolitan centres. Consequently, Correa concludes the analysis of the urbanization process in Third World countries. Due to capitalistic forces of accumulation and concentration, however, this process is regarded as inherently polarized. Hence, Correa postulates that assumptions of central place theory such as "autonomy" or "traditionality" of market systems; formal equity of market-participants; homogeneity of rural space; or rural centres that "serve" their hinterland, have to be rejected. In a recent paper, the Norwegian geographer peter Sjohatt (1984) also referred to central place theory in Third World marketing geography as a whole. As geographical research in Third World countries has become more and more concerned with the development process as polarized regional growth, classic central place theory, which is a typical static equilibrium theory, seems no longer really relevant. Sjoholt rather concludes that there is need of elaborating old and developing new analytical tools for marketing geography. To this end, in his opinion more empirical studies are needed, particularly into polarized central distribution systems as mechanisms of redistribution.

The present paper will incorporate both these claims. Firstly, It will discuss some new analytical tools from German develoapment theory. Secondly, It will present some empirical research from South

India to demonstrate the application of these tools.

'ARTICULATIONN' - APPROACH IN GERMAN DEVELOPMENT SOCIOLOGY

In the context of a worldwide discussion on modes of production in Third World countries (for India see:Bohle,1986 Harriss, 1982; Thorner, 1982). German development sociology has recently developed an approach which concentrates on the relation between subsistence economy and capitalism (Elwert,1982;1983). In this conception, both subsistence and market economy are subdivided into various socio-economic sectors which are defined by a specific mode of production. Examples of such sectors are peasant production, petty trade, migrant labour, indoor work, petty services etc. 8th the one hand, mechanised farming, wholesales trade, industrial work etc. on the other. Empirical analysis concentrates on the "articulation" between the various socio-economic sectors and on the consequences of this interrelationship It is mainly five points that are analysed in this connection :

transfers between subsistence and modern sectors, mainly transfers of commodities, capital and labour;
relations of authority or complemetarity which mobilize these transfers :
Conflict between different economic objectives or "rationalities" in the sectors;
conditions of stability or change in the relations between the sectors;
consequences of the relations for internal structures (that is social, economic, and also spatial structures); and last not least, for the living conditions of the population concerned.

Such conception which seeks to "translate" macro-theoretical approaches to the micro-level of individual villages or even households, seems highly relevant to the study of polarized distribution systems in Third World countries. I will try to demonstrate this by means of an empirical case study on fishmarketing in the Cauvery-Delta of Tamil Nadu. Before, I would like to give some idea of the general characteristics of mobile trade in Central Tamil Nadu, where I studied the weekly market systems of four districts and interviewed more than 1.500 weekly market traders (Bohle, 1985).

ROLE OF MOBILE TRADE IN CENTRAL TAMIL NADU

In the context of socio-economic and spatial polarisation in rural India, petty mobile trade in Central Tamil Nadu functions as a spatially decentralized distribution and marketing system for the rural poor. In many cases, weekly market trade also serves to accomodate marginal farmers and landless labourers. More than 75% of the traders interviewed had entered in trade within the last ten years; around one half of them belong to traditional farming castes.

South Indian weekly market trade appears as a typical case of "what has been called "survival - economy": different occupations are combined in the course of a week or seasonally: there is labour division within a single household, labour force is highly mobile; all activities are strategically oriented towards survival within an insecure environment. All this is typical of a predominant "search for security" (Ever and Elwert, 1983), where survival has absolute priority to income maximisation. Those who are fully dependent on trade find their work only on 2.9 days per week, on an average; around 70% of the mobile traders where found to live below the poverty line, only around 10% clearly above it.

Regarding the role of weekly market trade in relation to the wider economic system, it functioned as a subsystem of the entire distribution system, but, as a matter of fact, as a dependent subsystem which is controlled, financed, organised and dominated by urban wholesale trade. Recent processess such as growth, persistence or decline of regional weekly market systems or individual markets were found to be widely determined by the specific functions of weekly market trade for urban wholesale trade. Consequently, a spatially highly differentiated process of integration or disintegration of weekly market trade in relation to the overall distribution system, a process which also differed considerably from commodity to commodity was observed

CASE-STUDY: DRY FISH TRADE IN THE CAUVERY-DELTA

Dry-fish trade in the Cauvery-Delta of Tamil Nadu offers one example to demonstrate this process, there are 35 weekly markets in Thanjavur District, The majority of them are specialized; 85% of all stalls fall to the four main commodities, namely dry fish, vegetable, timber and second-hand clothes. As dry fish is ritually disreputable and of a penetrating smell, it is mainly consumed by low-caste, economically weak sections of the society: weekly markets are therefore especially suited for the sale of dry-fish.

Around 125 tons of dry-fish are produced weekly in the Cauvery-Delta. 75 tons are exported via Mayuram and Tirutturaippundi weekly markets (Fig - 1) to the large urban centres of Tamil Nadu, where it is mainly sold to the urban poor. There are another four weekly markets with whole-sale-trade, from where the remaining 50 tons of dry fish is distributed in the rural hinterland. It is evident from Fig-1 that these markets are located about 20-30 km. from the coast, where they function as mediators between coastal region and the interior country.

The interviews revealed that around 70% of all dry-fish, which is distributed in rural Thanjavur, is not sold directly from the producer to the consumer or from the producer via petty trade to the consumer, but is turned over via whole-sale traders. This proportion, however, varies considerably from region to region within the Delta, exhibiting a close connection between wholesale control, on the one hand, recent modernisation of fisheries on the other. In the New Belts, for example, nearly 100% of the dry fish reach the consumers via wholesale trade. Here, traditional fishing boats have largely been replaced by modern trawlers, and urban wholesale trade has heavily invested in this profitable business. Since, wholesale trade controls both fishing and marketing of fish, incase of repair, investment or losses, fisherman are provided with credit by the wholesale trader; as soon as they are indebted, they are bound to deliver their fish to this individual wholesaler only. Many of the modern boats even belong to wholesalers. In the process of marketing, coolies transport the fish to the urban wholesale stores by means of bicycles; from there, the fish is distributed by petty mobile traders to interior weekly markets or directly to the villages; these traders also live on credits and get their fish on a commission basis. Today, wholesale traders in dry fish constitute one of the richest groups of the districts; recently, they have even established a sort of syndicate in Pattukkottai to bar out-

FIG. 40.1

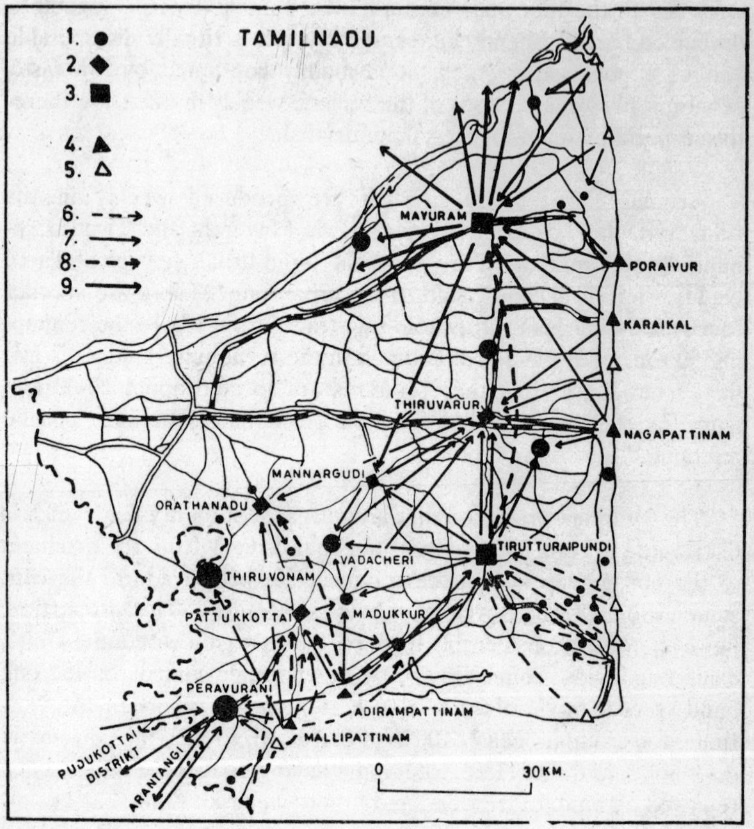

1 - Weekly markets with dry fish retail
2 - Retail and wholesale trade
3 - Additional export function
4 - Major fishing centre with wholesale
5 - Major fishing centre without wholesale
6 - Self marketing women traders
7 - Weekly market retail traders
8 - Wholesalers
9 - Metropolitan buying centre

siders from joining profitable dry-fish trade. Fisherman and petty traders, on the other hand, have remained as poor as before. Spatially, it is interesting to note that all those weekly markets have experienced growth in recent years which function as distribution centres for wholesale trade. In the New Delta the weekly market system thus becomes more and more stratified and hierarchical. Furthermore, we can observe that the market days of the retail markets are exactly coordinated to the periodicity of wholesale markets.

Contrary to this, the tail-end region of Southesast-Thanjavur exhibits direct forms of marketing between producer and consumer or between producer, petty trader and consumer. This is due to lack of roads, to heavy seasonal floodings and to fishing villages which are not suited for modernisation. Consequently, urban wholesale trade has no interest in this region. A dense network of small, unstratified and non-specialized weekly markets is predominant here.

CONCLUSION

From the perspective of the "articulation" between different socio-economic sectors, we can conclude that petty trade in dry-fish is multifariously integrated into and organized by a dominant modern mode of production, namely urban-based wholesale trade. This seems to be a general feature of the South Indian rural economy. The class of wholesale traders, which usually combines the functions of landlord, moneylender and merchant, bases its dominance mainly on the control of the rural sphere of production, that is agriculture, cattle-breeding and fisheries. Here, they control markets for the means of production, the means of subsistence; the markets for capital, land, and labour; and small the outlets for rural produce. Through mechanisms of credit and indebtedness, the relation between merchant-moneylender and small rural producer becomes stable and durable, The same is true to the distribution sphere and to the relation between petty trade and wholesale trade as revealed by my case studies. The latter control merchant-capital, market-channels and means of transportation; they supply pettty traders with commodities and money on conditions which they themselves dictate. The result of this "articulation" which is markedly an authority-dependency relationship is poverty and "survival economy" on the one side, wealth and accumulation on the other. Consequently, economic polarization in the sphere of distribution is even more marked in Tamil Nadu than in the sphere of production (Tables I,II).

TABLE 1 : POLARIZATION OF THE COMMERCIAL SECTOR OF TAMIL NADU

Year	1972/73
Number of taxed traders	188.957
Total Turnover	Rs.38.280.100.
Total Taxes	Rs.731.147
Proportion of	
Top 1,0%	45.3%
Top10%	77.0%
Lowest 50%	3.5%
Gini-Coefficient	0.740

Source: Harriss, B, 1981, p. 24

TABLE II : POLARIZATION OF THE AGRICULTURAL SECTOR OF TAMIL NADU

Year 1971	
Number of Landholdings	5.018.251 ha
Total Area of Landholding	7.542.415 ha
Proportion of the	
Top 1,0%	10.0%
10% 43.0%	
Lowest 50%	13.0%
Gini-coefficient	0.608

Source : Harriss,B, 1981,P.24

Such "articulation" has been intensified and further stabilized through the recent modernization of agriculture ("Green Revolution") cattle-breeding ("White Revolution") and fisheries ("Blue Revolution"). Surplus from the profitable new techniques has predominantly been invested in moneylending- or merchant-capital. The "efficiency" of the petty producer/trader which is, in the last analysis, based on "Survival economy" and chronical underconsumption, renders such investment more profitable than investment in agricultural or industrial production.

From this perspective, persistence and underdevelopment of marginal farmers, small fisherman and petty traders, as well as the economic and spatial polarization of the rural distribution system appear as a result of the very same form of a dependent relationship between subsistence economy and modern market forces.

FORTY ONE

Nandeshwar Sharma

Reorganising Commercial Complexes: A Core Mechanism of Rural Growth Process

RURAL DEVELOPMENT : A Growth Process Outcome

People in India compose a socio-cultural and techno-economic structure in which rural dominates. Of the two "basic forms of human settlement" - Urban and rural and the two equally fundamental " forms of human occupation" (Bose, 1976-p16) industry and agriculture, the latters correspond the Indian context the most. It is in tune with the fitness of the things, therefore, to invite deliberations on rural development from those who live in and feel rural as well as those who hear and compare rural the real. Development is a commonly used but ill-defined term often confused with semantics of planning and management. It has been referred, in the present context, to one event of "accredited accrual" (Sharma, 1984) caused by a process involving planning and management. These processes manifest in the concept of growth the outcome of which becomes development.

These are originally economic concepts in non-spatial context. They tend to be a geographic concept in spatial context only when prefixed by terms like rural or urban to denote growth form in physical expression. Rural development signifies the accrual of condition caused by a growth process leading activities in rural areas to flourish. The perceived growth process involves quantifiable as well as qualifiable change. Rural development signifies, in this sense, a "desired positive change in rural areas" (Mishra & Sundaram, 1979) which is never sudden and corresponds to inevitably a growth process outcome.

RURAL GROWTH PROCESS : An Exercise in Transformation

Development entails change through growth process and the growth process breeds transformation. Rural growth process exercises to accrue transformation in human behaviour and function in time and space perspectives. The stage, which transformation achieves at a time, in formal expression, manifests the growth process outcome. Rural growth process aims at transformation so as to raise the level of productive and consumptive efficiency. It represents the event which moulds, inescapably,the nature and form of development under the synergetic response of producer and consumer. This emphasises and validates the veracity of the mechanism through which growth output reaches the basket of consumers from the container of producer. The mechanism is is commercial organisation, which bridges the gulf existing between producer and consumer in the absence of mutual contacts as the two remain, invariably, simultaneously neither in time nor in space. Development has initiated and asserted transformation of non-commercial economies-stated now to be "exceptions to rub" to exist as "primitive activities" (Boyce, 1974 pp 117-123) in areas terraincognita-into commercial economies. No rural can afford to stay non-commercial. It embraces commerce as the third component of development to comply with the entire spectrum of growth processes that intervene between production and consumption. The relevance of commercial organisation hold good because it is not necessarily a non-spatial concept but is evident in space by acquiring space leading to the concept of commercial complexes. The whole growth process-development dynamics and the role of commercial complex can be comprehended in a flow chart.

COMMERCIALISATION :
A Core Mechanism of Rural Growth Process

Growth is essentially an economic concept. Production and consumption constitute the elemental emits of growth. Commercialisation happens, however, to be cinderella to these emits to compose the trinity on which growth process is set to move. Consumption being the "ultimate objective of all economic activity" (Nadda, 1983) commercialisation facilitates producers to produce more and to reach consumer through the mechanism of marketing. Commercialisation may be referred to the mechanism involving the "whole complex of processes that intervene between production and consumption" (Garnier & Delobez, 1979). It initiates and carries, thus, the concept of business in rural growth process. It represents an organisational and institutional business in which both the businesses of production and consumption are benefited at commercial scale. Rural growth process in business concept operates in 4 *Ms* formula : man - money - material - marketing band. This band creates a mechanism of rural growth process which manifests in transformation.

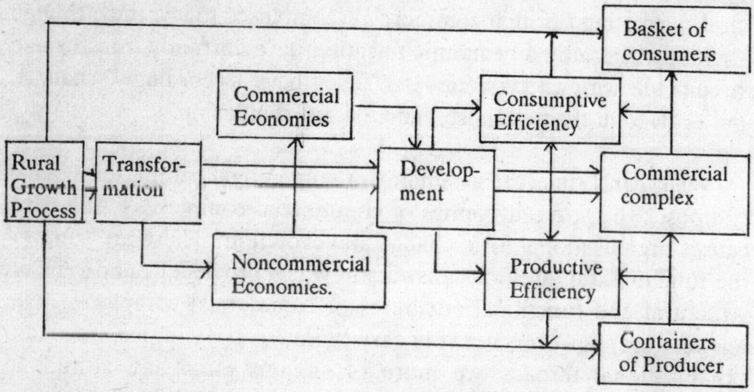

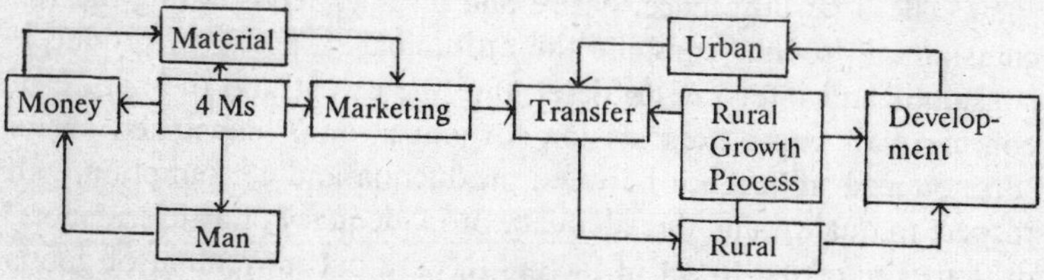

Every organisational and institutional business needs some situs or space. This situs develops to be what have been considered a commercial complex. Commercial complex may signify a point of location of organised infrastructure of human activities generating and sustaining the necessary mechanisms of exchange involving conflict-bargain -negotiation equation between either directly producer and consumer or through trader. It forms a place where use-value of materials changes into exchange-value conditioning marketing and thus the rural growth process.

COMMERCIAL COMPLEXES : Ground-View of Things

The concept of commercial complex may not entirely be understood as an innovation to rural growth process. Systems of exchange have always existed in the shape of gift and barter. The barter system at a comparatively large scale required a place where comparision among goods to be exchanged could occur. Any such "centrally agreed point" facilitating" bargaining and bartering" on the basis of value fixation and serving some "social function" conformed,to be rural market place" (Dilkinson, 1983). *Mandis*, *hats*, and *bazars* signified such points and they represent the organisational veracity of rural marketing through commercial complexes today, they, though originally, resembled economic purpose, have currently transformed to coincide with an economic act. They have, accordingly, changed and evolved in their purpose, function and dimension.

What constitutes the grounding of commercial complexes ? What composes the space dynamics of commercial complexes? And what causes organisational form change and evolution? These are some of the fundamental questions answers to which provide ground-view on structural and functional attributes of commercial complexes. The answers are, however, not very easy to find as the compositional and organisational threads are more of circumstantial and attitudinal spun. The 3 *Ds*-difference, desire and distance, constituting the circumstantial ground, combine the attitudinal response of producer, consumer and intervene to determine the extent and the nature of commercial complexes as an organisational construct. The "Pronounced" difference between production and consumption with respect to quality, and the adequacy or inadequacy of articles, "short" distance, referring to set of factors to ease out movement of goods and men, are said to be intensity inputs to commercialisation (Garnier & Delobez, 1979).

Commercial complex represents an economic and social need outcome and constitutes an ingredient of the total exchange system. Its structural and functional organisation over space responds to space adjusting and space intensification technologies. It grows and multiplies in response with technological changes and changes in economic and soc ial needs influencing the attitudinal adaptation of producer, consumer and trader - the fundamental active components of commerce. The entire dynamics of structural organisation of commercial complexes in spatial concept may be conceptual flow chart model that follows :

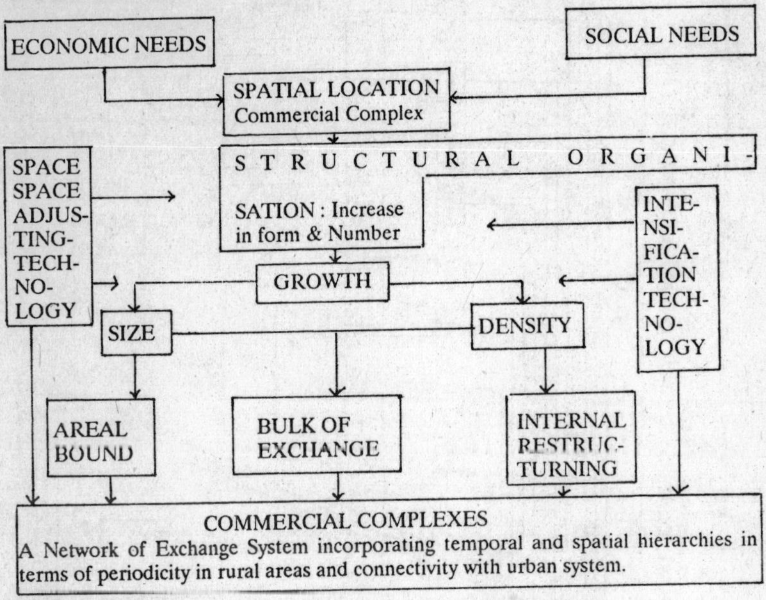

COMMERCIAL COMPLEXES : Organisational Frame in Indian Context

Commerce has proved to be a universal force behind socio-economic -structural organisations of a nation. It has generated and activated the vehicles of intermediaries between producers and consumers. It has produced platforms to negotiate with social and economic interests of producers and consumers which are simultaneously opposite and coincident. The emergence of commercial complexes has been, thus, a technical necessity of the society. Being, however, a reflection of a circumstantial and attitudinal outcome of the society in which it is implanted, the system of commercial complexes tends to fabricate the organisational network synchronizing the socio-economic and techno-political situations in national context.

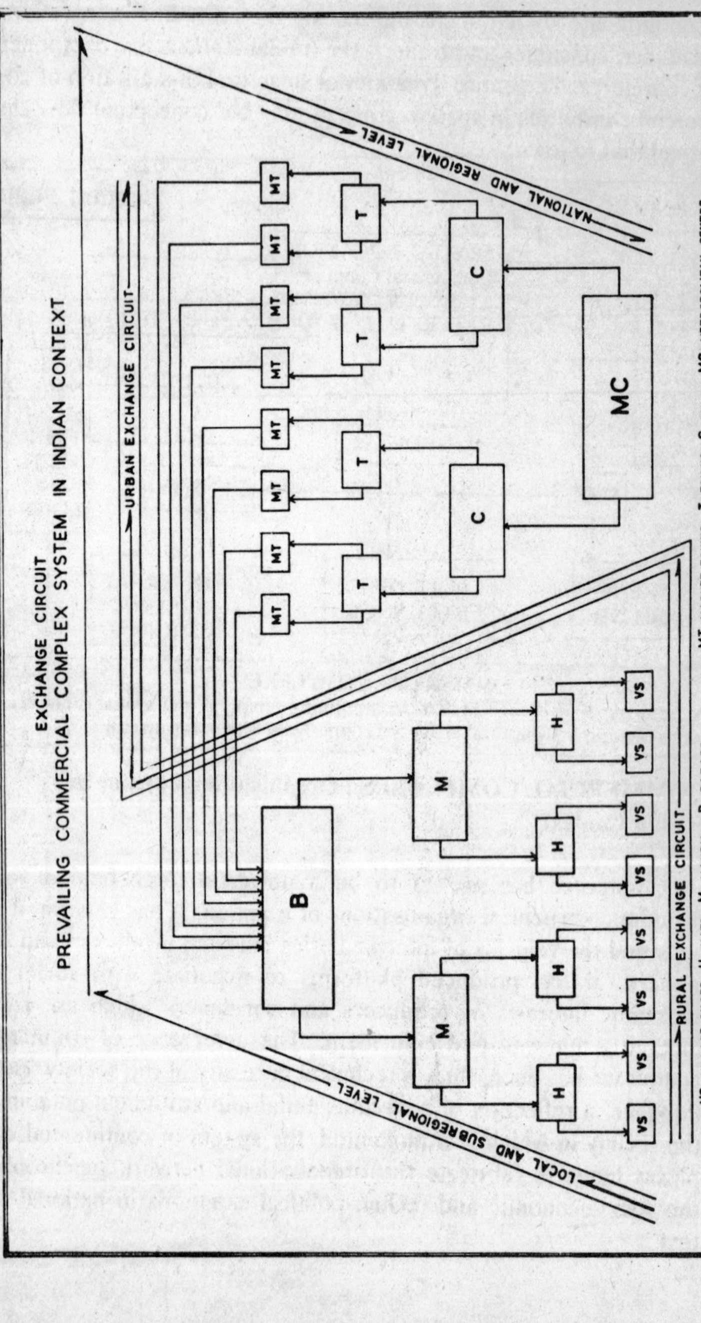

VS- VILLAGE SHOPS, H- HATS, M- MANDIS, B- BAZARS. MT- MARKET TOWNS, T- TOWNS, C- CITIES, MC- METROPOLITAN CENTRE.

FIG. 41.1

The commercial complex organisational frame in Indian context manifests through two distinctly knit exchange circuits: (i) the Rural Exchange circuit, and (ii) the Urban Exchange circuit. The two resemble, in morphogenetic appearance, with indigenous subsistence exchange quality and anglicised business exchange quality respectively. They conform to perform economic act respectively in local and regional settings. In a country where rural dominates urban, where people at different strata of economic progress need points of exchange frequently at regular time intervals and short distances and where such places serve not only economic functions but also social purposes, commercial complexes in rural exchange circuit are bound to be ubiquitous. In a country likewise where urban has made significant inroads, where rural-urban dichotomy has tended to fade and where a sense of interdependence has spread, commercial complexes in urban exchange circuit exhibit tendency to interweave a complete hierarchical organisational frame. India corresponds such as frame. Commercial complexes, through maintaining their individual identity at spatial hierarchy, form the part of interweaved exchange circuit. The contemporary organisational frame as commercial complexes create may conveniently be comprehended to produce a model (Fig. 1).

COMMERCIAL COMPLEXES : Reorganisational Divulge

A reorganisational divulge into commercial complex structure seems imperative on more than one count to foster the rural growth process:

i. Rural growth process ushers rural development.
ii. Rural growth process attaches wide significance to production and consumption technology.
iii. Locational and functional behaviour of commercial complexes combines people and technology in interweaving production technology, use technology and sale technology through producer-consumer-traders interface.
iv. By virtue of the possession of socio-economic vitality to stay and force to grow, commercial complexes happen to frequent both in time and space.
v. In being essential part of the socio-economic vitality to stay and force to grow, commercial complexes happen to fre-

quent both in time and space.

vi. Organisational structure of commercial complexes involves an inevitable spatial system hierarchy reflecting degree of incoherence in national context.

Rural growth process synchronizing change outcome necessitates, therefore, reorganisational divulge into commercial complex so as to provide a unified exchange system thrust to development at local, sub-regional, regional and national levels. The reorganisational divulge has to consider the issues of location of commercial complexes and those of their operational qualities. Reorganisation in this context has been viewed to be response function. Commercial complex locational response function hits, that may guide spatial redistribution, correspond to prefer locations that will respond to (i) transportation, (ii) territory , (iii) on-side resources I and (iv) socio-economic and institutional needs of producer, consumer and intermediaries the vehicles of rural growth process.

Rural growth envisages increase in productive and consumptive efficiency. The location of commercial complexes constitutes prerequisite to such increase. A commercial complex has, however, to be reorganised to confirm with the principle of triple reward release. The principle can be comprehended through following flow chart model.

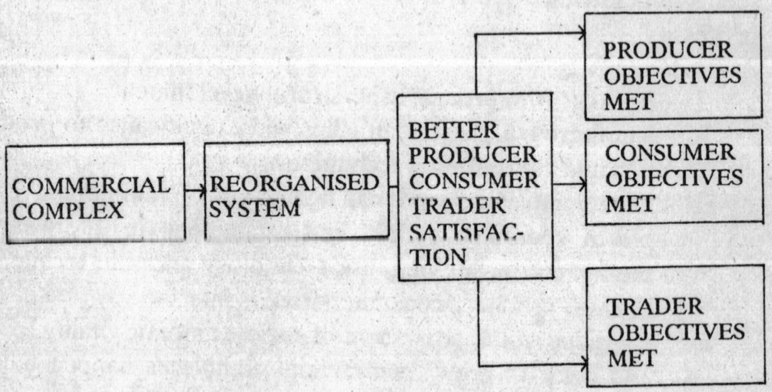

FIG.41.2

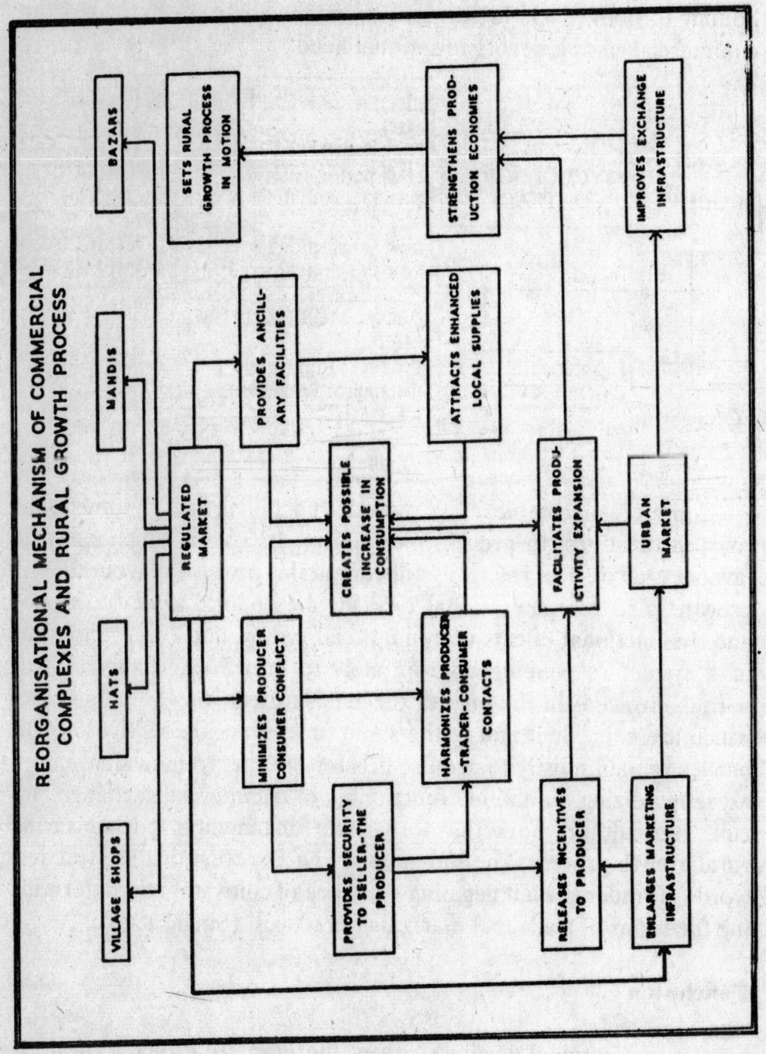

REORGANISATIONAL MECHANISM OF COMMERCIAL COMPLEXES AND RURAL GROWTH PROCESS

The extent to which the triple reward release satisfies the producer and consumer is determined by the role of the trader who intervenes the psychological and economic contract existing between producer and consumer. An another model emphasising equal honour to both psychological and economic contracts envisages the commercial complex reorganisational need.

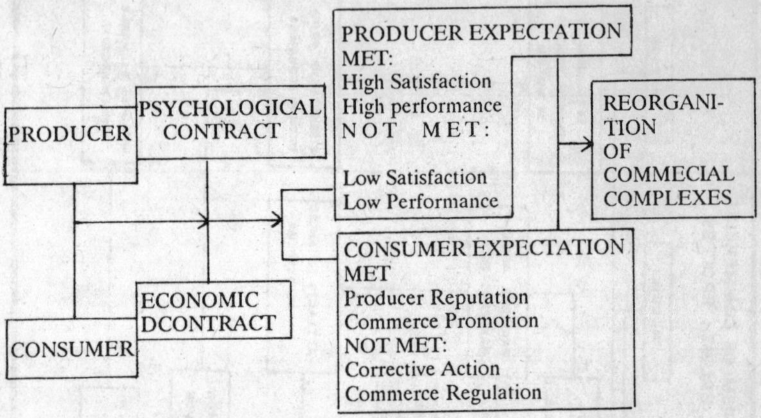

Commercial complexes play both functional and dysfunctional roles in rural growth process mechanism. Its role is functional if it favours growth. The role is dysfunctional if it proves unfavourable to growth. The reorganisational task involves appraisal of functional and dysfunctional effects of commercial system and comprehension of a system responding appropriately to growth mechanism. The parties involved in the growth mechanism bear, however, interests which are coincident and at the same time opposite. Motives of the parties remain mostly to acquire greater benefits to individual interest jeopardizing the unified functioning of commercial exchange circuit. Agricultural marketing forms the fundamental mechanism of rural growth process. The Indian experiences reveal that the will and words of trader prevail negating the voice of cultivators "in determining the terms of trade and marketing practices" (Singh, 1983).

Conclusion

Reorganisational divulge stresses, therefore, to evolve a rural exchange circuit so as to (i) ensure marketing surplus at local level, (ii) secure storage and conservation, (iii) provide ancillary facilities of transport, communication etc., (iv) secure even the availability of production inputs to producer, (v) provide producers and consumers opportunities to sell and buy at proper place and time with little risk of uncertainty and psychological and economic casualities, and (vi) develop regulatory checks on prevailing markets and regulated commercial complexes. The purpose should be to evolve a cumulative process of rural growth through the essential mechanism of commercial complex circuit. The reorganisational possibility of the core mechanism of rural growth process in the shape of commercial complex functional role has been comprehended to produce a model (Fig. 2). The model envisages the creative, protective and facilitative roles of reorganisational divulge into commercial complex structural and functional system.

FORTY TWO

Jagdish Singh

Dynamics of Rural Transformation in India

Lately there have been bewildering variety of conclusions appearing regarding the dimensions, temporal and regional variations as well as effective strategy for improving the lot of the poor. This paper, after an extensive investigation in the middle Ganga Plain, comes out with the conclusion that the rich have got richer, the poor with earning hands less poor while the poor without labour power have become destitutes.

The paper investigates deeper into the dynamics of rural transformation which reveals that; there is a nexus between the rural and urban life which is responsible for drawing resources out of the village community; there is an overall improvement in the living conditions, the magnitude varying according to the mix of endogenous-exogenous resources at the command of different groups and the participation of different socio-economic groups in the development process is uneven. the relative contribution being inverse to the beneficiary impact: the pool of formally educated unemployed youth belonging to the middle strata constitute an ever growing threat to village community, and there is a subtle process of land re-distribution in favour of the lower strata.

The paper is an attempt to fill the gap by assessing the impact of development efforts on different sections of rural society and to present a generalized model of the dynamics of rural transformation in its spatial-temporal dimension. The investigation is based on primary data collected at village level from each of the 38 districts comprising the middle Ganga Plain. The findings note that the material, living conditions of the rural population have improved in general. However, it not as that the rich have got richer, the poor with earning hands less poor while the poor without labour power have become destitutes.

The essentials of the dynamics of rural development have been analysed. The salient features of the schematic model of the dynamics of rural transformation reveal the socioeconomic reality of the rural population. The factors influencing the dynamics have been identified as natural hazards, infrastructure, migration of population, feudalistic capitatistic structure, policy implications etc. The strategy of rural transformation, will vary from region to region. Redistribution of land income, creation of infrastructure backed by appropriate technology, increased agricultural productivity and appropriate industries, generation of an atmosphere of competitive co-operation at intra and inter-group levels are some of the many suggestions made in the paper for rural transformation.

FORTY THREE

J.N.Pandey

A Strategy for Rural Development

Rural development is the current theme among planning experts and policy makers as a solution to the problems of poverty in developing countries. This is particularly advocated for Asian countries which generally possess a limited land area and a large and growing population, the bulk of them living at or near subsistence levels. To some extent perhaps, this reflects one of those periodical shifts in emphasis in the aims and strategies of planning for economic development. Problems of the rural poor now dominate discussions on development policy in the same way in which problems of industrialisatioin, international trade and aid transfers held the stage earlier.

The concept of rural development includes six elements, i.e. (i) Labour intensive productive agriculture, (ii) employment generating minor development works, (iii) small scale labour using farm based light industries, (iv) local self reliance, (v) institutional and organisational arrangements, and (vi) an appropriate hierarchy of development centres.

The rural development programme aims to integrate numerous disintegrated components responsible for socioeconomic backwardness of rural areas, especially economic, social and administrative. The mode and the level of the rural economy, the pattern of available resource utilisation and socio-politico attitude of the people are the primary considerations to formulate the strategies of rural development.

The main elements that have characterised rural development policies during the past 10 to 20 years have been extensively documented and commented upon by many observers. One was the assumption that while some of the problems of rural development, more particularly, agricultural development, could be tackled at the level of the individual farmers, other are best handled at a community or group level. Thus, the Indian Community Development Programme under-lined the possibilities and stressed the importance of village action to improve infrastructure, build up minor irrigation projects, establish common nurseries, provide drainage etc. all with a view to making agriculture more productive and to open up additional employment opportunities to the land-less people.

The second aspect that may be noted is from the midsixties. There has been a growing emphasis on improving the technological base of agriculture and allied activities. International transfer of technology in agriculture, primarily in the form of high yielding varieties of seeds, facilitated this orientation in policy for many of the countries involved apparently without their even having to go to the trouble of building up a viable research base indigenously.

In India there is a general concentration of spatial economy. Few metropolitan areas of the country control almost the whole economy of the nation. They have not proper links that exist, are exploitative in nature and are completely disadvantageous to the rural areas. Thus the impact of these centres are confined to a very narrow zone around them and they act against the process of decentralised concentration leading to a dual economy.

A sound policy for rural development will be one which leads to de-centralisation. In other words, which will link the village with service centre and growth points, and the growth points with growth centres, which in turn will be linked with growth poles. Rural development policy will envisage the creation or re-enforcing of a number of growth points which will function as service centres as well as growth generating centres within a community consisting a number of villalges.The development of growth points in rural area is very closely linked with the development of transportation.

It has come to be recognised that the village in the present stage of development scarcely provides in a great majority of cases, sufficient resource and viability to sustain comprehensive development. Even within the given development setup and without disturbing its pattern, it has been found necessary, therefore, to study the growth factors which enable the rural community to pick-up its viability. Thus planning for development must be based on the study of areas with social, economic and spatial interrelationships which have functional or systematic wholeness. It is important to keep in mind that in the larger frame work of national integration, the cohesive functional rural community is the essential building block. A number of these functional communities constitutes a sub region which will also provide a set of more complex services. The central service or functional village forms an integral element in rational allocation and mobilization of resources.

Problems relating to an improved system of resource use in the rural areas are not isolated but as part of a larger strategy of development for combating rural poverty. The rural development strategy must be based on the principle of utilising manpower to conserve and improve scarce resources, through the application of science and technology. There is every reason to expect that a massive programme of detailed reshaping and rationalisation of the physical facilities in the villages can generate enormous employment opportunities. This, and not make-believe public works programmes, holds the key to a solution of the problems of un-employment and lack of incomes to millions of rural people. On this basis, it may be possible even to offer a guarantee of employment,at suitable wage rates, to the rural unemployed. The strategy can thus be so designed that it confers benefits to all classes.

A development programme can be made broad based by developing avenues of production and employment other than cultivation of land. Besides expansion of activities connected with poultry, bee-keeping, carpentry and other such traditional avocations, a systematic, attempt at tapping locally available mineral, forest and other resources will need to be mounted. It is here that indiscriminate borrowing of technologies developed in the context of labour-scarce economies has to a certain extent, proved to be a stumbling block in using available resources to satisfy felt needs. Manufacturing plants are generally large in size. The process adopted also tend to be more mechanised and automatic than they ned be. A new orientation is needed to industrial policy so that units sizes and operational processes appropriate to the local environment are adopted. This will call for a corresponding science policy aimed at developing appropriate technologies, largely by indegenous effort. This was one of the fundamental tenets of the Gandhian philosophy of economic development. Modern agriculture, un-like traditional agriculture, needs a strong industrial base and an efficient delivery system for its success. The potential for developing smaller and more dispersed agro-industries should not be neglected,and should, on the contrary, be systematically identified for each local area and exploited to the full. This will include a whole range of units to (i) supply or service simple agricultural implements,(ii) to process agricultural produce, and (iii) to utilise by-products and waste-products in the production or processing of agricultural commodities.

A strategy of rural development based on a comprehensive survey of natural resources, their exploitation based on technologies appropriate to the local environment, mass mobilization through a process of education, all with a view to a scientific utilisation and equitable sharing of available resources, is sound conceptually.

Rural development needs a large educational-cum-mobilisation effort. It is for this reason that social and technological changes have to go hand in hand, if the objective of growth with social justice is to be attained. A cadre of scientists to extend and improve technologies of production is as important as a cadre of political workers to put through essential socio-economic changes.

FORTY FOUR

N.K. De

Jalpaiguri District: Ecological Studies for Commercial Activities and Rural Development

Introduction

Ecology is the study of the relationships between organisms and their environment, both animate and inanimate. The environment, however, means all the physical social and cultural factors and conditions influencing the existence or development of an organism or assemblege of organisms. The term rural means the countryside as distinguished from a city or town. It is essentially an area which is characterised by non-urban style of life, occupational structure, social organisations and settlement patern. The rural communities are fastened to their traditional forms and frames depending mainly on the physical environment.

The meaning of development is different to different intellectuals. It is, however, commonly accepted that the first objective of development should be to meet everyone's basic needs like food, clothing, shelter, education, health, sanitation, clean drinking water, public transport and so on. For rural development, the people in rural areas should have basis necessities of life, a good place to live and a clean enivironment where they can lead a life which gives them satisfaction and is also contributary to the onward march. Rural development is thus the multifaceted development of the rural economy by exploiting to the optimum the local resources in man, material, land and water on the basis of the local initiative and drive. Agricultural development is no doubt basis to not only development of the rural area but also to the development in the industrial sector. But rural development is larger than agricultural development. It is the interaction of all commercial/economic and social activities like agriculture, cottage industries, infrastructure, transport, labour education, housing etc. With the physical environment as it implies planning for a geographic area in all its aspects needed for modernization and betterment of living. Keeping this in mind, the district of Jalpaiguri (West Bengal) has been taken into consideration.

Study Area

The Jalpaiguri district is one of the northern districts of West Bengal bounded by the Lat 26° 16' N to 27° 00' N and long 88° 25' E to 89° 'E. The district has a total area of 6234 km^2 with a population of 22, 07, 087 as per 1981 census. About 70% of the total population is engaged in agricultural activities of which almost 50% is engaged in plantation and allied activities. Here land situation, relief, climate, drainage, soil and other socio-economic factors including the development of transport and market facilities strongly influence the types of land use on the basis of which the commercial activities of the district depends. There are 13 block namely Jalpaiguri, Rajgong, Mal, Metiali, Nagrakata, Dhupquri, Madarihat, Falakata, Kalachini, Kumargram and Alipurduar I & II.

Methodology

The following methods have been followed in the present study:

i) Pre-field method-This involves gaining knowledge of the area from existing reports, literatures, maps etc.

ii) Field work method: the physical, social, cultural, and commercial information are collected from the field.

iii) Post-field method: Analysis of the agricultural landuse patterns and other environmental attributes based on available data and field experiences.

iv) Finally, environmental planning of the district has been made based on the physical, socio-economic and land use potentiality of the area for future developmental purposes.

Environmental Factors

The overall economic development of the district under study is mainly governed by the physical environment. With the exception of the beds of slates, quartzites, dolomites and anthracite coal in the northern hilly tract, the district in general, is covered by alluvial deposits. Physiographically the distriict may be divided into three regions.

1) The northern hilly tract, 2) the foot hill in the middle, and 3) the plains in the south. The district is dissected by many north-south flowing parallel and subparellel hill streams. The district has a tropical monsoon type of climate. In general, high rainfall and high temperature are the characteristics of the district. The district is covered by the alluvial soils and the Moist Tropical Forest is predominent here. It covers about 148656.8 ha (i.e., 24.37%) of the district.

There are 754 villages and 14 towns including two municipal towns in the district. Furthermore, out of the total population of 220708 (1981) about 85%are rural. The density of population is only 353 per km^2 out of the 85 per cent rural population 70% is engaged in agricultural activities. Again, out of the 70% population engaged in agricultural activities 50% is under plantation cultivation and the remaining 20% is under field crops. A few metalled and unmetalled roads are the primary means of transportation. There are two important roads. (i) Assam-Bengal National Highway, and (2) the Eastern Railway which connects NewJalpaiguri and Gauhati. The economy of the district is not well developed as the people mainly depends on agriculture and as all the developmental activities are mainly dependent on agricultural resources. The district town of Jalpaiguri and the other local village and sub-divisional markets are the centres of commercial activities in the area.

Land Use:

The land use of Jalpaiguri district is very much varied in nature. Out of the total 6234 km^2 area, 24, 4% is under forest, 19.5% under tea garden, 35.9% under cultivation (field crops) and 19.2% under rivers, roads, settlement areas and towns etc.

Impact of environment on Landuse and Commercial Activities:

The use of the land in the north and south of the district varies depending on the nature of the parent material, terrain, relief, slope, hydrological conditions, drainage, rainfall, temperature, soils etc. and other socio-economic factors including road/transport and market facilities.

The northern hilly tracts with gritty parent material, high relief and high slope, dominated by very very coarse textured soils are covered mainly by forests (sal, sissu, siris, segun,etc.) Further south in the slopy undulating foothills with high rainfall and coarse textured, well drained highly leached soils, tea is mainly grown. Road and transport development is not significant in this hill section.

South of this sub-montane region with very gentle alluvial tracts (having loamy textured soils) field crops are grown extensively.

The percentage of land under field crops is high in Jalpaiguri (54.38%), Rajganj (46%), Falakata (61%), Mayanaguri (53%), Alipurduar 11 (76.65%). and Alipurduar I (46%) block where river in fine-textured alluvial soils are found.

The gardens cover large tracts of Maderihat (47.55%) Nagarakata (53.69%), Metaili (54.56%), Mal (33.68%) and Dhupguri (33.34%) block where where hilly and undulating sub-montane lands with rather coarse textured, well drained soils exist.

Kalchini (54.51%) and Kumargram (43.08%) have high percentages of land under forest followed by Alipurduar I (36.12%), Rajganj (26.32%) etc. The forests here are mainly concentrated in the foothills and in lands adjoining the rivers.

Because of the urban development, the percentage of non-agricultural area is highest in Jalpaiguri block which is situated on a plain land beside the river Tista.

The economy of the district is dependant on forest, Tea and

other agricultural crops. But the movement of these products again depend directly on the markets facilities and indirectly on the road and transport development and vice versa. The role of middle men in the exchange of products and other commercial activities is very important in the area.

Findings and Proposals:

The study of the ecological/environmental attributes is important because human activity is always disturbing the ecological balance and to check this imbalance environmental planning is a must. Based upon the physical attributes land resource potentialities in the district are evaluated and the lands of the district of Jalpaiguri are thus classified for future planning purposes (De, N.K. 1984). According to ecological attributes (Physical, Social, Cultural, Commercial etc.) there are three types of lands (i) the northern mountainous tract, (ii) the foothill tract in the middle, and (iii) the flat plains in the south.

In the district the agricultural a activities (mainly depending on the physical environment) and the social activities are to be taken in the integrated way both at local and state lelvels. A comprehensive plan of the agricultural activities for the development of rural economic conditions in the district is to be made in two parts (1) a short term plan aiming at self/sufficiency and to raise the standard of living of the people inhabiting the district, and (ii) a long term plan keeping in mind the state and national requirements.

Though the physical environment mainly controls the commercia' activities in the district, the interrelation of the economic and socia factors like agriculture, agro-based industries, infrastructure and services of the main centres (district) including road & transport, markets are to be improved along with the other subcentres (villages/block/thana levels) in the area, so that greater employment potentials are generated in the entire territory.

FORTY FIVE

S.K. Dikshit

Electoral Participation, Political Consciousness and Regional Development

Introduction

In the present paper an attempt has been made to analyse the relationship between electoral participation, political consciousness and regional development. The electoral participation in India has been measured through the voter participation, the degree of contest and the effective participation. This analysis reveals that areas where very high turnout of electoral participation is noted are comparatively more developed. These are Kerala, Tamil Nadu, West Bengal, Haryana, Punjab, Andhra Pradesh and some parts of Karnataka states. Areas where very low turnout has been noted are concentrated in backward regions of Orissa, Bihar, M.P. and Maharashtra.The spatial distribution of effective participation also matches with the above characteristics. The highest percentage of effective turnout, i.e. 99.96% is found in Lakshadweep island whereas the lowest percentage, i.e. 88.86% is found in the Baster constituency of M.P. Thus political consciousness seems to be correlated with the degree of development.

The basic aim of the electoral studies is to discern the electoral behaviour of an individual or of a social group. It is essential to examine the level of electoral participation to build and establish the proportions about relationships between the social characteristics and the electoral behaviour of geographical groupings of people. Electoral participation in a way, provides effective measure to assess the political consciousness. Which may lead to development.

Voter Participation:

The aggregate percentage of voter turnout in India at the 1980 elections was 56.92%. The trend of voter turnout clarifies the increasing interest of the people in elections in the country. It has been observed that in 1952 voter turnout was about 46%. Since then there has been a gradual increase in this figure which was as high as 63.61% in the 1984 elections. The effective participation range was between 95.5% (1957) to 97,6% (1980).

The study and analysis of the frequency distribution of constituencies under different categories of voter participation reveals the fact that there are 27 constituencies having voter turnout of more than 75% (Table-1). This category includes 15 constituencies of West Bengal, 4 of Tamil Nadu, 2 each of Manipur and Tripura and 1 each of Karnataka, Andaman, Lakshadweep and Pondicherry. The highest turnout of 84.68% and 88.78% was found in lakshadweep constituency at 6th and 7th Lok Sabha Election respectively. Similarly, the category of high turnout includes 22 constituencies of Tamil Nadu, 18 of West Bengal, 6 each of Maharashtra, Andhra Pradesh and Haryana, 5 each of Uttar Pradesh and Kerala, 4 each of Karnatak and Delhi. These constituencies have a higher percentage of urban population and the proportion of literacy is also higher. These constituencies may be said to be politically more conscious.

There are 53 constituencies in very low turnout category which includes 18 of U.P., 11 of Bihar, 8 of M.P., 5 of Orissa, 4 of Gujarat, 3 of Andhra Pradesh, 2 of Karnataka and 1 each of Assam and Maharashtra. These are mostly tribal and backward areas of the country where political consciousness is very poor. Six constituencies are very-very low turnout category. These are Singhbhum (S.T.) of Bihar, Koraput (S.T.), Naurangpur (S.T.) and Sundergarh (S.T.) of Orissa; Sikkim; and Chail (S.C.) of U.P. The lowest turnout, i.e. 25.11 and 25.70% in the country was found in Koraput (S.T.) constituency of Orissa in the 1977 and 1980 elections respectively. The moderate and low turnout areas are concentrated mostly at large parts of U.P., Rajasthan, Gujarat, Maharashtra, M.P., Himachal Pradesh etc.

TABEL I: VOTER PARTICIPATION IN THE 1980 ELECTIONS

State	Frequency distribution of constituencies						
	V.V.Low < 35%	V.Low 35-45	Low 45-55	Mod. 55-65	High 65-75	V.High > 75 %	Total
Andhra Pradesh	-	3	14	19	6	-	42
Assam	-	1	-	-	1	-	2
Bihar	1	11	22	18	2	-	54
Gujarat	-	4	6	14	2	-	26
Haryana	-	-	-	4	6	-	10
Himachal Pradesh	-	-	1	3	-	-	4
Jammu & Kashmir	-	-	-	5	-	-	5
Karnataka	-	2	6	15	4	1	28
Kerala	-	-	2	13	5	-	20
Madhya Pradesh	-	8	17	14	1	-	40
Maharashtra	-	1	20	21	6	-	48
Manipur	-	-	-	-	-	2	2
Meghalaya	-	-	1	-	-	-	1
Nagaland	-	-	-	-1	-	-	1
Orissa	3	5	9	4	-	-	21
Punjab	-	-	-	11	2	-	13
Rajasthan	-	-	14	11	-	-	25
Sikkim	1	-	-	-	-	-	1
Tamil Nadu	-	-	-	13	22	4	39
Tripura	-	-	-	-	-	-2	2
Uttar Pradesh	1	18	50	11	5	-	85
West Bengal	-	-	1	8	18	15	42
Andaman	-	-	-	-	-	1	1
Arunanchal	-	-	-	-	2	-	2
Chandigarh	-	-	-	-1	-	-	1
Dadra	-	-	-	-	1	-	1
Delhi	-	-	-	3	4	-	7
Goa	-	-	-	-	2	-	2
Lakshadweep	-	-	-	-	-	1	1
Mizoram	-	-	-	1	-	-	-
Pondicherry	-	-	-	-	-	1	1
India	6	53	163	190	89	27	528

EFFECTIVE PARTICIPATION:

Table-II shows the statewise frequency distribution of constituencies under various categories of effective turnout at the 7th. general election. The pattern is somewhat similar to that of voter turnout discussed above.

The constituencies under the high and very high categories are concentrated in developed and politically conscious regions of

Kerala, Lakshadweep, Karnataka, Haryana, Punjab etc. Tabel-II further reveals that there are 16 and 25 constituencies under the very-very low and very low categories respectively. These are mostly related to the backward regions of M.P., Orissa, Bihar, Arunachal, Dadra, Rajasthan, Andhra Pradesh, Gujarat, Manipur, U.P., Maharashtra, Karnataka, Meghalaya states. It establishes the relationship between effective turnout and political consciousness of the regions concerned.

TABLE II : EFFECTIVE PARTICIPATION

State	V.V.Low < 95%	V.Low 95-96	Low 96-97	Mod. 97-98	High 98-99	V.High > 99%	Total
Andhra Pradesh	-	1	15	18	8	-	42
Assam	-	-	-	1	1	-	2
Bihar	-	-	6	11	35	2	54
Gujarat	1	1	14	10	-	-	26
Haryana	-	-	-	9	1	-	10
Himachal Pradesh	-	-	-	1	3	-	4
Jammu & Kashmir	-	1	4	-	-	-	5
Karnataka	-	3	13	10	2	-	28
Kerala	-	-	-	-	7	13	20
Madhya Pradesh	5	6	14	14	1	-	40
Maharashtra	-	4	17	19	8	-	48
Manipur	-	1	1	-	-	-	2
Meghalaya	-	1	-	-	-	-	1
Nagaland	-	-	-	1	-	-	1
Orissa	8	4	5	4	-	-	21
Punjab	-	-	-	9	4	-	13
Rajasthan	-	2	3	12	8	-	25
Sikkim	-	-	-	1	-	-	1
Tamil Nadu	-	-	-	17	22	-	39
Tripura	-	-	-	-	2	-	2
Uttar Pradesh	-	-	14	43	28	-	85
West Bengal	-	1	4	26	11	-	42
Andaman	-	-	-	1	-	-	1
Arunanchal	1	-	1	-	-	-	2
Chandigarh	-	-	-	-	-1	-	1
Dadra	1	-	-	-	-	-	1
Delhi-	-	-	-	-	7	-	7
Goa	-	-	1	1	-	-	2
Lakshadweep	-	-	-	-	-	-	1
Mizoram	-	-	-	-	--	1	1
Pondicherry	-	-	1	-	-	-	1
India	16	25	113	208	149	17	528

THE DEGREE OF CONTEST:

The study and analysis of the participation of candidates and the degree of their contest is also very important in the study of geography of electoral participation. The candidates are the chief element and electoral tools, who activate, motivate an d mobilize the electors at a particular election. They also impress the voters with their personality cult, party performances and election issues. It has already been noted that the multi-party or higher degree of contest fails to provide a good opposition and the ruling party very easily manipulates to come in the power very regularly or very frequently. Table-III shows that higher contest regions are mostly spread over the northern part of the country including the states of U.P., Bihar, Haryana, Punjab, Delhi, Rajasthan, Maharashtra etc.

The analysis and examination of spatial distribution of higher degree of contest reveals the fact that these are mostly historical places rested to urban constituencies of the country where the literacy percentage is also higher. The people related to these constituencies are politically more conscious and take active part in the elections, which has now become the key of regional development. The increasing number of contestants from 6th to 7th Lok Sabha election, i.e. 2437 to 4628 is also an indicator of the growing political consciousness in the country.

Conclusion

There is definitely some relationship between political consciousness and regional development. Both seem to be mutually dependent. The re-framing and re-structuring of all modern states symbolizing the macro-regions of world are not only due to natural resources but by the efforts of the decision makers, who have adopted such decisions through elections to build and rebuild their nations. "When the nation has needed a leader with charisma, it has found or invented one. When the charismatic leader has erred it has chartised him or her. When leaders and institutions have failed to mediate the people have mediated through the ballot box and changed the entire landscape" (*The Times of India, Sunday Review*, January 30, 1983).

TABLE III: THE DEGREE OF CONTEST

States	Frequency distribution of constituencies						
	< 11 candi-dates	11-15 Cond.	16-20 Cond.	21-25 Cond.	26-30 Cond.	Above 30 cond.	Total
Andhra Pradesh	40	1	1	-	-	-	42
Assam	2	-	-	-	-	-	2
Bihar	30	16	6	1	1	-	54
Gujarat	24	2	-	-	-	-	26
Haryana	3	4	2	1	-	-	10
Himachal Pradesh	4	-	-	-	-	-	4
Jammu & Kashmir	6	-	-	-	-	-	6
Karnataka	26	1	1	-	-	-	28
Kerala	20	-	-	-	-	-	20
Madhya Pradesh	25	12	2	1	-	-	40
Maharashtra	37	8	2	1	-	-	48
Manipur	2	-	-	-	-	-	2
Meghalaya	1	-	-	-	-	-	1
Nagaland	1	-	-	-	-	-	1
Orissa	20	1	-	-	-	-	21
Punjab	7	3	2	1			
Rajasthan	16	8	-	1	-	-	25
Sikkim	1	-	-	-	-	-	1
Tamil Nadu	36	3	-	-	-	-	39
Trip2	-	-	-	-	-	-	2
Uttar Pradesh	45	22	10	4	3	1	85
West Bengal	39	2	1	-	-	-	42
Andaman	1	-	-	-	-	-	1
Arunanchal	2	-	-	-	-	-	2
Chandigarh	-	-	-	-	-	1	1
Dadra	1	-	-	-	-	-	1
Delhi	-	1	-	2	4	-	7
Goa	2	-	-	-	-	-	2
Lakshadweep	1	-	-	-	-	-	1
Mizoram	1	-	-	-	-	-	1
Pondicherry	1	-	-	-	-	-	1
Total	396	84	27	12	8	2	529

Source: Report on the 7th General Elections to Lok Sabha, pp.32-35.

The regional development of a country is mostly based on the representatives who have been sent to the government/Parliament. Whittlesey (1935) has pointed out that the government is the most effective geographic agent for the modification of landscape. Busteed (1975) has also stated that geography is profoundly affected by government, since the governments at present are the most effective geographic agents responsible for the location of various phenomena. The governments in most of the states all over the world are processed through the elections. Therefore, it may be said that the regional development would be possible with the development of political awareness and consciousness of the people.

In the present study it has been seen in the country that the politically more conscious regions of states like Kerala, West Bengal, Delhi, Punjab, Chandigarh, Lakshadweep, Tamil Nadu, Haryana, some parts of Karnataka, Maharashtra and Uttar Pradesh are among the development regions of the country.

CEREMONIES

V.K. Shrivastava

Introduction to the Conference

Respected Vice-chancellor, Professor B.M. Shukla, honourable chief guest Professor R.P. Mishra, Professor S.P. Negendra, Professor Ujagir Singh, distinguished delegates from India and abroad, ladies and gentlemen. It is may pleasant duty to introduce to you the Study Group on Geography of Commercial Activities and to inform you the background of the organization of this conference. In 1984, the 25th International Geographical Union held its Geographical Congress at Paris and at that time a Study Group was created under the title 'Geography of Commercial Activities'. Professor Alain Metton was elected Chairman of the Group and a Working Committee was formed. It was at that time that Professor Metton requested me to hold a conference of the Study Group out-side European countries and preferably in India. Taking that idea into my mind I discussed it with my colleagues in India and abroad and after getting their opinion, which was quite favourable, I approached the Vice-chancellor and the Head of the Department of Geography of Gorakhpur University and proposed this idea in April this year, that if possible attempts may be made to hold an International Conference at Gorakhpur. We all know that our University is not so well located to hold an international conference which may be convenient to the delegates from India and abroad. But still the Vice-chancellor graciously permitted me to go ahead with the preparations of the conference. Accordingly, we worked for about four to five months in organising this conference. Our greatest hurdle, I should say, was the timely permission from the Government of India because we cannot hold any international conference without the clearance from

Government of India. We approached the Government of India in June. Incidentally, the final permission from the Government and from the Reserve Bank of India India could be obtained on 9th. of December only. And it was only after 9th of December that we were in a position to give a green signal particularly to our foreign delegates. And I am very grateful that inspite of such a long delay a number of expected foreign delegates are with us this morning.

The theme of the conference is, (Commercial Activities and Rural Development) and it was our idea that because this University is situated in a rural area so the role of commercial activities is promoting development of this area may be crucial, and accordingly, we selected this theme and the Conference is now being held from December 21 to 23. We have divided it into four themes as follows:

- i Current Status and Trends of Researches in Commercial Geography and Rural Development,
- ii Analysis of Commercial Activities,
- iii Rural-urban Linkages and development
- iv Rural Development, Issues, Strategies and Planning Policy

We have received 43 papers and these papers will be discussed under various themes during these three days.

There will be a field trip of Gorakhpur city showing the commercial setting of this town to our delegates and there will be a field trip outside Gorakhpur showing the delegates nearby periodic and permanent markets and commercial centres of Gorakhpur and its environs.

On this occasion I not only thank the Vice-chancellor, the Pro-vice-chancellor, the Head of the Department but I also thank the gracious citizens of Gorakhpur, the North Eastern Railway, the Fertilizer Corporation of India, the Lions Club, Gorakhpur, Purvanchal, the All India Radio, Gorakhpur, the daily news-papers; Aaj, Dainik Jagran, Times of India, Northern India Patrika and the All India Radio, Govt. of U.P. and many other organizations who encouraged us and helped us in organising this conference inspite of our very very limited resources. Amongst us, ladies and gentlemen, we have 35 delegates present here and quite a few of them are expected this afternoon and tomorrow. Six other countries are represented here. West Germany, Sri Lanka, Malaysia, Thailand, Bangladesh and Nepal. Commonwealth Geographical Bureau, which is situated in London has been kind enough to send its representative to participate in this conference and Dr. C.P. Singh is with us as a representative of C.G.B. for south Asia. With this short introduction, dear friends, I apologise on behalf of the Head of the Department of Geography, Dr. Jagdish Singh, who had to be away from us on a very important assignment and I have to perform the function of the Head of the Department as well. He will be with us tomorrow and will be presiding on the final day session of this conference of Rural Development. Thank you all very much.

B.M. Shukla

Welcome Address

Professor R.P. Mishra, Mr. Pro-vice chancellor, my old friend from Banaras Hindu University, Professor Ujagir Singh, Dr. Shrivastava, distinguished delegates, ladies and gentlemen. I personally feel proud and it gives me a great sense of pleasure in welcoming such a distinguished gathering, where delegates not only from various parts of my own country but from other friendly countries have come here. When Dr.Shrivastava mentioned about this conference I congratulated him, I jumped over the idea and told him that these are the activities which any university should really stand for, should live for and I said go ahead. And inspite of the fact, as he has already mentioned here, that Gorakhpur cannot provide the facilities of five-star hotels, but at least the warmth of hospitality, although it may be a very simple one, but that warmth of genuine hospitality will be in no way less, in no measure less than what one can receive in large major towns. And, therefore, I think it was in the fitness of things that Dr.Shrivastava organised this symposium here and already he has mentioned that he has tried his best along with the cooperation of his colleagues to see that your stay is made comfortable and in the very beginning he has already given a hint that if there are any inconveniences here my friends you will kindly put up with them and excuse us for any shortcomings.

I would like to mention that Gorakhpur has obtained a name for itself because of certain historical reasons and factors for which those of us who are in *Purvanchal*, the area of eastern U.P is popularly known as *Purvanchal*, they are sure to feel proud of. But not only them, I think any Indian who has respect for this culture, who has respect for freedom movement, who has respect for all that India has stood for since ages, will have a great respect for the city of Gorakhpur and the entire region where it is situated, namely *Purvanchal*. Friends, it is this land, it is this area which has not only given to the sub-continent but to the world philosophies and messages which have stood the test of the time. The father of the nation, Mahatma Gandhi, his entire philosophy of truth and *Ahinsa*, if we look back, is a reflection of that age-old tradition, age-old philosophy of this region. Lord Buddha is not a small name, it goes much beyond the borders of our country. It practically covers the entire globe. Buddha was born at Kapilvastu in Basti which is one of the districts of this region and there is lot of dispute going on amongst the historians, but any way Lumbini which is in Nepal, if you go to the real geography of the region, the continuity of the region you find, leave aside international borders but the habit of the people, the climate, the way they live, if you find you can very well say that Buddha's philosophy emerged from this very region. And then he took his *mahanirvana* hardly 50 Km. from here, Kushinagar, a trip to which has been arranged by the convener where you yourself will have not only the pleasure and the great philosophical satisfaction of having visited the place where Lord Buddha took his *manhanirvana*. Fazilnagar is very much closely associated with the great personality, which gave the religion of the 'Jaina' the philosophy of Jainism. Apart from this if you look from a purely philosophical angle, at what is religion, what are castes, the only caste, the only religion is that of humanity. You find hardly 30 to 35 Km from here, west of Gorakhpur, a place 'Magahar' where saint Kabir lived. Kabir's philosophy, as I know has gone much beyond the borders of India. There are many countries where his work has been translated. I know scholars from other countries who have taken their doctorate in Kabir's philosophy. And then the name Gorakhpur, also you see that there is something as to how this name has come. Guru Gorakhnath, a very specialized sect of devotees of a particular clan, *Nath* sect as they are known, the *nath* community, one of the foremost proponents of particular philosophy. Guru Gorakhnath chose Gorakhpur for his meditation, for spreading the philosophy of this particular sect. Therefore,Gorakhpur got this name from Guru Gorakhnath's sect. This way you find that ideas which have really made India as one entity, which has permeated from the length and breadth of this country, you find that this region *purvanchal*, this area, this city has a claim, has a proud claim. Now if we come to the modern times, I must say that in this particular area, Gorakhpur city, although in shape, size, in its facilities, it is only a moderate one, but all the same, it is headquarters of the North Eastern Railway, it has an airforce base nearby in Kusumi. It also has a medical college, which is affiliated to this University. It has an engineering college and when you go, because you are going to discuss in this seminar commercial activity, I think Gorakhpur, this region, there must be papers about the commercial activities of this region also, you will find it does not lag behind in that also.We don't make any fantastic claim, sugar industry, you know very well that this area has so many sugar mills. We export sugar but we import sugar also. The whole trend has to go like that. One thing about which I would like to make a special reference is about the handicrafts, about the handwoven cloth which is very famous. This area is famous for its cloth production by the weavers themselves and it is an item of export. You will yourself appreciate when you have a look at the product being produced, here that have very artistic patterns. You have not come to a backward area but to an area which is rich in historical traditions, an area which has also the energies, and the enthusiasm to go ahead in the future.

Another thing which I would like to say before I close, is about our struggle for freedom for which this region takes rightfully a very important place. In India's struggle for freedom from foreign domination, this region has never lagged behind as compared to many parts in our own country. It has given people who have sacrificed their lives, it has given push to the entire mass movement. I am reminded of the days of my own experience when Pandit Jawahar Lal Nehru, who was our first Prime Minister, when he was jailed by the Britishers and he was kept in Gorakhpur jail for a couple of years. So that way you find that if you turn the pages of history and want to find contribution of this particular area and specially the city of Gorakhpur, it has never lagged behind.

Now friends with all these remarks I would only like to say that the conference which has been organised in this University, that will provide you a good opportunity of developing a greater comradelry between each one of you, greater understanding when you exchange thoughts, present you papers, the discussion which will be carried out here, that is bound to definitely be a matter of great satisfaction to you. I have absolutely no doubt in my mind that the few days that you are going to spend here my dear delegates you will find it most exciting and most rewarding and the discussion that will be carried out, I am quite sure will give you fresh food for thought so that the work goes on, academic ideas go on and the desire of carrying out further and further work to improve the lot of the society, because after all you are going to discuss commercial activities and rural development. Rural development is very dear to our hearts and this is where we want your impact as great geographers. Some healthy process has emerged for the past many years that practically all these ideas, all these disciplines, have telescoped together. In yester years geography was something different. In our days the concept of geography was something different. But now the concept of geography is quite different, which our learned Professor Mishra in his inaugural speech will let you know. In the development of any region, specially in rural development, geographers have to play a very important role. With that view in mind, I wish your conference a grand success and I welcome you to this University, to this town on behalf of all my university colleagues. Thank you very much.

R.P. Mishra

Inaugural address

Commercial Activities and Rural Development.

Ladies and gentlemen,

I am extremely grateful to Professor Shrivastava for giving me the opportunity to be with you this morning. I wish I could be with you for the three days you will be here but as Professor Shukla already mentioned the Vice-chancellors in Indian universities are no more to be academic. They are always fire fighting and the calibre that is needed of a vice-chancellor is not that of an academic man but something else, and to be away from the university is not very helpful that is why most of the time, vice-chancellors do away with the academic activities and be at the headquarters to extinguish the fire as it raises. I am, therefore, most grateful to you friends that I could get at least a glimpse of an opportunity of sharing a few thoughts with you. Geographers in this country have played a very significant role in the development process. A number of useful concepts have emerged from this country and as you all know and there is no development theory in the world which has not been used, experimented and implemented in this country. In fact most of the development concepts, particularly in the area of rural development were tested, experimented and implemented in this country before they were utilised in any other developing country of the world. It has been a testing ground and it is because of this that geographers are very much development-oriented. But there have been problems with geography and geographers which I would like to mention in a couple of minutes before I come to the main theme, particularly because it is not so important as to what we have done in the past as what we are doing at present and what future lies ahead of us.

I think in many areas of geography there is tremendous amount of stagnation and repeatition. It is particularly so in the field of rural development to which I have been more closely related or consistently related than to any other field of geography. During the last ten years if you look through the Ph.D theses that have been produced in this country on rural development by geographers you will see that at least forty per cent of these theses deal with the service centres, identification of service centres in a tahsil or in a block or in a district. As you appreciate the concept of growth centres and the rural service centres were so elaborately worked out by geographers in the late sixties and the seventies and since then we have not made the progress even by an inch. What the concepts were developed at that time, they are being repeatedly used in the same way. As in the area of urban development, the work on one particular theme for about 25 to 30 years to the extent that we became almost sterile in the field of urban geography. The same situation we have come to now in the field of rural development. There is need for correction. The societal needs and demands are changing very fast in this country. In fact the amount of development that has taken place in the country, particularly in the rural areas even in Gorakhpur, as Professor Shukla mentioned, which is supposed to be in a relatively backward region of the country. Eastern U.P., is a classic backward region of the country, but if you see the agricultural data of the last few years, if what is happening in this region continues to happen for another decade this region may become one of the most important agricultural regions of the country. It might not feed itself alone but may feed the whole of U.P., if the growth-rate of agricultural is the same as it has been for the last few years. This change is not so easily visible to many of us particulalry because we are part of the change. We are participating in the change in the development process and it does not come to us as a shock but rather it comes to us as a mild transformation, as the transformation in which we are ourselves the participants. We do not realise it. Because of this great change that has taken place in the whole country, particularly in the backward regions of the country, the needs and the demands of development are changing, both in theory and in practice. There is not only the dynamics of the economy that we have to take note, dynamics of the quality that we must take note, but also we must see that our discipline also becomes dynamic.The new concepts and theories emerge and the old ones, if necessary, are discarded or refined or further tested as we don't go on doing the same repetitive work changing only the taluka or the block or the district leaving the rest of the things the same. It is unfortunate that in many cases if you see the theses of the research work that is being done in many of the geography departments, I am not mentioning about Gorakhpur as such, because I have not seen many, but I think it must be the case here also, the conclusions of the research work are the same, instead of Gorakhpur district you have to say Deoria district or Pratapgarh district or Muzaffarnagar district and that is all. I think this is not going to lead us any where. This has not only brought bad name to our discipline but also bad name to the research work itself so that a thinking has emerged in the university circles that perhaps Ph.D. thesis is not essential any more in order to get into the university teaching job, because they have become so cheap. I must also mention and add here rather, that this is not the situation in geography alone. There are disciplines which are much worse and as a Vice-chancellor I think we have more opportunity to compare than those of us who are heads of departments or teachers of geography. Perhaps geography is much better, but we are not comparing ourselves with what is worst but we have to compare ourselves with what is the best because geography had always been a leading discipline and it must continue to lead in future also. So we have to develop centres of excellence in geography and I think in the next NAGI meeting that we are going to have in Banaras I think we should give thought to it so that our discipline does not become sterile, it continues to grow and we are in fore-front of the knowledge-building activity, knowledge-promotion activity and we are, if not ahead, abreast of the work that is going on in other disciplines.

Friends, now coming to the theme of this International Conference, i.e. Commercial Activity and Rural Development, I must admit that I have not been able to give thought, so whatever I am going to mention or I have mentioned, are just random ideas. As I mentioned to you the rural transformation that is taking place in this country is fantastic. And one of the indications is that there is tremendous amount of dissatisfaction in the society today. Some times dissatisfaction is interpreted as sign of frustration, as something which is happening in the society. But I would like to submit that there is a brighter side of the criticism, the frustration, that is visible in the society. The brighter side is that there is something good that is happening and this good that is happening is the one that is changing the whole social structure and not only the economic structure. We are challenging the norms of the society because the norms are inequatus not only in spatial terms but more so in social terms. Even the norms which are good and which we should retain and maintain and strengthen, are being challenged in the process because every thing must be in a inequatus society. Beneath or in social terms, beneath whatever is happening, whether you talk in spatial terms or in sectoral terms, of all that is happening, the confusion that is there, there is something to mention here that still I myself am not very clear what I am trying to say here.Let me make it clear about commercial activities and rural development. Is it only the market centres and the relation to rural development that we have to study. Is it only the locations of the market centres, the small towns, and the structure of these towns that we have to study. Or we have also to study the type of commercial development that is taking place in the rural areas and the implications of that type of development and the rural development and vice-versa. A small town emerges and becomes strengthened only in the region where the agricultural development has been speeded up, otherwise it does not. In other words, if the agricultural development takes place, if there is investment in agriculture to begin with, there is more surplus generated in the agricultural economy, then you see the emergence of road-side development, commercial, emergence of small towns which had emerged long long ago. Then if you reverse the order in the same area where tremendous amount of investment has been made in agriculture. If you compare two areas you find in one, the commercial activities have developed fast, in another they have not developed fast and in the third region one type of commercial activity has developed and in the fourth region another type of commercial activity has developed. And if you take these commercial activities into what now the well known theory that you have the production oriented tertiaries, let us that is emerging, which is not visible to us. It is not visible to us because we cannot see the present trends, subtarrenean trend easily because of the clattering of our mind with the details. It is through time that we see the main trends which have emerged through various years and decades. Present is always confusing and only when the present is past, the present become a long past then we see that what trends have been emerging through time and where we have reached. it is my firm feeling and also what I have realised through the empirical work that something very good is emerging in this country, not only in this country but in all the developing countries of the world. And what is that good that is emerging, I think, that is to be seen and brought to the size. Not only the frustration that appears on the surface, not only the bad things that appear on the surface, but something good, the great change, the revolution, the great movement, that is there that we are not seeing at all, and I think there geographers have a special role to play in this as social scientists to see what that movement is and that movement began as Prof. Shukla mentioned, before Independence movement and that is continuing and getting strength. I think only through time we will see in real terms what that movement is but the signs are clear and unless we do empirical research which will bring out those things, those real things that are emerging, the general movement that is going on for the last two or three decades, I think, we will be failing in our duty.

I would like to say that the consumption oriented tertiaries agricultural region, where the production oriented tertiaries have developed, that region has gone very well, and where only the consumption oriented commercial activities have developed that region has been much better exploited by the other regions. I am saying that much better exploited deliberately because when you see that the whole development from the national or macro-regional perspective, I think it is better for some one. So you have two types of commercial activities developing. One is the production oriented which the exchange of the goods and services of the type which go as input which evacuate the output and they all lead to development of the agricultural economy.Then you have another type which only causes exchange at local level. It does not leave anything in the region. It does not produce what you may call innovators. It does not create conditions. It does create schooling situations from which enterprenuers can emerge.

Despite the fact that agriculture has developed, and despite the fact that commercialization has taken place, that region has not developed and this you find very often in Eastern U.P. and in North Bihar. The other type production oriented you see in Karnataka where I worked for about 15 years and studied so deeply, Karnataka and Tamilnadu those regions for example. The production oriented commercial activities have developed faster, particularly in the irrigated areas. With the development of production oriented tertiaries, the secondary activities have also come up and the whole region has developed because the production oriented tertiaries also mean that these tertiaries will be produced somewhere and when the income is generated then that income is invested in that region. But there are also regions like Mandya district near Bangalore, where despite the fact that the green revolution practically came in 1930s, no secondary activities developed until 1972. But in the whole of this district, in the whole of this green revolution area, if you look into the structure of commercial activities that have developed in the rural areas they were all consumption oriented tertiaries. So there are different types of commercial activities that develop in rural areas for variety of reasons and these reasons have to be found out. And because of these variations in the nature of commercial activities that develop some rural areas grow and some rural areas don't grow. So it it not that any commercial activity that develop in rural areas necessarily leads to rapid economic and social development and change. Some where it is very rapid and somewhere it is very slow and somewhere it becomes very exploitative, particularly that you will see in the tribal areas of the country, like Bastar.

The Bastar is purely the consumption oriented tertiary that is developing at a very rapid rate, and more it has developed, more exploitation of the tribals has taken place. Because it is a network that has gone to these villages which was earlier at the district and higher level that has gone down to the village, and because of the strengthening of the network of exploitation the type or commercial activities that have lead to more exploitation of the people and the region. So at the cost of the Bastar district some other district, some other region of the State of Madhya Pradesh are growing.

So friends, there are tremendous amount of other areas where we need to pay our attention, and not confine ourselves, as we are doing , and I am specially talking to our younger friends, that just do some age-old methods and go finding out how many growth centres are there, how many service centres are there, how many villages should be there in a service centres and then you prepare theses and many of them are published, unfortunately. Then other thing that I would like to mention, that is the terms of trade. One or two papers I have received over here are related to the impact of international division of labour on the rural development. It is not only the international division of labour but also there is a national division of labour. That is the shadow of the international division of labour that has fallen on the national scene also. And the terms of trade as between the north and the south or even within south some times within the countries to some extent, are quite often exploitative.

The terms of trade between the region within the country they are also tending to be more and more exploitative as the development proceeds. I think it is the dynamics, the process that has to be seen rather than the statistics of geography. Then what is happening in the process of development both in terms of the quality and in terms of the economy when seen in the spatial terms. Where we are leading ourselves and the nation too, and what type of picture will emerge in the 21st century when we enter after 15 years? What types of spatial economy we will have? I think to analyse that we have to see the changes in the terms of trade that are taking place between the regions, between the commodities because there is no difference between the region and the commodity because there are certain regions which are specialised in certain commodities so even if we study the commodity still that study has spatial implication of it. We study the region also by studying the commodities. This is another area which needs to be given attention by the geographers and we must tell them now itself as to what type of regional structure we are leading to both at the micro level and at the macro level so that the policies that are formulated from year to year and at least every fifth years we also have our own input in that the geographers contribution continues to be of significance in the future also.

One more point and I will close now, it is about the tremendous transformation in the rural areas that is taking place particularly in the agricultural sector in the backward regions. I am specially mentioning because in the backward regions it is the agricultural sector which needs the buoyancy first as in east U.P. and in north Bihar.

You will be happy to know that probably if this trend continues as I mentioned eastern U.P. will feed the whole of U.P. after 10 years. So this buoyancy has led to tremendous amount of what I still call shift in the power structure in the rural regions of the country. We all remember pretty well that ours has been a feudal society. And the terminology in India used by the social scientist has been semi-feudal society. We call ourselves a semi-feudal society. We thought that as development proceeds the semi-feudualism will go down and ultimately it will disappear. The recent trend of the last five-six years is that semi-feudualism appears to be coming back in other forms. The number of people who are becoming landless in the rural areas is fantastic. It is not only in India, in our recent study of eight countries, Brazil, Nigeria, Philippines, China, Indonesia, Bangladesh, we found that in country after country this trend of polarization and marginalisation occurs. Polarization that is agricultural property is getting polarised, getting into fewer hands and a large number of people who were dependent on agriculture earlier, they are getting much polarised. Two volumes that we are just about to bring out clearly indicate that in all developing countries marginalisation process has become very strong. If the secondary sector is going very fast, rapidly, as it is in Europe and for a long time in the 19th century and in the early part of this century, probably things would have been different. But with the type of technology that we have at present it is not possible for us to increase employment in the secondary sector at a fast rate. One of the recent studies very clearly indicate that employment in the secondary sector, in the manufacturing sector has remained static in this country for the last twenty years and it is going to remain static in the future also. It does not mean that the value added has not increased. It does not mean that we have remained static industrially, in fact our production is growing very rapidly. We are very well-off industrially and the buoyancy that we need today, I think that the picture that will emerge by the turn of the century, I personally feel that this country will be a great industrial power. But it does not mean that the number of people, at least the percentage of people that are engaged in secondary sector would increase even in the next fifteen years. It will not. It can increase only if we try to keep ourselves abreast of the rest of the world in technology.

H.H. Giri

Votes of Thanks

It is my sincere duty to express a hearty vote of thanks to Professor B.M. Shukla, the Vice-chancellor of our University who has encouraged and helped us in holding this conference in our department. My heartfelt thanks are due to Professor R.P. Mishra, Vice-chancellor of Allahabad University, who has taken a great deal of trouble to come to this place and to inaugurate this conference. I am also thankful to our Pro-vice-chancellor Professor S.P. Nagendra who has helped at various levels in organising this conference. We are happy to note that Professor Ujagir Singh, our formers Head of the Department, had taken the trouble to come to this conference and to grace the occasion by his presence. I express my hearty thanks to all the foreign delegates specially to Dr.Mrs. Asmah Ahmad from Malaysia, to Dr. Nazrul Islam from Thailand, to Mrs. Ranasinghe from Sri Lanka, to Dr. Bohle from West Germany. Dr. M.P. Tripathi and his colleagues from our neighbouring country, Nepal, also deserve our thanks. We are grateful to them for coming here in such a large number and presenting papers. Many other delegates from foreign countries are expected to come this afternoon. I also thank all the delegates from our country, who have come, to mention a few, from Bardhman, Calcutta, Lucknow, Mithila, Meerut, Chandigarh, Baroda, Coimbatore, Shillong, Rajasthan, Madhya Pradesh, Maharastra and from other universities. I also express my sincere thanks to the distinguished guests and to honourable citizens of the town for their kind presence in this inaugural session of the conference. Our colleagues from the university have been kind enough to make this occassion a success by their benign presence and to them I also owe thanks. The research students of the Department, the office staff and other workers deserve a special mention because without their cooperation we might not have been able to organize this conference. I am also grateful to the representatives of All India Radio and news papers for giving this conference its due coverage.

In the end I thank all of you, ladies and gentlemen, for having come to this inaugural session and for having given the speakers a patient hearing.

Panel Discussion

A panel discussion was convened by the Association of Marketing Geographers of India, Gorakhpur, on the early evening of 22nd December.

The session was jointly chaired by Prof. A.B. Mukerji, Prof. J. Singh, Dr. H.M. Saxena, Dr. (Mrs.) Hemlata Ranasinghe and Dr. K.D. Sharma.

Initiating the discussion on research methodology and application of geography in solving the problems of the society, Professor A.B. Mukerji stressed upon the need for developing indigeneous research methodology based upon the micro and macro levels of study. Prof. Mukerji added that the research methodology and technique to be adopted should stem from empirical evidences gathered from field work.

Prof. J. Singh emphasised that a clear understanding of the concepts and theories of geography is the sine qua non for all geographical research.

Participating in the discussion Dr. V.K. Shrivastava called for a clarification in so far as the application of the concepts of central places, growth centres and service centres etc. were being made by Indian geographers in several studies. He pointed out that there was lack of awareness among geographers, particularly among younger ones, towards the theories as they actually are and as they are being applied.

Joining the discussion Professor D.K. Singh highlighted the role of modelling in research. He added that quantitative methods should be used only to the extent they helped in arriving at correct solutions. The insight and the judgement of the researcher should never be ignored.

Dr. H.M. Saxena highlighted some of the research problems faced by him in his research work on marketing geography. He was joined by Dr. S.C. Sharma who narrated the dilemma faced by a number of researchers in using or not using quantitative methods.

Dr. Mrs. Hemlata Ranasinghe put forward many examples of applied work done by the Sri Lankan geographers in their respective research fields and stressed that there was much more potential than normally thought of in so far as the utility of geographical research to society was concerned. Dr. K.D. Sharma spoke extensively on empirical work being done by young geographers in the remote Himalayan areas.

The panel discussion lasted for about one and a half hours and ended with the following recommendations:-

- i Market studies should be initiated at local and regional levels in different parts of India and the state governments may be requested to promote such activities;
- ii Field work should be given more emphasis in research work;
- iii Research projects should be conducted at an international level among countries of different economic status like India, African countries, South Asia, and France, U.K., Canada etc.

Field Excursion

A field trip was organised for the delegates in the afternoon of the first day of the conference. The delegates were taken around the commercial nuclei of Gorakhpur town and environs.

The delegates started the field-work from Gorakhnath Temple, the nucleus of the town also known as *purana* Gorakhpur. It provides a mix of territory activities based on general provision of goods and services. It has promoted secondary activities based on manufacture of handloom cloth which is also exported abroad. It is due to the existence of *julaha* population who have been traditional weavers. The impact of the temple on goods and services is confined within the huge temple-complex and along its fringe.

Alinagar was the next nucleus of business. It provides a cross-road location. An artery deals with building materials while the other specialises in domestic hardwares. Cloth and provision goods are developing along the east bound-road. The centre is occupied by a covered old vegetable market.

From Alinagar the study group moved through Buxipur crossing to Nakhas Chowk and then to Reti Chowk. These are the old and congested parts of the market places which were initiated nearly a 100 years ago. Ghantaghar chowk was the nearest spot from the banks of river Rapti which once flowed very close to it. River transport facility gave rise to the construction of shops, dharamshala and houses in this part. The linear pattern of shops-cum-residence is repeated throughout this stretch of nearly 3.5 Km.

The field trip further surveyed Ghosh Company crossing, Kutchery crossing and the modern market place known as Golghar. The delegates dispersed on Ganesh crossing of Golghar for their own shopping needs.

Report of the Closing Ceremony

The valedictory function was held on 23rd of December, 1985, in the late afternoon. The session was presided over by Dr.J. Singh. Professor S.P. Nagendra, Pro-VIce-chancellor of the University, and Professor L.B. Tripathi, Dean, Faculty of Arts, were the guests of honour. Dr. H. Lal presented a brief account of the three days of deliberations. He mentioned that in all 78 delegates attended the conference including delegates from West Germany, Sri Lanka, Malaysia, Bangladesh, Thailand and Nepal. Delegates from Pakistan, France, U.K. and Sweden could not attend due unavoidable circumstances. 43 papers were discussed in nine sessions. Dr. J. Singh, presiding over the session, apologized for his absence on the inaugural day. He appreciated the manner in which the conference was organised and the proceedings were conducted. He hailed the joint efforts made by the colleagues of the department and added that he was rather unaware of the potential of the department of geography.

Professor A.B. Mukherji initiated the reflections of the conference on behalf of the delegates. From academic discussions to field-trip, from accomodation to food and transport, he was all praise and was joined by the delegates present. He proposed that such conference/symposia should be organised every year under the auspices of the Association of Marketing Goegraphers of India. The proposal was unanimously accepted. Professor Nazrul Islam said that the academic outcome of the three days of deliberations would have far reaching consequences in streamlining the research themes and research methodology. Others who joined in reviewing the conference proceedings included Dr. S.C. Sharma, Dr. Mrs. Ranasinghe, Dr. Swaminathan and Dr. P.P. Rao. Professor L.B. Tripathi emphasised the role that geographers can play in planning commercial activities and development.

Professor S.P. Nagendra, put forward his assessment of the conference since the inauguration to the concluding session. He drew attention to the unifying role played by geographers in synthesizing the thoughts of social scientists and giving them a new dimension. He mentioned the areas where geographical thoughts come close to the thinking of the sociologists. As Pro-vice-chancellar he thanked all the delegates of the conference.

Recommendations of the Conference

The following recommendations to researchers, Universities and Governments were made by the conference :

i The role of market centres in rural development should be examined on regional levels.
ii Governments and academic bodies should integrate their activities in this field,
iii Field work should be given due emphasis in research work,
iv Research methodology should be oriented towards local conditions,
v Conferences on commercial activities and rural development should become annual phenomena in eastern U.P.
vi Developed and underdeveloped nations should exchange research projects and academicians for relevant research work.

Dr. V.K. Shrivastava, the Director of the conference, joined Professor Nagendra in expressing his gratefulness to all delegates. He expressed his thanks to the cooperation extended by the Vice-chancellor, Pro-Vice-chancellor, Registrar and other officers of the University in organising the conference. Govt. of India, Ministry of Human Resource Development, Govt. of Uttar Pradesh, the University Grants Commissions, the Indian council of Social Science Research, the Commonwealth Geographical Bureau, IGU study Group's President, Prof. A.Metton, All India Radio, Concept, New Delhi, News Media , staff members and students of the Department of Geography were all profusely thanked by the organisers of the conference.

APPENDIX - I

INTERNATIONAL GEOGRAPHICAL UNION "GEOGRAPHY OF COMMERCIAL ACTIVITIES"

Study Group

GOAL : To gather scholars from various countries for the exchange of ideas of empirical and theoretical studies by regular meetings and newsletters on the geography of the commercial activities in rural and urban areas in developing and industrialized countries.

Research Topics

1. To compare definitions, terminologies, classifications and geographical research methods of various forms of trade (shops, supermarkets, markets and other forms of trade) in each country. To establish an international terminology and list information sources.

2. To study retail trade : its adaptation to the diversification and changes of the urban and rural centres and types of economy.

3. To study supermarkets and shopping centres : their varying role according to the country where they are located, the spatial strategy of the firms and the new behaviour of customers.

4. To study the market trade (daily or periodic markets): its adaptation to the competition from other forms of trade and its importance for the social life of urban and rural areas.

5. To compare the effects of the legislation and the planning measures at the urban, regional and national levels and the various types of trade.

6. To study the changes of shopping behaviour among customers and their perception of various forms of shopping activities.

7. To examine the role of commercial activities in structuring various types of urban and rural areas, their influence on the landscape and the perception of the dwellers on the life of various social groups.

8. To study the evolution of the links between urban and rural areas and of the system of cities with regard to commercial geography.

Executive Committee

President : METTON A. (France) Depart. Geographie, Universite d'Orleans,.
Vice President : R.A. OBUDHO (Kenya) 45045 ORLEANS Cedex, France.
Members : R. DAVIES (England), E. GORMSEN (Germany), H. ISHIHARA (Japan), A. LOGAN (Australia), B. MERENNE-SCHOUMAKER (Belgium) C. NORDIN (Sweden), V.K. SHRIVASTAVA (India), MAC KIM (U.S.A.)

Participants: Adalemo I. A. (Nigeria), Bachelard M. (France), Beaujeu Garnier J. (France), Bonnain R. (france), Bondue J.P. (France), Cassou-Mount M. (France), Commercon N. (France), Cordeiro H.K. (Brasil), Delobez A. (France) Caenen R. (France) Nishikawa D. (Japan), Okuda Y. (Japan), Pallier G. (Germany), Seele E. (Germany), Sick W. (Germany), Sjoholt P. (Norway), Soumagne J. (France), Sporck J. A. (Belgium), Subbiah H. (India), Terasaka A. (Japan), Troin J.F. (France), Voudour N, (France), Wackermann G. (France), Zeller R.E. (U.S.A.)

INDEX